AFTER '08

Edited by Stephen McBride,
Rianne Mahon, and Gerard W. Boychuk

AFTER '08

Social Policy and the Global
Financial Crisis

UBCPress · Vancouver · Toronto

23 22 21 20 19 18 17 16 15   5 4 3 2 1

Printed in Canada on FSC-certified ancient-forest-free paper
(100% post-consumer recycled) that is processed chlorine- and acid-free.

Library and Archives Canada Cataloguing in Publication

After '08 : social policy and the global financial crisis / edited by Stephen McBride, Rianne Mahon, and Gerard W. Boychuk.

Includes bibliographical references and index.
Issued in print and electronic formats.
ISBN 978-0-7748-2963-2 (bound). – ISBN 978-0-7748-2965-6 (pdf)
ISBN 978-0-7748-2966-3 (epub)

1. Global Financial Crisis, 2008-2009 – Social aspects 2. Global Financial Crisis, 2008-2009 – Political aspects 3. Social policy – Economic aspects I. McBride, Stephen, editor II. Mahon, Rianne, editor III. Boychuk, Gerard William, editor

HB3717.2008A38 2015   330.9051   C2015-904565-7
                                                            C2015-904566-5

Canadä

UBC Press gratefully acknowledges the financial support for our publishing program of the Government of Canada (through the Canada Book Fund), the Canada Council for the Arts, and the British Columbia Arts Council.

This book has been published with the help of a grant from the Canadian Federation for the Humanities and Social Sciences, through the Awards to Scholarly Publications Program, using funds provided by the Social Sciences and Humanities Research Council of Canada.

UBC Press
The University of British Columbia
2029 West Mall
Vancouver, BC V6T 1Z2
www.ubcpress.ca

Contents

Tables and Figures

Acknowledgments

We gratefully acknowledge funding from the SSHRC Connections Grants program and the McMaster University Institute for Globalization and the Human Condition, which made it possible to hold a workshop at McMaster University in September 2013 at which draft versions of the chapters in this volume were discussed by participants. Andrea Rowe, Sorin Mitrea, and Bianca James provided invaluable assistance in organizing the workshop. We would also like to acknowledge financial support for preparation of the manuscript provided by the Balsillie School of International Affairs through its Publication Grant program.

AFTER '08

Introduction

RIANNE MAHON, GERARD W. BOYCHUK, AND STEPHEN McBRIDE

This book reflects on the impact on social policy of the global financial and economic crisis that began in 2007 and probes the extent to which the prospects for progressive social policy might have shifted since the onset of the crisis. In doing so, it asks two basic questions. First, to what extent has the neo-liberal landscape surrounding social policy shifted since the onset of the financial crisis? Second, is the direction that social policy has taken since the crisis sufficiently similar across countries and regions such that a typical trajectory of response can be identified, or has diversity in national experiences of the crisis produced a diversity of policy responses?

This volume examines whether neo-liberalism as an ideational paradigm has been challenged and whether alternatives to it are indeed emerging. We need to understand not only diverse crisis-driven policy responses but also how the crisis itself has been defined and understood by various actors (Farnsworth and Irving 2011). However, the volume also examines social policy "on the ground." In doing so, it looks at international organizations and nation-states, both of which are identified here as key actors determining whether, and to what degree, social policy stances, and social policy as delivered, have been changed by the crisis. Finally, the volume examines social policy developments in the "emerging" countries of the South as well as in advanced capitalist countries of the North from which the crisis originated. It thus speaks to the impact of the crisis and social policy responses in diverse parts of the world.

The Great Recession: Overarching Trends, Diverse National Experiences

The trajectory of the crisis that struck the global economy in 2007–8 is now well known. The sub-prime mortgage market in the United States collapsed, and defaults became common, revealing that banks and other financial institutions had lent vast sums backed by dubious or toxic assets of unknown value. In these circumstances, banks feared further defaults, lending to consumers, businesses, and other banks dried up, and economic activity slowed dramatically. Buyout and bailout measures were put in place to enhance liquidity in the economy, but in September 2008 Lehman Brothers filed for bankruptcy. The crisis in the financial sphere was then transmitted into the real economy. It soon emerged that European banks were also heavily exposed, and most countries entered recessions from which some have still to emerge.

Global recession soon followed. Despite its global reach, the crisis has had varied effects by country and region (Farnsworth and Irving, this volume). The Great Recession began at the centre, and the industrialized countries have been among the slowest to recover (Kahler and Lake 2013). Some summary statistics illustrate the variations within the group. Between 2007 and 2012, unemployment in the OECD area as a whole increased by 41 percent and for the eurozone by 49 percent. Yet, even within Western Europe, the range of unemployment change spanned from –37 percent (Germany) to +214 percent (Ireland). Similarly, the government debt-to-GDP ratio increased by 50 percent across the OECD and 47 percent within the eurozone but ranged from –27 percent for Norway to +351 percent for Ireland. The economies on the southern, western, and eastern peripheries of Europe were hard hit (Haggard 2013, 60–66), but for the most part the main Asian and Latin American countries were less severely affected, with the exception of countries heavily dependent on the United States (Mexico and Thailand). As we shall see, it is in these areas that governments have been increasing social expenditures.

To combat the approaching Great Recession, interest rates were reduced to historical lows, money creation through "quantitative easing" was pursued aggressively in some countries, notably the United States, and most countries engaged in Keynesian-style stimulus spending to help ease economic woes and jump-start recovery.[1] Thus, the initial reaction of states and international organizations to the crisis was to suspend practice based on the prevailing neoliberal theory and, instead, to engage in emergency reactions that included bailouts and de facto nationalization of banks and financial institutions coupled with significant spending to sustain demand.

Shortly following the initial response, however, the situation became much more complex. To illustrate, at the 2010 G20 meetings, there was a shift toward fiscal consolidation, deficit reduction, reducing debt-to-GDP ratios, structural labour market reforms, and measures to enhance investor confidence. Yet, in May 2012, G8 leaders called for a growth-led, rather than an austerity-induced, path to economic recovery. After the meeting, Germany's finance minister made it clear that Germany continued to position austerity as an essential precondition for growth (*Globe and Mail*, 23 May 2012). Indeed, within much of the European Union, a new Treaty on Stability, Coordination, and Governance in the Economic and Monetary Union had already been signed, requiring, when ratified, national budgets to be in balance or in surplus. If a member state deviates from this rule, then an automatic correction mechanism will be triggered. Those countries signing agreed to incorporate the "balanced budget rule" into national legislation, preferably at a constitutional level.[2]

If the technique of locking-in policy preferences to make them less susceptible to political change prevails, then the implications for social policy are ongoing budgetary stringency, program redesign to better reflect market principles, and disciplining of beneficiaries to reattach themselves to a (depressed) labour market.

Crisis, Continuity, and Change: Neo-Liberalism Reconstituted or a Polanyian Moment?

There is agreement that deep crises can be associated with fundamental (or paradigmatic) policy changes. Various concepts have been advanced to capture the moment at which such change occurs or at least seems possible. These concepts include "paradigm shift" (Hall 1993), "policy window" (Kingdon 1984), "critical juncture" (Hogan 2006), and "Polanyian moment" (Jenson, this volume). Typically, in these accounts, some exogenous shock creates the crisis in which a battle between competing solutions to the crisis ensues.

Crises are likely to generate both dynamics favouring innovation and dynamics reinforcing existing routines. The uncertainty endemic to a crisis can thus serve to "open politics to new possibilities while encouraging some political actors to return to older scripts based on a limited repertoire of political ideologies" (Kahler and Lake 2013, 22). However, there is no way to predict a priori the final balance between these contending sets of forces. The result might be significant change, or the pre-existing orthodoxy might be reconstituted and consolidated, representing an ideational path dependency that is resilient in the face of external shocks even if its hold is weakened and somewhat discredited as a result of them (Blyth 2001).

Neo-Liberalism Reconstituted

The neo-liberal paradigm has dominated policy making for decades at least in the global North and in the practice of international organizations such as the International Monetary Fund (IMF) and World Bank. In general, neo-liberalism consists of a number of mutually reinforcing policy goals, underpinned by a theory that emphasizes individualism, the sanctity and efficiency of private property rights, the rule of law, and a free market with a minimal but strong state (Gamble 1988; Harvey 2007). The neo-liberal program includes policies promoting these aims, such as privatization and deregulation, capital mobility and free trade, anti-inflation rather than full employment, and a limited and fiscally constrained state. Applied to social policy, it is defined by measures such as promotion of individual responsibility, including user-pay mechanisms, private delivery of services, attachment of strict conditions and obligations to receipt of benefits (e.g., workfare), and tougher qualification requirements and lower benefit levels for recipients of social programs.

Beyond these common themes, the neo-liberal package exhibits considerable variety by jurisdiction and over time.[3] Some argue that whole regions of the world, notably the East Asian developmental states (Evans and Sewell 2013), China (Cook and Lam 2011), and Latin America in the 2000s (Huber and Stephens 2012), either did not fully embrace, or later moved to abandon, the neo-liberal paradigm.

A considerable literature suggests, however, that the neo-liberal paradigm retains its dominant position post-crisis, most emphatically in its heartlands of North America and Western Europe. The implications for social policy are inherent in the austerity policies advocated by domestic elites and by some international organizations and are either imposed on states, as in the case of the peripheral states of Europe, or self-imposed, as with the United Kingdom, Canada, Germany, and other leading states. Sarah Babb's review of the attachment of international financial institutions to the Washington Consensus concludes that it might have been weakened, but no serious rival has emerged (Babb 2013). The chapters in this volume examine the degree to which, and the manner in which, neo-liberalism has survived the crisis.

· Rianne Mahon, Gerard W. Boychuk, and Stephen McBride

A "Polanyian Moment"? Financial Crisis as a "Turning Point" in Social Policy?

An alternative view, while not denying the crisis-prone nature of markets, emphasizes the capacity not of markets but of market societies to self-correct. Perhaps the most notable example is the work of Karl Polanyi. Since the financial crisis, there has been renewed interest in his work and its applicability to current conditions (Fraser 2013; Frerichs 2013; Kelsey 2013; Martin 2013; Özgür and Özel 2013; Polanyi Levitt 2013). As Kelsey (2013, 289) notes, Polanyi's analysis "resonates too closely with current conditions" to be easily dismissed, while Fraser (2013, 119–20) asserts that, "given these structural similarities, it is no surprise that many analysts of the present crisis are now returning to Polanyi's *magnum opus*." From the standpoint of this volume, then, a "Polanyian moment" involves an economic shock of the magnitude of the Great Recession that could alter the ever-shifting balance between societal forces in favour of further expansion of the free market and forces opposed to it.

Certainly, for Polanyi, nothing about the market is exogenous – the ostensibly "free" market is created by and embedded in society. Market societies are constituted by two opposing movements – one in favour of expanding the scope of the market and the other opposed to such an expansion. This opposition and the inextricable linkage between the market and society comprise the basis of his thesis of the "double movement," by which initiatives to expand the scope of the market simultaneously (and almost inevitably) generate a protective social reaction against the social dislocation thus created. As Block argues, for Polanyi, "it is inevitable that people will mobilize to protect themselves from these economic shocks" (2001, xxxiv).

For Polanyi, social policy was central in both preventing and facilitating development of the free market. It thus reflected the competitive dynamics among, and the shifting balance between, the laissez-faire movement and diverse protective societal responses. Given the capacity for social policy to constrain or expand the scope of the market, it was not a question of more or less intervention but the manner in which and the degree to which social policy served to either constrain or expand operation of the market.

Given that social dislocation arising from economic fluctuations is an important element in generating the tension between the free-market movement and protective social responses, it seems reasonable to ask whether the dislocation resulting from the Great Recession has shifted this balance. Since social policy has been a crucial venue in which these dynamics have played out, one can ask whether social policy shows any signs of a shift toward becoming more or less market conforming and whether there is a greater potential post-crisis that social policy will serve to constrain the role of the market.

Social Policy Ideas and Actors: International Organizations and Nation-States

The outcome of the competition between forces of change and forces of consolidation will be determined less by the quality of the ideas advanced and more by the ability of the actors supporting them to shape the narrative of the crisis (Jessop 2012; Utting, Razavi, and Varghese Buchholz 2012). In this volume, the key actors involved in shaping narratives and identifying solutions are international organizations and nation-states. Behind them, of course, lie a variety of social forces and interests.

Interactions among international organizations and nation-states in shaping policy responses to the crisis are complex; however, both are potentially important. International organizations played an important role in helping to establish the hegemony of neo-liberal ideas in the wake of the 1970s–early 1980s crisis. In particular, the international financial institutions (IFIs) – the IMF and World Bank – contributed to the imposition of the Washington Consensus on much of the global South as well as the "transition" countries of Eastern Europe. To the extent that social policy figured in the advice of the IFIs, it "favoured a residual or targeted approach to spending more reminiscent of the USA model" (Deacon 2007, 25). In contrast, the International Labour Organization (ILO), which had championed the extension of the Bismarckian social insurance model during the postwar period, sought to challenge the IFIs. It was able to use the occasion of the 2008 crisis to obtain UN sanction for its global social protection floor initiative, built on the principle of universality (see Deacon 2013 for more detail). One issue addressed in this volume is whether the ILO will be able to use the opportunity to alter the position of the IFIs.

Although, unlike in the 1930s, responses to contemporary economic crises thus have been, and are being, worked out in a transnational ideational context, policy decisions remain the preserve of states (Weyland 2009). Thus, though the international financial institutions with coercive powers can bring considerable pressure to bear on vulnerable countries (Ayhan and McBride, this volume), the ILO can use ratified conventions to apply moral pressure but is not in a position to counter national retrenchment policies. Starke, Kaasch, and van Hooren (2013) in fact suggest that the main contribution of international organizations such as the ILO and Economic Commission on Latin America

Rianne Mahon, Gerard W. Boychuk, and Stephen McBride

and the Caribbean is to the construction of a transnational political-intellectual climate.

The social policy situation on the ground in individual states is complex, and significant differences emerge when the industrial states of the OECD area are compared with the emerging economies of Asia and some parts of Latin America and Africa. Thus far, some studies of the impact of the crisis on social policies in Western Europe – particularly peripheral European countries but also core states such as the United Kingdom and Germany – indicate that neo-liberal austerity has led to retrenchment. At the same time, various scholars have argued that social policy restructuring goes beyond expansion versus retrenchment to include qualitative shifts from "passive" to "active" – that is, from protection from market-generated instability to a pro-employability stance – as well as from encompassing to selective programs (Bonoli and Natali 2012).

The "passive/active" distinction overlaps with the concept of "social invest-ment" (Jenson 2010). Both terms can mean workfarist policies designed to push (or draw) the unemployed and marginalized into an increasingly polarized labour market. At the same time, they can involve a combination of social in-vestment in human capital (for all) plus social protection, as outlined by Morel, Palier, and Palme (2012).These distinctions are important, especially in light of the claim that, since the 1990s, most Western European states have been fol-lowing a common trajectory of "active" reform (Crouch and Keune 2012; Hemerijck 2012; Hudson and Kühner 2011; Kosonen 2011).

The impact of previous crises can be seen most clearly in the developing world. In Asia, the situation is different partly as a result of learning from the financial crisis of 1997–99, which had a major effect on the region. The emerging economies of the region sanctioned relatively large fiscal stimulus packages. Of particular import was China's massive stimulus, which provided "a crucial public good to the entire region and unquestionably influencing its rapid re-covery" (Haggard 2013, 73).; there was also a strong social component to the stimulus programs (Haggard 2013, 73, 70).

Moreover, in contrast to Western European trends, social policy in key Asian countries, such as Korea, India, and China, has become more encompassing since the Asian financial crisis of 1997–99, even if, as Lee-Gong (2011) argues, the measures adopted fall short when it comes to social protection for "non-regular" workers. Korea has also embraced the idea of social investment, most notably in the expansion of child care (Peng 2011, 2014). Social policy develop-ment in China has moved it in the direction of the ILO's global social protection floor to the extent that it has encompassed formerly excluded groups, notably migrants, while also recognizing the potential contribution of social insurance to economic flexibility (Cook and Lam, this volume; Hong and Kongshøj, 2014). Nevertheless, social programs in both countries still fail to deal with the insecurity faced by a large "non-regular" labour force, which only serves to underline the importance of combining social protection with social investment while also developing measures to tackle the deepening problem of precarity that afflicts both North and South.

In the first decade of this century, the emerging countries of Latin America became important sites of social policy innovation in response to socio-economic and political impacts of the lost decade and crises of the 1990s. Most attention has been focused on the conditional cash transfer (CCT) programs pioneered by Brazil (Bolsa Familia) and Mexico (Oportunidades), noted for their marked social investment profiles. Huber and Stephens (2012) chart a similar pattern in the five countries – Brazil, Argentina, Chile, Costa Rica, and Uruguay – whose social policies they examined. The 2008 crisis did not halt the expansion of social policies in the region. As Cohen, Isaacman, and Cook (2012, 180) argue,

> in sharp contrast to both the stabilization period in Latin America and the implementation of austerity policies in the US and Western Europe more recently, a central assumption of policy reform has been a return to an expanded role of the state, which has been a crucial factor in the re-design and degree of active policy experimentation in Latin America. This role of the state has been emphasized by many observers, with the United Nations Economic Commission on Latin America and the Caribbean being the most consistent and well-grounded spokesman for this perspective in the region.

Although much remains to be accomplished if the deep inequality that has long plagued the region is to be overcome, it appears that, while most OECD countries are embracing austerity, key countries of the region are actively putting flesh on the kind of "inclusive growth" model discussed by Jenson (this volume).

The Volume

The chapters of this volume examine the degree to which the crisis has opened up significant opportunities for progressive social reform. The opening chapters frame the debate throughout the volume between those who argue that neo-liberalism is capable of ongoing renewal, and are thus skeptical about the degree to which the crisis has generated significant opportunities for social reform, and those who are more optimistic about the possibilities for new social policy initiatives to address deepening problems of inequality and poverty within and between countries.

Stephen McBride's opening chapter argues that, though neo-liberalism has been questioned more intensively than in the past, its predominance has not been successfully challenged. As a result, it remains relatively unshaken as the guide to action of important states and global institutions with important implications for all policy areas, including social policy. In contrast, Jane Jenson posits that we have reached another Polanyian moment in which a significant change of policy direction is occurring. Alongside the undeniable austerity-induced social policy cutbacks, coherent arguments for state spending in the name of social investment and inclusive growth have emerged from diverse sites – from northern-based international organizations such as the OECD to states in the global South.

Kevin Farnsworth and Zoë Irving suggest that "the" crisis is in fact best understood as a series of related crises that have hit different countries at different moments and with varying degrees of severity. In part, each country's response depends on a mix of the extent of financial integration, hence vulnerability; prior configurations of social policy, with more generous systems more capable of mitigating the impact; and current political alignments. Overall, they conclude, there are instances of expansionary social policy development in crisis responses; however, though the crisis has exposed the weaknesses of neo-liberalism, a credible alternative has yet to be established.

The second section focuses on international organizations and the role that they have played, and are playing, in establishing the parameters of the debate. Antje Vetterlein's chapter examines the stance taken by the IMF, which emerged as a key actor charged with forging a response to the crisis. Vetterlein shows that, contrary to its role in the Asian financial crisis, when the IMF was prepared to take social questions quite seriously, a recharged IMF moved to reassert its traditional approach. This means that it is prepared to leave social policies to the World Bank while it focuses on promoting macroeconomic stability and balance-of-payment problems even when doing so involves imposing austerity.

The IMF is not the only international organization that has seized the opportunity provided by the crisis. As Bob Deacon's chapter argues, the ILO was able to use its position within the UN system to advance its alternative to narrowly targeted social safety nets, the global social protection floor. The ILO envisages the global adoption of (nationally based) universal, tax-financed, social protection systems from birth to old age. Deacon recapitulates the story of how the ILO captured the global agenda after 2008 such that the social protection floor became the policy not only of the ILO but also of the G20, UNICEF, and even the World Bank. Deacon suggests that the ILO might be able to regain its lost role and contribute to a shift in global social policy in a progressive direction, but he concludes that such a shift will depend on a number of factors.

Nigel Haworth and Steve Hughes also argue that, in the longer term, the ILO's agenda might enjoy a resurgence. Their chapter focuses on the ILO's intervention in Greece as an example of the organization's importance in promoting employment and wage-led growth, social dialogue, and social justice. Nevertheless, a combination of factors challenges the short-term adoption of the ILO's preferred alternative: the orthodox economic and institutional underpinnings of neo-liberalism remain strong, and the willingness, let alone ability, of nation-states to commit to the ILO agenda can by no means be assumed.

Although the ILO might have gained some capacity to influence the World Bank's broad social policy perspective, a key question remains: what does the World Bank promote in practice? Anthony Hall's chapter suggests that it has used its financial and technical assistance programs to promote a policy idea pioneered by Mexico and Brazil: conditional cash transfers, which have also proven to be popular with client governments. Although CCTs can be seen as a prime example of social investment, they have caught on in a way that reinforces the emphasis on piecemeal programs focused on poverty, at the expense of the kind of universal and comprehensive approach advocated by the ILO.

Rianne Mahon's chapter marks the shift from global to regional and national scales and opens the section that examines social policy responses in key "emerging" countries. It focuses on a key think tank in Latin America, the Economic Commission for Latin America and the Caribbean (CEPAL). Mahon compares CEPAL's response to the crisis of the 1930s with the "lost decade" of the 1980s. In the present as in the past, the original concern was to develop the theoretical justification for the state's role in promoting domestic development. Over the past decade, inspired in part by UN rights-based discourse and European social democracy, and emboldened by the "pink tide" of electoral victories in the region, CEPAL, however, has developed a social policy perspective based on the principles of universality and comprehensiveness.

Although CEPAL's discourse parallels developments in Brazil, Costa Rica, Chile, Argentina, and Uruguay, as the analysis by Huber and Stephens (2012) suggests, Mexico – another major country in the region that has been actively involved in social policy innovation – has charted quite a different course from that championed by CEPAL. Lucy Luccisano and Laura Macdonald argue that

Mexico's initial response to the peso crisis of 1980 was to adopt a neo-liberal social policy model. In the 1990s, however, it developed its CCT program, Oportunidades, which combined a social investment orientation with a neo-liberal focus on the very poor. Its response to the 2008 financial crisis, however, involved a weakening of the social investment dimension of Oportunidades in favour of experimentation with a new social program focused on combatting hunger. The latter represents a return to clientelistic social policy as well as partial privatization through the involvement of multinational corporations.

Marlea Clarke's chapter argues that the end of apartheid in South Africa did open up a period of social policy innovation in that country but that the post-apartheid government's economic policy model gave rise to an employment crisis that existed long before the global economic crisis of 2008–9. The Great Recession has not only exacerbated these long-standing structural problems in the economy but also put the existing social security system under strain, exposing the gaps and limitations of the country's social assistance system. Clarke concludes that systemic reform is needed but likely impossible as long as the country retains its current economic model.

In China, the repercussions of the 2008 financial crisis are still being felt, though without the intensity experienced by many established welfare states. China's social policy "regime" is undergoing major transformations in response to changing economic, social, and political conditions. Sarah Cook and Wing Lam suggest that there are less direct ways in which the crisis might be influencing the direction of welfare reform as well as other drivers of reform. Overall, they argue, China's reforms are driven principally by the demands of its domestic structural transformation, including the management of inevitable social tensions. The financial crisis in effect was a significant hurdle, rather than a turning point, along a path that is still far from being clearly mapped out but on which the general direction is becoming clearer.

The final section returns to the original site of the Great Recession, the global North. Ayhan and McBride's chapter looks at three of the hard-hit European countries – Ireland, Greece, and Portugal – whose limited room for manoeuvre was further constrained by the severe conditions imposed by the "troika": the IMF, the European Central Bank, and the European Commission. Ayhan and McBride argue that their predicament, pre- and post-crisis, is best explained by the core-periphery relationship in the eurozone. In other words, the crisis and the conditions imposed by the troika exacerbated existing imbalances between the core and peripheral states and exposed the weaknesses in the constitution of the eurozone. As a result, in these three states, social policy has been sacrificed on the altar of austerity.

Australia, Canada, and the United Kingdom constitute the focus of Heather Whiteside's chapter. Whiteside argues that, though these countries could have opted for expansion, they chose austerity. Her central argument is that, in these three countries, austerity is strongly seen as a "common-sense" approach – albeit one that is non-hegemonic and highly contested and plays out in distinct national political contexts. Ron Labonté and Arne Ruckert's in-depth analysis of the Canadian case corroborates Whiteside's argument. Labonté and Ruckert argue that in Canada austerity does not represent a radical departure but reinforces neo-liberal trends existent before the onset of the crisis. The crisis simply provided a new justification for the deepening of neo-liberal social policy reforms. They then show how such policy choices have contributed to deepening health inequities.

The United States has charted a different course, opting for fiscal expansionism and shifting the overall US system of unemployment insurance benefits to a higher level of generosity than the Canadian system. Gerard Boychuk argues that the US social policy response to the crisis might not appear as a radical departure from the existing policy equilibrium since it can be seen as a strategy of social policy expansionism through stealth that has been significant nevertheless. Boychuk assesses the degree to which this can be seen as indicative of ideational and institutional shifts and considers the potential for future political coalitions that could sustain and deepen this turn in US social policy.

These chapters begin to answer the key questions outlined above. Has the broad neo-liberal landscape shifted as a result of the crisis? Is there a broad commonality across countries and regions in terms of the trajectory of policy responses, or are different national experiences and responses more accurately characterized by their degrees of diversity? It is to a consideration of the initial answers that the chapters collectively provide that we return in the conclusion.

Notes

1 A central bank implements quantitative easing by buying financial assets from commercial banks and other private institutions with newly created money. This increases the money supply by flooding financial institutions with capital, in an effort to promote increased lending and liquidity, thus stimulating the economy.
2 All members except the United Kingdom and Czech Republic signed the treaty.
3 As did the previously dominant Keynesian paradigm; see Esping-Andersen (1990).

References

Babb, Sarah. 2013. "The Washington Consensus as Transnational Policy Paradigm: Its Origins, Trajectory and Likely Successor." *Review of International Political Economy* 20, 2: 268-97.

Rianne Mahon, Gerard W. Boychuk, and Stephen McBride

Block, Fred. 2001. "Introduction." In *The Great Transformation: The Political and Economic Origins of Our Time,* by Karl Polanyi. Boston, MA: Beacon Press.

Blyth, Mark. 2001. "The Transformation of the Swedish Model: Economic Ideas, Distributional Conflict, and Institutional Change." *World Politics* 54: 1-26.

Bonoli, Giuliano, and David Natali, eds. 2012. *The Politics of the New Welfare State.* Oxford: Oxford University Press. http://dx.doi.org/10.1093/acprof:oso/9780199645244.001.0001.

Cohen, Michael, Tanushree Dutta Isaacman, and Mitchell Cook. 2012. "A Critical Juncture: Experimentation and Recovery." In *The Global Economic Crisis in Latin America: Impacts and Responses,* edited by Michael Cohen, 178-98. New York: Routledge.

Cook, Sarah, and Wing Lam. 2011. "China's Response to Crisis: What Role for Social Policy?" In *Social Policy in Challenging Times: Economic Crisis and Welfare Systems,* edited by Kevin Farnsworth and Zoë Irving 139-58. Bristol: Policy Press.

Crouch, Colin, and Maarten Keune. 2012. "The Governance of Economic Uncertainty: Beyond the 'New Social Risks' Analysis." In *The Politics of the New Welfare State,* edited by Giuliano Bonoli and David Natali, 45-67. Oxford: Oxford University Press. http://dx.doi.org/10.1093/acprof:oso/9780199645244.003.0003.

Deacon, Bob. 2007. *Global Social Policy and Governance.* London: Sage.

–. 2013. *Global Social Policy in the Making: The Foundations of the Social Protection Floor.* Bristol: Policy Press.

Esping-Andersen, G. 1990. *The Three Worlds of Welfare Capitalism.* Princeton: Princeton University Press.

Evans, Peter, and William H. Sewell, Jr. 2013. "Neoliberalism: Policy Regimes, International Regimes, and Social Effects." In *Social Resilience in the Neoliberal Era,* edited by Peter A. Hall and Michèle Lamont, 35-68. New York: Cambridge University Press.

Farnsworth, K., and Z. Irving. 2011. "Varieties of Crisis." In *Social Policy in Challenging Times: Economic Crisis and Welfare Systems,* edited by K. Farnsworth and Z. Irving, 1-30. Bristol: Policy Press. http://dx.doi.org/10.1332/policypress/9781847428288.003.0001.

Fraser, Nancy. 2013. "A Triple Movement? Parsing the Politics of Crisis after Polanyi." *New Left Review* 81: 119-32.

Frerichs, Sabine. 2013. "From Credit to Crisis: Max Weber, Karl Polanyi, and the Other Side of the Coin." *Journal of Law and Society* 40, 1: 7-26. http://dx.doi.org/10.1111/j.1467-6478.2013.00610.x.

Gamble, Andrew. 1988. *The Free Economy and the Strong State.* London: Macmillan.

Haggard, Stephan. 2013. "Politics in Hard Times Revisited: The 2008-9 Financial Crisis in Emerging Markets." In *Politics in the New Hard Times: The Great Recession in Comparative Perspective,* edited by M. Kahler and D.A. Lake, 52-74. Ithaca: Cornell University Press.

Hall, Peter. 1993. "Policy Paradigms, Social Learning, and the State: The Case of Economic Policy-Making in Britain." *Comparative Politics* 25, 3: 275-96. http://dx.doi.org/10.2307/422246.

Harvey, David. 2007. *A Brief History of Neoliberalism.* Oxford: Oxford University Press.

Hemerijck, Anton. 2012. "Stress-Testing the New Welfare State." In *The Politics of the New Welfare State,* edited by Giuliano Bonoli and David Natali, 68-90. Oxford: Oxford University Press. http://dx.doi.org/10.1093/acprof:oso/9780199645244.003.0004.

Hogan, John. 2006. "Remoulding the Critical Junctures Approach." *Canadian Journal of Political Science* 39, 3 (2006): 657-79.

Hong, Liu, and Kristian Kongshøj. 2014. "China's Welfare Reform: An Ambiguous Road toward a Social Protection Floor." *Global Social Policy* 14, 3: 352–68.

Huber, Evelyne, and John D. Stephens. 2012. *Democracy and the Left: Social Policy and Inequality in Latin America.* Chicago: University of Chicago Press. http://dx.doi.org/10.7208/chicago/9780226356556.001.0001.

Hudson, John, and Stefan Kühner. 2011. "Tiptoeing through Crisis? Re-Evaluating the German Social Model in Light of the Global Recession." In *Social Policy in Challenging Times: Economic Crisis and Welfare Systems,* edited by K. Farnsworth and Z. Irving, 159–80. Bristol: Policy Press. http://dx.doi.org/10.1332/policypress/9781847428288.003.0009.

Jenson, Jane. 2010. "Diffusing Ideas after Neoliberalism: The Social Investment Perspective in Europe and Latin America." *Global Social Policy* 10, 1: 59–84. http://dx.doi.org/10.1177/1468018109354813.

Jessop, B. 2012. "Narratives of Crisis and Crisis Response: Perspectives from North and South." In *The Global Crisis and Transformative Social Change,* edited by P. Utting, Rebecca Varghese Buchholz, and Shahra Razavi, 23–42. Basingstoke: Palgrave Macmillan. http://dx.doi.org/10.1057/9781137002501.0008.

Kahler, Miles, and David A. Lake, eds. 2013. *Politics in the New Hard Times: The Great Recession in Comparative Perspective.* Ithaca: Cornell University Press.

Kelsey, Jane. 2013. "Ulysses versus Polanyi: Can Embedded Neoliberalism Prevent a 'Great Transformation'?" In *Retrenchment or Renewal: Welfare States in Times of Economic Crisis,* edited by Guðmundur Jónsson and Kolbeinn Stefánsson, 273–92. Helsinki: Nordic Centre of Excellence Nordwel.

Kingdon, J. 1984. *Agendas, Alternatives, and Public Policies.* Boston: Little Brown and Company.

Kosonen, Pekka. 2011. "Experiences from Two Financial Crises in the Nordic Welfare States: 1990–93 and 2008–10 Compared." In *Social Policy in Challenging Times: Economic Crisis and Welfare Systems,* edited by K. Farnsworth and Z. Irving, 219-30. Bristol: Policy Press. http://dx.doi.org/10.1332/policypress/9781847428288.003.0012.

Lee-Gong, Eunna. 2011. "South Korea after the 1997 Economic Crisis: A "Paradigm Shift?" In *Social Policy in Challenging Times: Economic Crisis and Welfare Systems,* edited by K. Farnsworth and Z. Irving, 119-38. Bristol: Policy Press. http://dx.doi.org/10.1332/policypress/9781847428288.003.0007.

Martin, Lisa. 2013. "Polanyi's Revenge." *Perspectives on Politics* 11, 1: 177–86. http://dx.doi.org/10.1017/S1537592712003404.

Morel, Nathalie, Bruno Palier, and Joakim Palme. 2012. "Social Investment: A Paradigm in Search of a New Economic Model and Political Mobilisation." In *Towards a Social Investment Welfare State? Ideas, Policies, and Challenges,* edited by N. Morel, B. Palier, and J. Palme, 353-76. Bristol: Policy Press.

Özgür, Gökcer, and Hüseyin Özel. 2013. "Double Movement, Globalization, and the Crisis." *American Journal of Economics and Sociology* 72, 4: 892–916. http://dx.doi.org/10.1111/ajes.12030.

Peng, Ito. 2011. "Social Investment Policy in South Korea." In *Feminist Ethics and Social Policy: Towards a New Global Political Economy of Care,* edited by Rianne Mahon and Fiona Robinson, 94–110. Vancouver: UBC Press.

–. 2014. "The 'New' Social Investment Policies in Japan and South Korea." *Global Social Policy* 14, 3: 389–405.

Polanyi, Karl. 2001. *The Great Transformation: The Political and Economic Origins of Our Time.* Boston: Beacon Press.

Polanyi Levitt, Kari. 2013. *From the Great Transformation to the Great Financialization: On Karl Polanyi and Other Essays.* Halifax: Fernwood.

Starke, Peter, Alexandra Kaasch, and Franca van Hooren. 2013. *The Welfare State as Crisis Manager: Explaining the Diversity of Policy Responses to Economic Crisis.* Houndmills: Palgrave Macmillan. http://dx.doi.org/10.1057/9781137314840.

Utting, P., S. Razavi, and R. Varghese Buchholz. 2012. "Overview: Social and Political Dimensions of the Global Crisis: Possible Futures." In *The Global Crisis and Transformative Social Change,* edited by P. Utting Rebecca Varghese Bucholz and Shahra Razavi 1–22. Basingstoke: Palgrave Macmillan. http://dx.doi.org/10.1057/97811370 02501.0007.

Weyland, Kurt. 2009. *Bounded Rationality and Policy Diffusion: Social Sector Reform in Latin America.* Princeton: Princeton University Press. http://dx.doi.org/10.1515/9781400828067.

1

Neo-Liberalism in Question?

STEPHEN McBRIDE

The starting point of this chapter is that neo-liberalism ought to be in question since the implementation of this policy paradigm is responsible for recurrent crises,[1] including from 2007 to 2008, the most serious financial and economic crisis since the Great Depression. However, I argue here that there has been little deviation from neo-liberalism, especially in the heartlands of that doctrine. Among the implications for social policy are ongoing budgetary constraints and austerity, since they have been the neo-liberal response to the crisis. Critics might have questioned neo-liberalism, and some alternatives have been put forward, but they have lacked the traction to displace the dominant paradigm. Given the severity of the shock to the neo-liberal system, this requires examination.

This chapter begins by reviewing expectations that crises can provoke paradigm shifts. I then touch on why it matters for social and other policy areas whether neo-liberalism has been transcended. Then I develop the argument that neo-liberalism remains firmly entrenched, notwithstanding the development and articulation of alternatives. I also review explanations of neo-liberalism's durability in the face of a major crisis.

Crises and Policy Change

It is widely accepted that crises merely create the opportunities for replacing one policy paradigm with another but do not guarantee it (see Farnsworth and Irving 2011; Utting, Razavi, and Varghese Buchholz 2012a).[2] A number of factors will explain whether a crisis is transformed into a critical juncture that triggers fundamental policy change. Much of the policy change literature depicts a crisis that leads to a critical juncture as an "exogenous shock," a challenge posed by events, natural or political, that lie outside the boundaries of the existing policy system itself.[3] Examples might include natural disasters, the economic effects of security-related events such as the oil price increases in the 1970s, or the financial crisis that led to an economic crisis in 2007–8. Policy change is understood as a historical and evolutionary process punctuated by exogenous shock, conflict, and competition, which generate possibilities for paradigmatic change. This orthodoxy is rooted in seminal works by Baumgartner and Jones (1991, 1993) and Hall (1993) and identifies exogenous shocks or "focusing events" or "policy windows" (Kingdon 1984) as generating the conditions, including greater scope for agency (Katznelson 2003), under which more dramatic and paradigmatic policy and institutional transformations can occur. Stiglitz (2011, 169) notes that orthodox economics similarly must resort to external explanations for crises – according to the model and its assumptions, there is no room for such dislocations to develop, so they must come from outside the system itself.

Such change does not happen automatically, as the reference to agency signifies. Different actors dispute the causes of the crisis, they present different narratives and solutions, and the process by which the extent of change is furthered or blocked is inherently political, not "scientific" as based on superior ideas, analyses, or prescriptions (Hall 1993, 280). As Robert Cox (1981, 128) put it in a different context, "theory is always for someone and some purpose." The outcome depends on the alignment of political and social forces. On the global scale, Deacon (2012, 81) reminds us of the relevance of both ideas and interests, referring to the "discourse or hegemonic struggle through which different interests and actors jostle to be in the driver's seat of ideas and world views."

Interpreting the Crisis

Nonetheless, it might be argued that ideas and interpretations do matter in their own right. The rhetorical conversion of the current crisis from one of the (private) financial sector, underpinned by poor regulation and predatory behaviour, into a sovereign debt crisis, for which public authorities are responsible, and to which public sector austerity is the solution, is revealing. To the extent that this interpretation has taken hold, whatever its empirical foundation or lack thereof, it becomes a material factor in addressing the crisis.

Stephen McBride

The empirical basis for reframing the crisis in this way has been challenged. Ian Gough (2011, 53–58) has identified the drivers of increased public debt since the crisis occurred. They consist of the costs of governments' financial interventions to avert collapse of the banking and financial sector and the costs of fiscal stimulus to prevent depression and mass unemployment. The impact of automatic stabilizers such as unemployment insurance and increased social spending resulting from the effects of recessions was also important, along with the impact of slower or negative growth on tax revenues. It is important to note that all of these drivers of increased public (sovereign) debt are related to the crisis resulting from implementation of the dominant neo-liberal paradigm. Yet the policy solution widely advanced, public sector austerity, is entirely consistent with that paradigm and, resting on the implied proposition that sovereign debt results from state profligacy to which spending curbs provide the answer, evades the question of responsibility for the crisis (see Blyth 2013, 5–6). Since much sovereign debt in reality is socialized private debt, or the result of emergency measures taken to moderate the effects of a private sector crisis, successfully reframing the issue in this way is a discursive achievement.

This is particularly true since it has been accomplished as the intellectual case for austerity has disintegrated. In this context, the austerity "solution" can be defined, following international organizations' and states' practices, as comprising "fiscal consolidation" and structural reforms. Fiscal consolidation means getting state budgets back into balance within a reasonable period and reducing public debt as a percentage of GDP (OECD 2012b). Structural reforms include public efficiency, privatization of public services, and reduction of public subsidies. Structural reforms of social policy programs include changing disability and health compensation, eliminating early retirement schemes, reducing employment benefits, and ending short-work schemes (OECD 2012b). Much of the current debate has focused on the fiscal consolidation part of the equation. Widely cited papers by Reinhart and Rogoff (2010a, 2010b) claim that, once public debt reached 90 percent of GDP, growth fell dramatically. But Herndon, Ash, and Pollin (2013) probed the numbers and concluded that, "when properly calculated, the average real GDP growth rate for countries carrying a public-debt-to-GDP ratio of over 90 percent is actually 2.2 percent, not −0.1 percent as published in Reinhart and Rogoff. That is, average GDP growth at public debt/GDP ratios over 90 percent is not dramatically different than when debt/GDP ratios are lower." Similarly, Mark Blyth (2013) has convincingly demonstrated that austerity never works in the way that it is proclaimed to work by its advocates. Yet, as we shall see below, the policies espoused by states and key international organizations remain relatively impervious to the critique and the evidence on which austerity is based.

In explaining all of this, we can conclude that, though ideas genuinely do matter, they do not have autonomous impacts. Utting, Razavi, and Varghese Buchholz (2012a) note that structural changes in the economy – global production chains that focus on export-led growth, trade and investment liberalization, privatization (all central aspects of the neo-liberal paradigm) – have weakened governments and their perceptions of which choices are available to them. As well, Utting, Razavi, and Varghese Buchholz (2012a, 4) established that elites have "shown remarkable capacity to shape the post-crisis recovery process" through instrumental power (being directly involved in decision making) and discursive power (being able to frame how the crisis and responses to it are understood).

Is the Dominant Paradigm Changing or Being Reconstituted?

The concept of paradigm change or shift has been widely applied in the social sciences since Peter Hall's (1993) typology of policy change. The typology differentiates between first- and second-order changes that occur *within* a given paradigm and third-order changes when, as happens rarely, the entire policy paradigm shifts and the goals, as well as the instruments and settings, are transformed. There are operational difficulties in applying this approach to change. As Schmidt (2011, 39) observed, it can be difficult to know when paradigms have shifted and to understand why and how these shifts have occurred.[4] This is true whether paradigm change is envisaged as an "episodic rupture" or an "evolutionary process" (Skogstad and Schmidt 2011, 10). Indeed, counterposing the two options in this way confines the more dramatic episodic rupture to an excessively narrow range of cases and might not be an accurate depiction of what happens in those shifts. Acknowledging that identifying whether paradigm change is in progress is an inexact science, there still seems to be value in trying to establish the degree to which the neo-liberal paradigm is being challenged or reconstituted. It matters because the nature of the dominant paradigm is laden with consequences for social, political, and economic life.

At one level, neo-liberalism consists of a number of mutually reinforcing policy goals, underpinned by a theory that emphasizes individualism, the sanctity and efficiency of private property rights, the rule of law, a free market, and a minimal but strong state that guarantees preservation of the other rights and institutions (Gamble 1988; Harvey 2007). The neo-liberal program could be

Stephen McBride

sketched, then, as comprising policies promoting these aims. In the social policy sphere, these aims include the transfer of risk from society to the individual and a consequent restructuring of programs to tighten or impose conditions, such as preparation for labour market participation in exchange for receipt of benefits. The broader policy agenda includes privatization and deregulation; capital mobility and free trade; preservation of the value of money (i.e., an anti-inflation focus); a limited and fiscally constrained state (to keep taxes low), even in times of prosperity, but one nevertheless effective in reinforcing market relations; flexible labour markets to empower capital; and acceptance of market outcomes, including inequality.

Clearly, the list does contain most of the basic elements of neo-liberalism. But these elements, and the means of achieving them, are hardly static or frozen in time or space. The prominence of any one of them varies similarly. Partly because of the many crises that it has created, neo-liberalism is a dynamic construction constantly reinventing and reconstituting itself as new challenges arise. The neo-liberal package exhibits considerable variety by jurisdiction and over time.[5] However, the concept is worth retaining since there has been continuity of the fundamentals over the entire period that it has been dominant: budgetary austerity, implementation of regressive taxation, deregulation and reregulation, privatization, liberalization, determination to keep inflation under control even if at the expense of high unemployment, individual activation (as with welfare or "workfare" programs) rather than social compensation in the face of systemic problems such as unemployment, and free trade and capital mobility.

Moreover, these policies have been associated with a variety of outcomes meaning that the issue of whether the dominant paradigm is being reconstituted or replaced is of some consequence for the future of society. Interconnected outcomes associated with neo-liberalism include diminished democracy and depoliticization (Hay 2007; Offe 2013). These effects are associated partly with what Hay calls the "demonization" of politics resulting from neo-liberalism's close affinity with public choice theory and partly with institutional developments that increasingly place important powers in locations remote from and unaccountable to citizens (McBride 2010). The emphasis on markets has been depicted as an obfuscation behind which lies the rise of corporate power (Crouch 2011, 2013; Wilks 2013), within which finance predominates (Dumenil and Levy 2011), and in the face of which governments are ineffective. Socially, the welfare state has been displaced by the workfare state (MacLeavy 2010); policies aimed at full employment and economic security in the labour market have been abandoned (McBride 1992) and replaced by ones aimed at flexibility, with a consequent degradation of work and rise of precarious employment (Standing 1999; Schafer and Streeck 2013) and a promotion of inequality (Wilkinson and Pickett 2010, Chapter 16).

Questioning Neo-Liberalism

There is certainly evidence that since the 2007–8 crisis neo-liberalism has been questioned by a variety of intellectuals, social forces, some states and their leaders, and international organizations. Indeed, it was not without critics before the crisis.

Intellectuals and Social Forces

Heterodox economists (e.g., Quiggin 2010; Stanford 2008) are long-standing critics. Discrediting of the Reinhart-Rogoff thesis is one accomplishment of this school, and, though Blyth is a political scientist, his work on austerity should also be mentioned here. The group of critical economists has expanded, however, with the addition of voices such as Nobel Prize winners Paul Krugman (2013) and Joseph Stiglitz (2012) calling for fiscal stimulus as a response to the crisis and critiquing the austerity response and key assumptions of the prevailing economic model (Stiglitz 2011).

There have been massive protests and demonstrations in a number of countries. Icelandic voters refused to assume responsibility for the profligate and insolvent banking sector, and the government imposed capital controls to deter capital flight. From a position of structural weakness, labour has clearly sought to promote alternative ideas to resolve the crisis on terms more favourable to labour (McBride and Smith 2013). At the global level, this includes trying to influence the policy positions of international organizations, such as the ILO and OECD, in which labour, as a result of its strength in earlier periods, has representation. Global organizations such as the IMF, G8, and G20 have also been lobbied. Global labour officials sometimes depict their activities in a Gramscian sense as a struggle for hegemony: "Organized labour, political movements, and critical academic research and thinking, and also media and journalism [are involved in] trying to change the hegemonic discourse ... The ILO has the opportunity to bring some arguments for ... the kind of macroeconomic policies conducive to growth, which we can bring into the debate ... It's a complex process and you need alliances" (confidential telephone interview, ILO official, 7 November 2012, cited in McBride and Smith 2013, 221).

States and International Organizations

Even before this crisis struck there was evidence that the neo-liberal consensus was being rejected in parts of the world where international organizations had imposed it as part of structural adjustment programs and conditionalities attached to them. In Latin America, governments were elected on programs that explicitly rejected the neo-liberal Washington Consensus (Silva 2009). Since the crisis, election results in Greece, where the left-wing Syriza made major gains, and France, where a Socialist Party president, François Hollande, was elected, spawned hopes that a change of course would occur. Certainly, in the case of France, such hopes were dashed by the Hollande government's record in office. Elsewhere, some state leaders have been critical of the turn to austerity. For example, Brazil's president commented that "austerity by itself only generates more recession and more jobs' losses" because making budget adjustments "is not efficient unless practiced in the framework of growth."[6] In international forums, the United States has advocated stimulus over austerity, though domestically, after the initial fiscal stimulus program, political deadlock has meant an emphasis on monetary stimulus through quantitative easing. The size of the fiscal stimulus has been criticized as inadequate and its distribution between tax cuts and actual spending undesirable (Kregel 2011); however, some economists argue that the real stimulus was much higher than the $800 billion American Recovery and Reinvestment Act once measures such as unemployment insurance extensions and payroll tax cuts are factored into the equation.[7]

Other features of the neo-liberal package connected to capital mobility have come under fire. Some South American states have attempted to escape from the investor-state dispute procedures characteristic of international and bilateral investment agreements. Interest in controls on capital mobility has grown. Ministers from emerging nations denounced an IMF plan to limit capital controls to last-resort measures for countries facing volatile capital flows (Reddy 2011). Furthermore, there are limited signs that central propositions of neo-liberalism are being rethought by some states and other actors. For example, in April 2011, the government of Australia announced that it would no longer include investor-state arbitration provisions in its future economic agreements (Australian Trade Policy Statement, 12 April 2011).

Notwithstanding states' commitments to free trade (a crucial part of the neo-liberal package), the European Union has complained about increasing trade restrictions. Almost 700 new measures have been identified since October 2008, when the European Commission started monitoring global protectionist trends.

According to EU Trade Commissioner Karel De Gucht, "All of us need to stick to our pledge to fight back against protectionism. It is worrisome to see so many restrictive measures still being adopted and virtually none abolished ... The G20 agreed a long time ago to avoid protectionist tendencies because we all know these only hurt the global recovery in the long run."[8] In addition, some of the institutions and policies of neo-liberal globalism have encountered an impasse in terms of their further development. The best example is the Doha round of WTO negotiations, launched in November 2001; it was protracted, and many of the items originally envisaged were absent when the final agreement was signed in 2013. Even so, a multilateral agreement was signed, and many other regional and bilateral trade negotiations are under way.

Some international organizations have clearly diverged, at least in part, from neo-liberal orthodoxy. Although hardly presenting a full alternative macroeconomic paradigm in its publications, the ILO has been a voice for fiscal stimulus and social protection (see McBride and Merolli 2013), and it has "influenced other international agencies, such as the World Bank and G20, in the area of social protection (Deacon, this volume).[9] In Latin America, CEPAL has developed alternative perspectives with a strong social dimension (Mahon, this volume). The IMF has admitted that its zeal for austerity was sometimes mistaken, and it has issued a working paper acknowledging that its earlier advice was faulty because of underestimating the multiplier effect of reductions in government spending. Instead of a multiplier of 0.5, it seemed that the correct figure was as high as 1.5. In other words, for every dollar cut, $1.50 would be lost in output (see Blanchard and Leigh 2013). In these circumstances, austerity policies could well be excessive. The IMF advised the United Kingdom, for example, to consider slowing the pace of cuts, advice that the British government made clear it would reject.[10] Similarly, IMF economists have recognized that fiscal consolidation has adverse effects on demand and therefore on growth (Blanchard 2012). However, though the IMF might have become more flexible in its thinking about austerity, this flexibility mainly pertains to speed and size, not to the goal of fiscal consolidation itself. When a former IMF official claimed that policies imposed on Ireland by the troika had failed and that there was a need for alternatives to austerity, the IMF made clear its disagreement.[11]

Summing up, we can see numerous forms of criticism and some concrete measures that chip away at part of the neo-liberal edifice. But, as the next section outlines, there are few signs of a coherent, unified alternative or, at least outside Latin America, the kind of social coalition that could mount a serious challenge to the dominant neo-liberal ideas.

Neo-Liberalism in Question?

Intellectuals and Social Forces

Reviewing the impact of the voices questioning neo-liberalism does not support the conclusion that its hegemony is in peril. Labour might have expressed, at least in part, an alternative vision for the global economy, but it lacks power nationally and particularly internationally. During the neo-liberal era, labour was weakened significantly. In the OECD area, trade union density fell from about 36 percent in the mid-1970s to 17.5 percent in 2010 (OECD 2012a). Strike activity declined steadily over the same period. The OECD (2007) noted that the strike rate had roughly halved in each decade since the early 1980s. Politically, labour's great political forces of the past century are largely gone, as with the communist parties of Western Europe, or they are thoroughly integrated into the prevailing paradigm, as with almost all social democratic parties. Labour's voice is easy to disregard.

No significant business interests have defected from the neo-liberal strategy. Social movements opposed to neo-liberal globalization have occasionally won victories, for example in helping to block the adoption of the Multilateral Agreement on Investment in the 1990s. But, for the most part, they wage defensive battles. Moreover, they have failed to aggregate disparate demands into a coherent alternative.[12]

Notwithstanding dissident economists and other critics, there has been no change of mind on economic fundamentals among neo-liberal elites, particularly those in Europe. Nor has any alternative political force been able to wrest the initiative from those who have presided over the crisis-prone neo-liberal era. Thus, almost before stimulus programs had time to take effect, policy discussions turned to the issue of how quickly they could be terminated and "sound" budgetary policies restored. Efforts to significantly reform global financial governance made only limited headway.

In short, neo-liberal rule seems to be on the point of repeating its recent history by attempting to use the crises that its policies have regularly created to push its agenda to the next stage. Austerity will negatively affect social policy. Public debt will be used to further contract the social role of the state. This means, of course, that the policies and institutions that led to the meltdown remain in place and that some are even being extended. This can be seen in other policy areas too. For example, as multilateral trade negotiations have become more difficult, there has been a proliferation of regional (e.g., Trans Pacific Partnership) and bilateral trade negotiations (e.g., Canada-European Union,[13] European Union-United States).

States and International Organizations

Neither leading states nor economically important international organizations have defected from support for the neo-liberal package. This is exemplified by international organizations that rely on moral suasion, such as the OECD; those that play a coordinating role, such as the G20; and those that have coercive power, actually or potentially, such as the European Union, European Central Bank (ECB), and IMF.

As the introduction to this volume indicates, the OECD is a complex organization, and the publications and statements of its various sections are not always in harmony. In dealing with the crisis, however, the pronouncements of its Economics Department are probably the most important. Initially, the OECD supported the US government's capital investments in domestic financial institutions (OECD 2008a) and various reforms governing the conduct of financial institutions (OECD 2008b).[14] However, far from advocating a systemic alternative, the OECD's position was one of adjustment of the current instruments – first-order change in Hall's typology. Overall, the organization was supportive of fiscal stimulus as long as it was "timely, targeted and temporary" (OECD 2009b). From the first, limits to spending and a clear plan to scale back spending as the economy recovered were central to the OECD's advice to member states (OECD 2009a). Market liberalization remained at the heart of the OECD plan. The organization warned against overregulation, supported keeping markets open, and fostered privatization.

By the end of 2010, the OECD was clear that the time for extraordinary measures had ended and that the time for austerity had begun: "Many countries will have to face up to severe macroeconomic imbalances during the recovery period and beyond" (OECD 2010a). The organization positioned fiscal consolidation, with clear and negative implications for the funding of social programs, and structural reform as the two approaches that states needed to take. Structural reform would include increasing public efficiency, privatizing public services, reducing public subsidies, reforming disability and health compensation, eliminating early retirement schemes, reducing employment benefits, and ending short-work schemes (OECD 2012c). These changes were likely to restructure social programs in more residual directions than formerly, including through greater use of means testing, tighter eligibility requirements, substitution of conditional benefits for those based on rights or entitlement, encouragement of market-like provision of benefits through new public management techniques, and outright privatization of service provision. Such measures threaten existing concepts of the welfare state, including those articulated as part of the European social union (see Hermann 2013). OECD reports claimed that countries with high employment protection legislation experienced a much higher rise in structural unemployment and that "structural unemployment in countries with flexible labour and product markets is likely to be relatively untouched by economic downturns" (Furceri and Mourougane 2009, 3). Consequently, the OECD emphasized the importance of "willingness to work" conditions on social assistance and unemployment and the need to avoid early retirement plans or expansion of long-term disability. All of this is entirely consistent with pre-crisis thinking.

In the crisis and post-crisis period, the G20 assumed increased importance, partially displacing the older G7 and G8. This reflected the rise of strong developing states such as Brazil and China, with somewhat different agendas than the countries of North America, Europe, and Japan, which had held undisputed sway over the global political economy. Yet the impact of the G20 is ambiguous. G8 and G20 leaders' summit communiqués tend to be general, typically promoting job creation and growth *and* fiscal consolidation, stimulus *and* austerity, without clearly defining the lines or sequencing between them. More concretely, the G20 finance ministers' communiqués highlight the transition in prescriptions from the 2008–9 period to 2010 and beyond. In 2008–9, the ministers upheld the need for coordinated demand-stimulus in conjunction with reduced interest rates, financial institution recapitalization, and regulation of the financial sector. From about 2010 on, there was a shift toward fiscal consolidation, deficit reduction, reduction of debt-to-GDP ratios, structural labour market reforms, and measures to buttress investor confidence.

The European Union and Central Bank have been among the strongest advocates of austerity. This advocacy can be seen clearly in the conditions imposed in exchange for financial assistance. In the case of the peripheral countries of Europe, the IMF is a partner in these arrangements, forming, with the European Commission and the ECB, the troika (see Ayhan and McBride, this volume). The theoretical basis of imposed austerity on peripheral Europe is that cutting government deficits and debt will reassure financial markets, thus lowering borrowing costs, and lead to renewed economic growth. The painful social impact of austerity is acknowledged but deemed necessary (Blackstone 2012). Even in cases in which the European Commission has relaxed its stance by giving countries more time to bring deficits under control, this leniency has been balanced by insistence on other neo-liberal measures – structural reforms of labour markets and pension systems and other social programs (Dalton and Stevis 2013). Similarly, though some EU documents (e.g., *Europe 2020*; see

European Commission 2010) prioritize "inclusive growth" and a variety of social measures, it has been suggested that the real priority is fiscal consolidation, wage moderation, and supply-side measures on job creation despite the demand-deficient nature of current unemployment (Leschke, Theodoropoulou, and Watt 2012). In short, there is little sign of any serious rethinking of the neo-liberal nostrums that have guided EU policy to date. Similarly, Sarah Babb's careful application of the notion of policy paradigms to the global level is instructive. Babb assesses the degree to which international financial institutions (IFIs) such as the World Bank and IMF have diverged from the neo-liberal Washington Consensus and concludes that both they and the states that to a degree challenged features of the consensus have enacted changes but that they do not amount to a paradigm shift (2013, 285–92). Thus, though criticism of the liberal paradigm, never absent during its long period of hegemony, might have intensified since the crisis (and in some parts of the world since previous crises), it remains relatively unshaken as the guide to action of important states and global institutions (see Crouch 2011; Peck 2013), with important and challenging implications for all policy areas, including social policy.

Explanations

Some explanations for policy continuity rely on cognitive lock-in by decision makers – a phenomenon that can be used to explain path dependency. It might be that only in the context of a major and unpredictable, or unpredicted, exogenous shock does the range of possible choices open up and a new direction become possible. Even so, the odds remain stacked in favour of continuity. Veto players can block significant change from occurring (Hirschi and Widmer 2010; Tsebelis 1995, 2002; Zohlnhöfer 2009). There can be congruence among players who opt not to disturb the status quo (Coyle and Wildavsky 1987; Tsebelis 2002; Wildavsky 1982; Zohlnhöfer 2009). These factors do bring in agency and power to a degree. Others, for example Blyth (2001), emphasize ideational practices. He suggests that ideas function in three ways in contexts of shock: as institutional blueprints, as weapons, and as cognitive locks. The third, cognitive locks, or constraints on the range of policy options that agents perceive are at their disposal (Blyth 2001), is of most interest in the current situation. Cognitive locking-in suggests that policy change does not inevitably follow from crisis and shock, because policy makers operate with strong cognitive attachments to existing policy preferences and ideas. Thus, in the context of shock, policy makers debate and define the parameters of potential responses within cognitive, rather than structural, boundaries (Blyth 2001; Starke, Kaasch, and van Hooren 2013, 182–84).

Still, these psychological explanations are unsatisfactory in that they leave out the "elephant in the room" – power and interests. True, in mainstream accounts of policy change, the activities of advocacy coalitions, veto players, or policy entrepreneurs do sometimes feature, thus putting agency into the equation. But these theories do not sufficiently address systemic political economy and the instrumental and structural power wielded by those who forged the neo-liberal era and continue to benefit from it.

It is easy to forget how central the weakening of labour was to the triumph of neo-liberalism. This was accomplished through coercion, as with the Professional Air Traffic Controllers Organization (PATCO) and National Union of Mineworkers (NUM) disputes, through allowing unemployment to rise (McBride 1992),[15] through globalization permitting the relocation of production and the threat of capital flight, through policies to render labour markets flexible, and so on. The weakening of labour was accompanied by entrenchment of the power of capital, and the outcomes of this shift in power can be traced in trends in income and wealth inequality and social mobility. Although the composition of capital might have evolved, with many pointing to the increased significance of finance, there is little or no evidence to suggest that its predominance has been undermined. The ability of finance to ensure that its losses in successive financial crises of the neo-liberal era are socialized indicates the contrary. Certainly, the insistence on austerity as a response to the 2007–8 crisis has been explained in terms of the class forces demanding it (Crotty 2012; Johnson and Kwak 2012).

The degree to which neo-liberalism has been structurally and institutionally locked-in to the political and economic structures at both state and international levels also might help to explain its resilience. Devices such as central bank independence; international agreements that restricted trade and investment options for states; removal of much control of monetary policy, including the option of devaluation, as with the eurozone; and fiscal policy options through Europe's Stability and Growth Pact all play their parts. Given the remoteness (from democratic accountability) of many of these institutional innovations, and the fact that the rules that they embody favour capital, the persistence of the neo-liberal paradigm is unsurprising. In that sense, the new constitutionalism of the neo-liberal order is working according to plan. Its effects include insulating (private) capital from government (i.e., public) regulation; locating key powers in ways that are remote from popular pressure and democratic influence; "locking-in" the neo-liberal content of globalization by embedding rules in international treaties; and creating agreements that are difficult to change. Underpinning these trends is the enhanced structural power of private capital (Gill 1992; Gill and Law 1989; Harmes 2006; McBride 2010), especially finance.

Notes

1 Deep recessions in the early 1980s and 1990s and periodic financial crises (e.g., Mexico in 1994–95, East Asia in 1997–98, Russia in 1998, Turkey in 2000, and Argentina in 2001–3).

2 The concept of policy paradigm includes an economic and capital accumulation strategy. See McBride and Whiteside (2011, Chapter 2).

3 Like many of the terms used in the literature, "critical juncture" has been described as overly descriptive and "underspecified"; see Hogan (2006).

4 For a sophisticated review of the literature on policy paradigms and paradigm shifts, see Skogstad and Schmidt (2011).

5 As did the previously dominant Keynesian paradigm; see Esping-Andersen (1990). In neo-liberalism, examples of modification and adjustment can be seen as policy learning and adjustment in the face of crisis. For example, Peck and Tickell (2002) describe three phases of neo-liberalism as it evolved from an intellectual rival to Keynesianism in the 1970s to a set of policy prescriptions in the 1980s dealing with problems of global stagflation and distinguish between roll-back and roll-out policies. The roll-back concept refers to the partial demolition or reduction of the key institutions and programs of the Keynesian era. The roll-out concept, on the other hand, identifies a phase of constructing new institutions and programs that embed the neo-liberal approach to governance (see Whiteside 2013).

6 Comment made on 13 December 2012; see http://en.mercopress.com/2012/12/13/rousseff -warns-austerity-measures-alone-are-not-sufficient-to-address-economic-crises.

7 See http://dailycaller.com/2012/08/06/analysis-real-stimulus-spending-is-at-least-2-5-trillion-since-2008/; also see Boychuk (this volume).

8 See http://europa.eu/rapid/press-release_IP-13-807_en.htm.

9 The adoption of a global social protection floor represents a significant development. Whether it is one that really breaks with the dominant paradigm is more open to question (see Mestrum 2013).

10 See http://www.bbc.co.uk/news/business-22623519; and http://online.wsj.com/article/BT-CO-20130419-708495.html.

11 See http://www.rte.ie/news/2013/0722/463911-budget/.

12 A Brazilian trade union leader noted that he had counted the agenda items raised at a large meeting of social movements and unions; there were over 900 items. See Halimi (2013, 13).

13 An agreement in principle was announced on 18 October 2013.

14 For a fuller account, see McBride and Merolli (2013).

15 In an interesting interview, Sir Alan Budd, special adviser to the Treasury Board under Prime Minister Thatcher, alluded to this possibility: "The nightmare I sometimes have,

about this whole experience, runs as follows. I was involved in making a number of proposals which were partly at least adopted by the government and put in play by the government. Now, my worry is as follows – that there may have been people making the actual policy decisions, or people behind them or people behind them, who never believed for a moment that this was the correct way to bring down inflation. They did, however, see that it would be a very, very good way to raise unemployment, and raising unemployment was an extremely desirable way of reducing the strength of the working classes – if you like, that what was engineered there in Marxist terms was a crisis of capitalism which re-created a reserve army of labour and has allowed the capitalists to make high profits ever since. Now again, I would not say I believe that story, but when I really worry about all this, I worry whether that indeed was really what was going on." See http://www.youtube.com/watch?v=sdZp5iw-UEo.

References

Babb, Sarah. 2013. "The Washington Consensus as Transnational Policy Paradigm: Its Origins, Trajectory, and Likely Successor." *Review of International Political Economy* 20, 2: 268–97. http://dx.doi.org/10.1080/09692290.2011.640435.

Baumgartner, F.R., and B.D. Jones. 1991. "Agenda Dynamics and Policy Subsystems." *Journal of Politics* 53, 4: 1044–74. http://dx.doi.org/10.2307/2131866.

–. 1993. *Agendas and Instability in American Politics*. Chicago: University of Chicago Press.

Blackstone, Barry. 2012. "ECB Chief Defends Austerity Measures." http://online.wsj.com/article/SB10001424127887324677204578185631431132060.html.

Blanchard, Olivier. 2012. "Driving the Global Economy with the Brakes On." *IMF Direct*, 24 January. http://blog-imfdirect.imf.org/2012/01/24/driving-the-global-economy-with-the-brakes-on/.

Blanchard, Olivier, and Daniel Leigh. 2013. "Growth Forecast Errors and Fiscal Multipliers." *IMF Working Paper* 13, 1: 1. http://dx.doi.org/10.5089/9781475576443.001.

Blyth, Mark. 2001. "The Transformation of the Swedish Model: Economic Ideas, Distributional Conflict, and Institutional Change." *World Politics* 54, 1: 1–26. http://dx.doi.org/10.1353/wp.2001.0020.

–. 2013. *Austerity: The History of a Dangerous Idea*. Oxford: Oxford University Press.

Cox, R. 1981. "Social Forces, States, and World Orders: Beyond International Relations Theory." *Millennium* 10, 2: 126–55. http://dx.doi.org/10.1177/03058298810100020501.

Coyle, D., and A. Wildavsky. 1987. "Requisites of Radical Reform." *Journal of Policy Analysis and Management* 7, 1: 1–16. http://dx.doi.org/10.2307/3323347.

Crotty, James. 2012. "The Great Austerity War: What Caused the US Deficit Crisis and Who Should Pay to Fix It?" *Cambridge Journal of Economics* 36, 1: 79–104. http://dx.doi.org/10.1093/cje/ber029.

Crouch, Colin. 2011. *The Strange Non-Death of Neoliberalism*. Cambridge, UK: Polity.

–. 2013. "From Markets versus States to Corporations versus Civil Society." In *Politics in an Age of Austerity*, edited by Armin Schafer and Wolfgang Streeck, 219-38. Cambridge, UK: Polity.

Dalton, Matthew, and Matina Stevis. 2013. "EU Eases Austerity Goals for Six Nations." http://stream.wsj.com/story/latest-headlines/SS-2-63399/SS-2-242024/.

Deacon, Bob. 2012. "Shifting Global Social Policy Discourse and Governance in Times of Crisis." In *The Global Crisis and Transformative Social Change*, edited by P. Utting,

S. Razavi, and R. Varghese Buchholz. London: Palgrave Macmillan and UNRISD. http://dx.doi.org/10.1057/9781137002501.0011.

Dumenil, Gerard, and Dominique Levy. 2011. *The Crisis of Neoliberalism*. Cambridge, MA: Harvard University Press.

Esping-Andersen, G. 1990. *The Three Worlds of Welfare Capitalism*. Princeton: Princeton University Press.

European Commission. 2010. *Europe 2020*. Brussels: European Commission

Farnsworth, K., and Z. Irving, eds. 2011. *Social Policy in Challenging Times: Economic Crisis and Welfare Systems*. Bristol: Policy Press. http://dx.doi.org/10.1332/policypress/9781847428288.001.0001.

Furceri, Davide, and Annabelle Mourougane. 2009. "How do Institutions Affect Structural Unemployment in Times of Crises?" Economics Department Working Papers, OECD, Paris.

Gamble, Andrew. 1988. *The Free Economy and the Strong State*. London: Macmillan.

Gill, Stephen. 1992. "Economic Globalization and the Internationalization of Authority: Limits and Contradictions." *Geoforum* 23, 3: 269–83. http://dx.doi.org/10.1016/0016-7185(92)90042-3.

Gill, Stephen, and David Law. 1989. "Global Hegemony and the Structural Power of Capital." *International Studies Quarterly* 33, 4: 475–99. http://dx.doi.org/10.2307/2600523.

Gough, I. 2011. "From Financial Crisis to Fiscal Crisis." In *Social Policy in Challenging Times: Economic Crisis and Welfare Systems*, edited by K. Farnsworth and Z. Irving, 49-64. Bristol: Policy Press. http://dx.doi.org/10.1332/policypress/9781847428288.003.0003.

Halimi, Serge. 2013. "We Can't Go on like This." *Le monde diplomatique*, 13 September.

Hall, Peter. 1993. "Policy Paradigms, Social Learning, and the State: The Case of Economic Policy-Making in Britain." *Comparative Politics* 25, 3: 275–96. http://dx.doi.org/10.2307/422246.

Harmes, Adam. 2006. "Neoliberalism and Multilevel Governance." *Review of International Political Economy* 13, 5: 725–49. http://dx.doi.org/10.1080/09692290600950621.

Harvey, David. 2007. *A Brief History of Neoliberalism*. Oxford: Oxford University Press.

Hay, Colin. 2007. *Why We Hate Politics*. Cambridge, UK: Polity.

Hermann, Christoph. 2013. "Crisis, Structural Reform, and the Dismantling of the European Social Model(s)." Working Paper No. 26, Institute for International Political Economy, Berlin.

Herndon, Thomas, Michael Ash, and Robert Pollin. 2013. "Does High Public Debt Consistently Stifle Economic Growth: A Critique of Reinhart and Rogoff." Working Paper 322, Political Economy Research Institute, University of Massachusetts.

Hirschi, C., and T. Widmer. 2010. "Policy Change and Policy Stasis: Comparing Swiss Foreign Policy toward South Africa (1968–94) and Iraq (1990–91)." *Policy Studies Journal: The Journal of the Policy Studies Organization* 38, 3: 537–63. http://dx.doi.org/10.1111/j.1541-0072.2010.00373.x.

Hogan, John. 2006. "Remoulding the Critical Junctures Approach." *Canadian Journal of Political Science* 39, 3: 657–79. http://dx.doi.org/10.1017/S0008423906060203.

Johnson, Simon, and James Kwak. 2012. *13 Bankers: The Wall Street Takeover and the New Meltdown*. New York: Pantheon.

Katznelson, I. 2003. "Periodization and Preferences: Reflections on Purposive Action in Comparative Historical Social Science." In *Comparative Historical Analysis in the Social*

Sciences, edited by J. Mahoney and D. Rueschmeyer, 270–302. New York: Cambridge University Press. http://dx.doi.org/10.1017/CBO9780511803963.009.

Kingdon, J. 1984. *Agendas, Alternatives, and Public Policies*. Boston: Little Brown and Company.

Kregel, J. 2011. "Resolving the US Financial Crisis: Politics Dominates Economics in the New Political Economy." *PSL Quarterly Review* 64: 23–37.

Krugman, Paul. 2013. *End This Depression Now!* New York: W.W. Norton.

Leschke, Janine, Sotiria Theodoropoulou, and Andrew Watt. 2012. "How Do Economic Governance Reforms and Austerity Measures Affect Inclusive Growth as Formulated in the *Europe 2020* Strategy?" In *A Triumph of Failed Ideas: European Models of Capitalism in the Crisis*, edited by Steffen Lehdorff, 243–81. Brussels: European Trade Union Institute.

MacLeavy, Julie. 2010. "Remaking the Welfare State: From Safety Net to Trampoline." In *The Rise and Fall of Neoliberalism: The Collapse of an Economic Order?*, edited by Kean Birch and Vlad Mykhnenko, 133–50. London: Zed Books.

McBride, Stephen. 1992. *Not Working: State, Unemployment, and Neo-Conservatism in Canada*. Toronto: University of Toronto Press.

–. 2010. "The New Constitutionalism: International and Private Rule in the New Global Order." In *Relations of Global Power: Neoliberal Order and Disorder*, edited by Gary Teeple and Stephen McBride, 19-40. Toronto: University of Toronto Press.

McBride, Stephen, and Jessica Merolli. 2013. "Alternatives to Austerity? Post-Crisis Policy Advice from Global Institutions." *Global Social Policy* 13, 3: 299–320. http://dx.doi.org/10.1177/1468018113499980.

McBride, Stephen, and Scott Smith. 2013. "In the Shadow of Crisis: Economic Orthodoxy and the Response of Global Labour." *Global Labour Journal*, 4, 3: 206-29.

McBride, Stephen, and Heather Whiteside. 2011. *Private Affluence, Public Austerity: Economic Crisis and Democratic Malaise in Canada*. Halifax: Fernwood.

Mestrum, Francine. 2013. "Social Protection Floor: Beyond Poverty Reduction?" Global Social Justice. http://www.globalsocialjustice.eu/index.php?option=com_content&id =223:social-protection-floor-beyond-poverty-reduction&Itemid=6.

OECD. 2007. "Strikes." In *Society at a Glance* 2006 OECD Social Indicators: OECD Social Indicators. OECD Publishing. http://dx.doi.org/10.1787/soc_glance-2006-34- en p.110.

–. 2008a. Statement by the Secretary-General of the OECD on the Financial Crisis and its Aftermath. OECD: Paris.

–. 2008b. Address by Angel Gurría, OECD Secretary-General. Presented at the Enlarged Parliamentary Assembly of the Council of Europe, 8 October, Strasbourg.

–. 2009a. *Economic Policy Reforms 2009*. Paris: OECD.

–. 2009b. *OECD Economic Outlook: Interim Reform March 2009*. Paris: OECD.

–. 2010a. OECD Economic Outlook Vol 1. Paris: OECD.

–. 2012a. *Trade Union Density 1975-2011*. Paris: OECD.

–. 2012b. *Fiscal Consolidation: How Much, How Fast, and by What Means?* Paris: OECD.

–. 2012c. Going for Growth Report 2009. Paris: OECD.

Offe, Claus. 2013. "Participatory Inequality in the Austerity State: A Supply-Side Approach." In *Politics in an Age of Austerity*, edited by Armin Schafer and Wolfgang Streeck, 196–218. Cambridge, UK: Polity.

Peck, Jamie. 2013. "Explaining (with) Neoliberalism." *Territory, Politics, Governance* 1, 2: 132–57. http://dx.doi.org/10.1080/21622671.2013.785365.

Peck, Jamie, and Adam Tickell. 2002. "Neoliberalizing Space." *Antipode* 34, 3: 380–404. http://dx.doi.org/10.1111/1467-8330.00247.

Quiggin, John. 2010. *Zombie Economics: How Dead Ideas Still Walk among Us*. Princeton: Princeton University Press.

Reddy, Sudeep. 2011. "Emerging Nations Reject Capital Plan." *Wall Street Journal Internet Edition*. http://www.wsj.com/articles/SB10001424052748703702004576268980074855142.

Reinhart, C.M., and K.S. Rogoff. 2010a. "Growth in a Time of Debt." *American Economic Review* 100: 573-78.

–. 2010b. "Growth in a Time of Debt." Working Paper 15639, National Bureau of Economic Research. http://www.nber.org/papers/w15639.

Schafer, Armin, and Wolfgang Streeck, eds. 2013. *Politics in an Age of Austerity*. Cambridge, UK: Polity.

Schmidt, Vivien A. 2011. "Reconciling Ideas and Institutions through Discursive Institutionalism." In *Ideas and Politics in Social Science Research*, edited by Daniel Béland and Robert Henry Cox, 47–64. New York: Oxford University Press.

Silva, Eduardo. 2009. *Challenging Neoliberalism in Latin America*. Cambridge, UK: Cambridge University Press. http://dx.doi.org/10.1017/CBO9780511803222.

Skogstad, Grace, and Vivien A. Schmidt. 2011. "Introduction: Policy Paradigms, Transnationalism, and Domestic Politics." In *Policy Paradigms, Transnationalism, and Domestic Politics*, edited by Grace Skogstad, 3-35. Toronto: University of Toronto Press.

Standing, Guy. 1999. *Global Labour Flexibility: Seeking Distributive Justice*. Basingstoke: Macmillan.

Stanford, Jim. 2008. *Economics for Everyone*. Halifax: Fernwood.

Starke, Peter, Alexandra Kaasch, and Franca van Hooren. 2013. *The Welfare State as Crisis Manager: Explaining the Diversity of Policy Responses to Economic Crisis*. London: Palgrave Macmillan. http://dx.doi.org/10.1057/9781137314840.

Stiglitz, Joseph E. 2011. "Rethinking Macroeconomics: What Went Wrong and How to Fix It." *Global Policy* 2, 2: 165–75. http://dx.doi.org/10.1111/j.1758-5899.2011.00095.x.

–. 2012. *The Price of Inequality*. London: Penguin.

Tsebelis, G. 1995. "Decision Making in Political Systems: Veto Players in Presidentialism, Parliamentarism, Multicameralism, and Multipartism." *British Journal of Political Science* 25, 2: 289–325. http://dx.doi.org/10.1017/S0007123400007225.

–. 2002. *Veto Players: How Political Institutions Work*. Princeton: Princeton University Press.

Utting, P., S. Razavi, and R. Varghese Buchholz. 2012a. "Overview: Social and Political Dimensions of the Global Crisis: Possible Futures." In *The Global Crisis and Transformative Social Change*, edited by P. Utting, S. Razavi, and R. Varghese Buchholz, 1–22. Basingstoke: Palgrave Macmillan. http://dx.doi.org/10.1057/9781137002501.0007.

Whiteside, Heather. 2013. "The Pathology of Profitable Partnerships: Dispossession, Marketization, and Canadian P3 Hospitals." PhD diss., Simon Fraser University.

Wildavsky, A. 1982. "The Three Cultures." *Public Interest* 69: 45–58.

Wilkinson, Richard, and Kate Pickett. 2010. *The Spirit Level: Why Equality Is Better for Everyone*. London: Penguin.

Wilks, Stephen. 2013. *The Political Power of the Business Corporation*. Cheltenham: Edward Elgar. http://dx.doi.org/10.4337/9781849807326.

Zohlnhöfer, R. 2009. "How Politics Matter When Policies Change: Understanding Policy Change as a Political Problem." *Journal of Comparative Policy Analysis: Research and Practice* 11, 1: 97–115. http://dx.doi.org/10.1080/13876980802648300.

2

Broadening the Frame
Inclusive Growth and the Social
Investment Perspective

JANE JENSON

Any great economic crisis provokes two types of assessment by social policy analysts. The Great Depression of the 1930s brought skyrocketing unemployment, and social policy was in tatters. Since 2008, Greece has provided another chilling example of the costs of economic crisis, with its massive and rapid increases in unemployment and poverty, in part following from radical cutbacks in public spending. A first assessment, then, is that crisis threatens social policy. And this conclusion is correct.

A second assessment might be simultaneously correct, however. Great crises have been moments of huge social innovation. Karl Polanyi (1944) reviewed decades of economic liberalization and market building to develop and refine his argument that the workings of an expanding and supposedly "self-regulating market" provoked a response that focused on preserving the social fabric, what we might call social cohesion. Subsequently, numerous analyses have traced the construction over the Great Depression and Second World War of what are termed Keynesian welfare regimes. As Weir and Skocpol (1985, 108) described these years, "coherent economic arguments were developed to justify government spending not merely (in timeworn fashion) as a humanitarian response to emergency, but also as a proper strategy of national macroeconomic management in advanced capitalism." We might ask, then, whether the last number of years, including the post-2007 crisis, are already laying the foundation for such a Polanyian moment, one that would put neo-liberalism to rest and generate social policy innovation.

This chapter argues that, for a number of years before 2007 and into the aftermath of the crisis, we can find the promotion of economic arguments for state spending, in the name of both economic stabilization and better social policy. This is no return to a Keynesian welfare regime, to be sure. Nonetheless, these conversations take the form of a geographic as well as trans-sector extension of the policy frame of "inclusive growth" and the incorporation within it of the social investment perspective on social policy. In some policy communities, arguments go well beyond the "humanitarian response to emergency" and even beyond a focus on poverty. They seek to provide propositions for reducing the inequality that is a major legacy of the neo-liberal years in many countries.

Compared with the 1930s and 1940s, however, neither the institutional locales nor the actors are the same. Although national states are by no means sidelined in policy actions, international organizations and transnational policy communities built over the past seventy years have generated wide-reaching policy networks and formidable policy legacies that shape interventions. Another contrast is geographical. Early transnational policy communities as well as institutional settings were overwhelmingly populated by concerns about and actors from what we now term the "global North." Policy diffusion, to the extent that it occurred (e.g., to Latin America), was distinctly unidirectional toward the "global South." I will document that ideas and interpretive frames now travel from South to North and within the South.

Analytical Comments

For decades, analysts have sought the best way to understand public policy development. Concentrating on the broad area of social policy, we can observe abandonment of the structuralist argument that welfare state development depended on economic growth, and a turn to political factors to account for both the timing and characteristics of welfare regimes. Historical institutionalism made significant early contributions. Whereas a first branch often focused on continuity, a second branch always asked about change and the contribution of ideas to change (Thelen and Steinmo 1992, 13–14). Both now have a change-oriented focus, often seeking to assess the effects of globalization, of neo-liberalism, of Europeanization, and so on. Although the "continuity" group has made strides in describing change (e.g., Streeck and Thelen 2005), the "ideas" group unfortunately has diverged in some cases from the key insight of historical institutionalism that ideas do not "do" anything, that they must be understood as socially and institutionally anchored.[1]

This chapter therefore returns to one of historical institutionalism's basic insights, that there is representational content to *any* action, whether of policy makers or citizens, of national agencies or international organizations. Actors' representations of who they are, what they want, and more broadly what the "world looks like" shape their identities and the definitions of their interests as well as their strategies (Jenson 1990). Yet actors are also constrained by structured relations in a universe of political discourse shaped by institutionalized power relations and patterns of interest driven in part by policy legacies. The universe of political discourse bounds ideas as well as interests and institutions.

There are conditions, of course, under which the universe of political discourse is less stable, in which paradigms can be more easily altered (Jenson 1990, 663–64). Times of economic crisis have been conjunctures in which new ideas and interests institutionalize (e.g., Hall 1993; Weir and Skocpol 1985). Some institutional configurations, such as federalism, can also foster a more open universe of political discourse (Banting and Myles 2013). Altered patterns of power relations within governments can also destabilize the universe of political discourse (Mahon 1977). For example, during the years of high neoliberalism, reconfigured power within states gave finance ministries a preponderant influence on social policy directions, while social ministries faded into the background (Jenson 2012b). It is essential, therefore, to map this universe with care and without presuppositions.

Such a mapping approach is easily extended beyond national settings to the policy perspectives of international organizations and the universe of political discourse within which they operate. Just as national policies can alter over time, break with previously selected paths or continue along them, innovate or stagnate, so too can policies promoted by international organizations and transnational networks. As with national (or subnational) states, the fluidity of stances of international organizations is also an empirical question. There is no valid reason to assume that they are more or less likely to modify their policy stances than any other kind of institution.[2]

With these analytical premises in mind, I examine in this chapter the encounter in the current social policy discursive universe of two ideational constructions that international institutions have increasingly promoted together and in interaction with each other. One is "inclusive growth," and the other is "social investment." A range of international and supranational institutions is engaged in the incorporation of what originally developed as a perspective for modernizing welfare states into an economic frame initially proposed for addressing economic issues in the global South.

Jane Jenson

Inclusive Growth Spreads: From "Pro-Poor" to "the Socials"

The universe of political discourse is being altered; inequality is increasingly accused of hindering development in the North as well as the South. The OECD's (2008, 2011) path-breaking publications documenting escalating inequality are part of a blurring of regional boundaries within policy communities as well as a refocusing of attention from so-called structural impediments to consequences of recent policy. Part of this swing was the 2013 launch of the OECD's Initiative on Inclusive Growth, which explicitly called attention to rising inequality in the North and South and proposed an inclusive growth strategy to limit negative effects.[3]

The campaign for inclusive growth began in the development community a number of years ago. As Ianchovichina and Lundstrom (2009, 2) write of the World Bank's 2008 Commission on Growth and Development, "the commission notes that inclusiveness – a concept that encompasses equity, equality of opportunity, and protection in market and employment transitions – is an essential ingredient of any successful growth strategy. [It] considers systematic inequality of opportunity 'toxic' as it will derail the growth process through political channels or conflict." Both the World Bank and the OECD were ultimately concerned with the high costs of political opposition, as they had been in the first half of the 1990s. Then they proposed "social cohesion" as the remedy (Jenson 1998, 5–6); now it is "inclusive growth."

Although much of the discussion of inclusive growth still focuses on production and trade, the distribution of resources and power is a growing part of the conversation (see, e.g., Ianchovichina and Lundstrom 2009; OECD 2013; Ranieri and Ramos 2013). This attention to inequalities in distribution of income and power has led, in turn, to proposals for better social protection across the world, including a social protection floor (ILO 2011). It has taken several years, however, for this link between growth and inequality to be made.

Poverty as the Problem

In the mid-1990s, a congeries of interconnected challenges preoccupied policy communities. Even before the Asian economic crisis of 1997, neo-liberal policy prescriptions were giving way to concern at both national and international levels that poverty was soaring. Within the institutions working in the global South, attention to the issue of poverty rose. The World Bank, for example, "redefined its official mission as 'working for a world free of poverty'" (Noël and Thérien 2008, 183) under the presidency of James Wolfensohn that began in 1995. In these early years, the focus was primarily on the negative consequences of a decade of neo-liberalism, especially for the South (and particularly Africa), for poor and low-income earners in all regions of the world, and for children. The OECD Development Assistance Committee published its *Shaping the 21st Century* at mid-decade, saying that, "clearly, we need to sustain and increase official development assistance if we expect to see a reversal of the growing marginalisation of the poor and achieve progress toward realistic goals of human development" (OECD Development Assistance Committee 1996, 16). It is interesting – and very relevant – to note that this report identified an additional outcome; it described the "greater similarity in the policies of industrialised and developing countries" (5).

At the same time as the OECD's development branch was laying bare the consequences of poverty in "developing countries," the secretariat was calling on members of the OECD to rethink structural adjustment practices that might be leading to outcomes (termed "social exclusion") menacing economic growth and well-being. The organization had been a fervent proponent of neo-liberal-style labour market interventions in the 1980s and early 1990s, but it undertook a course adjustment in the face of concerns about social cohesion, instability, and the social as well as political costs of the structural adjustments that it had been promoting (Mahon 2008).[4] This modification led to attention to poverty and strategies to limit social exclusion.

The diagnostic rested on several arguments for why poverty should be reduced. One was simply to ensure social rights and equity. Another was to protect the gains associated with globalization from the braking effects of social upheaval, environmental degradation, and so on. A third was to protect the North's welfare state from itself by judicious policy reforms (especially of pension and unemployment programs that consumed large amounts of state revenue) and by new policy commitments and instruments to confront the "new social risks." Nonetheless, these social policy innovators were still treating social concerns and challenges as a weight on the economy, albeit one that had to be borne – and lightened – in order to achieve larger goals. In other words, the fear was that "the social" could brake "the economic" if countries and international organizations continued with the policies of the neo-liberal decades.

By the first decade of the new century, then, analysts could point to what is called "a global anti-poverty consensus." It could be described as a "rediscovery" of poverty (Staab and Gerhard 2010, 1), bringing a wave of attention to what have been called "pro-poor" policies or the "poverty reduction paradigm." This concern about poverty shaped policy interventions in both the North and the South. Nonetheless, the "anti-poverty" label did not lead to any single social policy prescription for "after neo-liberalism."

Jane Jenson

Seeking the Appropriate "Social" Intervention

When political discourse turned to *what to do* about poverty, how to combat or reduce it, there was often a turn to one of the "socials" – social inclusion, social cohesion, and social capital. Proposals to promote social capital tended to focus on combatting poverty by strengthening individuals' ties to each other (Szreter and Woolcock 2004 provide an overview). The other two concepts, however, rested on the assumption that addressing relations among individuals or families would be inadequate. Both included an institutional analysis that prescribed intervention by governments, non-governmental organizations, and international agencies in order to fight poverty and social exclusion. The turn to these concepts in the universe of political discourse traversed the traditional divide between "developed" and "developing" worlds.

These analyses of *how* the "socials" might reduce poverty all explicitly identified a relationship between lagging social development, whether measured by poverty or social exclusion, and economic well-being and growth. As they did so, spending on social programs eventually lost its status as a "cost to be borne" and became a positive contribution to the present and future well-being of northern and southern societies. Concomitantly, an additional "social" began to overtake the others. This was "social investment." Such an investment was presented by enthusiasts as a "productive factor" rather than a burden (Vandenbroucke, Hemerijck, and Palier 2011).

This addition brings to the universe of political discourse a compelling idea about *where* policy interventions should be directed. The calling card of social investment is that it is "child centred." In particular, the perspective everywhere contains a commitment to human capital formation, from early childhood through the stages of formal education. Investments in child care and schooling are identified as good for children's human capital accumulation and as supports for the labour market participation of their parents, particularly their mothers (Jenson 2001; Michel and Peng 2012).

The Social Investment Perspective for "after Neo-Liberalism"

In many ways, the discourse of and prescriptions for social investment are innovative. They retrieve a certain amount of legitimacy for state action after the assaults of neo-liberalism, though by no means do they represent a full return to principles of the Keynesian welfare regimes of the post-1945 years.[5] The perspective reworks basic notions about how to achieve a measure of income security and how to ensure care for dependants, thereby also providing answers different from the citizenship regimes of the post-1945 years (Jenson 2012a). In many countries, these earlier regimes rested on a male-breadwinner model, promoting "full employment" for (the male half of) the population and assuming that most care for dependants (children and vulnerable adults) would be provided privately in the home. The social investment perspective represents another social policy regime, in which the state has a degree of responsibility for both limiting poverty and ensuring adequate amounts of social care (Jenson and Levi 2013).

These principles contrast with several premises of neo-liberalism. Neo-liberals had popularized the diagnosis that social spending and state intervention were in conflict with economic prosperity, and the state as the generator of such spending was labelled the source of the problems of many countries. Markets ought to be the distributors of well-being, families responsible for their own opportunities, and the community sector the final safety net. The social investment perspective offers an alternative vision of the role of each sector of any society – market, state, community, and family. The social investment perspective abandons the precept of neo-liberalism that assigned responsibility for both income and care to the private realms of the market and the family or, if need be, to the third sector of community-based provision. Particularly relevant is the return in the social investment perspective to an emphasis on the role of the state in ensuring that adequate investments are made. The state is not meant simply to spend, however; it is to make wise "investments."

The social investment perspective has been advanced by governments of different ideological orientations. In Latin America, for example, this approach was proclaimed by the right-leaning Peruvian government of Alan Garcia, whose 2007 anti-poverty law asserted that "we have to move from a vision based on social spending to one based on social investment" (quoted in Jenson 2010, 63). But it was also present in Brazil, governed by the leftist president Lula da Silva, where there was a consensus that "the government has the duty of designing social protection policies that will redistribute part of the country's wealth while making sure that families can invest in children's education to improve the country's future prospects" (Morais de Sa e Silva 2010, 149).

International and supranational organizations called on their member states to be more proactive and make social investments. The final communiqué of the OECD social ministers in 2005 sketched an active role for the thirty-two member countries: "Social policies must be pro-active, stressing investment in people's capabilities and the realisation of their potential, not merely insuring against misfortune."[6] When the European Union finally made its commitment

Jane Jenson

to a social investment package in 2013 (Kvist 2013, 92), it called on its member states to be social investors of this type: "Social investment means enhancing people's capacities and supporting their participation in society and the labour market. This will benefit individuals' prosperity, boost the economy and help the EU emerge from the crisis stronger, more cohesive and more competitive." Although the European Union sees benefits for all categories of the population, the first beneficiaries of its social investment package are "children and young people [via] early intervention and other measures to break inter-generational cycles of disadvantage" (European Commission 2013a). This is because the new social risks that social investment is meant to address "weigh most heavily on the younger cohorts" (Vandenbroucke, Hemerijck, and Palier 2011, 6).

Despite the relegitimation of state action and the emphasis on new public spending, the social investment perspective assumes, as did both post-1945 welfare regimes and neo-liberalism, that the market should be the main source of well-being. A major premise is that employed parents provide better child raising than do those in workless families. Thus, the perspective puts a heavy emphasis on fostering paid employment and other forms of market income for families. But, whereas neo-liberals assumed that market participation was an easy solution, the social investment perspective includes a suspicion that the market might not produce sufficient income for everyone. The working poor can exist (Morel, Palier, and Palme 2012, 361–62). In addition, informal markets so prevalent in many countries do not provide income and stability to limit poverty. Social exclusion might be the result, therefore, of real social problems that require more than simply a job.

There is a basic recognition, in the perspective, that opportunities – and increasingly capabilities – are neither equally nor equitably distributed. Here we find the clearest link to the notion of inclusive growth.

Inclusive Growth: A Larger Frame for the Social Investment Perspective

The move toward placing the social investment perspective within a frame of inclusive growth took place even as the crisis unfolded after 2007 and shook European certainties (Ross 2011, Part III). Precepts of social policy were re-examined. At this time, and despite fears of high costs and public sector deficits, inclusive growth and the social investment perspective began to be jointly conjugated by international organizations such as OECD and UN agencies as well as the European Union.[7]

The social investment perspective provides more guidance to policy makers than does a simple "pro-poor" approach. It focuses on the *how* of social policy interventions (human capital development and activation policies) and for *whom* (children, including preschoolers, and their parents).[8] Since its earliest days, the social investment perspective contained a premise that the whole society would benefit from investments in individual children, resting on the assumption that breaking the intergenerational transmission of disadvantage (poverty) would be a general benefit (Jenson and Saint-Martin 2006, 435). The strongest form of the argument was internal to the field of social policy, that social investments now would reduce the costs of social programs in the future as well as provide a solid financial foundation for them via the increase in labour force participation and a higher birth rate. This argument internal to the domain of social policy is well summarized by the dedication of one of the founding documents of the social investment perspective: "For today's children who will provide for our welfare when we are old. It is for you – and hence for ourselves – that we desire the best possible welfare state" (Esping-Andersen et al. 2002, v). This stance is sometimes also captured by the sentence "good pension policies – like good health policies – begin at birth" (Vandenbroucke, Hemerijck, and Palier 2011, 6).

Incorporating the social investment perspective into the inclusive growth approach places it in a more encompassing discursive frame, relying on economic analysis as well as social justice arguments, about why social policy interventions of this type are worth undertaking. This frame lengthens the list of identified advantages, adding to those habitually identified by advocates of the social investment perspective. It makes broader claims about the dangers of rising or intensive inequality and about the advantages of less inequality. Thus, more than poverty and exclusion must be targeted by social investments. Inadequate opportunities for employment, and for the education assumed to open them up, are diagnosed as the problem.

A particular notion of equality is central here: equality of opportunity. The concept of inclusive growth rests on an analytical understanding of the effects of inequality.[9] Ifzal Ali (2007, 14) sets out clearly the connections between social investment premises (and the practices that follow from them) and inclusive growth: "Inclusive growth is not based on a redistributive approach to addressing inequality. Rather, it focuses on creating opportunities and ensuring equal access to them. Equality of access to opportunities will hinge on larger investments in augmenting human capacities, including those of the poor, whose main asset – labor – would then be productively employed." Equality of results is not the goal.[10]

Jane Jenson

To be sure, poverty is often a sign of inequality, but pro-poor interventions target only the margins of society. These margins are identified by a measure of their distance from a statistical norm, the amount of income (e.g., a dollar a day) or an average of the society (e.g., 50 or 60 percent below the median). In contrast, those who advocate inclusive growth pay more attention to the distribution of income, including its dispersion at the high as well as the low end. The GINI coefficient rather than the national median or an absolute dollar amount is the preferred indicator.

Calls for inclusive growth began to be heard within the universe of political discourse as the crisis was addressed by policy communities. Several examples are relevant here.

The IPC-IG

Thinking about the distinction between older approaches, such as pro-poor and inclusive growth, has been essential for the International Policy Centre for Inclusive Growth (IPC-IG) of the United Nations Development Programme (UNDP), if only because it has experienced an identity shift. The group was originally called the International Poverty Centre and focused on anti-poverty perspectives. It promotes inclusive growth now but without abandoning its roots in work on the "socials." Inequality is diagnosed as the problem because it may generate effects that brake development, social as well as economic. In a summary text dedicated to clarifying the meaning of inclusive growth, we read that, "although some inclusive growth definitions are interchangeable with absolute pro-poor growth, most understand that reducing both poverty and inequality is at the heart of the meaning of inclusive growth" (Ranieri and Ramos 2013). Similarly, the concept note prepared for a 2010 workshop covering Brazil, China, India, and South Africa said that "the concept of Inclusive Growth appears as a common thread in these countries' national development strategies, in so far as social inclusion is not dismissed as a compensatory measure or as a mere by-product of growth, but is considered as both its driving force and its principal goal."[11] The same organization is the primary South-South diffuser of the social investment perspective via its promotion of Brazil's model of conditional cash transfers (Ancelovici and Jenson 2013, 306–7).

The European Union

The policy discourse of the European Union in its *Europe 2020* ten-year strategy to replace the *Lisbon Strategy* of 2000 aims to promote, among other things, inclusive growth.[12] It defines inclusive growth as a return to well-functioning economies and social cohesion: "Inclusive growth means empowering people through high levels of employment, investing in skills, fighting poverty and modernising labour markets, training and social protection systems so as to help people anticipate and manage change, and build a cohesive society" (European Commission 2010).

Initially, *Europe 2020* focused on poverty reduction, with a commitment to there being "at least 20 million fewer people in or at risk of poverty and social exclusion."[13] It fell back, in other words, on a pro-poor agenda. But the strategic document was much criticized for being an inadequate social strategy and for putting the emphasis more on the health of the economy than on that of the people.[14] Three years later the discourse was adjusted. In 2013, the European Union formally and explicitly embraced the social investment perspective by issuing its Social Investment Package, and the president of the European Commission intoned that, "indeed, it is precisely those countries with the most effective social protection systems and with the most developed social partnerships that are amongst the most successful and competitive economies in the world" (quoted in Kvist 2013, 91–92).

The OECD
Whereas its path-breaking initial analysis of *Growing Inequality* (OECD 2008) made no link to inclusive growth, by 2011 and *Divided We Stand* (OECD 2011) the discursive universe of the OECD was connecting the two. Secretary-General Angel Gurría had a somewhat cheerleading version: "Without a comprehensive strategy for inclusive growth, inequality will continue to rise. We need to put better policies for better lives at the centre of our policy efforts, while providing people with hope and equal opportunities. This report provides powerful evidence of the need to 'go social!'" (OECD 2011, 19). The sober OECD analytical narrative said the same thing (OECD 2011, 41). When it came time to make policy recommendations, the authors of *Divided We Stand* turned to the standard tool of the social investment approach – investments in human capital so as to maximize access to employment in a more equal way (OECD 2011, 40–41). By 2013, the OECD (2013, 1) had an inclusive growth agenda that included the practices of social investment: "Investment in people underlies the OECD's 'go social' principle of economic and governance reforms, while systemic public policy changes align with the Organisation's 'go structural' principle."

The ILO and WHO
The Bachelet Report calling for a worldwide social protection floor (SPF) also argued consistently that inequality and poverty were problems and dangers.

Jane Jenson

According to the report, a SPF could "kick-start a virtuous circle of development that provides an exit route from poverty and inequality, and towards long-term economic resilience and inclusive growth" (ILO 2011, 12). Here too social investment was prescribed as a solution; social rights to early childhood education and adequate family income were provided as examples of how to construct the SPF. For the Bachelet Report, social policy has been explicitly repositioned as a driver of growth and a shield for economies as well as people during economic crises.[15]

Differences, Polysemy, and Discursive Policy Legacies

The social policy discursive universe of these institutions has been altered, and the global universe of political discourse has shifted along with these modifications. Policy communities promote the social investment perspective across the North and in parts of the South. They advocate different policy instruments but share a common goal of breaking the intergenerational cycle of disadvantage by expanding opportunities (Jenson 2010). This chapter documents an incorporation of this social policy perspective into the larger policy frame of the inclusive growth approach, because the social investment perspective provides a prescription for reducing inequalities. The two discourses are commensurate.

These international and supranational organizations have not all adjusted their discursive worlds to the same extent and in the same ways, however. Polysemy remains. For example, the European Union's commitment to inclusive growth appeared with *Europe 2020:* "Inclusive growth – a high-employment economy delivering economic, social and territorial cohesion" (European Commission 2010, 17). In effect, the formulation involves a simple combination of ideas about social inclusion (primarily via employment) and growth (via innovation and technological change). The labour market remains at the core of policy prescriptions. The document says nothing about economic inequality.[16] Thus, the Social Investment Package derived from the *Europe 2020* strategy does not focus on inequality either. Indeed, it does not even mention the standard trope of promoting equal opportunity.

The Bachelet Report, for its part, prescribes standard social investment instruments for achieving its goals. However, it was unable to abandon the long-standing pro-poor discourse so widespread in the development communities of the global South. As a result, it almost always used the couplet "poverty and inequality." Nor does the report focus on equality (with the exception of several mentions of gender equality). Its attention goes to the negative effects of and therefore the need to combat inequalities. This trope is now a consensual one in the public health domain among those analyzing the social determinants of health.

It is the OECD that makes the strongest and most explicit link among inclusive growth, social investment policies, and inequality. It arrived at the notion of inclusive growth after its analysis of rising inequalities was completed. Thus, it calls for inclusive growth to tackle these inequalities. Education, including in early childhood, emerges as the solution (OECD 2013).

These different ways of conjugating inclusive growth and social investment are the result of discursive and policy legacies. Neither discourse nor policy instruments can be simply abandoned in the search for solutions to economic crisis. They must be reworked, and this can be more or less easy for any institution to achieve.

Some legacies provide more resources and useful tools than do others for making any particular shift within the organization's discursive universe. The OECD, as an organization dominated by economists and with an economic mandate, could "go social" by displaying the non-controversial analytical tool of the GINI coefficient. It has, in other words, a long-standing legitimate vocabulary to document the correlation between inequality – and especially inequality across time – and other negative outcomes. It can also range widely across the globe, using the same indicator for northern, southern, and emerging economies. Moreover, as the OECD itself expanded to incorporate middle-income countries, including several that had long been categorized in the "developing" category, it began to break down divisions within intellectual and management organizational charts as well as its discursive categories between northern and southern analyses. It could then position itself better to speak to the world: "The global community is calling for change – for solutions that foster economic growth in a more inclusive manner, where the gap between the rich and the poor is less pronounced and the 'growth dividend' is shared in a fairer way. The OECD stands ready to respond."[17]

Resulting from a commission struck jointly by the ILO and WHO, the Bachelet Report came from different analytical traditions and faced other constraints. It provides the least coherence in the combination of inclusive growth and the social investment perspective. This does not mean that the report and its analysis are not coherent; it means, rather, that the conjugation of the two concepts is not always fluid. The commission's understanding of inequalities was drawn primarily from the policy community promoting attention to the social determinants of health. The notion that inequalities translate into physical costs was married to an understanding of social protection transfers as buffers in times of economic crisis. The latter forced attention to many more social policy interventions than those usually composing the child-focused social investment perspective. Pensions and access to health care, for example, were central to the definition of a social protection floor developed by the report.

For its part, the European Union also had to deal with discursive legacies that left the two concepts sitting uncomfortably together. In this case, it was the absence of any real experience of manipulating the concept of inclusive growth and a long-standing practice of distributing consideration of social and economic policies among different institutional locations. There has long been a tension between the "social" machinery and the financial powers in the Directorate-General for Economic and Financial Affairs (ECFIN) and elsewhere. This tension remained in the European strategy. In winter 2012, for example, the president of the European Central Bank was widely quoted as saying that the European social model was "already gone."[18] Then, harking back to long-standing neo-liberal views on the European labour market, he identified changes in the direction of labour market flexibility as the solution. In contrast, analyses coming from the social policy community have been focused on distribution, poverty, and so on. Thus, the discursive universe of the European Union continues to house varied prescriptions for responding to crisis. In addition, because it is not simply an international organization but a supranational one with significant discursive input from member states, its discourse ranges widely indeed. Some still seek to promote equality within their societies, while others are not yet convinced that greater inequality has costs. Not surprisingly, even when the Commission is speaking only for itself, trying to summarize all of this in a forward-directed narrative leads to discursive gymnastics.

In this polysemy, however, we do see movement across these institutions, despite their different identities and interests, toward incorporation of the social investment perspective into an inclusive growth frame. This convergence within the broader international universe of political discourse is helped by the characteristics of the concepts themselves. The lineage of each is post-neo-liberal. Neither seeks to return to the equality discourse of earlier decades. Fighting inequality is by no means the opposite of ensuring equality. The first requires actions to limit effects, whereas the second requires intervention to ensure a particular outcome.

Both of these post-neo-liberal concepts rest on similar projects of reducing poverty and inequality and of promoting social inclusion via employment. Both seek to maximize employment rates. However, there is also – in the North as in the South – recognition of certain market failures that require new forms of social protection. Indeed, recognition of the limits of the formal sector marks a break with long-standing assumptions about social protection from the twentieth century that made formal employment (or its absence) the trigger for accessing benefits. There has been a widespread turn toward both breaking down barriers to receiving benefits between those in the formal and those in the informal sectors and providing supplements to the inadequate wages received through paid work in the formal sector.

The reason that it is possible to embed the social investment perspective in the inclusive growth approach is also clear when the time horizon of each is examined. Both are ontologically focused on the future more than on the present. The concept of "growth" makes sense only by thinking across time, whereas "investments" are always made now for some future payoff. In their very natures, the two are compatible, and the intersection of their guiding principles and cross-regional convergence are visible in the way that time is treated in each.

This conjugation is moving us toward a Polanyian moment marrying economic and social goals in the universe of political discourse. The second set of goals is no longer hostage to the first, as was the case under neo-liberalism. Nor is the state an illegitimate actor, as it was in the neo-liberal discourse and its universe. This is not, however, a return to the past, to previous understandings of state-society relations or of large social goals such as equality. Laments for this past should not disguise what is new, no matter how much polysemy it might involve.

Notes ·

1 From the beginning, Hall and Taylor (1998, 962) noted the legacy of this "ideas" group: "There is potential in historical institutionalism for the character of the discursive processes through which individuals interact to affect the outcomes that ensue. This follows, in large measure, from their vision of the preferences of the individual as multifaceted or ambiguous and thus something that can be conditioned by active processes of discussion or contestation." There is no need, in other words, for a "discursive institutionalism." For further critique of the misleading tendency to give autonomy to "ideas" or "discourse," see Jenson and Mérand (2010).

2 Put another way, we cannot assert, as Béland and Orenstein (2013) do, that international organizations are "flexible" by nature or more likely to change than any other policy institution. Variation can only be empirically determined, in the same way that their influence must also be empirically assessed.

3 See the video *Making Growth Inclusive to Tackle Rising Inequality,* https://www.youtube.com/watch?v=b69-NrgYev4, whose images of poverty as well as policy are drawn from OECD member countries and from non-members in the global South or emerging economies. For the initiative, see http://www.oecd.org/fr/sites/inclusivegrowth/.

4   For the OECD's role in launching the social cohesion discussion, see Jenson (1998).
5   Jenson (2010) compares these three social policy moments. Mahon (2010) and Peng (2011) also discuss the differences between neo-liberalism and the social investment perspective.
6   http://www.oecd.org/els/meetingofoecdsocialaffairsministers2005-extendingopportunities howactivesocialpolicycanbenefitusall-finalcommunique.htm.
7   Both the UN Capital Development Fund (UNCDF 2013) and the United Nations Research Institute for Social Development (UNRISD 2010) focus on combatting inequality at least in part via public investments.
8   This "child-centred" approach is evident in the discourse of the European Union, which issued, along with its Social Investment Package, a Recommendation by the European Commission (2013b) about investing in children. Although a Recommendation does not carry a legal obligation, it is stronger than a simple analysis or set of suggested actions.
9   Not all versions of an inclusive growth analysis anchor problem identification and diagnosis in the effects of inequalities. Some focus on productivity, trade, and employment (e.g., Lederman 2011). Another World Bank publication defines inclusive growth as "sustained," broadly based, and focused on employment more than "direct income redistribution, as a means of increasing incomes for excluded groups" (PRMED 2009). Both of these World Bank publications go out of their way to distinguish between pro-poor strategies and inclusive growth, seeing the latter as being driven by jobs, trade, and technology and the former as being about something else.
10 Concern more with outcomes than with opportunities leads analysts directly and correctly to criticisms of the social investment approach (e.g., Cantillon and Van Lancker 2013).
11 See http://www.ipc-undp.org/conference/workshop_ig/concept_note.pdf.
12 See http://ec.europa.eu/europe2020/index_en.htm.
13 http://ec.europa.eu/europe2020/targets/eu-targets/.
14 See, for example, the report of the EU consultation process and the criticisms raised, http://eurofound.europa.eu/observatories/eurwork/articles/other/debate-about-social-dimension-of-europe-2020-strategy.
15 The general analysis of the problem, right from the start of the analysis, is that "inequality is widening and continues to do so at unacceptable and unsustainable levels. High inequality combined with a lack of adequate social protection mechanisms threaten[s] social cohesion and political stability worldwide ... An economic growth pattern based on income and asset concentration and social exclusion is neither economically viable nor socially desirable" (ILO 2011, 2).
16 "Gender equality" was mentioned both as a long-standing EU commitment and as a basis for achieving inclusive growth, while "health inequalities" got a mention.
17 http://www.oecd.org/inclusive-growth/.
18 This was an interview with the *Wall Street Journal,* http://blogs.wsj.com/eurocrisis/2012/02/23/qa-ecb-president-mario-draghi/.

References

Ali, Ifzal. 2007. "Inequality and the Imperative for Inclusive Growth in Asia." *Asian Development Review* 24, 2: 1–16.
Ancelovici, Marcos, and Jane Jenson. 2013. "Standardization for Transnational Diffusion: The Case of Truth Commissions and Conditional Cash Transfers." *International Journal of Sociology* 7, 3: 294–312.

Banting, Keith, and John Myles. 2013. "Introduction: Inequality and the Fading of Redistributive Politics." In *Inequality and the Fading of Redistributive Politics*, edited by Keith Banting and John Myles, 1-39. Vancouver: UBC Press.

Béland, Daniel, and Michael Orenstein. 2013. "International Organizations as Policy Actors: An Ideational Approach." *Global Social Policy* 13, 2: 125-43. http://dx.doi.org/10. 1177/1468018113484608.

Cantillon, Bea, and Wim Van Lancker. 2013. "Three Shortcomings of the Social Investment Perspective." *Social Policy and Society* 12, 4: 553-64. http://dx.doi.org/10.1017/ S1474746413000080.

Esping-Andersen, Gøsta, Duncan Gallie, Anton Hemerijck, and John Myles. 2002. *Why We Need a New Welfare State*. Oxford: Oxford University Press. http://dx.doi.org/10.1 093/0199256438.001.0001.

European Commission. 2010. *A Strategy for Smart, Sustainable, and Inclusive Growth*. COM (2010) 2020 final.

–. 2013a. *Towards Social Investment for Growth and Cohesion – Including Implementing the European Social Fund 2014-2020*. COM (2013) 83 final.

–. 2013b. *Investing in Children: Breaking the Cycle of Disadvantage*. COM (2013) 778 final.

Hall, Peter A. 1993. "Policy Paradigms, Social Learning, and the State: The Case of Economic Policymaking in Britain." *Comparative Politics* 25, 3: 275-96. http://dx.doi.org/10.2307/ 422246.

Hall, Peter A., and Rosemary C.R. Taylor. 1998. "The Potential of Historical Institutionalism: A Response to Hay and Wincott." *Political Studies* 46, 5: 958-62. http://dx.doi. org/10.1111/1467-9248.00178.

Ianchovichina, Elena, and Susanna Lundstrom. 2009. "Inclusive Growth Analytics: Framework and Application." Policy Research Working Paper 4851, World Bank, Washington.

ILO. 2011. *Social Protection Floor for a Fair and Inclusive Globalization* [Bachelet Report]. Geneva: ILO.

Jenson, Jane. 1990. "Representations in Crisis: The Roots of Canada's Permeable Fordism." *Canadian Journal of Political Science* 23, 4: 653-83.

–. 1998. *Mapping Social Cohesion*. Ottawa: CPRN. http://www.cprn.org/doc.cfm?doc= 180&l=en.

–. 2001. "Re-Thinking Equality and Equity: Canadian Children and the Social Union." In *Democratic Equality: What Went Wrong?*, edited by Ed Broadbent, 111-29. Toronto: University of Toronto Press.

–. 2010. "Diffusing Ideas for after Neo-Liberalism: The Social Investment Perspective in Europe and Latin America." *Global Social Policy* 10, 1: 59-84. http://dx.doi.org/10. 1177/1468018109354813.

–. 2012a. "Redesigning Citizenship Regimes after Neoliberalism: Moving towards Social Investment." In *Towards a Social Investment Welfare State? Ideas, Policies, and Challenges*, edited by Nathalie Morel, Bruno Palier, and Joakim Palme, 61-90. Bristol: Policy Press.

–. 2012b. "A New Politics for the Social Investment Perspective: Objectives, Instruments, and Areas of Intervention in Welfare Regimes." In *The Politics of the New Welfare State*, edited by Giuliano Bonoli and David Natali, 21-44. Oxford: Oxford University Press. http://dx.doi.org/10.1093/acprof:oso/9780199645244.003.0002.

Jenson, Jane, and Ron Levi. 2013. "Narratives and Regimes of Social and Human Rights: The Jackpines of the Neoliberal Era." In *Social Resilience in the Neoliberal Era*, edited by

Peter A. Hall and Michèle Lamont, 69–98. New York: Cambridge University Press. http://dx.doi.org/10.1017/CBO9781139542425.006.

Jenson, Jane, and Frédéric Mérand. 2010. "Sociology, Institutionalism, and the European Union." *Comparative European Politics* 8, 1: 74–92. http://dx.doi.org/10.1057/cep.2010.5.

Jenson, Jane, and Denis Saint-Martin. 2006. "Building Blocks for a New Social Architecture: The LEGO™ Paradigm of an Active Society." *Policy and Politics* 34, 3: 429–51. http://dx.doi.org/10.1332/030557306777695325.

Kvist, Jon. 2013. "The Post-Crisis European Social Model: Developing or Dismantling Social Investments?" *Journal of International and Comparative Social Policy* 29, 1: 91–107. http://dx.doi.org/10.1080/21699763.2013.809666.

Lederman, Daniel. 2011. "International Trade and Inclusive Growth: A Primer for Busy Policy Analysts." Policy Research Working Paper 5886, International Trade Department, World Bank, Washington.

Mahon, Rianne. 1977. *Canadian Public Policy: The Unequal Structure of Representation*. Toronto: University of Toronto Press.

–. 2008. "Babies and Bosses: Gendering the OECD's Social Policy Discourse." In *The OECD and Transnational Governance*, edited by Rianne Mahon and Stephen McBride, 260–75. Vancouver: UBC Press.

–. 2010. "After-Neoliberalism? The OECD, the World Bank, and the Child." *Global Social Policy* 10, 2: 172–92. http://dx.doi.org/10.1177/1468018110366615.

Michel, Sonya, and Ito Peng. 2012. "All in the Family? Migrants, Nationhood, and Care Regimes in Asia and North America." *Journal of European Social Policy* 22, 4: 406–18. http://dx.doi.org/10.1177/0958928712449774.

Morais de Sa e Silva, Michelle G. 2010. "Conditional Cash Transfers and Education: United in Theory, Divorced in Policy." PhD diss., Columbia University.

Morel, Nathalie, Bruno Palier, and Joakim Palme, eds. 2012. *Towards a Social Investment Welfare State? Ideas, Policies, and Challenges*. Bristol: Policy Press.

Noël, Alain, and Jean-Philippe Thérien. 2008. *Left and Right in Global Politics*. Cambridge, UK: Cambridge University Press. http://dx.doi.org/10.1017/CBO9780511790751.

OECD. 2008. *Growing Unequal*. Paris: OECD.

–. 2011. *Divided We Stand*. Paris: OECD.

–. 2013. *OECD Workshop on Inclusive Growth 3 April 2013. Session Notes*. Paris: OECD.

OECD Development Assistance Committee. 1996. *Shaping the 21st Century: The Contribution of Development Co-Operation*. Paris: OECD.

Peng, Ito. 2011. "The Good, the Bad, and the Confusing: The Political Economy of Social Care Expansion in South Korea." *Development and Change* 42, 4: 905–23. http://dx.doi.org/10.1111/j.1467-7660.2011.01724.x.

Polanyi, Karl. 1944. *The Great Transformation: The Political and Economic Origins of Our Time*. Boston: Beacon.

PRMED (Economic Policy and Debt Department, World Bank). 2009. *What Is Inclusive Growth?* http://siteresources.worldbank.org/INTDEBTDEPT/Resources/468980-1218567884549/WhatIsInclusiveGrowth20081230.pdf.

Ranieri, Rafael, and Raquel Almeida Ramos. 2013. "After All, What Is Inclusive Growth?" IPC-IG One-Pager 188.

Ross, George. 2011. *The European Union and Its Crises through the Eyes of the Brussels' Elite*. Houndmills: Palgrave Macmillan.

Staab, Silke, and Roberto Gerhard. 2010. "Childcare Service Expansion in Chile and Mexico: For Women or Children or Both?" Gender and Development Programme Paper 10, UNRISD, Geneva.

Streeck, Wolfgang, and Kathleen Thelen, eds. 2005. *Beyond Continuity: Institutional Change in Advanced Political Economies.* New York: Oxford University Press.

Szreter, Simon, and Michael Woolcock. 2004. "Health by Association? Social Capital, Social Theory, and the Political Economy of Public Health." *International Journal of Epidemiology* 33, 4: 650–67. http://dx.doi.org/10.1093/ije/dyh013.

Thelen, Kathleen, and Sven Steinmo. 1992. "Historical Institutionalism in Comparative Politics." In *Structuring Politics: Historical Institutionalism in Comparative Perspective,* edited by Sven Steinmo, Kathleen Thelen, and Frank Longstreth, 1–32. Cambridge, UK: Cambridge University Press.

UNCDF. 2013. *Inclusive Future: Inequality, Inclusive Growth, and the Post-2015 Framework.* New York: UNCDF.

UNRISD. 2010. *Combatting Poverty and Inequality: Structural Change, Social Policy, and Politics.* Geneva: UNRISD.

Vandenbroucke, Frank, Anton Hemerijck, and Bruno Palier. 2011. "The EU Needs a Social Investment Pact." Observatoire social européen Opinion Paper 5, OSE, Brussels.

Weir, Margaret, and Theda Skocpol. 1985. "State Structures and the Possibilities for 'Keynesian' Responses to the Great Depression in Sweden, Britain, and the United States." In *Bringing the State Back In,* edited by Peter Evans, Dietrich Rueschemeyer, and Theda Skocpol, 107-68. Cambridge, UK: Cambridge University Press. http://dx.doi.org/10.1017/CBO9780511628283.006.

3

A New Era for Social Policy?
Welfare States and the Financial Crisis

KEVIN FARNSWORTH AND ZOË IRVING

No period in history is likely to prove to be quite so significant for quite so many welfare systems as the economic crisis that struck in the late 2000s (Farnsworth and Irving 2012). The effects on welfare states have been varied, devastating for some, insignificant for others. However, the full impact of the crisis continues to unfold, and its aftershocks are likely to be felt for years, even decades, ahead. State borrowing, associated with the direct and indirect costs of the crisis, has risen dramatically in the majority of welfare states and is set to do so until at least 2018. It is against this backdrop that a number of governments have embarked on severe spending cuts in public services, including welfare provision. According to the IMF (2009, 2013), only massive cuts in state expenditures between now and 2030 will facilitate a real reduction of the currently high and growing levels of national debt borne by many states. The welfare state of the future will depend on the ability and willingness of governments (and citizens) to continue to borrow and/or maintain high levels of debt in order to finance social policies. But the crisis might also present opportunities for new debates on public policy and for an expansion in welfare states. As Bermeo and Pontusson (2012a, 1) put it, "crises are surely periods of peril, but they also facilitate change." In the context of deep cuts to welfare expenditures in some states, it is worth remembering that economic and political crisis in the past, from the Great Depression to the Second World War, facilitated the expansion of social policies. Welfare states also appear to have survived previous challenges, including the age of "limits" (Palier 2006) and the period of continual austerity from the 1980s identified by Pierson (1994). Focusing on the prospects for progress or regress of welfare states, this chapter begins with some discussion of how crises and their impacts have been explained; it then traces the origins and trajectory of the post-2007–8 economic crisis, from the banking crisis to the eurozone crisis. It argues that different welfare states have fared differently, partly because their existing configurations helped to mediate and manage the crises as they struck. The chapter goes on to illustrate how some welfare states have utilized political agency in order to operationalize their own particular national responses to the crisis, whereas in other states national politics have had much less impact; national decision making has been dominated by domestic economic circumstances and overriding international political constraints. The chapter also argues, however, that the international discourse on the crisis has been, at times, incoherent and confusing. The final discussion considers whether we are now at a new crossroads as far as social policy is concerned, with the persistence of defunct and failing "old" ideas and few "new" ideas to usher in a period of more progressive welfare state development in advanced economies.

Understanding the Impact of Crisis on Welfare States

The key question, following from Bermeo and Pontusson's (2012) quotation above, is whether the current crisis will result in change that is conducive to welfare state stability and/or growth. The immediate backdrop to the post-2007–8 crisis has some unique features that might yet prove to be decisive in shaping the future of social policy. First, the post-2008 crisis had the biggest impacts on some of the most mature welfare states and was more widespread than the crises that affected East Asia and the Nordic countries in the 1990s. Second, public expenditure levels were much higher in these mature welfare systems than they had been when the same states had faced past crises of comparable magnitude. As the proponents of historical institutionalism argue (Steinmo, Thelen, and Longstreth 1992), crisis periods create new opportunities and new challenges that are often enough to divert the paths of capitalist welfare states. During "normal" times, welfare states tend to follow their historically determined trajectories, but during periods of crisis – political or economic and "internal" or "external" – welfare states might deviate, moving in a new temporary or permanent direction. In such circumstances, policies are likely to be more path-breaking (Pierson 1994), less about "muddling through" and more about locating new ways of responding to changed circumstances. However, we argue here that these changed circumstances are not identical

Kevin Farnsworth and Zoë Irving

across states because the national impacts of what is often referred to as "the global economic crisis" have not been universally experienced.

The history of social policy analysis is certainly not lacking discussion of crisis moments and predictions of the end of the welfare state. The issue of welfare state crisis was of particular interest in the 1970s, notably among the neo-Marxist left. Linked to discussions of crisis, and its imprudent under-pinnings, is the spectre of "austerity" – and Paul Pierson (1998) wrote of a state of permanent austerity in affluent democracies over a decade before the present "age of austerity."

For each author who has predicted the demise of the welfare state during periods of crisis, there are others who, on looking at the evidence, seek to explain why, in the face of economic and political challenges, including the spectre of globalization, the welfare state continues to survive and, in some cases, thrive. Certainly, any comparative analysis of overall public expenditure levels in the key areas of social policy suggests that social spending is far more robust than we might assume at times. National expenditures in welfare states, in fact, have either increased or at least remained stable since their inception.

Explanations of the apparent resilience of the welfare state have been many and varied: its popularity among citizens, policy legacies (which get in the way of rapid short-term changes), institutional sclerosis (the tendency of an en-trenched interest to defend its "patch"), and the accusation that the irreconcil-able challenges of social policy tend to be exaggerated and, while they might result in welfare reform, leave welfare states broadly intact.

The present age of crisis and austerity reflects a similar pattern of debate. Although there has been no shortage of those who have documented reforms (Farnsworth and Irving 2011; Hemerijck 2013; Palier 2010; Taylor-Gooby 2013), there has been some disagreement over whether or not the crisis has led to a drift toward austerity (Starke, Kaasch, and van Hooren 2013; van Kersbergen, Vis, and Hemerijck 2014). Importantly, the debate between those who argue that the crisis led to austerity (and, by implication, a likely demise of the welfare state as we know it) and those who argue not is becoming caught up in a false dichotomy; as van Kersbergen, Vis, and Hemerijck (2014) ask, "is it empirically the case that retrenchment is the only show left in town? If it is, then the measures of governments' responses taken since 2010 – when the Euro or sovereign debt crisis kicked in – should be solely of the retrenchment or cost containment type. We should not find measures aimed at compensation or social investment."

But categorizing spending in this way is rarely so straightforward, and in any case overall fiscal austerity might well coexist with welfare expansion in other areas, especially where measures aimed at compensation or social investment are electorally popular or where the compensatory measures might make deeper cuts elsewhere more palatable. In arguing that Armingeon (2013) is wrong to assert that "austerity is the only game in town," van Kersbergen, Vis, and Hemerijck (2014) look for indications of deviation from "austerity" messages and question whether "all reform measures [should] be typified as retrenchment or cost containment[.] Or is there also room for social investment policies or more compensatory measures?"

Of course, both positions could be right. Their differences largely depend on how austerity is viewed and defined, and neither van Kersbergen, Vis, and Hemerijck (2014) nor Armingeon (2013) define what they mean by austerity, beyond its reference to cuts in state expenditures. The following discussion proceeds with an understanding of austerity as more than a retrenchment/investment response based on simple accounting or even, with a longer-term objective, preferred strategies for growth. In the following sections, we demonstrate that, though these are the points around which debate is mostly concentrated, the complexity surrounding welfare states' present and future cannot be fully explained by existing assumptions of what different "types" of welfare state would do, because the crisis, or in fact the crises, are nationally differentiated in timing, scope, and scale. The austerity "response" to the various forms and depths of crises, we argue, is equally differentiated, partly because of these differences of crisis and partly because of the broader patterns of domestic and international power relations and the political opportunities and challenges that each variety of crisis actuates.

Differentiating "the Crisis"

The global crisis, in fact, was not one crisis but a series of crises that struck in waves and, while it might yet become more global, has exhibited certain geopolitical qualities, varying in terms of its impact on different parts of the world and according to the level of financial integration among countries. Although we would expect welfare states to have changed direction in the face of the crisis, since its strength and nature varied among states, we would also expect to see wide variation in social policy responses. To understand the pressure for change within and among states, we have to understand more about the differences among pre-crisis capitalisms and the ways in which social policies helped to mediate and/or intensify the crisis. The most recent crisis also occurred against a general backdrop largely unfavourable to welfare expansion, including relatively weak trade unions, more flexible labour markets, a larger financial and

Kevin Farnsworth and Zoë Irving

services sector relative to manufacturing, growing levels of home ownership, increasing levels of economic inequality, and aging populations, all set within a period of neo-liberal globalization. These various factors helped to determine not only the way in which the crisis was mediated and managed in different states but even whether and how the crisis struck in the first place. In the following, we discuss the various waves of the crisis before we discuss their impacts.

The banking crisis that began in the United States in 2007 represented the first wave of the global crisis. Its origins were in the bursting of the US housing market bubble. The immediate effect from falling house prices in the United States was a massive devaluation of mortgage-backed securities, most of which were held by banks, including foreign banks. As the Financial Crisis Inquiry Commission (2011, xviii) put it,

> more than 30 years of deregulation and reliance on self-regulation by
> financial institutions, championed by former Federal Reserve chairman
> Alan Greenspan and others, supported by successive administrations and
> Congresses, and actively pushed by the powerful financial industry at every
> turn, had stripped away key safeguards, which could have helped avoid
> catastrophe. This approach had opened up gaps in oversight of critical areas
> with trillions of dollars at risk, such as the shadow banking system and
> over-the-counter derivatives markets.

A high proportion of international financial capital was based on what turned out to be overvalued mortgage products. Thus, the US crisis was primarily caused by inadequate regulations within American financial markets, and its contagion outside the United States was the failure of banking regulations elsewhere. The reason that the banking crisis spread so quickly to Western Europe but had less effect on Canada than the United Kingdom, Ireland, and Iceland, for instance, was a set of tighter regulations in the former. The banking crises in the latter were caused primarily by a failure of regulations governing international banking practices, whereas the ability of a range of countries – including the closest neighbours (Canada and Mexico) of the United States and other countries within the European Union – to virtually escape the crisis was due largely to tighter regulations and far less internationalized financial markets. It is useful to note that some of the hardest hit economies in the "crisis" – Greece, Portugal, and Spain – were virtually unaffected by the banking crisis. For some, the crisis created new opportunities. Santander, one of Spain's largest banks prior to the crisis, was able to capitalize on the crisis by taking over a number of crisis-hit banks in Europe, becoming one of the largest high-street banks in the United Kingdom.

The variable costs of the banking crisis on different states are captured in Table 3.1. The table illustrates the enormous costs of the various measures borne by governments in their efforts to rescue the financial sector. The actual costs of some of these measures are still unknown since governments will likely recoup some costs in due course. As the IMF has pointed out, the amounts recovered from the sale of assets, such as shares, is unlikely to result in anything approaching their total costs, let alone the costs of servicing the debts necessary to purchase them. The IMF (2009) estimates that layout recovery rates during economic crises tend to be about 51 percent in developed economies compared with about 13 percent in emerging economies. Guarantees might also bring with them zero or only marginal costs since, in most instances, corporations will remain solvent and governments will not have to make good the "insurance" policies that they have effectively put in place. However, there is a value to the private sector in both the purchase of assets and the guarantees issued by governments even if the eventual net costs to the state are negligible, just as any form of insurance or temporary loan has value.

Taken together, the value of the support packages put in place in 2008–9 ranged from 0 percent of GDP in several countries to 267 percent of GDP in Ireland. The value of the packages in the United States and United Kingdom was over 80 percent of GDP. In Greece and Italy, two of the hardest hit countries in the second and third waves of the crisis, the costs of the banking crisis were 6.5 percent and 4 percent GDP, respectively. More important in terms of the real costs to governments was the amount spent on upfront financing. In Italy and Japan, upfront financing was equivalent to less than 1 percent of GDP, whereas in Greece upfront costs were equivalent to 5.4 percent of GDP. In France, the cost was less than 2 percent of GDP, whereas in the United States and Canada upfront financing was close to 10 percent of GDP. The real outlier here was the United Kingdom, where the upfront costs of the crisis were equivalent to 19 percent of GDP, just less than half of the entire cost of combined government expenditures in an average year. Of course, the eventual costs of the crisis went beyond bailing out the financial sector to losses in tax revenues as the crisis spread to the wider economy.

The impact of the economic crisis, the ensuing recession, and the various rescue measures on public finances has been huge. Fiscal balances (the difference between taxation and spending) declined sharply and are not set to recover for several years. Debt has also risen sharply. Average net debt in the G7 countries

Kevin Farnsworth and Zoë Irving

Table 3.1

Headline support for the financial sector in the aftermath of the crisis, 2008–10 (% GDP)

	Capital injection	Purchase of assets and lending by treasury	Central bank support provided with treasury backing	Liquidity provision and other support by central bank	Guarantees	Total	Upfront government financing
				Finance and banking sectors			
Argentina	0.0	0.9	0.0	0.0	0.0	0.9	0.0
Australia	0.0	0.7	0.0	0.0	8.8	9.5	0.7
Austria	5.3	3.5	0.0	0.0	26.6	35.4	8.9
Belgium	4.8	0.0	0.0	0.0	26.4	31.1	4.8
Brazil	0.0	0.0	0.0	1.5	0.0	1.5	0.0
Canada	0.9	8.8	0.0	1.9	13.5	25.1	9.8
China	0.0	0.0	0.0	0.0	0.0	0.0	0.0
France	1.4	1.3	0.0	0.0	16.4	19.2	1.6
Germany	3.8	0.4	0.0	0.0	18.0	22.2	3.7
Greece	2.1	3.3	0.0	0.0	6.2	11.5	5.4
Hungary	1.1	2.2	0.0	4.8	1.1	9.2	3.3
India	0.4	0.0	0.0	6.3	0.0	6.7	0.4
Indonesia	0.0	0.0	0.0	0.0	0.1	0.1	0.1
Ireland	5.4	0.0	0.0	0.0	261.0	267.0	5.4
Italy	0.8	0.0	0.0	2.5	0.0	3.3	0.8
Japan	2.4	11.4	0.0	1.2	7.3	22.2	0.8
Korea	2.5	5.0	0.0	0.2	12.7	20.4	0.3

	Finance and banking sectors						
	Capital injection	Purchase of assets and lending by treasury	Central bank support provided with treasury backing	Liquidity provision and other support by central bank	Guarantees	Total	Upfront government financing
Netherlands	3.4	2.8	0.0	0.0	33.9	40.1	6.2
Norway	2.0	15.8	0.0	0.0	0.0	17.7	15.8
Poland	0.0	0.0	0.0	0.0	3.2	3.2	0.0
Portugal	2.4	0.0	0.0	0.0	12.0	14.4	2.4
Russia	0.6	0.5	0.4	7.6	0.5	9.6	1.7
Saudi Arabia	0.0	1.2	0.0	0.0	n.a.	1.2	1.2
Spain	0.0	4.6	0.0	0.0	18.3	22.8	4.6
Sweden	2.1	4.8	0.0	15.4	47.5	69.7	5.2
Switzerland	1.1	0.0	0.0	7.2	0.0	8.3	1.1
Turkey	0.0	0.3	0.0	0.0	0.0	0.3	0.0
United Kingdom	3.9	13.8	12.8	0.0	51.1	81.6	18.9
United States	4.6	2.3	0.7	41.9	31.4	81.0	7.5

Source: IMF (2010).

in 2007 was 55 percent of GDP, 73 percent of GDP by 2009, and had grown to over 90 percent of GDP by 2012. It is projected to remain at this level for the foreseeable future (see Table 3.2).

The second wave of the crisis began with the "Great Recession" from 2009 on. During the decade leading up to the crisis, most developed economies had enjoyed a long period of stability and growth. But by 2009 the majority of countries were in recession. The economic slowdown had an immediate impact on exporting states in particular, including Germany, China, and Japan, and spread throughout the eurozone. The banking crisis had second-order effects in that it led to a liquidity crisis as banks became reluctant to lend to consumers and to each other. As credit dried up, consumption dried up, and the economic slowdown accelerated. Declining demand and large-scale business failures meant that the Great Recession morphed into the third wave of the crisis in states that struggled to put in place effective measures to stem it.

The third wave of the crisis, linked to the first and second waves, describes the period of fiscal crisis that has gripped a number of welfare states from 2010 on. The global economic slowdown and recession led to a fall in tax revenues that, when accompanied by the costs of the financial bailouts in some countries and the costs of social welfare commitments in others, led to growing deficits. In countries with already high levels of government debt, the depth of the crisis only increased. The first wave of the crisis imposed huge financial costs on the worst hit states and led to greater levels of borrowing. The second wave resulted in a drop in tax revenues that forced governments to borrow heavily in states that had not experienced the first wave. Slowing economies also resulted in large-scale job losses, which in turn resulted in higher levels of unemployment and higher social welfare bills. In states that had already suffered significantly from the first wave, the second wave only added to the costs and debts already accumulated.

The fourth wave of the crisis – the European sovereign debt crisis – began in late 2009. It gave way to further economic instability and uncertainty across Europe (mirroring the earlier banking crisis), especially in Portugal, Spain, Italy, Ireland, and Greece. Of these countries, only Ireland had suffered significantly from the first wave, but all five countries suffered in subsequent waves. The net result was that they breached the conditions of their membership in the eurozone, and, given that they did not have the option available to sovereign currency countries of printing money and/or adjusting interest rates, they presented greater risks for would-be lenders operating within global bond markets. Their only option, other than seeking withdrawal from the eurozone and defaulting on their existing debts, was to seek bailouts from the European

Table 3.2
Net debt, OECD countries, 2006-18

	2006	2007	2008	2009	2010	2011	2012	2013	2014*	2015*	2016*	2017*	2018*
Australia	-6.3	-7.3	-5.3	-0.6	4.0	8.1	11.6	12.7	12.5	11.6	10.8	9.8	5.6
Austria	43.1	40.9	42.0	49.2	52.6	52.2	53.5	54.0	53.4	52.4	51.6	50.4	49.2
Belgium	77.0	73.1	73.3	79.5	79.7	81.2	83.3	84.3	84.3	83.8	82.7	80.9	78.7
Canada	26.3	22.9	22.4	27.7	29.7	32.3	34.6	35.9	36.6	36.7	36.3	35.6	34.9
Denmark	1.9	-3.8	-6.1	-4.5	-1.6	3.3	7.6	10.3	12.2	13.7	14.0	14.2	14.0
Estonia	-2.5	-4.0	-4.7	-2.3	-2.8	-0.4	2.5	4.1	3.8	3.6	3.4	3.2	3.0
Finland	-69.4	-72.5	-52.3	-62.8	-65.5	-54.0	-50.9	-47.5	-44.6	-42.3	-40.3	-38.6	-37.1
France	59.6	59.6	62.3	72.0	76.1	78.8	84.1	86.5	87.8	87.8	86.6	84.5	81.8
Germany	53.0	50.6	50.1	56.7	56.3	55.3	57.2	56.2	54.7	53.5	51.9	51.7	51.4
Greece	107.3	107.0	112.0	128.9	146.9	168.3	155.4	176.1	172.2	166.0	156.8	147.6	138.1
Iceland	7.8	10.8	41.8	55.7	59.9	66.7	68.2	62.2	59.3	56.8	53.9	51.0	47.5
Ireland	12.4	11.4	23.0	41.8	74.5	94.9	102.3	106.2	107.5	105.6	102.8	99.4	96.0
Israel	74.8	69.2	69.1	70.8	69.2	68.9	70.1	70.3	69.3	68.3	67.2	66.4	65.6
Italy	89.3	86.9	88.8	97.2	99.2	99.7	103.2	105.8	106.0	105.4	104.1	102.4	100.8
Japan	81.0	80.5	95.3	106.2	113.1	127.4	134.3	143.4	146.7	149.5	151.4	153.0	154.8
Korea	29.4	28.7	28.8	32.3	32.1	32.9	32.2	31.1	29.3	27.4	25.6	23.8	22.0
Netherlands	24.5	21.6	20.6	22.8	26.0	28.3	32.5	35.5	38.4	40.6	42.4	43.5	43.9
New Zealand	8.8	6.5	7.4	11.7	17.0	22.2	26.4	28.8	29.8	30.0	29.8	28.7	26.9
Norway	-133.5	-138.8	-123.7	-154.8	-163.8	-157.8	-165.5	-175.0	-180.8	-184.9	-187.4	-188.2	-187.7

Portugal	58.6	63.7	67.4	79.0	88.8	97.5	111.6	115.0	116.5	115.6	113.2	110.7	108.0
Spain	30.7	26.7	30.8	42.5	49.8	57.5	71.9	79.1	84.7	88.6	91.9	95.2	98.2
Sweden	−14.0	−17.4	−12.5	−19.6	−20.9	−18.4	−17.6	−16.3	−15.1	−15.6	−16.6	−17.6	−18.5
Switzerland	39.7	32.0	29.4	28.7	28.0	28.2	28.3	27.8	26.9	26.3	26.1	25.9	25.7
United Kingdom	37.8	38.0	48.1	63.2	72.9	77.7	82.8	86.1	89.6	92.2	93.2	92.8	91.1
United States	48.4	48.0	54.0	66.7	75.1	82.4	87.9	89.0	89.7	88.6	87.6	86.9	86.6
Average	48.2	46.3	51.9	62.4	67.5	72.7	77.4	78.1	79.1	79.0	78.6	78.1	77.6
Euro area	54.3	52.1	54.0	62.3	65.5	67.8	71.9	73.9	74.5	74.4	73.6	72.9	72.0
G7	55.5	54.4	61.0	72.7	78.9	85.2	90.4	91.5	92.6	92.4	91.8	91.4	91.0
G20	53.1	51.8	58.1	69.4	74.8	80.5	85.2	86.1	86.9	86.7	86.0	85.5	84.9

* = Projections

Source: Fiscal Monitor (2013, Table 4).

Central Bank, which they did. And this assistance, which came in the form of loans, also came with strict conditions (we will return to this point).

These, then, are the major episodes of the crisis. Each wave brought new pressure to bear on welfare states. But in examining the impacts, another piece of the puzzle needs to be examined: that is, how welfare states shaped the waves of the crisis as it unfolded.

Varieties of Welfare, Varieties of Crisis

An examination of the impact of the economic crisis on welfare states is important, but equally important is a greater understanding of how existing configurations of social policy helped to mediate the various waves as they hit nation-states. First, the most comprehensive systems provided natural stabilizing effects as economies were hit by the Great Recession. Claimants and budgets change in line with levels of employment and unemployment, increasing during economic downturns and decreasing during periods of growth. Developed social security systems helped a number of countries to avoid what would otherwise have turned into economic depressions (see Starke, Kaasch, and van Hooren 2013). Without the modest levels of economic stability afforded by state social protection measures, many more citizens would have lost their homes, and the recession would have been deeper and more prolonged by a total collapse of consumption. Without these measures, political legitimacy would also have been damaged. States that did not have such systems in place sought to introduce new schemes (as in the case of China) or extend existing ones (as in the case of the United States).

Second, the distribution of tax liabilities prior to the crisis was important. Governments already failing to spread the tax base more broadly and managing to run budget surpluses in the years running up to the crisis – an unprecedented period of growth for many countries – were more vulnerable in the face of fiscal tightening as the recession hit. Persuading citizens already faced with greater levels of instability and uncertainty in employment markets that they should pay higher taxes in order to increase the sustainability of public policy in the long term would have presented serious political challenges. Spending cuts appeared to be more appealing to politicians, especially those on the right, and easier to sell to the electorate.

Third, housing markets, in particular the extent to which home owners were indebted and their ability to meet their mortgage payments, were heavily implicated in the initial US housing crisis – the index case in the subsequent spread of financial contagion. The US housing market is distinguished by heavy reliance

Kevin Farnsworth and Zoë Irving

on owner occupation, extremely small social housing provision, and relatively few regulations in the private rental sector (OECD 2011a). This housing market combined with relatively few regulations within the mortgage market, which had encouraged the proliferation of sub-prime mortgages among households highly likely to struggle to meet their payments. Unlike in a number of other states, the US benefits system also has no provision for covering mortgage costs, making eviction more likely. The collapse of the US housing market was made more likely and more devastating in terms of its wider impact on the United States and beyond because of the lack of protections in its social welfare system. Notably, other countries hit in the first wave of the crisis (Iceland, Ireland, and the United Kingdom) were also characterized by high levels of housing indebtedness and overinflated property markets.

Fourth, income levels and inequality were also directly implicated in causing the crisis, in part because of the reasons outlined above, in part because falling incomes have been shored up by growing levels of personal debt, not just mortgage debts but also credit card debts and personal loans. Part of the explanation for this is that the share of national income accruing to citizens in the form of wages and salaries has fallen since the 1970s across OECD countries, from an average of 68 percent to less than 55 percent, with the rest going to profits (see Glyn 2006). Income inequality has also increased since the 1980s across all OECD economies. And the crisis appears to be widening the divide between highest and lowest incomes still further; referring to data from Saez (2013), Oxfam (2013) reports that, in the United States for example, "the wealthiest one per cent captured 95 per cent of post-financial crisis growth since 2009, while the bottom 90 per cent became poorer." The major bulwark against growing inequality, of course, is the welfare state. Redistributive taxation coupled with comprehensive social and labour policies prevents the gap between rich and poor from becoming ever wider. It also increases economic stability and sustainability through wage-funded consumption. Economic growth since the 1980s was achieved, despite the fall in incomes, by rapidly rising personal debt, as already noted, but particularly in the years immediately preceding the crisis from 2000 to 2007, when global average household debt rose 80 percent (Credit Suisse AG Research Institute 2013).

Fifth, and more generally, there is a relationship between the type of welfare state within a nation-state and the overall regulatory regime. The literature on capitalism provides evidence suggesting that states that tend to have loose regulations on capital also tend to have the least generous welfare systems (e.g., Hall and Soskice 2001). Where loose regulations on capital have been extended to the banking sector, especially where the relative size of the financial sector is large, as in the United Kingdom and Ireland, the banking crisis in particular was more significant.

Structural Constraints on the Road to Austerity

Much of the debate surrounding the direction of policy making in the era of crisis has focused on the political dimension and the extent to which politics still matter. The implication, if politics do not matter, is that policy is shaped more by economic structures than by political agency. This is an important debate, but it fails to recognize the variability in the ability of countries to act. Some governments have simply had much less political space in which to deal with the crisis than others. Here the structural constraints have varied: a lack of lending capacity, intolerably high interest rates, low pre-crisis growth rates, or high pre-crisis debt rates. Also important is how much governments have been able to shift the bad debts of their banking sectors onto their own balance sheets (Blyth 2013). And then there are particular constraints faced by governments that have effectively undermined the political space in which to manoeuvre by locking themselves into austerity. The effect, as Streeck and Shafer (2013) put it, is to deny choice to electorates and to incapacitate democracy.

All democratic countries have faced elections since the onset of the earliest banking crisis, and some faced elections soon after they experienced the effects of the crisis. In the United Kingdom, the election in 2010 was fought over the basis of the timing and depth of spending cuts. The election was won by a Conservative-led coalition government, which imposed deep cuts within weeks of coming to power. Similar swings to the right were also witnessed across Europe as incumbent parties, which just happened to be primarily parties on the left, were framed by opposition parties as being culpable in contributing to the crisis and/or recession. In the United States in 2008 and Japan in 2009, centre-left parties won strong mandates, but domestic politics and confrontations within different parts of the legislature – the House of Representatives in the former, the Upper House in the latter – curtailed welfare expansion (Bermeo and Pontusson 2012).

Of the four countries most affected by the first wave, the banking crisis, Iceland and Ireland suffered the deepest subsequent recessions, whereas the United States was the quickest to emerge from negative growth in 2009. Although Iceland suffered a deeper economic recession than the United Kingdom or United States, it returned to growth in 2010. In the United Kingdom and Ireland, the recession was more pronounced, and both countries suffered a double-dip

Kevin Farnsworth and Zoë Irving

recession in 2011–12. The key difference among these four countries is that Iceland alone avoided engaging in a massive bailout of its banking sector. In the United Kingdom, United States, and Ireland, the banks were considered too big to fail. In Iceland, they were too big to bail! In terms of debt levels alone, therefore, its decision to allow its banks to default on their liabilities meant that Iceland faced lower debt levels and thus had more options than the other three countries. The crisis in Iceland undermined neo-liberalism and provided a spur to centre-left politics, resulting in the election of a centre-left coalition in 2009 that, in turn, facilitated a short-lived progressive challenge to the version of austerity promulgated in the other countries. The paradox is that, by 2013, the broad economic outlook was brighter for the country, and this facilitated the re-election of a centre-right government, on a platform of ending austerity.

The left in the United States, in the guise of the Democrats, was similarly able to capitalize on the crisis in order to expand social security benefits. Politics were important after the banking crisis in expanding social welfare, but the Republicans, under the "neo-liberal" George Bush, had already agreed to sign off on significant stimulus measures by the time of the election in 2008, including an extension of unemployment compensation.[1] Where politics have played a bigger role is in the rise of a form of libertarianism within the Republican Party that, at the time of writing, is forcing President Obama to agree to widespread spending cuts in exchange for Republican willingness to approve an extension of the government's borrowing capacity. In this context, the politics of the Republican Party are having an increasing influence on the Democrats. In this respect, the fiscal crisis and the political responses to it have proven to be almost as decisive for the United States as the initial banking crisis.

Limiting our focus to the four banking crisis countries, Ireland faced the greatest external constraints on its social policies because of its membership in the eurozone and its subsequent IMF/ECB loan facility. Membership in the eurozone meant that Ireland was unable to borrow more heavily in the usual ways, and it lacked the ability of sovereign currency states to print money – a policy pursued vigorously by the United Kingdom and United States. Prior to the crisis, Ireland had sought to encourage corporate investment through minimal regulations and low levels of corporate taxation, policies that exposed the country to greater risks than other nations. In common with other eurozone economies, Ireland also experienced a relatively deep and prolonged recession. Coupled with its limited options for stimulating the economy – essentially limited to further reductions in taxes – these factors ensured that Ireland experienced a deeper fiscal crisis than either the United States or the United

Kingdom. A growing deficit forced Ireland to seek assistance from the IMF and ECB, and the resulting "conditionality" imposed deep cuts on welfare expenditures (see below).

In the United Kingdom, the timing of the general election was such that the economy had already gone into deep recession, a fact that the Conservative and Liberal Democrat opposition parties were able to exploit to their advantage. The outcome was not clearly in favour of any of the major parties, but the Conservatives, as the largest party, were able to form a coalition with the Liberal Democrats. Although prior to the election of 2010 all of the major parties had agreed that cuts in public expenditures would be necessary eventually, only the Conservative Party advocated immediate and massive cuts, a policy that it implemented once it formed the coalition government merely days after the election. The coalition government continued with austerity measures even in the face of widespread criticism that such policies had plunged the United Kingdom back into recession in 2011. Moreover, political statements made by the prime minister, David Cameron, in 2013 confirmed that austerity was part of a bigger political project. Along with his chancellor of the exchequer, he stated that the government would maintain low levels of public expenditure even when the economy had recovered. Given that the coalition government was not constrained by membership in the eurozone, and did not share with the Obama government the political barriers presented by the second chamber, the UK coalition government had more freedom to pursue its own political agenda compared with many other governments.

The National Politics of Austerity

In the United States, the crisis helped to usher in the Democrats in 2008 and again in 2012. This period of relative political stability has helped to maintain stimulus measures in the United States longer than in many other economies. It has also led to a perverse situation in which the United States has effectively led in cautioning against austerity and promoting stimulus measures, whereas the European Union and Canada have actively promoted deeper cuts in public expenditure. In contrast, in some nations, in particular the United Kingdom and Ireland, along with Canada, the crisis has been used by powers antipathetic to state welfare to undertake just such a reversal, utilizing the window of opportunity to further protect the interests of the most privileged in society. Although the long-term distributive outcome has yet to become clear, early indications are that the limited gains in terms of social equality in these three liberal welfare states will now regress and that, in wider Europe, the "social dimension" of European integration is under threat (Degryse, Jepsen, and Pochet 2013).

Thus, a range of austerity arguments is playing out at the international level and in different countries. An OECD (2011b) assessment of countries "at risk" gives an idea of differences in approach to restoring public finances and, we suggest, feeds into the idea that austerity has a distinct character depending on the particular national combination of economics and politics, not necessarily a combination that fits the traditional family of nations or welfare capitalism literature. The OECD assessment, however, reports on fiscal consolidation requirements rather than long-term political projects of governments, which we suggest broadly place countries in one of three groups.

In the eurozone economies most severely affected by debt-related crises, governments have alluded to structural constraints that make the imposition of severe cuts inevitable. In these countries, austerity measures have been introduced not on the basis that there are grave problems with "welfare" per se but on the basis that the demands of current market and economic conditions must be met (Greece, Ireland, Portugal, Spain, and Italy).[2] In a second group, a number of economies have sought to capitalize on the "age of austerity" to cut expenditures even when economic conditions have not demanded it. The arguments in these economies are that other countries with high levels of debt and expenditure are imposing huge cuts and that, in order to avoid the same fate, some fiscal strengthening, which involves spending cuts, needs to be implemented. This argument has gained the most ground in the United Kingdom, Canada, Sweden, Germany, and the Netherlands. Were the United Kingdom a member of the eurozone, it would face pressures similar to those faced by Ireland in particular, but it is included in this second group because of the size of its "preemptive cuts." Finally, a third group includes France, Japan, and the United States, where there have been fewer cuts and more limited interest in the age of austerity. These three countries are all in the OECD's "in trouble but not doing much about it" category, but they have very different and country-specific factors that help to explain their lack of explicit adoption of the austerity agenda. In the French case, the notion of austerity is politically volatile, and only since 2013 has the government sought to combine substantial spending cuts (though not initially specifically targeted at social protection and welfare services) and a rise in the value-added tax with the more progressive tax increases that characterized its early response. Japan's situation was complicated by the 2011 tsunami and its aftermath, and its recovery has been hampered by economic stagnation that predated the later impact of the financial crisis. Japan is an interesting case in that it pursued austerity briefly in 2012 but abandoned it with a change of government in 2013. It also has exceptionally high levels of public debt, but because most of it is financed by national savers it faces fewer international pressures (Blyth 2013). As the most powerful national player, but one with overwhelming domestic struggles, the United States has voiced one of the most consistent arguments against austerity. The following statement by Jack Lew (2013), secretary of the US Treasury, captures the position well:

> To remain on the path of continued growth, we need to avoid self-inflicted wounds while we are still trying to make up lost ground ... And job growth would be faster if the across-the-board cuts ... were replaced by a more balanced path of fiscal consolidation. [We need] investments in centres of excellence for advanced manufacturing, in job training, in education and in clean energy ... And more work remains to be done to bring down the number of long-term unemployed. Similarly, for global growth to be sustainable, other G20 nations must pursue macroeconomic policies that are centred on increasing domestic demand and employment. The eurozone's first priority is to maintain financial stability ... As a result, Europe is now in a position where it can put greater priority on boosting demand and addressing unemployment levels that have reached historic highs.

Despite this general view, after a period of expansion, in its domestic policies the United States has embarked on a program of large cuts, forced on the Democrats by the rise of the right. Figure 3.1 provides an overview of the measures introduced in selected countries that represent the kind of retrenchment associated with austerity.

The ultimate illustration of how structural constraints have undermined national politics is illustrated by the effective installation of unelected political leaders in Greece and Italy. In Greece, a former member of the European Central Bank was "imposed" to replace the elected prime minister in 2011, while in Italy a former European commissioner replaced the democratically elected prime minister. Politics can matter in such circumstances, but national politics appear to matter far less than one might assume. In such circumstances, international (or world regional) politics appear to matter more.

Exogenous Constraints

International politics also count in setting the environment within which national politics take place, even where there is a lack of "formal" power. But here the international response to crisis and austerity has lacked coherence and clarity.

Figure 3.1
Overview of austerity measures in selected countries 2008-11

Denmark
- Austerity plan seeks €3.2 billion in cuts in budget consolidation
- Unemployment benefits to be cut back to two years (from four years)
- Public sector to lose 20,000 jobs
- Child benefits to be reduced by 5 percent
- Ministerial salaries to be cut by 5 percent

Finland
- Government jobs to be cut by 5,000 by 2014
- Plan to raise retirement age from sixty-three to sixty-five
- Tax increase on energy to raise €750 million and increase in excise duties to raise €100 million
- VAT rise of 1 percent

France
- Plan for €65 billion in savings by 2016
- Plan to raise retirement age to sixty-two (from sixty) from 2018 on and to delay state pension until sixty-seven (from sixty-five)
- Aim to close tax loopholes, withdraw economic stimulus measures, and introduce income tax rise of 1 percent on highest earners
- Three-year freeze on public sector spending from 2011 on
- VAT on many goods and services (except essentials such as food) to be raised from 5.5 percent to 7.0 percent
- Corporate tax on companies with a turnover of more than €250 million a year to be temporarily raised by 5 percent
- Employees' pension contributions to be increased to 10.55 percent (from 7.85 percent)

Germany
- Plan to cut budget deficit by record €80 billion a year by 2014
- Planned cuts to defence (reducing the armed services by 40,000 troops)
- Civil service jobs to be cut by 10,000 by 2014 and some bonuses for civil servants to be suspended in 2011
- Cuts in subsidies to parents
- Increase in tax on nuclear energy

Greece
- €110 billion EU/IMF bailout in 2010 followed by further deal in 2011 to include private bank creditor "haircut" of 50 percent on returns
- New property tax and VAT raised by 4 percent
- Freeze on civil service recruitment until 2014 and suspension of 30,000 civil servants on partial pay
- Removal of bonuses and cuts in public sector worker allowances of 8 percent
- Unemployment increased to 18.4 percent by 2011
- Privatization through sales of public assets such as postal, water, and rail services expected to raise €35 billion
- Retirement age to be increased from sixty-one to sixty-three

Ireland
- €85 billion EU/IMF bailout in 2010 (repayable over seven and a half years initially, later extended to fifteen years)
- Cost of bank bailout €46 billion since 2008, estimated to rise to €70 billion after March 2011 because of further bank recapitalization
- Budget pledge to reduce deficit by €6 billion in 2011
- Government spending cut by €4 billion
- Minimum-wage cut from €8.65 to €7.65 per hour
- Cut of 5 percent in public sector wages
- Capital gains and capital acquisitions taxes to be increased by 25 percent
- Social welfare cut by €760 million, including a 4 percent cut in unemployment programs
- Child benefits reduced by €16 per month
- Tax increases in excise on cigarettes
- Carbon tax of €15 per ton of CO_2 and a new water tax to be imposed
- Capital investment cut by €960 million

Italy
- Government approved austerity measures of €24 billion for 2011–12
- €70 billion to be saved through health-care fees, cuts to family tax benefits and pensions of higher earners, and cuts to local authorities of €13 billion
- Planned savings of a further €58.9 billion through sales and wealth tax and provisions to reduce tax evasion
- Public salaries frozen for three years, one employee to be replaced for every five who leave, cuts of 5–10 percent for higher public sector pay (over €90,000)

Netherlands
- Centre-right coalition plan to cut budget by €18 billion by 2015

Portugal
- Aim to get the budget deficit down to 5.9 percent of GDP this year (2011)
- EU/IMF bailout of €78 billion in 2010
- Public salaries frozen and social programs cut
- Five percent cut for top earners in public sector
- Privatization program includes seventeen public enterprises
- VAT increased by 1 percent
- Income and corporate taxes to be raised by 2–5 percent
- Military budget cut back and capital investment in transport postponed

Spain
- Unemployment highest in European Union at 21 percent, with 46 percent youth unemployment
- Socialist government's austerity budget for 2011 included an increase in higher-rate income tax and 8 percent in spending cuts
- Public sector's workers pay cut by 5 percent and salaries frozen for 2011
- Retirement age raised to sixty-seven
- Tax on tobacco increased to 28 percent

Kevin Farnsworth and Zoë Irving

- Socialist government and opposition agreed in 2011 to a "golden rule" in the constitution to keep future budget deficits to a strict limit
- Privatizations planned (e.g., lottery and airport authority) and infrastructure budget cut by 30 percent

United Kingdom
- Conservative-Liberal Democrat coalition government announced the biggest cuts in state spending since Second World War
- Retirement age to increase to sixty-six by 2020
- VAT increased by 2.5 percent (to 20 percent)
- Savings estimated at about £83 billion over four years; plan to cut 490,000 public sector jobs
- Most government departments to face budget cuts of 19 percent on average and up to 25 percent
- Unemployment at 2.62 million (8.2 percent), highest level since 1994
- Youth unemployment over 1 million (21 percent)

Romania
- Government proposed wage cuts of 25 percent and pension cuts of 15 percent in May 2010
- Police officers went on strike over the 25 percent pay cut
- Economy shrank more than 7 percent in 2009, and IMF bailout used to cover wage bill
- VAT increased by 5 percent

Sources: The European Institute, www.europeaninstitute.org/April-2011/eu-austerity-country -by-country-updated-421; BBC News Europe, www.bbc.co.uk/news/10162176.

According to the IMF, in order to balance budgets and pare back debts to a "moderate level" equal to about 60 percent of GDP, governments need to impose deep spending cuts over the next twenty years. Still, given that the crisis has not had even impacts on countries, the remedial measures prescribed by the IMF are not universal either. Mirroring the finding relating to historical and recent patterns in state aid, economies that historically have had lower levels of public expenditure have been hardest hit by the crisis. This can be illustrated by plotting average public expenditures between 2000 and 2008 against the IMF's target fiscal adjustment rate. This rate is the amount of adjustment needed in public finances between 2010 and 2020 in order to reduce national deficits to zero by 2030. The IMF-required adjustment is the greatest in countries with lower levels of public expenditure: the United States, Greece, Spain, Ireland, Japan, and the United Kingdom. Countries with historically high levels of public expenditure – Denmark, Sweden, Finland, France, Austria, and Belgium – require much less austerity (indeed, Denmark can afford to increase its expenditure slightly) (see Farnsworth and Irving 2011, Figure 1.2). If followed, the result of such fiscal adjustment would be to place an even wider gap between the most comprehensive and the more residualist welfare states.

What is important to stress here is that the policy prescriptions of the ECB, European Union, and IMF are based on a particular (ideological) interpretation of the problems of debt, the desirability of public services, and particular assessments of the economic and social costs and benefits of dramatic cuts in public expenditures and/or tax increases. This is clear if we consider international discourse since the first wave of the crisis, which at times has been incoherent and inconsistent. Jose Manuel Barroso, president of the European Commission, for instance, moved from his statement in September 2010 that "there is also no such thing as a 'free deficit'" to a position in October 2011 in which he stated that "to focus solely on cuts suggests that government overspending was the only source of the crisis."[3] Having also acknowledged that both financial regulation and "political will" were implicated in the crisis, by 2013 Barroso had softened his position further still, to the point where he admitted that, though "this policy [austerity] is fundamentally right, I think it has reached its limits in many respects."[4]

The explanation of what Bermeo and Pontusson (2012) refer to as the Janus-faced quality of the EU position is that the recommendations or stipulations of the European Union with regard to the crisis have varied among member states. For those that remained fiscally solvent, or those that lie outside the single currency, the union has been less important in shaping national policies and priorities. For those that have sought assistance from the union and IMF, the union has assumed "formidable new powers of surveillance and policy constraint" (Bermeo and Pontusson 2012). And here the conditions that have been imposed on Greece, Ireland, Italy, and Spain are relatively consistent and largely unchallenged. The IMF (2013), however, in a rare admission of failure, suggests that the conditions imposed on Greece in particular did not achieve the desired effects of restoring market confidence and growth and instead created high unemployment and a deeper recession.

The incoherence of the IMF's position on Greece was replicated in its commentary on the United Kingdom. The IMF heaped praise on the strength and credibility of UK austerity measures in 2010, to the extent that Martin Wolf, a senior columnist at the *Financial Times,* stated that the assessment amounted to a "love letter" rather than a simple appraisal.[5] Just one year later, however, Christine Lagarde, president of the IMF, argued that European countries ought to be shifting from austerity measures to the drivers of growth.[6]

The OECD appears to be similarly torn between prescribing heavy doses of fiscal consolidation (OECD 2011b) and the need for countries to attend to "the

Kevin Farnsworth and Zoë Irving

human and social dimension of the crisis" through employment and social policy intervention, particularly in the context of rising inequality and the "unravelling" of the "social compact" (OECD 2009). As is so often the case in global policy discourse, there appears to be a mismatch between one set of policy prescriptions – in this case austerity – and another – social harmony and effective social policies.

Concluding Thoughts

One of the key debates in the post-crisis period has centred on the extent to which the crisis and austerity are game-changers as far as social policy is concerned, capable of transforming, disrupting, or even dismantling welfare states. The question is whether economic crises provide the political capacity and space to create a paradigm shift, a radical transformation of the way that the welfare state is viewed and economic policy is managed.

The evidence considered here suggests that the crisis has indeed had a major impact on some welfare states. Generally, studying the economic measures, political and public discourse, and events that continue to unfold, the impact is spreading and increasing over time as national strategies combine to create world regional effects. In a range of developing countries, the evidence remains unclear (Barrientos 2011), but more recently there have been signs that the ripples of the Great Recession are spreading to a number of countries that had previously fared reasonably well –notably India. Thus, though there are some generalized crisis effects at the global level that relate to what Walden Bello (2013) describes as "chain-gang economics," more significant are the range and patterning of effects and responses at the national level and how they interact with the particular international constraints acting on domestic policy making.

Our analysis suggests that, in understanding the true impact of the period since 2007, it is not enough to identify "the crisis" as everything and anything that has changed in the global economy. Neither is it sensible now to simply amass measures of spending to calculate whether or not there has been retrenchment and from this analysis establish both a country's adherence (or not) to the austerity agenda and the future stability of its welfare state. We have argued that there is not a universal crisis in either economic or political terms but a series of related but different crises, each of which has had differing effects on and consequences for the social policy trajectories of different welfare states.

Some effects could be argued to be more predictable than others – the banking crisis clearly having greater impacts in countries more deeply integrated with the global financial system and where the financial sector played a more significant role in the national economy. These countries were obviously more likely to be liberal economies since less regulation promoted the establishment and growth of their financial networks. However, beyond this, the standard classifications of worlds of welfare become less helpful in explaining subsequent welfare reforms, and, though the distinction between the coordinated market economies and liberal market economies provides a basis for understanding existing national configurations, it too is more limited in explaining the emerging varieties of austerity. The reason is that austerity is much more than a rational economic response to a straightforward economic setback.

We understand austerity as a political response to the economics of crisis. The response might be undertaken at the international level rather than the national level, thus imposing "constraints" at the latter level. Yet austerity refers to more than cuts in public expenditure. It describes a particular approach to public expenditure and implies a particular reading and understanding of economics and social relations. Although austerity has been presented as a pragmatic response to objective economic facts, the way in which it has played out demonstrates that it is anything but. Austerity is also a political project (see Farnsworth and Irving 2012). The evidence considered above does not necessarily imply that austerity has emerged as a new paradigm in the organization of public policy, but it might in the future. Austerity, as Armingeon (2013) recognizes, is deeply neo-liberal, but it is most powerful because it can be disguised as non-ideological. It can be, and has been, "sold" as a pragmatic response to the economic climate. It can be used, as it has been in the United Kingdom and Canada, to galvanize political support for cutting public expenditures and dismantling social obligations. It can also be employed for other ends, of course. Some countries have engaged in more moderate cuts but distanced themselves from the austerity agenda (e.g., Sweden). Some governments have engaged in large-scale expenditure cuts but deny that they are employing austerity measures for fear of losing electoral support (e.g., Italy). Not all austerity policies are linked to cutting back expenditures, and the pursuit of austerity does not necessarily imply cuts to all areas of public and social policy. It is also important to bear in mind that, in many countries, planned austerity cuts have yet to be fully introduced. Given fiscal crisis and debt, austerity of some form or another is likely to remain for some time an important backdrop against which social policy is made in perhaps the majority of welfare states.

Perhaps this lack of coherence in responses to crises should be expected given that, in key ways, a lack of effective coordination among nation-states was the catalyst for the events since 2007. Certainly, there have been some surprises in the global discourse, the biggest of which has been the apparent swing toward

Keynesianism in the "liberal" United States and toward monetarism in the traditionally social democratic European Union. What the incoherent global message on social policy signals is a current vacuum in strategy in which the weaknesses of neo-liberalism have been exposed but for which an alternative vision of social policy has yet to be established. We can only hope that, when the moment comes, the new vision is as progressive as it is radical and as dominant as the neo-liberal model that it replaces. The alternative is the reascendance of neo-liberalism, which would signify that, for the growth of welfare states at least, the crisis has truly gone to waste.

Notes

1 http://www.fas.org/sgp/crs/misc/RL34340.pdf.
2 In the other European Union countries, the austerity program in Greece has been framed as a necessary response to welfare-related profligacy.
3 http://europa.eu/rapid/press-release_SPEECH-10-494_en.htm.
4 http://europa.eu/rapid/press-release_MEMO-13-368_en.htm.
5 Martin Wolf, 2010. "The IMF's foolish praise for austerity." *Financial Times.* September 30, 2010.
6 http://mobile.reuters.com/article/businessNews/idUSTRE7830W220110904?irpc=932.

References

Armingeon, Klaus. 2013. "Breaking with the Past? Why the Global Financial Crisis Led to Austerity Policies but Not to the Modernization of the Welfare State." In *The Welfare State Reader,* 3rd ed., edited by C. Pierson, F.G. Castles, and I.K. Naumann, 214–26. London: Blackwell.

Barrientos, A. 2011. "Poverty, the Crisis, and Social Policy." In *Social Policy in Challenging Times: Economic Crisis and Welfare Systems,* edited by K. Farnsworth and Z. Irving, 101–18. Bristol: Policy Press. http://dx.doi.org/10.1332/policypress/9781847428288.003.0006.

Bello, W. 2013. *Capitalism's Last Stand? Deglobalization in the Age of Austerity.* London: Zed Books.

Bermeo, Nancy Gina, and Jonas Pontusson. 2012. *Coping with Crisis: Government Reactions to the Great Recession.* New York: Russell Sage Foundation.

Blyth, M. 2013. *Austerity: The History of a Dangerous Idea.* Oxford: Oxford University Press.

Credit Suisse AG Research Institute. 2013. *Global Wealth Report 2013.* Zurich: Credit Suisse AG Research Institute.

Degryse, C., M. Jepsen, and P. Pochet. 2013. "The Euro Crisis and Its Impact on National and European Social Policies." Working Paper 2013.05, European Trade Union Institute, Brussels. http://dx.doi.org/10.2139/ssrn.2342095.

Farnsworth, K., and Z. Irving, eds. 2011. *Social Policy in Challenging Times: Economic Crisis and Welfare Systems.* Bristol: Policy Press. http://dx.doi.org/10.1332/policypr ess/9781847428288.001.0001.

–. 2012. "Varieties of Crisis, Varieties of Austerity: Social Policy in Challenging Times." *Journal of Poverty and Social Justice* 20, 2: 133–47. http://dx.doi.org/10.1332/1759827 12X652041.

Financial Crisis Inquiry Commission (FCIC). 2011. *Financial Crisis Inquiry Report.* Washington, DC: FCIC.

Glyn, A. 2006. *Capitalism Unleashed.* Oxford: Oxford University Press.

Hall, P., and D. Soskice, eds. 2001. *Varieties of Capitalism: The Institutional Foundations of Comparative Advantage.* Oxford: Oxford University Press.

Hemerijck, A. 2013. *Changing Welfare States.* Oxford: Oxford University Press.

IMF. 2009. *The State of Public Finances.* Washington, DC: IMF.

–. 2013. *Fiscal Monitor.* Washington, DC: IMF.

Lew, Jack. 2013. "Put Job Creation at the Heart of the Global Recovery." *Financial Times,* 18 July.

OECD. 2009. *Tackling the Jobs Crisis: The Labour Market and Social Policy Response, OECD Labour and Employment Ministerial Meeting, 28–29 September.* Paris: OECD.

–. 2011a. *Economic Policy Reforms 2011: Going for Growth.* Paris: OECD. http://www.oecd.org/newsroom/46917384.pdf.

–. 2011b. *Restoring Public Finances: OECD Working Party of Senior Budget Officials, Public Governance and Territorial Development Directorate.* Paris: OECD.

Oxfam. 2013. "Working for the Few: Political Capture and Economic Inequality." Oxfam briefing paper. http://policy-practice.oxfam.org.uk/publications/working-for-the-few-political-capture-and-economic-inequality-311312.

Palier, B. 2006. "Beyond Retrenchment: Four Problems in Current Welfare State Research and One Suggestion on How to Overcome Them." In *The Welfare State Reader,* 2nd ed., edited by P. Pierson and F.G. Castles, 358-74. Cambridge, UK: Policy Press.

–, ed. 2010. *A Long Good Bye to Bismarck? The Politics of Welfare Reform in Continental Europe.* Amsterdam: Amsterdam University Press. http://dx.doi.org/10.5117/9789089642349.

Pierson, Paul. 1994. *Dismantling the Welfare State.* Cambridge, UK: Cambridge University Press. http://dx.doi.org/10.1017/CBO9780511805288.

–. 1998. "Irresistible Forces, Immovable Objects: Post-Industrial Welfare States Confront Permanent Austerity." *Journal of European Public Policy* 5, 4: 539–60. http://dx.doi.org/10.1080/13501769880000011.

Saez, E. 2013. *Striking It Richer: The Evolution of Top Incomes in the United States (Updated with 2012 Preliminary Estimates).* Berkeley: Department of Economics, University of California. http://elsa.berkeley.edu/saez/saez-UStopincomes-2012.pdf.

Starke, P., A. Kaasch, and F. van Hooren. 2013. *The Welfare State as Crisis Manager: Explaining the Diversity of Policy Responses to Economic Crisis.* Basingstoke: Palgrave Macmillan. http://dx.doi.org/10.1057/9781137314840.

Steinmo, S., K. Thelen, and F. Longstreth, eds. 1992. *Structuring Politics: Historical Institutionalism in Comparative Analysis.* Cambridge, UK: Cambridge University Press. http://dx.doi.org/10.1017/CBO9780511528125.

Streeck, W., and A. Shafer. 2013. *Politics in the Age of Austerity.* London: Wiley.

Taylor-Gooby, P. 2013. *The Double Crisis of the Welfare State and What We Can Do about It.* Basingstoke: Palgrave Macmillan. http://dx.doi.org/10.1057/9781137328113.

van Kersbergen, K., B. Vis, and A. Hemerijck. 2014. "The Great Recession and Welfare State Reform: Is Retrenchment Really the Only Game Left in Town?" *Social Policy and Administration* 48, 7: 883–904. http://dx.doi.org/10.1111/spol.12063.

PART 2: INTERNATIONAL ORGANIZATIONS

4

Understanding Policy Change as Position-Taking
The IMF and Social Policies in Times of Crisis

ANTJE VETTERLEIN

In its programs targeting low-income countries (LICs), the IMF has promoted social safety nets since the early 1990s to mitigate detrimental effects of structural adjustment on the poor (IMF 1993). However, a major turn-around in its position occurred in the wake of the Asian financial crisis, when the IMF joined the World Bank's Poverty Reduction Strategy Paper (PRSP) initiative. Suddenly, the IMF departed from its firm conviction that sound economic policies and an increase in economic growth are the best social policies and began to promote poverty reduction as one of its priority objectives (IMF 2000). This new focus also caused significant operational changes within the organization.

Contrary to the Asian financial crisis, in response to the most recent crisis, the IMF did not move significantly toward an increased social agenda. The reason lies in the organization's changed power position vis-à-vis other actors in the organizational field of social policies and poverty. While the run-up to the Asian financial crisis was characterized by the IMF's decreasing importance and an ever-increasing legitimacy gap, enhanced by the IMF's inability to tackle the crisis appropriately, the latest crisis presented itself almost as the complete opposite, boosting the IMF's position as the most important actor in dealing with the crisis and enhancing its financial resources. This had consequences, in turn, for how the IMF reacted to the crisis. In general, the organization is known to be slow to adapt to pressure and engage in innovative policy reform (Vetterlein 2010; Vetterlein and Moschella 2014). In contrast to the World Bank, in which policy reform is more often initiated internally and from the bottom up, the IMF usually reacts to external pressure from the top down (member states) and thus adapts to its environment rather than innovatively and proactively changes policies (Park and Vetterlein 2010). The specific circumstances of the 1997 crisis, also called a "legitimacy crisis" (Seabrooke 2007), however, provided the opportunity for significant change by opening up to alternative policy ideas from NGOs and other actors critical of the IMF's social policy position. In contrast, the recent crisis enabled the IMF to reinforce its position on poverty and to ignore alternative viewpoints, especially those of NGOs.

This chapter contributes to the literature on international organization (IO) policy change anchored in the field of international relations (IR). Although there is considerable debate over the main driving forces for IO change, most studies agree that external shocks such as political or financial crises trigger fast and more significant change, even in organizations such as the IMF that usually manage to resist pressure. Yet, as the editors of this volume also ask, is this always the case? I argue that change can vary on a continuum from being minor policy adjustments and adaptations to being rather transformative innovations. My assumption is that variation in response, in terms of how deep change goes, can be referred back to different positions that the IO takes in the field.

The chapter is structured as follows. After a brief review of the existing IR literature on IO policy change, I elaborate the theoretical framework that guides the empirical analysis. This shows how introducing the notion of an IO's position-taking in its organizational field enhances our understanding of the nature of IO policy responses. The following section gives a detailed picture of the IMF's social policy engagements post-crises and how these engagements have changed over time. I conclude the chapter by reflecting on the findings at both the theoretical level and at the policy level.

Policy Change as Position-Taking

The IO literature on policy change has been asking how, when, and why change occurs in IOs (Barnett and Coleman 2005). A major part of the field is framed in terms of a rationalist-constructivist divide. On the one hand, principal-agent (PA) models account for IO policy change either by the power of member states to dictate their interests (Koremenos, Lipson, and Snidal 2001) or by "agency slack" in IOs (Hawkins et al. 2006; Nielson and Tierney 2003). On the other hand, constructivists refer to organization-internal factors, especially organizational culture, to account for change (see, e.g., Chwieroth 2010; Lipson 2007; Momani 2005; Park 2010; Steffek 2010; Weaver 2008; Willets 2000). I argue, however, that the situation is characterized by multicausality. All of these factors identified by IO scholars, such as NGO pressure, internal norm entrepreneurs, powerful member states, and IO autonomy, are usually simultaneously present and interact with each other. The challenge is to identify the conditions under which they work.

One point that most IR scholars would agree on is that crisis situations trigger fast and major changes in IOs since they create uncertainty and/or legitimacy problems that in turn allow for new policy ideas to gain traction. But is this really the case? Streeck (2009, chapter 15), for instance, argues that the exogenous shock of Germany's unification in 1990 did not lead to radical changes in its social system but reinforced gradual changes long under way in West Germany. Vetterlein and Moschella (2014) also show that exogenous shocks do not always lead to rapid policy change in IOs. In other words, it might be legitimate to assume that, even in crisis situations, the nature of policy responses can vary.

Current IO studies are not able to address the nature of change because they fail to problematize policy change as such. Change is assumed to take place (or not), yet the content of change or its qualitative nature is overlooked. The nature of change, however, can vary on numerous dimensions, such as speed, depth, or direction (Viola and Rixen 2013).[1] This chapter focuses on the depth of change, arguing that change can vary from minor adjustments to major policy shifts. Measuring change is a tricky endeavour and can be perceived as a matter of theoretical perspective (Capano and Howlett 2009, 7), but the employment of a comparative approach makes it possible to identify relative differences. Inspired by Hall's (1993) distinction among first-, second-, and third-order change in the settings, instruments, and goals of a policy, I distinguish among discursive, policy, and operational change. Changes in statements in speeches or reports presented to the outside world are regarded as minor changes. Changes in policy instruments or newly introduced policy tools denote medium changes, whereas changes in regulations that guide the organization's and staff's conduct are defined as major changes.

Drawing on Bourdieu-inspired organizational studies, I argue that variation in the depth of change is related to the IO's position-taking in its field. Bourdieu defines field as "structured spaces of positions (or posts) whose properties depend on their position within these spaces and which can be analyzed independently of the characteristics of their occupants (which are partly determined by them)" (1993, 72). A field is characterized by the positions that these organizations occupy, which are related to the resources or capital that they possess. IO action therefore has to be understood in reference to the position that an IO occupies in the field of structural relations and not its observation of and response to other actors' behaviours or signals. In the case of the World Bank, for instance, NGOs are generally more successful in being heard compared with the IMF (Park and Vetterlein 2010). Yet, as Vetterlein and Moschella (2014) show, the power (or capital) that NGOs possess vis-à-vis the IMF also depends on the IMF's position in the field based on its expertise (or cultural capital) in the respective policy area. This also implies that an organization's position is not fixed but depends on the relations and positioning of other actors in the field. Because its policy responses can change over time, they have to be analyzed in relation to the specific situation in which they occur.

Field is thus theorized as a space where a struggle is constantly ongoing among the participating actors over the respective policy (object), leading to temporarily stable and dominant policy norms and rules – also called a process of structuration (Fligstein 2008; Giddens 1984). A field has three defining characteristics: a specific object around which the field constitutes itself or what is "at stake" (i.e., the policy); power relations among the relevant actors in the field; and emerging norms and rules, related to the object, that become the temporary "rules of the game" over time. The theoretical expectation is that the power position of the IO matters with respect to the outcome of this process of structuration in a particular policy field.

If we understand the action of an IO as being determined by its position in the field, then being in a weaker or more powerful position changes the conditions under which it engages in policy change, which in turn affects the degree of change. In other words, IOs do not simply possess power (or not); their positioning varies depending on the relation of their positions relative to other actors in the field. The concept of field also suggests the utility of a comparison of an IO's positioning in different situations of policy change. I thus examine the power position of the IMF in different situations of policy change and the process of social interaction between the organization and its fields that shapes the content of policy responses.

IOs do not just possess a position in the field but also assume such positions in an act of "position-taking" (Bourdieu and Wacquant 1992). By taking a position, an IO acquires certain capital. Position-takings are specific actions – such as a product, service, argument, or, as in our case, policy – that derive meaning in relation to other such position-takings in the field. Bourdieu (1996) provides the example of firms that, in the business field, take positions by branding their products. Another example, in the name of CSR activities, is that firms can engage in social responsibility by donating money or engaging more thoroughly in community projects. By choosing one activity over the other, they

Antje Vetterlein

assume a certain position. Yet this act is not just the result of a deliberate choice. Position-takings can derive from past positions as well as specific context conditions.

Built on this theoretical framework, an organization's position is defined as the temporary status granted to an organization based on the capital that it holds relevant within the respective field (Bourdieu 1993). This can be perceived as a property that is not given but derives from past behaviours and interactions. Yet, it is also related to the perceptions of all field actors. The position of an organization can vary from powerful to weak, based on its recognition in the field as having the ability to determine the 'rules of the game' or as marginal to the process of structuration. The assumption is that organizations in powerful positions interact less with other actors in the field and are able to shape the policy content to their liking, avoiding as much change as possible; whereas weakly positioned organizations are more receptive to other actors including those advocating alternative policy ideas. The organization's position is related to the capital it possesses within a particular field. This capital can be of three different kinds – financial independence, confidence in its expertise and competence, and perceived legitimacy.

In what follows, I compare the IMF's policy response in two different crisis situations. As we will see, different degrees of depth follow from the organization's position in its field.

The IMF and Social Policies in Times of Crisis

The financial crises in 1997 and 2007 raised concerns about their social impacts on the most vulnerable people in the world. As the organization primarily responsible for dealing with economic and financial crises, the IMF came under fire. Yet, contrary to what some critics say about it, the organization had already positioned itself on social and poverty issues before those crises. As I argue elsewhere (Vetterlein 2010), the IMF's engagement with social policies can be seen as falling into three different periods. Throughout the 1980s, the organization's main position was that sound economic policies lead to economic growth, seen as the best vehicle to reduce poverty. Therefore, social policies as such are not only unnecessary but also perceived as detrimental to growth since they divert resources away from investment, the major driver of growth. Although this was the basic understanding within the IMF, in the face of growing criticism of its programs as well as their adverse impacts on poor people, at the end of the 1980s the organization acknowledged that its adjustment programs had income-distributional effects (e.g., Heller et al. 1988). Some in-house research was conducted to find a way to operationalize poverty and income distribution. The results, presented to the Executive Board, led to the decision that the IMF should continue to rely on World Bank data and expertise with regard to poverty and that social issues should not be linked to conditionality (Boughton 2001). In the end, the IMF's operational solution for dealing with LICs led to two new lending facilities, the structural adjustment facility (SAF) in 1986 followed by the enhanced structural adjustment facility (ESAF) in 1987. Both offered favourable terms for loans tailored to LICs and technical advice regarding subsidies and government expenditures but did not explicitly address social issues.

Although "the social" did not figure prominently during the 1980s on the discursive, policy, or operational level, the 1990s witnessed a change. Pressured by other IOs, mainly the United Nations and World Bank, the IMF found a way to incorporate social safety nets (SSNs) into its policy advice (e.g., IMF 1993). This policy tool was meant to mitigate the adverse social effects of IMF programs on some people in developing countries. The respective countries' existing social policies were seen as the basis on which to build, supplemented by new tools that would "include a mix of limited subsidies on basic necessities (particularly basic foodstuffs), social security arrangements (such as pensions and unemployment benefits), and possibly public works programs adapted for this purpose" (IMF 1993, 23). Furthermore, "it is important for countries to establish cost-effective permanent social security measures to deal with 'normal' contingencies" (ibid., 3). The IMF saw additional possibilities to integrate a minimum set of such measures into economic reform programs (ibid., 20). The two basic underlying assumptions remained – first, that economic growth is the best engine to achieve poverty reduction – with one qualification: some social policies can foster economic growth. Second, poverty reduction and social policies remain in the World Bank's area of expertise, and the IMF should not get too involved in this area.

This brief account shows that even without major crises the IMF had responded to the changing discourse of development and assumed a position with regard to its role in social policies and poverty reduction. Aligning its reaction to its original organizational mandate, the IMF incorporated social issues into its economic framework by arguing that social policies support economic development. Yet, the main assumption that economic growth is the best means to achieve poverty reduction prevailed throughout the 1990s even though the discourse of development changed significantly around that time. In 1995, the World Summit on Social Development adopted the Copenhagen Declaration

Antje Vetterlein

and a Program of Action stressing the objectives of poverty reduction, full employment, and just and safe societies. The United Nations proposed a human development approach. NGOs, in particular the Fifty Years Is Enough campaign, increasingly challenged the IMF for paying insufficient attention to issues of poverty. Although these criticisms triggered some changes in the World Bank, they did not seem to have an impact on the IMF. The decisive shift in the IMF's behaviour toward social issues took place only in 1999 when the organization agreed to participate in the World Bank–initiated PRSP program. This change, triggered by the Asian financial crisis, led to significant reforms at the operational level because of the IMF's weak power position prior to the crisis.

The IMF's Turn to Poverty Reduction

During the 1990s, the IMF was in crisis, scoring rather low on the three kinds of capital. With regard to *legitimacy,* the IMF was a target of major NGO campaigns that criticized the organization for its lack of social consciousness and anti-development policies. From the other end of the political spectrum, criticism mounted against the organization as no longer being necessary as a lending organization. Both arguments questioned the IMF's *expertise* and *competence* in development aid. The right argued that the market would work much better than the IMF since private sector lending and foreign direct investment would more efficiently stimulate developing country markets (Bird 1991). The left suggested that the IMF's questionable approach to development had failed to generate economic growth and to decrease poverty in developing countries. Related to the IMF's decreasing legitimacy and waning confidence in its competence was deterioration of its *economic capital.* While the IMF depends on fees paid by borrowing countries (Woods 2010), major borrowers were increasingly turning elsewhere for funding, unsatisfied with the IMF's continued use of conditionality and its lack of a more democratic structure (legitimacy). Moreover, the G7 members failed to develop new strategies to pay for the organization. Thus, the IMF itself ran into a financial crisis.

Its weak position was well reflected in the 1998 external review of its structural adjustment lending. In 1996, the Executive Board asked for a review of the ESAF – the first time that an IMF program was *externally* assessed. The final review heavily criticized IMF practice in LICs, highlighting three points: first, IMF programs lacked ownership, which in turn led to implementation problems; second, social and poverty issues were insufficiently addressed in structural adjustment lending; and third, there was a lack of cooperation among different donors, in particular the World Bank. The report concluded with the following objectives: "[to] better focus ESAF by improving protections for the poor, by improving the cooperation with other international financial organizations and bilateral donors, and by strengthening 'ownership'" (Botchwey et al. 1998, Part 1, 4).

The report further decreased the organization's self-confidence and thus its relative position. Although the points made were similar to previous criticisms, that this evaluation was carried out by Kwesi Botchwey, a highly regarded economist (and former finance minister of Ghana), who had worked for the IMF before, made it resonate much more within the organization than any NGO protest. The report further damaged the IMF by revealing it to be an arrogant organization that imposed its values on developing countries (interview with IMF staff, April 2004).

The IMF lost more capital when the 1997 financial crisis hit East Asia. In the beginning, this crisis was considered solely a *financial* crisis and as such reflective of the IMF's inability to deal with the situation. Criticism from all sides increased. This experience hit the organization's self-esteem hard, and the IMF had to admit that its models did not work across the board. Criticism escalated as the crisis came to be characterized as a social catastrophe.[2] In this situation of high-level external pressure and high organizational uncertainty, Michel Camdessus argued for a social pillar within the international financial system (see Gupta et al. 2000). The IMF's weak position thus led to its opening up to other actors in the field (see Hibben 2015), in particular the World Bank. Consequently, the IMF agreed to participate in the World Bank's PRSP initiative, and this triggered operational changes in its attitude toward social policies and poverty reduction for the first time in IMF history.

In line with the new PRSP process, the IMF renamed its concessional lending tool from ESAF to PRGF, poverty reduction and growth facility. The website description of this new facility mentioned poverty reduction as the *first* of the PRGF's seven key features, signalling the IMF's changed focus (interview with IMF staff, April 2004). Poverty reduction became more central in the organization. Instead of referring to the World Bank on social issues, the IMF's role in poverty reduction was now openly debated inside the organization (interview with IMF staff, April 2004). This changing discourse was also apparent in IMF publications. Research papers began to address the relationship between growth and poverty, noting that "the causality could well go the other way. In such cases, poverty reduction could in fact be necessary to implement stable macroeconomic policies or to achieve higher growth" (IMF and World Bank 2001, 5). This signified a turn-around in the IMF understanding of development.

Antje Vetterlein

Also, as a new policy tool, the PRGF changed common practice in the IMF. The PRSPs are operational papers, decisively different from their predecessors, the Policy Framework Papers (PFPs), under SAF and ESAF. Not only is poverty reduction the main focus of PRSPs, but also they are much more comprehensive, since they entail a complete assessment of the country's poverty situation and the identification of priority areas and specific targets in line with the Millennium Development Goals (MDGs). They further specify indicators to monitor poverty reduction performance and collect information on all development aid present in the country, listing different donors and projects. The time frame is longer than that under structural adjustment lending. Finally, the PRSPs have to include a section indicating that all stakeholders were able to participate in development of the strategy. Thus, instead of a tripartite paper written by the IMF and World Bank in consultation with the president and finance minister of the country, the PRSP process requires all stakeholders to voice their opinions, including NGOs and beneficiaries.

In these ways, the IMF's participation in the PRSP initiative managed to address all three critical aspects: enhancing country ownership instead of imposing development strategies, increasing the focus on poverty and social development, and collaborating with all other development stakeholders, in particular the World Bank, to enhance donor harmonization by offering *one* strategy for the country.

These changes had impacts on the IMF's operational reality. Three changes are important to note. First, PRSPs state precise quantitative targets and performance criteria and aim to monitor the budget allocation. For the first time, these targets were incorporated into conditionality guidelines for IMF resources (Gupta et al. 2000, 22). Second, such an approach required the collection of social indicators and poverty measurements along with an *ex ante* social impact analysis and monitoring. Therefore, in 2004, the IMF established its own unit on poverty and social impact analysis (PSIA) within the Fiscal Affairs Department (FAD). Again, though this issue had been discussed in the late 1970s and again in the late 1980s, it was always concluded that the IMF should rely on World Bank data on poverty (Boughton 2001; interview with IMF staff, March 2004). Third, several social scientists were engaged as consultants to IMF economists on the social aspects of their country missions.

Many of these reforms at the operational level had been debated in the past but always rejected. Such fundamental operational changes were possible because of the special situation in which the organization saw itself prior to and during the 1997 crisis. Its waning importance in the run-up to the crisis had already put the IMF in a weak position. The organization clearly needed to think about reform. The commissioning of an external review revealed member country dissatisfaction with IMF performance in LICs and changed the IMF's relationship with critics in the field. The Asian financial crisis worsened the IMF's situation. As a result of its bad performance, confidence continued to decline, and this had an impact on the IMF's perception of its position. The decision to join the PRSP initiative has to be understood against this backdrop. Publication of the external review coincided with the financial crisis, putting pressure on the IMF to react quickly to the criticism that this was also a social crisis. Under pressure, its uncertainty about how to react and the decline in support from all sides significantly weakened its position, putting other actors in the field in a better position to dominate the struggle over the rules of the game. The World Bank, on the forefront in these processes, proposed the PRSP initiative, which the IMF quickly joined as a smart way to address criticisms in the external review of ESAF. This in turn triggered significant operational changes.

The question is how much these changes signified a new "rule of the game." Although operational changes were made, the new development ideas were much contested within the IMF. For instance, Managing Director Horst Köhler's (2000–4) proposal to hire more non-economists was rejected by the Executive Board (interview, 16 March 2004). The non-economists hired were financed not by the IMF but by the British Department for International Development. Moreover, a number of directors on the board continued the well-known discourse on the IMF and poverty, arguing "that the IMF should not allow its primary mandate to be diluted"; rather, it should contribute "to poverty reduction mainly through its support of economic policies that provide a conducive environment for sustained growth" (Gupta et al. 2000, 28). Furthermore, "in the family of international organizations, the social components of country programs are primarily the responsibility of the World Bank and other organizations, not the IMF" (ibid., 1). Interviews with IMF staff in March 2004 confirmed these observations of internal skepticism (see also Hibben 2015).

Paradigm Maintenance in the 2007 Financial Crisis
The IMF's silence on necessary reforms in the immediate aftermath of the Asian financial crisis is remarkable. Its responses to the affected Asian countries not only led to doubts regarding its expertise but also "left it branded 'illegitimate' even by mainstream economists" (Woods 2010, 52), while the lack of change to its governance structure to reflect the growing weight of emerging market economies contributed to its decreasing legitimacy. This had further economic consequences since major clients, such as Russia, Argentina, and Brazil, sought

Antje Vetterlein

other financial sources, leading to further decreases in IMF income. A shortfall of US$400 million was estimated for 2010, prompting the organization to lay off up to 400 staff members (ibid.). In this situation, Dominique Strauss-Kahn took over as managing director (in 2007) and announced far-reaching reforms to address the three forms of capital on which the IMF scored so low: decreasing finances or economic capital, the lack of confidence in its competence after the Asian financial crisis, and the growing perception of its illegitimacy given the changes in the global economy.

In response, two types of reforms were initiated *prior* to the 2007 crisis: financial reform and governance reform. The main objectives of the financial reform were to increase the IMF's financial independence and enhance its predictability and flexibility. In general, the IMF has three sources of income: that earned from the fees that borrowers pay for their loans, used to pay for administrative costs; that earned from credit lines provided by "New Agreements to Borrow" (NAB) and "General Agreements to Borrow" (GAB); and that earned from independent resources, such as quota-based capital as well as gold holdings. Based on the recommendations of a group of experts (The Committee 2007), the following reforms were agreed to: create an endowment with the profits of 403.3 metric tons of gold, establish investment authority, and charge service fees for the PRGF trust fund. The expectation was that these reforms would generate about US$300 million within a few years. They were designed to enhance the IMF's financial independence from member countries, both from borrowers and from lenders, and thus enhance its position based on economic capital.

Governance reforms started in 2006 at the annual meetings of the IMF and the World Bank in Singapore. Four of the most underrepresented countries – Korea, Turkey, China, and Mexico – received an immediate and ad hoc increase of their quotas, which meant an increase in their voting power and access to resources. Four other reform proposals were made and adopted two years later: a new quota formula; another round of ad hoc quota increases in accordance with the new formula; a tripling of basic votes; and a strengthening of African countries' representation on the Executive Board (IMF 2008). These reforms signified a total shift of voting power in the IMF of 5.4 percent. Individual countries benefited from increases in quota shares, such as China (+50 percent), Korea (+106 percent), and India, Brazil, and Mexico (+40 percent each). Some countries eligible for a quota increase, such as Germany, Japan, and the United States, passed on a part of it (Woods 2010). As the IMF itself announced in 2008, these "far-reaching" changes were an attempt to re-establish its "credibility and legitimacy."

These reforms were all under way when the financial crisis of 2007 hit. This crisis came in two waves: first, following the breakdown of Lehman Brothers in September 2008, a credit crunch across countries that had engaged in global banking; second, and consequently, a deterioration of the real economy since global trade decreased, spreading recession globally. In response, the G20 Action Plan made the IMF the core institution for coordinating emergency measures and thus significantly enhanced its power position. The G20 held three meetings to discuss further action, in November 2008 in Washington, DC, in April 2009 in London, and in November 2009 in Pittsburgh. At the first meeting, the G20 agreed on an Action Plan that set the framework to deal with the crisis, regulate global finance, support the poorest countries affected, and reform IOs. Part of this plan was also to delegate specific tasks to different IOs, among them the IMF. In the April meeting, the resources given to these institutions were increased to enable them to fulfill their tasks, significantly boosting the IMF's role. The G20 announced an increase in IMF funding of about US$750 billion. In addition, the emerging market economies of China, Brazil, and India promised major contributions. These plans were then reviewed in Pittsburgh.

Initially, the consequences of the crisis for LICs were not entirely clear. Yet, in their 2009 *Global Monitoring Report,* the World Bank and IMF called it a "development emergency." In London, the G20 came to the same conclusion, acknowledging the "disproportionate impact on the vulnerable in the poorest countries and recognis[ing their] collective responsibility."[3] The resources pledged to the IMF in the wake of the crisis were also meant to enhance support for social protection, trade, and concessional lending. Indeed, the IMF presented itself as the "knight in shining armour" and lent record amounts to its members, basically doubling their access to resources. Concessional lending for the LICs was increased by doubling the PRGF and exogenous shocks facility (ESF). About US$6 billion was used for this from the sales of IMF gold, bilateral contributions, and internal resources (Woods 2010). Yet this sum was rather small compared with the more than US$750 billion made ready for NAB-participating members. Furthermore, comparing IMF activities in LICs with loans given to European countries and emerging market economies, most of the loans given in 2009 post-crisis were made to European countries (79 percent); only about 3 percent were committed to African countries (ibid., 58). The IMF indeed estimated at the end of 2009 that it would be able to provide only up to a third of the new financing needs of LICs. Other organizations, in particular the World Bank (which did not receive new funding after the crisis), tried to raise awareness of this fact, and President Zoellick called for a vulnerability fund for the poorest countries (World Bank Group 2009).

Antje Vetterlein

Apart from these lending activities, what has changed in terms of the IMF's position on social issues and poverty reduction? The biggest change was the 2010 replacement of the PRGF by three new lending facilities, the extended credit facility (ECF), the rapid credit facility (RCF), and the standby credit facility (SCF). Remarkable here is the lack of emphasis on poverty reduction. This is obvious in the facilities' titles compared with the previous crisis, when the very phrase "poverty reduction" was celebrated as a success by the supporters of a reformed IMF (interviews with IMF staff, 2004 and 2008). The factsheets describing these facilities also bear testimony to a noticeable reduction in the focus on poverty since the emphasis is now on flexibility and streamlining conditionality to meet country-specific needs. That might not come as a surprise given the IMF's interpretation of the crisis. Although the IMF labelled the crisis a "development emergency," looking at individual statements by the managing director or other staff members, it becomes clear that the IMF defined the impact of the financial crisis in developing countries as an economic problem. Introducing the proposal to replace the PRGF in spring 2009, Strauss-Kahn did not mention social policies at all.[4] This is particularly striking compared with Camdessus's reaction to the Asian financial crisis a decade prior. For the IMF, the crisis was interpreted as an economic issue characterized by falling trade because of a decrease in global demands, decreasing foreign direct investment, remittances, and lesser aid flows.[5]

These changes are not only discursive. IMF operations also changed with the introduction of these new facilities. While the PRSP process was comprehensive, including all development stakeholders in drafting a strategy paper that served as an operational paper for the World Bank and IMF,[6] the new facilities decoupled the IMF lending facility from this process and only loosely referred to the PRSPs. For instance, the ECF reads as follows:

> ECF-supported programs should be based on the country's own development strategy and aim to safeguard social objectives. Related documentation requirements have been made more flexible, by allowing the program documents of countries that have a valid poverty reduction strategy paper covering a year from the date of the program review to describe how the current fiscal budget, the upcoming fiscal budget (if available), and the planned structural reforms advance implementation of a country's poverty reduction strategy.[7]

For the other two, the SCF and RCF, no PRSP is required.[8] That does not mean that the IMF turned around when it comes to poverty issues and social policies. All three facilities point out that loans and conditionality should be aligned with the economic growth and poverty reduction plans of the respective country. In fact, the IMF further developed its social spending targets (Clegg 2014). This was not a new idea but a continuation of what had been developed in the late 1990s with the introduction of social benchmarks to its conditionality.

In other words, the changes in 2009–10 were rather minimal compared with those in 1999. We can observe a reinforcement of what had been thus far developed but with a reduced focus on poverty. The enhanced power position of the IMF made it possible to return to the perception that, though social issues might be important, they do not belong in IMF policies. The lack of interaction with other actors in the field is remarkable in this respect. Hibben (2015, 18) provides empirical evidence that NGOs played a smaller role in the IMF's reaction to the crisis in 2009 than in 1999.

Conclusion

Comparing the IMF's response to the latest major financial crises in terms of its social policies, this chapter's contribution is twofold, at both a theoretical level and a policy level. Theoretically, I have shown that shock events such as major crises do not always lead to major changes in IOs. Rather, it is the position that the organization assumes in its field that is a crucial component of explaining its response, or position-taking, in crisis situations. A weak position, based on different types of capital, means that the organization is more open to other actors in the field, or, put differently, those actors have more leverage to promote their ideas. We have seen how, in the 1997 crisis, the IMF worked with the World Bank and NGOs. In this situation of a high degree of criticism, increasing uncertainty, and immense pressure to act quickly, the IMF agreed to what was offered as a policy solution. The situation in 2007–8 was different. The IMF had started to re-establish its power position. The crisis actually contributed to its increasing importance since the G20 made the organization the core player in dealing with it. In this situation, no major changes happened in terms of social policies. In each instance of policy change in IOs, many factors are at work, and it is therefore difficult to single out one, such as leadership, NGO pressure, member states' power, or organizational culture. A relational approach, understanding the organization to be embedded in a field in which other actors also take positions, might therefore be a more appropriate way to study IO policy change. Further empirical research is necessary to refine these arguments.

Antje Vetterlein

On the policy level, tracing the IMF's role in LICs, we can see its approach to social policies and positions with regard to poverty reduction in developing countries. The brief historical account has shown that the IMF has been concerned with social issues early on even though this concern was not reflected in its policies. Adoption of the social safety net approach in the 1990s was the first "real" engagement, yet the IMF did not change its practice or its main assumption about economic growth being the main driver of poverty reduction. More significant changes took place at the end of the 1990s in the wake of the Asian financial crisis and in the situation of losing its power position. Yet the newly established understanding of development as a holistic process that would require incorporating social policies into a macroeconomic framework never took hold. Right from the start, the IMF's participation in the PRSP process was perceived critically inside the organization. Instead of going down that road, the IMF – once in a better position again – re-established its "old" approach to social issues and poverty, which means that social policies are World Bank business, whereas the IMF deals with macroeconomic stability and balance-of-payment problems.

Notes

1   In particular, institutionalism has provided a sound conceptualization of the variation of policy change (see, e.g., Campbell 2004). Since Streeck and Thelen (2005), for instance, we know not to confuse speed and depth of change, meaning that even incremental and slow-moving changes can be transformative. Similarly, depth needs to be more qualified in terms of direction of change since change can reinforce but also undermine particular policies (Viola and Rixen 2013).

2   The description of one of the interviewees who went on a mission to East Asia with James D. Wolfensohn at the time of the crisis points out that in the beginning everyone, including the governments of the affected countries, was on the financial side. But after making Wolfensohn aware of the social costs of the crisis, the tone of the debate changed. A press conference took place, and the crisis was reframed as a social crisis. Also within the IMF, the East Asian crisis from then on was conceived as a social crisis.

3   London Summit Communiqué (2009), http://www.londonsummit.gov.uk/resources/en/news/15766232/communiqué-020409.

4   See http://www.imf.org/external/np/speeches/2009/031009.htm.

5   See http://www.imf.org/external/np/seminars/eng/2010/lic/.

6   It had to be aligned to the Country Assistant Strategy of the World Bank and the "letter of intent" in the IMF.

7   http://www.imf.org/external/np/exr/facts/ecf.htm.

8   For the RCF, see http://www.imf.org/external/np/exr/facts/rcf.htm. For the SCF, see http://www.imf.org/external/np/exr/facts/scf.htm.

References

Barnett, M., and L. Coleman. 2005. "Designing Police: Interpol and the Study of Change in International Organizations." *International Studies Quarterly* 49 (4): 593–619.

Bird, G. 1991. "The IMF in the 1990s: Forward to the Past or Back to the Future?" ODI Working Paper 46, London.

Botchwey, K. Paul Collier, Jan Willem Gunning, and Koichi Hamada. 1998. *Report of the Group of Independent Persons Appointed to Conduct an Evaluation of Certain Aspects of the Enhanced Structural Adjustment Facility.* Washington, DC: IMF.

Boughton, J. 2001. *Silent Revolution: The International Monetary Fund, 1979–1989.* Washington, DC: IMF.

Bourdieu, P. 1993. "Some Properties of Fields." In *Sociology in Question*, translated by Richard Nice, 72–77. London: SAGE.

–. 1996. *The Rules of Art: Genesis and Structure of the Literary Field*, translated by Susan Emanuel. Stanford: Stanford University Press.

Bourdieu, P., and L. Wacquant. 1992. *An Invitation to Reflexive Sociology.* Chicago: University of Chicago Press.

Campbell, J.L. 2004. *Institutional Change and Globalization.* Princeton: Princeton University Press.

Capano, G., and M. Howlett. 2009. "Introduction: The Multidimensional World of Policy Dynamics." In *European and North American Policy Change: Drivers and Dynamics*, edited by G. Capano and M. Howlett, 1–12. London: Routledge.

Chwieroth, J.M. 2010. *Capital Ideas: The IMF and the Rise of Financial Liberalization.* Princeton: Princeton University Press.

Clegg, L. 2014. "Social Spending Targets in IMF Concessional Lending: US Domestic Politics and the Institutional Foundations of Rapid Operational Change." *Review of International Political Economy* 21 (3): 735–63.

The Committee. 2007. *Final Report.* Washington, DC: Committee to Study Sustainable Long-Term Financing of the IMF.

Fligstein, N. 2008. "Fields, Power, and Social Skill: A Critical Analysis of the New Institutionalisms." *International Public Management Review* 9: 227–53.

Giddens, A. 1984. *Constitution of Society. Outline of the Theory of Structuration.* Cambridge, UK: Polity Press.

Gupta, S. Louis Dicks-Mireaux, Ritha Khemani, Calvin McDonald, and Marijn Verhoeven 2000. "Social Issues in IMF-Supported Programs." Occasional Paper No. 191. Washington, DC: IMF.

Hall, P.A. 1993. "Policy Paradigms, Social Learning, and the State: The Case of Economic Policymaking in Britain." *Comparative Politics* 25 (3): 275–96.

Hawkins, D.G., D.A. Lake, D.L. Nielson, and M.J. Tierney, eds. 2006. *Delegation and Agency in International Organizations.* Cambridge, UK: Cambridge University Press.

Heller, P.S., and A. Lans Bovenberg, Thanos Catsambas, Ke-Young Chu, and Parthasarathi Shome 1988. "The Implications of Fund-Supported Adjustment Programs for Poverty: Experiences in Selected Countries." Occasional Paper No. 58. Washington, DC: IMF.

Hibben, M. 2015. "Coalitions of Change: Explaining IMF Low-Income Country Reform in the Post-Washington Consensus." *Journal of International Relations and Development* 18 (2): 202–26.

IMF. 1993. "*Social Safety Net in Economic Reform.*" Internal Document EBS/93/34. Washington, DC: IMF.

–. 2000. *World Summit for Social Development and Beyond* June 2000 Follow-Up. IMF Initiatives in Support of Social Development, *submitted to the UN;* December 6, 2000, Washington, DC: IMF.

–. 2008. "Transcript of a Conference Call by Senior IMF Officials on Board of Governors Vote Quota and Voice." http://www.imf.org/external/np/tr/2008/tr080429a.htm.

IMF and World Bank. 2001. *Macroeconomic Policy and Poverty Reduction.* Washington, DC: World Bank.

Koremenos, B., C. Lipson, and D. Snidal. 2001. "The Rational Design of International Institutions." *International Organization* 55 (4): 761–800.

Lipson, M. 2007. "Peacekeeping: Organized Hypocrisy?" *European Journal of International Relations* 13 (1): 5–34.

Momani, B. 2005. "Limits on Streamlining Fund Conditionality: The International Monetary Fund's Organizational Culture." *Journal of International Relations and Development* 8 (2): 142–63.

Nielson, D.L., and M.J. Tierney. 2003. "Delegation to International Organizations: Agency Theory and World Bank Environmental Reform." *International Organization* 57 (2): 241–76.

Park, S. 2010. *The World Bank Group and Environmentalists: Changing International Organisation Identities.* Manchester: Manchester University Press.

Park, S., and A. Vetterlein, eds. 2010. *Owning Development: Creating Global Policy Norms in the World Bank and the IMF.* Cambridge, UK: Cambridge University Press.

Seabrooke, L. 2007. "Legitimacy Gaps in the World Economy: Explaining the Sources of the IMF's Legitimacy Crisis." *International Politics* 44: 250–68.

Steffek, J. 2010. "Explaining Patterns of Transnational Participation: The Role of Policy Fields." In *Transnational Actors in Global Governance: Patterns, Explanations, and Implications,* edited by C. Jonsson and J. Tallberg, 67–87. Basingstoke: Palgrave Macmillan.

Strauss-Kahn. Dominique, 2009. *Changes: Successful Partnerships for Africa's Growth Challenge,* Remarks by Dominique Strauss-Kahn, Managing Director of the International Monetary Fund, Dar es Salaam, Tanzania, March 10, 2009, available at: http://www.imf.org/external/np/speeches/2009/031009.htm.

Streeck, W. 2009. *Re-Forming Capitalism: Institutional Change in the German Political Economy.* Oxford: Oxford University Press.

Streeck, W., and K. Thelen, eds. 2005. *Beyond Continuity: Institutional Change in Advanced Political Economies.* Oxford: Oxford University Press.

Vetterlein, A. 2010. "Lacking Ownership: The IMF and Its Engagement with Social Development as a Global Policy Norm." In *Owning Development: Creating Global Policy Norms in the IMF and the World Bank,* edited by S. Park and A. Vetterlein, 93–112. Cambridge, UK: Cambridge University Press.

Vetterlein, A., and M. Moschella. 2014. "International Organizations and Organizational Fields: Explaining Policy Change in the IMF." *European Political Science Review* 6 (1): 143–65.

Viola, L., and T. Rixen. 2013. "Historical Institutionalism and International Relations: Conceptualizing Change in International Institutions." Unpublished manuscript, Wissenschaftszentrum Berlin fuer Sozialforschung, Berlin.

Weaver, C.E. 2008. *Hypocrisy Trap: The World Bank and the Poverty of Reform.* Princeton: Princeton University Press.

Willets, P. 2000. "From 'Consultative Arrangements' to 'Partnership': The Changing Status of NGOs in Diplomacy at the UN." *Global Governance* 6 (2): 191–212.

Woods, N. 2010. "Global Governance after the Financial Crisis: A New Multilateralism or the Last Gasp of the Great Powers?" *Global Policy* 1 (1): 51–63.

World Bank Group. 2009. "Zoellick Calls for New Vulnerability Fund Ahead of Davos Forum." 30 January 2009. http://go.worldbank.org/76E1GRKBN0.

World Bank and IMF. 2009. *Global Monitoring Report 2009: A Development Emergency.* Washington, DC: World Bank and IMF.

Antje Vetterlein

5

The ILO and Social Protection Policy after the Global Financial Crisis
A Challenge to the World Bank

BOB DEACON

This chapter first rehearses the historical contest between the World Bank and ILO in terms of their recommendations to countries about social protection, in particular pension policy.[1] It then reviews recent developments in World Bank social protection policy following the global economic crisis of 2008. Similarly, it examines recent developments within the ILO concerning its post-crisis approach to social protection and pension policy. Recapitulated is the story of how the ILO captured the global agenda on the social protection floor (SPF) after 2008 such that the SPF became not only ILO but also G20, UNICEF, UN, and World Bank policy. Creation of the Social Protection Inter-Agency Cooperation Board is then explained. The chapter then asks what the prospects are for global policy synergy around the concepts of the SPF given this new board jointly chaired by the World Bank and ILO. The chapter suggests that the ILO might be able to regain its lost role and contribute to a shift in global social policy in a progressive direction, but this depends on a number of factors.

The Historical Rivalry between the ILO and World Bank

As Orenstein and I have written (2014) (also see Deacon 2007), efforts to create a global pension policy began toward the end of the Second World War as Allied leaders considered ways to better regulate the world economic system. A top-level conference in 1943 put the ILO in charge of developing a postwar social policy. This new policy encouraged all countries to implement state-administered pensions and unemployment insurance, public health systems, and social assistance in the interest of social peace. The ILO's Declaration of Philadelphia became the blueprint for this new global social policy order. The ILO vigorously pursued this agenda worldwide by advising countries on social policy development, organizing high-profile regional conferences, and spreading this new vision of social policy, including state-managed, pay-as-you-go pension insurance. Prior to the Second World War, countries in Europe, North America, and Latin America had already established national pension systems. They were revised according to the new ILO model. After the war, state-managed, pay-as-you-go pension systems quickly became standard practice worldwide. This practice was not to last.

Collapse of the communist project in the former Soviet Union saw the dramatic emergence of a transnational campaign for pension reform led by the World Bank. This campaign, launched in 1994 with the publication of *Averting the Old Age Crisis* (World Bank 1994), advocated pension reform worldwide to cope with an emerging demographic "crisis" of aging people in developed countries and soon in many developing countries. It argued that, whereas most pay-as-you-go or social security–type pension systems had been established under more favourable demographic conditions, economic development, improved medical care, and falling birth rates had reduced the proportion of workers contributing to pension beneficiaries in many countries, particularly in Europe. As people lived longer and had fewer children, pay-as-you-go pension systems suffered from growing fiscal pressure. To support a growing proportion of older persons living longer and longer in retirement, the World Bank report argued, payroll tax rates had to rise, pension ages had to increase, or benefit levels had to fall. The fourth and most controversial possibility introduced in the report was to fully or partially replace pay-as-you-go pension systems with ones based on private, individual, pension savings accounts. Prefunding seeks to ameliorate the budget crisis of pay-as-you-go systems by providing benefits from an individual's own mandatory savings. The World Bank report argued that private savings accounts are a superior method of providing income-related benefits, since private sector managers can achieve higher rates of return on investments than state social security administrations. In addition, the report argued, private pension funds provide an important source of capital for investment in emerging market economies. Creating such funds can spur economic growth and increase standards of living across the board. The influence of the World Bank was instrumental in driving this pension policy reform in many countries in several continents between the 1990s and 2000s, criticisms of the World Bank policy articulated by the ILO and others notwithstanding. The question now is whether the global economic crisis of 2008 both dented the World Bank's enthusiasm for its privatization policy and provided a renewed opportunity for the ILO to regain its role as *the* global Ministry of Social Security articulating a more progressive pension and social protection policy.

The Global Economic Crisis and Social Protection Policy

The World Bank

The World Bank's zeal for privatizing pensions actually lessened even before the onset of the global economic crisis. It has been argued (Orenstein and Deacon 2014) that 2005 was a critical year for pension privatization discourse globally for at least three reasons. First, 2005 was the year in which President George W. Bush's efforts to privatize the US social security system failed. Second, 2005 was the year in which the Chilean system (the first case of privatized pensions) was reformed anew under progressive Chilean president Michelle Bachelet. Third, 2005 was the year in which several new World Bank publications caused the organization to back away from its strong support for pension privatization. Doubts had set in about the efficacy of the private savings system in poorly regulated countries.

However, the global economic crisis played its part too. Orenstein and I (2014) note that, during the global financial crisis, countries began to reconsider pension privatization from two perspectives: first, they questioned whether they could sustain the borrowing needed to finance the transition to the new system; second, they considered confiscating balances in individual accounts in order to pay down government debt. In addition, evidence was emerging of the failure of the new private contribution schemes to provide adequate pensions for many. Perhaps most satisfying from the standpoint of those who had long argued against privatization was the climb down, or mea culpa, expressed by Robert Holzmann, one of its main advocates. In the wake of the global financial crisis impacts on the sustainability and utility of private defined contribution pension schemes, his work focused on social pensions. *Closing the Coverage Gap: The Role of Social Pensions and Other Retirement Income Transfers* captures well the reasons why a reliance on schemes of either the defined benefit or the defined contribution kind has limitations:

> Many of the problems behind low coverage rates in low- and middle-income countries are structural, cannot be resolved overnight, and fall outside the scope of social protection policy. A sustained expansion of the contributory system in the average low- or middle-income country would require fundamental changes in the productive structure of the economy and the functioning

of its product and labor markets ... Against this background, social pensions and other retirement transfers emerge as an important instrument
for bridging the coverage gap – at least for the time being – by focusing on
individuals with no or limited saving capacity, who are more likely to be
outside the contributory system. (Holzmann, Robalino, and Takayama
2009, 18)

Noteworthy in this context is the World Bank's concern that defined contribution pension schemes might not provide decent pensions for those forced
to retire during the crisis. That this in turn might encourage countries to reverse
recent reforms, setting up private schemes and returning to state pay-as-you-go
schemes, prompted the World Bank to caution against radical reversal and to
offer public subsidies for a short while to those affected.[2]

It was with the hindsight of this economic crisis, the unsatisfactory experiences of the new pension schemes in some countries, and the knowledge that
some privatizing reforms had been reversed that the new *Social Protection and
Labor Strategy (SPL)* of the World Bank, under the direction of Arup Banerji
(Holzmann having left), was drafted in 2012. Banerji ran his own consultations
on drafting a new *SPL* for 2012–22. The proposed strategy (World Bank 2011)
then argued for an approach to social protection made up of prevention (insurance), protection (assistance), and promotion (human capital formation
through conditional cash transfers, employment creation, and public works).
It had little to say about pensions in its first version. Commenting on the first
draft, the social security policy team within the ILO (2011c, 2) concluded that,

after decades of ... controversial discourse and debate on pensions and
safety net policies, this Note embodies a welcome departure from the ways
of the past. It embodies a major turning point and a bold change of direction
in the World Bank's social protection strategy, even if it does not explicitly
advertise it ... Regrettably the concept note does not explicitly acknowledge
its conceptual proximity to the positions of UN agencies ... However, the
new policy may give rise to the optimistic expectation that the Bank would
now be in a position to become a much more active partner.

The final draft of the new World Bank *SPL* was circulated for final feedback
on 16 March 2012 (World Bank 2012a) and officially launched at the time of
the World Bank and IMF meetings in April 2012 (World Bank 2012b). Its main
messages and slogans had shifted from the earlier formulation of the three
Ps to the less alliterative formulation of R (resilience), E (equity), and O

(opportunity). Resilience was still associated with insurance, equity with assistance, and opportunity with work and human capital development. It advanced a life cycle approach with interventions in the field of opportunity focused on childhood, youth, and working life; those in the field of resilience focused on working life, old age, and disability; and those in the field of equity, such as social pensions, focused on all stages of the life cycle.

In the field of pension policy, in which the World Bank was strongly criticized by the ILO and others for advocating for privately managed defined contribution schemes, the new *SPL* policy retreats to a much more cautious, pragmatic approach within which the case for tax-based social pensions is given more prominence. Thus, we read that "the World Bank's advice will be pragmatic and context-specific, focused on balancing coverage and adequacy of pensions with financial viability, closely guided by the country's demographic/aging profile, its social contract, its fiscal capabilities and regulatory/administrative capacity. The right 'portfolio' of pensions programs will depend very much on these country-specific conditions" (World Bank 2012a, 32). The "background paper" on pensions by Dorfman and Palacios (2012) stressed coverage, adequacy, and sustainability. Echoing the pragmatic approach of the broader social protection strategy, it now acknowledges that the question of coverage cannot wait for new contributory pension schemes to mature. Dorfman and Palacios (2012, 20) conclude that,

> even if labor force coverage rates were to increase dramatically in the short run, this would not address the needs of those that do not have sufficient time to accumulate enough to generate adequate pensions ... Social assistance, through general safety net programs or categorical targeting is an increasingly popular response to the coverage gap. For older workers that do not have enough time to accumulate pensions in contributory programs, this is the only option available.

Thus, it was in the context of the global economic crisis that the World Bank moved away from a dogmatic pension policy and toward a recognition of the urgency and importance of social pensions for those excluded from either pay-as-you-go pensions or private defined contribution systems.

The ILO

Parallels with the shifts in ILO policy are noteworthy. Just as the World Bank's new pragmatism reflected the retreat of some countries from earlier privatizing reforms and the introduction in Chile, for example, of social pensions, so too the ILO's new Social Protection Policy and Strategy came to be built upon the new approaches to social protection developed in practice.

Barrientos and Hulme (2008, 3) note that "the concept and practice of social protection in developing countries have advanced at an astonishing pace over the last decade or so ... Social protection practice has also changed from a focus on short term social safety nets and social funds to a much broader armoury of policies and programmes." This "quiet revolution," as they term it, was the bottom-up rediscovery in the global South of the importance of cash transfers, often distributed universally to categories of recipients. This process took place over several continents, but of prime importance was the move within Latin America to establish conditional cash transfers (CCTs), encouraging school and clinic attendance, and the move in Africa to establish social pensions, sometimes universally, which would also serve as means of child support since many grandchildren were cared for by grandparents because of the deaths from HIV and AIDS of parents. The point in the context of this chapter is that, historically, social protection in Latin America focused on workers in formal employment. The majority of the region's population was excluded from public social protection. But, by the mid-1990s, the new democratic governments had to engage with the strong popular demand for more universal forms of social protection.

How did the ILO respond to this move given its historical defence and promulgation of only contributory pensions available to a very small percentage of the population in many countries? In my book on the emergence of the ILO's social protection floor policy (Deacon 2013), I explore in detail the varied responses discussed and pursued by various sections of what, between 2000 and 2005, was a fragmented Social Security Department. It was only after Michael Cichon became director of the reformed department that the policy drive toward social protection for all residents (not even just citizens, let alone just workers) was quickly advanced. It was his drive that encouraged rethinking inside the ILO (just as there had been pre-crisis changes in thinking inside the World Bank) combined with the impact of the 2008 crisis (discussed below) that would cement the new policy emphasizing universal tax-based social transfers not only for pensioners but also for children and other categories.

Cichon decided to use the mainstream practice of the ILO, that of promulgating standards, conventions, and recommendations, and apply it not only to the 20 percent of the world's workers who were formal employees but also to 100 percent of the world's residents. In other words, he was to break from the Bismarckian background of the ILO and argue for a new ILO convention or recommendation for people. Cichon was to base his case that the ILO should develop an instrument concerned with the social protection of all residents on the pre-existing, but oft-forgotten, ILO Recommendations 67 and 69 of 1944, the Income Security Recommendation and the Medical Care Recommendation, respectively, which addressed the needs of all people, not just workers. He would come to argue that such an SPF was consistent with human rights and was needed, affordable, and doable. His task was made much easier because by 2005 the concept of the "global social floor" upon which the concept of the "social protection floor" was to be built had already become mainstream within the ILO following Somavia's important report (ILO 2004) produced by the World Commission on the Social Dimension of Globalization.

The global economic crisis of 2008, combined with the fortuitous circumstance of the ILO happening to hold the rotating chair of the High Level Panel on Programmes of the UN Chief Executives Board, gave a further boost to the SPF policy. A meeting of the UN Chief Executives Board (UNCEB) for Coordination was held in Paris later in April 2009 and generated the CEB issue paper "The Global Financial Crisis and Its Impact on the Work of the UN System." The report called for work toward a global SPF that would ensure "access to basic social services, shelter, and empowerment and protection of the poor and vulnerable" (UNCEB 2009, 31). The ILO and WHO would lead on this UN Social Protection Floor Initiative (UNSPF-I) policy, supported by a host of other agencies, including UNICEF and UNDESA. The global social floor had become UN policy, at least in terms of the UNCEB, even before it became formal ILO policy. That was to happen in 2012 when, after two International Labour Conferences devoted to the topic, the ILO's recommendation on SPFs was agreed on without a vote against.

Formally speaking, there are twin aspects of the new ILO social security policy. The official strategy is set out in *Social Security for All: Building Social Protection Floors and Comprehensive Social Security Systems* (ILO 2012a), which reaffirms "the ILO's two-dimensional strategy ... Its horizontal dimension aims at establishing and maintaining social protection floors as a fundamental element of national social security systems. The vertical dimension aims at pursuing strategies for the extension of social security that progressively ensure higher levels of social security to as many people as possible, guided by ILO social security standards."

The Global Social Protection Agenda and World Bank Cooperation

Rethinking ideas within both the World Bank and the ILO combined with the impact of the global economic crisis, which propelled concerns about tax-based social pensions to the fore, has led to much greater policy synergy between the two IOs. The ILO was instrumental in bringing this apparent synergy about. Once the UN Chief Executives Board had established the UN Social Protection Floor Initiative, the ILO effectively ran it. In 2009, 2010, and 2011, meetings were convened in the ILO Turin Training Centre of many UN agencies, including the World Bank, and many INGOs to advance a common view of the social protection floor. This created a framework of consensus that Arup Banerji had to take account of when he took on the task of formulating the World Bank's new *Social Protection and Labor Strategy*. His first draft mentioned the ILO/UN SPF policy in a footnote though fell short of formally endorsing it. Pressure on the World Bank was to grow, however.

During this period, from late 2011 to early 2012, the issue of closer cooperation between the ILO and World Bank on social protection policy was pursued actively at different levels and in different modes by the ILO. On the one hand, Cichon and his close colleagues held regular meetings with Banerji in Washington; on the other, the ILO Director General DG level ensured that the final version of the Bachelet Report launched in New York on 27 October 2011 contained this exhortation: "We recommend that the social protection floor approach be fully integrated into the World Bank Social Protection Strategy 2012–2020 as well as in the social protection technical assistance programmes implemented by the regional development banks" (ILO 2011a, 95). This exhortation did seem to have an impact. A new section of the final version of the World Bank's *SPL, A Global Challenge: An Emerging Consensus,* noted that there was growing international concern to centre-stage the social protection floor. The section noted that

> this emerging global consensus is manifested in numerous country actions and global initiatives, including the prominent One-UN Social Protection Floor initiative (SPF-I), adopted by the United Nations Chief Executives Board in April 2009 (box 3.1). The SPL strategy and engagement is consistent with these core principles of the SPF-I, particularly through the strategy's emphasis on building inclusive, productive, responsive SPL programs and systems tailored to country circumstances. The World Bank has been a strategic partner in the One-UN Social Protection Floor initiative (SPF-I), and has an important role to play both in helping countries who sign on to the SPF-I to operationalize it and in knowledge sharing. (World Bank 2012b, 11)

It was one thing for the ILO to influence World Bank policy in this way, but it would take more to ensure that the World Bank actually sat down at the same table as the ILO in working out how both organizations might deliver SPFs in countries. It was determined work by the ILO at the G20 that brought about the creation of the Social Protection Inter-Agency Cooperation Board (SPIAC-B) that would be jointly chaired by the ILO and World Bank. The earlier invitation to the ILO to sit at the G20 table was crucial in providing this role for it. The ILO became involved in the G20 at the Pittsburgh summit under UK official convenorship but hosted by Obama for the United States. President Lula of Brazil requested the ILO's formal membership at the table, and Obama agreed (Kirton 2011). Subsequently, the 2010 G20 summit in Seoul under the Korean leadership took the issue of longer-term development rather than short-term crisis seriously and concluded with creation of the Seoul Development Consensus. This consensus was accompanied by a nine-point detailed action plan; the development "pillars" included work on job creation, domestic resource mobilization, infrastructure investment, and so on. The sixth pillar was to become an important vehicle for influencing social protection policy. Joint responsibility was given to the UNDP and ILO under action 1 of the sixth pillar, entitled Resilient Growth (overseen by Australia, Indonesia, and Italy), for the production by June 2011 of a report[3] "identifying lessons learned from use of social protection mechanisms in developing countries (and) prepare best practice guidelines" (ILO 2011d).

The scene was therefore set for the ILO to play a significant part in the 2011 French G20. A combination of the experience already gained of the G20 process, the resolve of the French president to table the issue of social protection, the opportunity provided by the upcoming Bachelet Report on the subject, and partly fortuitous and partly well-planned connections between the ILO and French government would secure a significant advance. The French government's public statement on G20 priorities introduced by Sarkozy at a press conference in February 2011 mentioned that

> France would like to promote a "Social Protection Floor" at an international
> level, whose goal would be to a) ensure universal access to essential social
> services such as education and training, as well as health care and employ-
> ment, b) provide citizens with essential social transfers to give them income
> and livelihood security for accessing essential services. The Floor would
> include social benefits for children, working age individuals who do not
> have a minimum income, seniors and those with disabilities.[4]

Clearly, already at this stage, somebody within the Social Security Department of the ILO had the ear of the French government. The words used were too similar to be coincidental. In fact, there were parallel connections. Christien Jacquier, a French national within Cichon's department, worked closely with the representative of the French Ministry of Labour in the French consulate in Geneva. Jacquier was about to retire but was asked to stay on till at least the end of the G20 Labour Ministers Conference held in September 2011. At the same time, Martin Hirsch, already an active member of the Social Protection Advisory Committee (which generated the Bachelet Report), had the ear of the French president. Hirsch himself was to publish in France a book on the social protection floor (2011). Vinicius Pinheiro, a member of the ILO's DG cabinet with Jacquier, was ILO Sherpa at the G20 Labour Ministers Conference, and it all worked like clockwork. An advance copy of the Bachelet Report (ILO 2011b) was rushed out in limited numbers for delegates with an additional section, not included in precisely that form in the final published version, listing a number of recommendations addressed to the G20. Among them were recommendations not only to establish social protection floors but also to design innovative international funding to support low-income countries and a coordination mechanism to include the ILO, UNDP, UNICEF, WHO, UNESCO, World Bank, regional banks, and IMF, building on the SPF initiative to enhance global policy coherence.

The conclusions of the G20 Labour and Employment Ministers Conference therefore predictably recommended (G20 2011a, paragraph 15) that the G20 help to "develop nationally defined social protection floors with a view to achieving strong, sustainable and balanced economic growth and social cohesion." It went on to say that the floors should include "access to health care, income security for the elderly and persons with disabilities, child benefits and income security for the unemployed and working poor," and it echoed the points about innovative funding, global policy coherence, and so on.

It was one thing to get the ILO's views through the Labour Ministers Conference. Would it be so easy to keep them in the final summit communiqué after Cannes in November? However, once again, in part because of the work of the ILO Sherpa, many of the labour ministers' conclusions were endorsed by the heads of state. Paragraph 6 restated upfront that "we recognize the importance of social protection floors in each of our countries, adapted to national situations" (G20 2011b). Of equal importance was paragraph 31, calling on "international organizations, especially the UN, WTO, the ILO, the WB, the IMF and the OECD, to enhance their dialogue and cooperation, including on the social impact of economic policies, and to intensify their cooperation."

To cut a long story short (Deacon 2013), it was eventually resolved between the ILO and World Bank that a new Social Protection Coordinating Board (G20 2012, paragraph 12) should be established and

> chaired by the *ILO and the World Bank* and include representatives of IMF, UN-DESA, UNDP, UNICEF, WHO, Regional Development Banks, Regional Economic Commissions, other relevant international organizations and, *as appropriate,* bilateral institutions from G20 and non G20 countries working internationally at country level on social protection advocacy, financing and/or technical advice. Social partners and other organizations, including large NGOs with a major work program in social protection, *could* have observer status.

So it was that SPIAC-B was born.[5] However, it would initially further complicate rather than simplify the global governance of social protection. The complication was that the terms of reference of SPIAC-B focused not just on the SPF (the job of the already existing UNSPF-I mechanisms) but also on social protection more generally. Nevertheless, the point is that the ILO, in effect, succeeded via the G20 in forcing the World Bank to work with it on global and national social protection policy. It first met in July 2012 (ILO 2012b). Unfortunately, between December 2012 and September 2013, the ILO was without a head of social security (Cichon retired), and no meeting of the UNSPF initiative was convened either. In this interregnum, it seemed that Arup Banerji was trying to weaken the influence on the World Bank of SPIAC-B.

The World Bank took the opportunity of this interregnum to advance a proposal for a totally new process called the Social Protection Assessment of Results and Country Systems (SPARCS) convening two meetings of all the same agencies who had been involved with the SPIAC-B, ignoring the ILO SPF assessment tools for helping countries work out the cost of the gaps in their SPFs and seemingly not using SPF as a benchmark. This situation confronted Isabel Ortiz, the new director of the newly named Social Protection Department of the ILO in October 2013. At the meeting of SPIAC-B in that October Ortiz "demanded" a change of name and governance of SPARCS. It was agreed that SPARCS was renamed SPIA,[6] or Social Protection Interagency Assessment, and SPIA will be governed as a SPIAC-B task group. At the same time the ILO will lead another SPIAC-B task group focused on national dialogue, social protection role in national development strategies, and fiscal space. It was also resolved that because SPIAC-B is not a SPF instrument the UNSPF-I group that had driven the UN SPF agenda after the global economic crisis might need to be re-launched. The joint steerage by the ILO and the Bank of the agency charged by the G20 for the better governance of social protection is now a fact.

Implications and Conclusions

What can we conclude about (a) whether the ILO is once again an important, perhaps the most important, international social protection agency, (b) whether it has managed to place at centre stage a new, more progressive, social protection policy, and (c) what this implies for the future of global social governance and global social protection policy? Insofar as it can be concluded that a change in the content and governance of global social protection policy has come about, why is this, and what part did the global economic crisis play?

The period near the end of the previous century, when the World Bank dominated the global pension debate and engineered a huge shift away from state pay-as-you-go pensions and toward partial or full private pensions with defined contributions and no guarantees on benefit levels, has come to an end. On that policy, it is in full retreat. In its place has emerged, driven by the ILO, a new focus, relevant for much of the developing world, on universal social pensions and universal social protection floors paid for out of progressive taxation with international support for those countries unable to cover the full initial costs. The World Bank has found itself signed up to that agenda and is being urged to refrain from the language of targeted safety nets. Its compliance goes only so far. When acting alone, outside the constraints of the new Social Protection Inter-Agency Cooperation Board, it reverts to type. The ILO, in the past few years, has driven this global agenda toward social protection floors despite the continued imbalance of funds going to the two organizations from donor countries. To a large extent, the ILO is once again *the* global Ministry of Social Protection. There is debate about the adequacy of the social protection floors, about the danger that they might be regarded as minimal, and about how universal they should be. The point is that the terms of the global social protection debate have shifted to the terrain laid down not by the World Bank but by the ILO.

In my 2007 book, I argued that global social governance was constituted of a contest among agencies for the right to shape global social policy and for the content of that policy. This remains partly true, but we have witnessed a partial coming together of the social protection policies of both the World Bank and the ILO recently, as analyzed here. What I did not foresee or fully explore in the 2007 book was the role of the G20 as a new centre of global

Bob Deacon

economic and social policy making. Catapulted to the centre of events by the 2009 crisis, the G20 then went on in Seoul in 2010, Cannes in 2011, and Mexico in 2012 to rapidly develop a large portfolio of economic and social policies and commitments that demands a radical rethinking of how we characterize the global social governance system. The nine pillars of its development agenda agreed to in Seoul became the vehicle that the ILO used to push the G20 to call for greater international coordination. Has the United Nations come out weaker or stronger from the actions of the G20? Pascal Lamy noted already in 2009 that he saw

a new triangle of global governance emerging that we need to strengthen. On one side of the triangle lies the G20, providing political leadership and policy direction. On another side lie member-driven international organizations providing expertise and specialized inputs whether rules, policies or programmes. The third side of the triangle is the G-192, the United Nations, providing a forum for accountability.[7]

From the account given above, it seems that, though the aspiration to G20 accountability through the United Nations has yet to be realized, the UN social agencies have been strengthened by the decisions of the G20. I noted the workings of the G20 Development Working Group, which in its short life had required the ILO, UNDP, IMF, World Bank, and other social agencies to report on a whole raft of issues. Regarding the ILO in particular, it was called on to be involved in a report to finance ministers on job creation (with the IMF, OECD, and World Bank); a report to employment ministers on the Task Force on Youth Unemployment and several related issues connecting employment, social protection, and growth (with the OECD and IMF); a report for the Development Working Group on skills development (with the OECD, World Bank, and UNESCO); and a report for the Development Working Group on private investment and job creation (with the UNCTAD, UNDP, World Bank, and OECD). This is both remarkable and unprecedented. The ILO has been strengthened by this.

In terms of the debate set up in the opening chapter of this book, this chapter suggests at least the possibility that a "Polanyian moment," as described by Jenson, might be upon us in which coherent policy alternatives are being articulated for both the content of global social protection policy and its governance. The ILO is shaping this new post–neo-liberal agenda not only in the field of social protection focused on here but also in terms of the concomitant policy fields of fiscal policy, anti-austerity policy, job creation, and global social justice.

At the same time, the World Bank has lost its dominance in the global discourse on social policy. Attention now has to focus on whether the G20 chooses to make further use of the ILO, how the United Nations and ECOSOC relate to the G20, and whether the rest of the UN system can be prevailed on in the UN post-2015 development agenda to accept the firm advice of the ILO that the new agenda should have central to it targets for countries to lay down social protection floors and to include the associated policy imperatives of creating fiscal space to help contribute to the realization in practice of the right of all to social protection.

Why have these changes arisen? Was the global economic crisis a central factor in shifting debate and policy? In 2013, I argued, following the agency, structure, institutions, and discourse framework of Jessop and colleagues, that the changes in global economic and social structure brought about by and associated with the crisis of 2008 played their parts in this shift in global policy. This social structural consideration is only one of the factors driving change. The SPF policy of the ILO resulted from the intersection of the *biographies* and careers of individuals who drove the agenda through the ILO (Cichon and others) with the *idea* that the world needed a global social floor (which had been debated at least since 2000), an idea whose time had come with the new *circumstances* of the 2008 global economic crisis (and the social protection revolution in the global South), which provided the opportunity for the ILO to ensure that the idea could find a home inside the *institution* of the ILO and indeed the wider global governance framework. An echo can be found, I suggest, in terms of the World Bank. Key personnel changes among its social protection professionals (*biographies*) generated a shift in World Bank pension and social protection thinking (*ideas*) prior to the crisis, but the crisis (*circumstances*) pushed these changes further, and, once the ILO through the G20 (*institutions*) had forced the World Bank into a closer relationship with a new global governance mechanism, it found itself somewhat constrained.

Notes

1 This chapter is based on my recent book (2013) and my chapter with Orenstein (2014).
2 http://siteresources.worldbank.org/INTPENSIONS/Resources/395443-1121194657824/PRPNote-Financial_Crisis_12-10-2008.pdf.
3 Published subsequently as ILO-UNDP 2011.
4 http://www.g20.utoronto.ca/2011/sarkozy-g20finance-110218.html.
5 The revised name and acronym were agreed to at the first meeting of the SPIB, on 2 July 2012.
6 See GSP Digest, Social Protection section, *Global Social Policy*, 14 (1): 149.
7 http://www.wto.org/english/news_e/sppl_e/sppl132_e.htm.

References

Barrientos, A., and D. Hulme. 2008. "Protection for the Poor and Poorest in Developing Countries: Reflections on a Quiet Revolution." Working Paper 30, Brookings World Poverty Institute, Manchester.

Deacon, B. 2007. *Global Social Policy and Governance*. London: Sage.

–. 2013. *Global Social Policy in the Making: The Foundations of the Social Protection Floor.* Bristol: Policy Press. http://dx.doi.org/10.1332/policypress/9781447312338.001.0001.

Dorfman, M., and R. Palacios. 2012. "World Bank Support for Pensions and Social Security." Background paper for the World Bank 2012–22 *Social Protection and Labor Strategy*, World Bank, Washington, DC.

G20. 2011a. "G20 Meeting of Labour and Employment Ministers in Paris 26–27 September 2011, Communiqué."

–. 2011b. "G20 Heads of State Meeting in Cannes, 3–4 November 2011: Final Communiqué."

–. 2012. "G20 Development Working Group (DWG): Growth with Resilience Pillar." Inter-agency Coordination on Social Protection, note submitted to the second meeting of the G20 DWG, 19–20 March.

Hirsch, M. 2011. *Secu objectif monde le defi universel de la protection social.* Paris: Parti Stock. www.editions-stock.fr.

Holzmann, Robert, D.A. Robalino, and N.Takayama, eds. 2009. *Closing the Coverage Gap: The Role of Social Pensions and Other Retirement Income Transfers.* Washington, DC: World Bank. http://www-wds.worldbank.org/external/default/main?pagePK=641930 27&piPK=64187937&theSitePK=523679&menuPK=64187510&searchMenuPK= 57313&theSitePK=523679&entityID=000333038_2009073023543&searchMenuPK =57313&theSitePK=523679.

ILO. 2004. *A Fair Globalization: Creating Opportunities for All: Report of the World Commission on the Social Dimension of Globalization.* Geneva: ILO.

–. 2011a. *Social Protection Floor for a Fair and Inclusive Globalization: Report of the Advisory Group Chaired by Michelle Bachelet.* Geneva: ILO.

–. 2011b. *Bachelet Report G20 Version.* Geneva: ILO.

–. 2011c. *ILO Comments on the World Bank's Strategy Concept Note: "Building Resilience and Opportunity: The World Bank's Social Protection and Labor Strategy 2012–2020."* Geneva: ILO Social Security Department.

– 2011d. *'ILO and G20; Dawn at Cannes?'* Presentation by G20 ILO Sherpas to the ILO, 23 November.

–. 2012a. *The Strategy of the International Labour Organization: Social Security for All: Building Social Protection Floors and Comprehensive Social Security Systems.* Geneva: ILO.

–. 2012b. "1st Social Protection Inter-Agency Cooperation Board Meeting." ww.ilo.org/ newyork/issues-at-work/social-protection/social-protection-inter-agency-cooperation -board/first-meeting/WCMS_226913/lang--en/index.htm.

ILO-UNDP. 2011. "Inclusive and Resilient Development: The Role of Social Protection." A paper prepared by ILO and UNDP for the G20 Development Working Group, 2010–11.

Kirton, J. 2011. "Development Governance, 1999–2011: Increase, Institutionalization, Impact." Paper presented at The Global Development Agenda after the Great Recession of 2008–2009," Employment Policy Department, ILO, Geneva.

Orenstein, M., and B. Deacon. 2014. "Global Pensions and Social Protection Policy." In *Understanding Global Social Policy,* 2nd ed., edited by N. Yeates, 187-208. Bristol: Policy Press.

UNCEB. 2009. "The Global Financial Crisis and Its Impact on the Work of the UN System." UNCEB Issue Paper.

World Bank. 1994. *Averting the Old Age Crisis*. Washington, DC: World Bank.

–. 2011. *Building Resilience and Opportunity: The World Bank's Social Protection and Labor Strategy 2012–2020*. 1st draft. Washington, DC: World Bank.

–. 2012a. *Resilience, Equity, and Opportunity: The World Bank's Social Protection and Labor Strategy 2012–2022*. 3rd draft. Washington, DC: World Bank.

–. 2012b. *Resilience, Equity, and Opportunity: The World Bank's Social Protection and Labor Strategy*. Washington, DC: World Bank.

6

The ILO, Greece, and Social Dialogue in the Aftermath of the GFC

NIGEL HAWORTH AND STEVE HUGHES

This chapter considers the development and implementation of the ILO's response to the global financial crisis (GFC), focusing on its attempt to sustain a social dialogue approach to the Greek crisis. We argue that the ILO's intervention in Greece reflects an often understated importance of the ILO in promoting policies that emphasize employment and wage-led growth, social dialogue, and social justice. The post-GFC role of the ILO reflects a combination of historical presence, vision, leadership, and capacity in the organization (see Deacon 2013). That role explicitly proposes policy settings – at national, supranational, and global levels – at odds with the dominant post-1970s neo-liberal agenda.

We also argue that, despite the coherence and grounding of the ILO's alternative policy settings, a combination of factors challenges short-term adoption of ILO settings. First, the orthodox economic and institutional underpinnings of neo-liberalism remain strong and are not easily displaced in the short term at either the national level or the international level. Second, the need for short-term policy interventions militates against the longer-term horizons associated with social dialogue-based solutions. Third, the preparedness of national agendas to commit to the ILO agenda is neither uniform nor necessarily sophisticated. Equally, we argue that, in the longer term, the ILO's agenda might enjoy a resurgence.

Background

Understanding the role of the ILO in the aftermath of the GFC will benefit from some historical background. That background – a long history of institutional adaptation and adjustment to changing world conditions, while consistently maintaining a proud commitment to tripartitism and social dialogue – emphasizes the double-edged impact post-2008 of the GFC on the ILO. The moment was both a threat to and an opportunity for the ILO. In the aftermath of the GFC, the centrality of a jobs-led growth model was not certain, particularly after three decades of neo-liberal policy hegemony. For all that, the policy vacuum left by the intensity and reach of the crisis provided an opportunity for the ILO to present at the highest level its alternative policy proposals to respond to the GFC.

The ILO in many ways was an unlikely survivor of the failed League of Nations. It survived that unhappy experiment in global governance because of the interplay of three conscious strategies – autonomy, presence, and relevance (Haworth and Hughes 2012, 206) – and, no doubt, an element of serendipity. *Autonomy* refers to the political coup that allowed membership of the ILO without being a member of the league (thus providing distance between the two organizations and an institutional "space" for the ILO beyond the league). *Presence* refers to a deliberate strategy to ground the ILO in national circumstances by, for example, mobilizing public opinion in nations around the ILO agenda. *Relevance* refers to the ILO's adoption and active promotion of a "Keynesian" model for recovery during the interwar depression. In many ways, that interplay defines the ILO's engagement with individual countries still. We focus here on relevance and presence.

Relevance
Traditionally, relevance had numerous dimensions. For example, it involved the configuration of the ILO's institutions in a way that delivered useful analysis and information. It required the ILO to develop a strong technical and policy-oriented skill base. The ILO's tripartite model lent itself to discussion of ways to overcome growing class conflict over the impact of the interwar crisis. Then the ILO positioned itself as a unique organization in which the strains and stresses created by the crisis could be addressed in terms of well-grounded information and constructive outcomes and in terms of what we now understand as "social dialogue." Key to this was the success of maintaining worker participation in the ILO. The search for contemporary relevance drove its response to the 2008 crisis. Prior to that crisis, and in an extended period since the late 1970s, the ILO had been coming to terms with a range of pressing challenges – globalization, the rise of neo-liberalism, the fall of the communist order, and internal organizational difficulties, to name but the most important – that in turn gave rise to the current (and somewhat controversial) Decent

Work agenda and its four pillars: labour standards, employment creation, social protection, and social dialogue (ILO 2001; Hughes and Haworth 2011).

The GFC was yet another challenge but also provided an important opportunity for the ILO to contribute positively to global responses to the crisis. Juan Somavia – then the director general – worked hard to engage with, first, the Bretton Woods organizations and, second, the G20. This engagement, on the whole, has been successful. The ILO produced a technical overview of the employment impacts of the 2008 crisis following calls made by the G20 leaders at their April 2009 London Summit on Growth, Stability, and Jobs. The ILO was invited to bring a report to the Pittsburgh G20 meeting later that year, arguably establishing the ILO at the "top table" of global institutions in a manner similar to establishment of the organization as a relevant and technically competent body during the interwar depression. The ILO has also been active in the European Union and elsewhere as it presses its employment-led approach to a rebuilt global economy.

There is little doubt that the GFC posed both a challenge to and an opportunity for the ILO. It was forced to act because the feared post-crisis resurgence of neo-liberal crisis responses would have further threatened the ILO tradition of social dialogue, generally under attack since the 1970s. The absence (at least in the short term) of responses such as a strong policy voice then created a policy vacuum into which the ILO's jobs-led model of growth could be inserted. Director General Somavia seized that opportunity with the G20 and European Union. The ILO displayed deft political skills in seizing that opportunity, skills that derived from a long history of adaptation to changing political realities.

Underpinning the post-GFC engagement with the G20 was the ILO's development of a Global Jobs Pact in 2009 (ILO 2009). It emphasized the impacts of the crisis on labour markets, highlighting the long-term damage done by unemployment, developing Decent Work–based responses to those impacts, and, simultaneously, providing a technical rationale for engagement with the G20. The principal objective of the Global Jobs Pact was to reduce the time lag between economic recovery and recovery in the employment market. According to ILO estimates, even if a global recovery were to take hold, the global economy would need to create 440 million new jobs over the period to 2020 just to keep pace with 45 million new entrants into the global jobs market annually (ILO-IMF 2010, 59). Also linked to the employment focus of the Global Jobs Pact was the perennial ILO focus on full employment, a concern about "jobless growth," and, in the context of emerging challenges to neo-liberal orthodoxy, a debate on wage-led growth. With comparisons between the Great Depression of the 1930s and the 2007–9 crises recurring among G20 leaders, the social and political consequences of high levels of unemployment were underlined in ILO reports and helped to shift the G20 toward a more coordinated response to the crisis. Now as then, high unemployment and growing income inequality are key determinants of the deterioration of social stability (IILS 2010). Somavia saw in the crisis a major opportunity for the ILO to contribute to recovery and consolidate the relevance and status of the organization and its work.

Presence

Traditionally, the search for presence caused the ILO to extend its growing relevance beyond the narrow, controlling interests of European nations. Over the years, directors general realized that an ILO bound by European interests could not survive and, by means of delegations and frequent international contacts, sought to engage many more countries in the ILO. In this strategy, the organization cultivated the key mass medium then available – the newspaper – taking particular care that leading newspapers around the world were well informed of the ILO's work. In time, this strategy bore much fruit, including US membership but also a strong ILO presence in Latin America and elsewhere. This success was achieved despite the need to overcome problems such as a lack of knowledge about the ILO and concerns over the cost of membership.

Presence remains a key strategic goal of the ILO in the modern era. It has a network of regional offices across the globe and, in a variety of ways, engages with the tripartite actors at national levels across its membership. A contemporary example of this is the Decent Work Country Programmes established as the main vehicle for delivery of ILO support to countries (ILO 2011f). The programs are intended to support development goals in member countries but serve a parallel purpose in establishing the ILO as an actor in domestic labour market and social policy debates. The interplay of presence and relevance – in this case in terms of the skills and knowledge that the ILO brings to domestic tripartite discussions – is a hallmark of ILO practice.

Presence also occurs in reverse. In particular, tripartite partners in the national sphere have recourse to the ILO by means of a complaints mechanism. Articles 22–34 of the ILO Constitution establish a process by which a country can be investigated and sanctioned for non-compliance with any ILO convention that the country has ratified. Hence, any of the tripartite parties can file a complaint with the ILO, which, in turn, can lead to a commission of inquiry and even a referral to the International Court of Justice. When a country fails to comply with ILO-sanctioned recommendations from a commission of inquiry, or recommendations from the court, the ILO's governing body "may

Nigel Haworth and Steve Hughes

recommend to the Conference such action as it may deem wise and expedient to secure compliance therewith (ILO 1919, Article 33)." The ILO relies primarily on moral suasion and the power of its social dialogue tradition to bring recalcitrant countries into compliance with its conventions.

Relevance and Presence in Contemporary Greece?

The 2009 (Panhellenic Socialist Movement) government inherited from its predecessor what might be described as the perfect political and economic storm – a country already wracked by civil unrest over long-term attempts to impose structural adjustment and a country that had increased its deficit spending and now had to respond to the immediate impacts of the global crisis, which focused in policy terms primarily on debt. The new government was met by credit downgrades as a result of international fears about the size and repayment of Greek debt. It faced internal pressure to enact draconian adjustment policies and increasing opposition, within PASOK and on the streets, to such measures. Upon election, a first round of spending cuts was proposed, followed by a second round in January 2010. People took to the streets again throughout February and on into March.

By early 2010, the eurozone had become seriously concerned about the prospect of a Greek default. When, in March 2010, a third round of spending cuts was introduced, and once again mass demonstrations followed, European leaders expressed serious concern about the "contagious" effect of the Greek crisis. Out of this concern emerged the Memorandum of Economic and Financial Policies (MEFP), managed by the "troika" of the European Union (EU), European Central Bank (ECB), and IMF. The MEFP required further structural adjustment measures, which led to sustained popular militancy throughout the rest of 2010. The troika's expectations also included labour market reform. The manner of achieving such goals was left up to the Greek government to determine.

By the beginning of 2011, the Greek crisis had deepened considerably. The troika argued that Greece was not acting rapidly enough on the adjustment front, a concern compounded by the impact of the Greek crisis in the eurozone. A second bailout was agreed to in July 2011, but credit-rating agencies responded with further downgrades of both the government and the banking sector as confidence in the political will to meet the troika's requirements decayed further. In November, faced with an ever-worsening political and economic crisis, the PASOK government gave way to a national unity government led, somewhat controversially, by an ex–vice-president of the ECB and the governor of the Bank of Greece, Lucas Papademos. This, then, was the volatile and complex economic and political environment into which the ILO intervened in 2011.

Social Dialogue in Greece

As the GFC took hold, Greece was marked by a weak state, a fragmented civil society, a low trust relationship with the tripartite actors, and a weak tradition of social dialogue (Featherstone 2005). We suggest, first, that key actors in Greece tended to see reform in zero-sum terms, with the outcomes of reform sustaining a more uneven distribution of material benefits, perhaps to the advantage of the current "winners." Hence, the incentives for the "losers" to cooperate with the process were low. Second, the government pursued ambiguous and inconsistent strategies because it had divided and possibly irreconcilable goals: cost saving, maintaining internal political harmony, maintaining the ruling party in power, and meeting EU requirements (especially financial ones). Third, government actors in charge of reform initiatives made strategic miscalculations, undermining their cause (raising the issue of governance capacity). Fourth, the strategies of the main unions displayed unity, consistency, defensiveness, and clear self-interest, thus compounding the challenges identified above. Employers played a less active role in general.

Moreover, social dialogue is weak in Greece, and EU attempts to build dialogue have been relatively ineffectual. Formally, Greece has a clear social dialogue framework operating at three levels: participation in commissions, advisory groups, and similar activities; collective bargaining of the National General Collective Agreement; and operation of the Economic and Social Council (Government of Greece 2007). Much activity takes place at each level, yet outcomes are described officially as difficult, time consuming, variable in terms of quality, and prone to failure (Government of Greece 2007; Zambarloukou 2006). This view is supported by other analyses of social dialogue in Greece. For example, studies report, *inter alia*, the limited participation of social partners in EU mechanisms (Gold 2007); the importance of national collective bargaining procedures compared with concertation (Karamessini 2008; Kornelakis 2011; Zambarloukou 2006); the continuation of class politics in preference to social dialogue traditions (Karamessini 2008; Kritsantonis 1998); the historical development of unions as a barrier to understanding of, or willingness to participate in, dialogue (Zambarloukou 2006); the limited effect of the European Union's social dialogue approach in Greece (Sakellaropoulos 2007); the adverse impact of "disjointed corporatism" on Greek social dialogue (Lavdas 2005); and

Nigel Haworth and Steve Hughes

the impact of imperfectly represented legitimate interests in trade unions on union performance and openness (Matsaganis 2007).

A further difficulty has been identified in the scope and importance of small and medium-sized enterprises (SMEs) in the Greek economy (Interview, 20 September, ILO 2011e). More than 96.5 percent of Greek enterprises are micro-companies employing nine or fewer workers and provide 57.6 percent of total employment (European Commission 2011). Social dialogue, arguably, is best suited to economies in which there is a concentration of employment in large enterprises and in which union representation is strong and creates an important foundation for dialogue. In this view, a stronger, better-established tradition of dialogue would require new forms of collective organization and representation that encompass the SME sector.

The ILO, the 2008 Global Crisis, and Greece

The ILO's intervention in Greece in 2011 had its origins in 2010.[1] In July, the General Workers Confederation of Greece (GSEE), supported by the International Trade Union Confederation (ITUC) and the European Trade Union Committee (ETUC), lodged a formal complaint with the ILO's Committee of Experts. In its deliberations in late 2010, the committee recognized that this was a complaint of a different order from the norm. The wider political implications of the Greek crisis were well established by then. The complaint was not simply about the local implications of the MEFP for employment and social protection, or even the future of social dialogue, in Greece. It had the potential to be a test case for the ILO as it observed similar crisis responses emerging internationally. By 2010, debt management and structural adjustment were replacing the initial deficit-financing model for overcoming the crisis. The potential for the Greek situation to be reproduced elsewhere was apparent to members of the committee. The support given to the complaint by ITUC and ETUC reinforced its high profile.

The Committee of Experts responded carefully. It noted the GSEE's complaints, particularly as they reflected concerns about the impact of the MEFP. It noted the legislative measures introduced in Greece to give effect to the MEFP, along with other adjustment measures. It focused on the GSEE's particular concerns about the effect of the MEFP and associated measures on collective bargaining, especially in relation to sector arrangements and the National General Collective Agreement. It noted union concerns about the impact of structural adjustment measures on social dialogue, on minimum wages and conditions, on conditions for younger workers, and on wage reductions.

The Committee of Experts emphasized the need for "full and frank" consultations by the government with employers' and workers' organizations on collective-bargaining arrangements, stating that their restriction should be an exceptional measure, of short duration, and with associated measures to protect workers' living standards. Further information, especially from the government, was canvassed. The committee also noted the "portmanteau" nature of the complaint in that the revision of collective-bargaining arrangements had an impact on Greece's observance of a wide range of conventions. It then arrived at its key conclusion:

> In light of the complexity and pervasiveness of the measures adopted in the framework of the support mechanism, which touch upon a number of ILO Conventions ratified by Greece, the Committee invites the Government to avail itself of the technical assistance of the Office and to accept a high-level mission to facilitate a comprehensive understanding of the issues, before the examination by the Committee of the impact of the measures in question on the application of this Convention, as well as other Conventions ratified by Greece. (ILO 2011a, 83)

The recommendation of "a high-level mission" highlighted the committee's understanding of the importance and complexity of the Greek case. Such missions are not common, usually reserved for challenging or complex circumstances.

The Greek case was then debated at length at the International Labour Conference in June 2011. The Greek government representative accepted that the MEFP required a variety of significant and contentious changes – for example, public sector cuts, changes in wage setting, and reform of the social security system. She also noted that the National General Collective Agreement remained in force, that its terms could not be changed, and that the principle of free collective bargaining was untarnished. She highlighted the 2010 private sector agreement between the GSEE and employers as evidence of this. She defended many of the other emergency measures brought in as a result of the MEFP. For example, changes to the minimum conditions for young workers were presented as opening up job opportunities for them. Arbitrary public sector wage cuts were necessary for a reduction in government expenditure. She praised the social partners' "outstanding responsibility in supporting the national effort to overcome the economic crisis, which was accompanied by the increase of unemployment and strong signs of economic recession, threatening social coherence of the country" (ILO 2011b, 68), and she concluded on a message of *force majeure* – there was no alternative in a crisis of this magnitude.

The workers' representative highlighted the volume and nature of the arbitrary changes made as a result of the MEFP, arguing that the reforms, *inter alia*, were disproportionate in effect, introduced without consultation with the social partners, attacked workers' rights, and contradicted Greece's commitments to the ILO. The employers' representative took a constitutional approach, noting in particular three things. First, in the absence of a formal reply to the complaint from the Greek government, the discussion could not be well informed and balanced. Second, the discussion should focus narrowly on the technical aspects of the convention under discussion, thus not moving into the broader issues raised by the complaint. Third, were constitutional requirements such that the whole discussion was inadmissible?

The subsequent discussion supported the idea of a high-level ILO mission to Greece in which the technical expertise associated with the ILO was given particular status. Moreover, in a significant departure from ILO tradition and practice, the conference considered that contact with the IMF and European Union would also assist the mission in its understanding of the situation (ILO 2011b, 72). Reference to the IMF and European Union significantly raised the stakes associated with the Greek complaint. We have seen that the complaint had been understood by the Committee of Experts to be a test case for the ILO's response to post-2008 structural adjustment measures at the country level. How the ILO handled the Greek complaint would be watched carefully both inside the organization and beyond it. Involving the IMF and European Union in the mission's work raised the profile of the Greek complaint to a higher level still, for it placed at centre stage the relationship between other "top tier" international agencies and the ILO, a core issue for the ILO and its leadership.

Meetings on the Greek crisis between the ILO and, respectively, the European Union and IMF took place in late 2011. From an ILO perspective, both meetings were seen as positive. The European Union showed itself to be open to discussion on key issues such as fostering a social dialogue approach to the crisis and the mechanisms for extending social dialogue into the SME sector. The meeting with the IMF covered similar ground in a constructive manner, in line with the strengthened institutional linkages between the two agencies. The precariousness of the Greek situation was a pervasive feature of both meetings (Interviews, ILO, December 2011).

ILO officials had no doubt about the significance of the conference's conclusion on the Greek complaint. They understood that the desire by the workers' party to highlight the role of the IMF and European Union in the Greek case was linked to a "politics of exposure," for the workers' party saw in the MEFP a model that might be transferred elsewhere. At its 2010 Vancouver conference,

ITUC had made "the universal and full respect of workers'" fundamental rights a key goal of its activities for a new model of globalization, including in its work with the IFIs and WTO (ITUC 2010), and had invited the IMF's Dominique Strauss-Kahn to address the conference. Included in the Vancouver discussions was an explicit recognition that, on the one hand, under Stauss-Kahn, the IMF had become more "open" to labour issues and that, on the other, the European Union and ECB were more "closed" in that respect.

ILO officials understood the view that, in the Greek case, the two European elements of the troika were likely to place more emphasis on economic require-ments than on inclusionary or social dialogue opportunities, an understanding in tune with other analyses of contemporary EU priorities (e.g., Meardi 2011). Moreover, ILO officials were conscious of the view that the European Union was institutionally challenged by the impact of the debt crisis in general and by the Greek situation in particular and that, as a result, political leadership gave way to economic leadership, in which a hard-line structural adjustment position in the Directorate General of Economic and Financial Affairs dominated.

The ILO mission to Greece carried a dual burden. On the one hand, it represented the only international organization in which worker complaints about the impacts of structural adjustment would be addressed in a tripartite manner and in full recognition of the right to take issue with such impacts. Expectations would be vested in the mission, especially by workers. On the other hand, there is no established mechanism to address such complaints when they arise from the impacts of supranational arrangements. The ILO can operate at the member state level, and assess what happens at that level, but its mandate and operating principles are not geared to a situation in which the member state acts under duress from such arrangements. To date, there is no governance framework across international agencies that permits the assess-ment and negotiation of such supranational, transinstitutional arrangements.

The Broader Context of Social Dialogue

The challenges faced by the ILO in Greece were not isolated (see Ayhan and McBride, this volume).[2] The 2008 crisis precipitated a similar destabilization of social dialogue in other countries sorely afflicted by the crisis and required by international pressure to address debt problems (Natali and Pochet 2009). It is useful to look at other cases in order to establish a general argument about the difficulties faced by the ILO's social dialogue model as a result of the GFC. This examination will allow us to extend our conclusions beyond the case of Greece.

In Italy, social dialogue, broadly a positive feature in Italian employment relations in the 1990s, has more recently been defined by conflict (Regini and Colombo 2011; Rychley 2009). Prior to the crisis, employer and union parties were sufficiently strong and committed to dialogue to engage in bipartite discussions. The role of the government, in general, was weaker than that of the other two parties. In the 1990s, the EU commitment to dialogue, coupled with economic challenges, drove discussions. Dialogue took place at several levels – nationally, regionally, on a bipartite basis, and in the public sector, while collective bargaining was limited to sector and second-tier, company-level bargaining by the 1993 tripartite agreement. This agreement was an important example of "concertation" and for some a turning point in the reform of Italian employment relations. Its success gave rise to subsequent agreements on pension reform (1995), labour market reform (1996), and economic growth (1998).

In the 2000s, but prior to the crisis, dialogue was marked by controversy and greater difficulty in sustaining its progress. The Pact for Italy (2002) was a tripartite attempt to chart a course for income policy, employment measures, and improved production performance. However, the Italian General Confederation of Labour (CGIL), the left-oriented *central* union, did not sign the pact, substantially weakening its impact. In 2007, there was further controversy over proposed adjustments to pensions, welfare provision, and labour market measures. Thus, when the crisis hit Italy, dialogue was already subject to challenge. In November 2008, the centre-right government in power since May launched a first tranche of anti-crisis measures in the face of a prognosis of declining GDP and a rapid rise in company failure and unemployment. The focus was on economic recovery – sustaining wage levels and domestic demand, improved training, reduced tax burden for companies, and measures to encourage productivity improvement. Union responses were mixed, with the CGIL taking a particularly critical line, offering its own, far more radical, anti-crisis plan.

However, conflict became more marked over proposals to reform the provisions of the 1993 tripartite agreement. Reform had been a topic for discussion frequently after 1993, particularly around the Giugni Report in 1997 and 1998. Battle lines were drawn in key areas, especially wage outcomes and the benefits of sector versus company-level bargaining. Debate on the bargaining structure grew in 2008. Unions continued to support the two-tier model, with the CGIL strongly in favour of the priority of sector bargaining. The CGIL effectively withdrew from the discussion in late 2008, leaving other unions to continue a debate with employers, who were seeking major changes to bargaining arrangements. When, in January 2009, some union bodies and the main employer groups agreed to a reform of collective bargaining, the CGIL, believing that the agreement was designed to weaken unions and collective bargaining, refused to sign it, despite having come back to the table. Undoubtedly, a key impact of the 2009 agreement was a weakening of social dialogue in Italy, for it took collective bargaining out of macroeconomic policy, reduced the impact of collective bargaining, and relied instead on automatic wage increases contingent on the economy's performance.

Throughout 2009, bargaining became more difficult as an effect of the January agreement. However, core sectoral agreements were signed throughout the year with the participation of the CGIL and with the exception of the important metalworking sector agreement. As the year progressed, the impact of the crisis became more profound, leading the government to introduce a range of measures designed to provide support for those most affected. Little improvement followed in 2010. And so, in October 2010, the social partners established a working party to look at wide-ranging reforms, including productivity improvement, needed to extricate Italy from the crisis. All key partners were involved, including the CGIL. Reports suggest that the working party sought to be a way forward for the social partners after a period of growing conflict. It seemed that social dialogue was emerging as a mechanism for discussion of shared ways through the crisis.

However, in September 2011, two months before its fall from power, the government acted to destabilize greatly social dialogue. It introduced measures to allow company and local agreements to break from national and sectoral agreements in key areas such as working hours, contract forms, and workplace reform. The CGIL reacted with strike action and the threat of legal action, while responses to the measure more generally within the union movement suggested a fractioning of union perspectives. Meanwhile, employers were disappointed that the measure went no further.

In November 2011, Mario Monti was elevated to power and immediately began reforms, including an austerity package, social security reform, changes in pension provision, and superannuation arrangements and support for SMEs. Strike action ensued, and employer representatives praised the reform. In January 2012, following other austerity measures, the Monti government introduced a project to reform radically labour law, especially the Article 18 employment stability provision. Major industrial unrest followed, and subsequently to a chorus of complaints from employers and international commentators, Monti watered down his proposals, in part as a compromise to allow other measures to proceed. The "backdown," as supporters of radical labour

Nigel Haworth and Steve Hughes

market reform saw it, was an effect of power relations, not an outcome of "concertation."

Events in Spain have taken a similar path (Campos Lima and Martin Artiles 2011; Rohfler 2012). Prior to the crisis, social dialogue enjoyed some success in terms of outcome and process. The outcome was social dialogue declarations in 2004 and 2008 with high levels of buy-in from the organizations comprising the social partners. Dialogue addressed broad issues well beyond employment relations, including economic sustainability, competitiveness, company performance, and fairness in employment. A number of agreements addressed labour market (2006), social security (2006), and dependant care (2008) issues. Social dialogue also contributed to measures on training and development, equal opportunity, and work-life balance. Industrial conflict was declining, apart from the "blip" created by the 2002 general strike. Collective bargaining was bounded by the regularly renewed multisectoral collective bargaining agreement (AINC). Spain's economic performance up to 2007 was positive. A socialist government, considered to be pro-dialogue, was re-elected in 2008. In July 2008, the social partners, led by the government, confirmed their commitment to dialogue. In sum, prior to the crisis, social dialogue was an emerging force in Spain.

By early 2009, dialogue was in retreat, primarily because of tensions caused among the social partners by the impact of the crisis. Employers' calls for changes in collective agreements were met by union determination to protect wages and conditions. Despite the signing by the social partners of a Declaration of Principles for Stimulating the Economy, Employment, Competitiveness, and Social Progress, the 2009 renewal of the AINC was severely disrupted by employer demands for changes in agreements and union concerns that wages would be cut and domestic demand reduced. Moreover, the unions argued that the government should take a stronger position in the organization and delivery of social dialogue, a clear statement of concern that the crisis was marginalizing dialogue in government thinking. By mid-2009, social dialogue was in abeyance as the government and unions refused to meet the demands of employers for reduced social security contributions and greater employment flexibility thought likely to lead to greater employment insecurity.

Unfortunately, the impact of the crisis increased in Spain, and the country became the focus of international concern in terms of its debt levels. Thus, in mid-2010, the minority socialist government sought to introduce drastic cuts to reduce the public deficit, including reductions in social provisions and the first public sector pay cuts since the end of the Franco era. These measures were not sufficient to placate international fears, and the government, with EU support, introduced even larger cuts and arbitrary reforms of employment relations. The latter promoted more company-level bargaining, streamlined bargaining procedures, and improved flexibility. Political opposition was widespread in the parliamentary process, particularly to a proposed pension freeze, and both of the key union bodies vehemently objected, calling for industrial action in June.

By early 2011, circumstances had changed. The urgency of the crisis, and the recognition that action was needed, brought the social partners together again, initially on the issue of pension reform and then on broader industrial and labour market issues. The resulting agreements covered growth, active employment policies, and guaranteed pensions. Apart from pressure from the crisis and external forces, the government appears to have been the driver of this process since it required agreements that could be presented externally as confidence building. Rather like the origins of the Irish partnership model, the burgeoning crisis was concentrating efforts among the social partners to find effective solutions.

In November 2011, a conservative government came to power in a general election and, in February 2012, introduced legislation to promote a greater level of decentralization in bargaining and reduced employment protection (Fernandez Rodriguez and Martinez Lucio 2013). The model proposed owes much to 1980s and 1990s free-market employment relations traditions, highlighting inefficiencies caused by bargaining arrangements, promoting greater levels of employment flexibility, and seeking to free employers from costs and institutional arrangements that create inefficiencies. Unsurprisingly, the union movement opposed these measures, while employers welcomed them heartily. Social dialogue in Spain is once more in crisis.

These brief vignettes of social dialogue in Italy and Spain display much in common with the Greek example. While displaying superficial differences in terms of the timing and nature of social dialogue's dilemma, they suggest that, in economies in which a combination of strong external pressure for debt reduction and fragile or developing social dialogue exists, the weight (external and domestic) of political and institutional pressure for change is inexorable. If social dialogue helps that change to occur, as we have seen on occasion in both Italy and Spain, so be it. However, social dialogue can be jettisoned easily, by the government or employers in particular, if such an alignment is not possible. ILO or other interventions in either Italy or Spain would face many, if not all, of the challenges thrown up by the Greek case.

Nigel Haworth and Steve Hughes

Discussion

We noted in our introduction that, first, the orthodox economic and institutional underpinnings of neo-liberalism remain strong and are not easily displaced in the short term at either the national level or the international level. Second, the need for short-term policy interventions militates against the longer-term horizons associated with social dialogue–based solutions. Third, the preparedness of national agendas to commit to the ILO agenda is neither uniform nor necessarily sophisticated. The Greek case study, supported by the vignettes from Italy and Spain, bears out these points.

The report of the ILO's high-level mission to Greece, undertaken in September 2011, captured starkly the challenges facing the traditional ILO model of social dialogue, labour standards, and social justice (ILO 2011e). The mission concluded that it had "been left with the impression that unprecedented changes are being introduced in the Greek labour market institutions in a manner which seems to be disconnected from Greek realities, thereby weakening, among other things, the impact and real effects of the reforms." Moreover, "it is essential at this time of crisis to allow the Greek social partners and the Government the necessary space to find common solutions to problems that they all seem to acknowledge, in a manner which corresponds to the country's conditions and international obligations."

The sense that an inappropriate and ill-sequenced and -managed mix of policies was being introduced in Greece was pervasive in the report. The mission manifested "deep concern" about changes in the employment relations framework that threatened established relationships among the social partners (especially the move to enterprise agreements signalled in October 2011). The destabilizing "spillover" of such changes into broader political unrest was noted. The impact of changes in wage-setting and related institutions and protections on standards of living was given prominence, as were gender implications of emergency reforms (e.g., the impact of state sector redundancies on women's employment). A marker was set down in relation to the implications for poverty levels of changes in the social security system. The mission noted the paucity of references to employment measures in troika documentation and thinking and offered to Greece ILO political and technical assistance in reasserting a focus on employment creation.

The reader is struck by the asymmetry between the policies of the troika – in substance, configuration, and sequencing – and the model preferred by the

ILO, the model underpinning the logic of the report. Two worlds collide in Greece – the essentially neo-liberal, macrolevel reform model enjoined by the troika and the Keynesian social dialogue model of the ILO. In terms of economic power and effective status, the former was superior, requiring the ILO team to engage carefully in order to retain credibility.

The ILO must operate by suasion, influence, and presentation of data-backed arguments that provide to the social partners in a member state (and, in this case, the troika) a rationale for new strategies and changed behaviours. Such methods take time and a process of iteration, whereby the logic of the ILO's argument is established in social partners' thinking. At the time of writing (early 2014), despite ongoing efforts by the ILO, a social dialogue–based, long-term approach to the effects of the crisis remains elusive.

Is the evidence from Greece, and that from Spain and Italy, in line, then, with either of the two interpretations that inform this volume – a Polanyian double movement and a resilient neo-liberalism? The simple but correct answer is that it is too early to tell. Much depends on the perspective adopted. In the narrow context of our case study economies, and in the short term (i.e., the period since 2008), the difficulties faced by the ILO's model for growth might indicate a resilient neo-liberalism. Suggestions abound that world society has fallen back into pre-2008 patterns of behaviour, particularly in the finance sector. The implication is often drawn that it has failed to learn from the 2008 crisis, has not sought an alternative model such as that proposed by the ILO, and is heading toward another crisis. We favour, however, a longer-term and broader perspective. We look to various sources of ideas about long-term, sustained shifts in economic and social policy that, to some extent at least, contradict the narrow view. Examples include Blanchard's leadership on an alternative perspective on macroeconomic settings from the heart of the IMF, Ostry and colleagues' work on inequality, from the same source, emerging analysis of wage-led growth, and, perhaps most surprising, the World Economic Forum's recent and trenchant concern about the rise of inequality (see Blanchard et al. 2012; Lavoie and Stockhammer 2014; Ostry et al. 2014; WEF 2014). This broad tradition variously argues that the GFC is a game-changer in policy terms, and a key aspect of that change is social inclusion, in part from a strong emphasis on jobs, redistribution, and social dialogue. The current period, therefore, is marked by conflict between contending paradigms, the outcome of which is unclear. In our view, this conflict is likely to be long term, exacerbated by the equally important impact of global economic integration and consequent shifts in economic power, production systems, and labour utilization. Although one cannot foretell the outcome of the complex interplay between the GFC and

Nigel Haworth and Steve Hughes

its consequences, on the one hand, and globalization, on the other, we suggest that it is certainly too early to predict victory for a resilient neo-liberalism.

It would be a brave and ahistorical position to assume that the passage of time will not create circumstances in which social dialogue finds a central role. Deacon (2013) has highlighted the challenges facing the ILO on this front, much as we do. At the heart of the ILO perspective exists the profound belief that economic and political sustainability requires effective social dialogue. Dialogue creates and sustains consensual outcomes that are embedded institutionally and ideologically. That social dialogue, in a post-GFC context, must encompass not only the workforce and employment relations but also wider concerns about, for example, social security, democratic institutions, and social justice. Such issues might appear to be of secondary importance in the first flush of policy responses after a GFC or similar crisis but rapidly become key elements in the configuration of post-crisis reconstruction. As we have concluded, it is too early to determine the fate of the ILO's social dialogue model, but any attempt to write its obituary will be premature.

Notes

1 This section is drawn from previous unpublished papers on the Greek crisis, and a significant portion of this section derives from interviews conducted at the ILO in late 2011.
2 A significant element of the following Italian and Spanish vignettes is assembled from data abstracted from the European Industrial Relations Observatory Online.

References

Blanchard, O., D. Romer, M. Spence, and J. Stiglitz. 2012. *In the Wake of the Crisis: Leading Economists Reassess Economic Policy.* Cambridge, MA: MIT Press.

Campos Lima, M., and A. Martin Artiles. 2011. "Crisis and Trade Union Challenges in Portugal and Spain: Between General Strikes and Social Pacts." *European Journal of Industrial Relations* 17, 3: 387–402.

Deacon, B. 2013. *Making Global Social Policy: Towards the Social Protection Floor.* Bristol: Policy Press. http://dx.doi.org/10.1332/policypress/9781447312338.001.0001.

European Commission. 2011. *Small Business Act Fact Sheet 2010/2011.* Directorate General Enterprise and Industry. http://ec.europa.eu/enterprise/policies/sme/facts-figures-analysis/performance-review/files/countries-sheets/2010-2011/greece_en.pdf

Featherstone, K. 2005. "'Soft' Co-Ordination Meets 'Hard' Politics: The European Union and Pension Reform in Greece." *Journal of European Public Policy* 12, 4: 733–50. http://dx.doi.org/10.1080/13501760500160631.

Fernandez Rodriguez, C., and M. Martinez Lucio. 2013. "Narratives, Myths, and Prejudice in Understanding Employment Systems: The Case of Rigidities, Dismissals, and Flexibility in Spain." *Economic and Industrial Democracy* 34, 2: 313-36. http://eid.sagepub.com/content/34/2/313.abstract.

Gold, M. 2007. "The European Works Council Directive: Changing Rationales for EU Regulation of Employee Participation." In *European Works Councils and the Problem of European Identity,* edited by M. Whittall, H. Knudsen, and F. Huijen. London: Routledge.

Government of Greece. 2007. *About GREECE.* Athens: General Secretariat of Communication, General Secretariat of Information.

Haworth, N., and S. Hughes. 2012. "The International Labour Organisation." In *Handbook of Institutional Approaches to International Business,* 204-18, edited by Geoff Wood and Mehmet Demirbag. London: Edward Elgar. http://dx.doi.org/10.4337/9781849807692.00014.

Hughes, S., and N. Haworth. 2011. "Decent Work and Poverty Reduction Strategies." *Industrial Relations/Relations industrielles* 66, 1: 34–53. http://dx.doi.org/10.7202/1005104ar.

IILS. 2010. "From One Crisis to the Next," World of Work Report, International Institute for Labour Studies, International Labour Office, Geneva.

ILO. 1919. Constitution. http://www.ilo.org/dyn/normlex/en/f?p=1000:62:0::NO:62:P62_LIST_ENTRIE_ID:2453907:NO.

–. 2001. *Reducing the Decent Work Deficit – A Global Challenge.* Report of the Director General. Geneva: ILO, 89th Session.

–. 2009. *Global Jobs Pact.* http://www.ilo.org/jobspact/lang--en/index.htm.

–. 2011a. *Report of the Committee of Experts on the Application of Conventions and Recommendations: Report III (Part 1A), International Labour Conference.* http://www.ilo.org/wcmsp5/groups/public/---ed_norm/---relconf/documents/meetingdocument/wcms_151556.pdf.

–. 2011b. *Information and Reports on the Application of Conventions and Recommendations: Report of the Committee on the Application of Standards (Part Two), Provisional Record, International Labour Conference.* http://www.ilo.org/wcmsp5/groups/public/---ed_norm/---relconf/documents/meetingdocument/wcms_157818.pdf.

–. 2011c. *World of Work Report 2011 – Making Markets Work for Jobs.* http://www.ilo.org/global/publications/ilo-bookstore/order-online/books/WCMS_166021/lang--en/index.htm.

–. 2011d. *Director General Speech to European Parliament.* http://www.ilo.org/global/about-the-ilo/media-centre/statements-and-speeches/WCMS_162828/lang--en/index.htm.

–. 2011e. *Report on the High Level Mission to Greece (Athens, 19–23 September).* http://www.ilo.org/global/standards/WCMS_170433/lang--it/index.htm.

–. 2011f. *Decent Work Country Programmes: A Guidebook.* http://www.ilo.org/public/english/bureau/program/dwcp/download/dwcpguidebookv3.pdf.

ILO-IMF. 2010. "The Challenges of Growth, Employment, and Social Cohesion." Report to the Joint ILO-IMF Conference, Oslo, Norway http://osloconference2010.org/index.htm.

ITUC. 2010. *Second ITUC World Congress.* http://www.ituc-csi.org/congress.html.

Karamessini, M. 2008. "Continuity and Change in the Southern European Social Model." *International Labour Review* 147, 1: 43–70. http://dx.doi.org/10.1111/j.1564-913X.2008.00023.x.

Kornelakis, A. 2011. "Dual Convergence or Hybridization? Institutional Change in Italy and Greece from the Varieties of Capitalism Perspective." *CEU Political Science Journal* 6, 1: 47–82.

Kritsantonis, R.D. 1998. "Greece: The Maturing of the System." In *Changing Industrial Relations in Europe,* edited by A. Ferner and R. Hyman, 504–28. Oxford: Blackwell.

Nigel Haworth and Steve Hughes

Lavdas, K. 2005. "Interest Groups in Disjointed Corporatism: Social Dialogue in Greece and European Competitive Corporatism." *West European Politics* 28, 2: 297–316. http://dx.doi.org/10.1080/01402380500059769.

Lavoie, M., and E. Stockhammer, eds. 2014. *Wage-Led Growth: An Equitable Strategy for Economic Recovery.* Geneva: ILO.

Matsaganis, M. 2007. "Union Structures and Pension Outcomes." *British Journal of Industrial Relations* 45, 3: 537–55. http://dx.doi.org/10.1111/j.1467-8543.2007.00627.x.

Meardi, G. 2011. *Social Failures of EU Enlargement.* London: Routledge.

Natali, D., and P. Pochet. 2009. "The Evolution of Social Pacts in the EMU Era: What Types of Institutionalization?" *European Journal of Industrial Relations* 15, 2: 147–66. http://dx.doi.org/10.1177/0959680109103606.

Ostry, J., A. Berg, and C. Tsangarides. 2014. "Redistribution, Inequality, and Growth." IMF Staff Discussion Paper SDN/14/02, IMF, Washington, DC.

Regini, M., and S. Colombo. 2011. "Italy: The Rise and Decline of Social Pacts." In *Social Pacts in Europe: Emergence, Evolution, and Institutionalization,* edited by S. Avdagic, M. Rhodes, and J. Visser, 118–46. Oxford: Oxford University Press. http://dx.doi.org/10.1093/acprof:oso/9780199590742.003.0006.

Rohfler, S. 2012. "Perspectives on Social Pacts in Spain: Social Dialogue and the Social Partners." *Management Review* 23, 1: 49–65.

Rychley, L. 2009. "Social Dialogue in Times of Crisis."Dialogue Working Paper No. 1, International Labour Office, Geneva.

Sakellaropoulos, T. 2007. "Greece: The Quest for National Welfare Expansion through More Social Europe." In *The Europeanisation of Social Protection,* Bristol: The Policy Press, edited by J. Kvist and J. Sarri, 211-28. Bristol: The Policy Press.

World Economic Forum. 2014. "Global Risks 2014." World Economic Forum, Geneva.

Zambarloukou, S. 2006. "Collective Bargaining and Social Pacts: Greece in Comparative Perspective." *European Journal of Industrial Relations* 12, 2: 211–29. http://dx.doi.org/10.1177/0959680106065042.

7

It Takes Two to Tango
Conditional Cash Transfers, Social Policy, and the Globalizing Role of the World Bank

ANTHONY HALL

No social policy has seen such a dramatic expansion in recent years as conditional cash transfers (CCTs). These programs are designed to assist the very poor, who typically work outside the formal employment sector and are not covered by conventional social insurance. Cash transfers are non-contributory and based on the premise that acute poverty can be directly addressed by supplementing the incomes of selected poor households previously excluded from "mainstream" social policy. Regular payments are made in exchange for parental commitment to adopting human capital–strengthening measures, such as regularly sending their children to school and participating in preventive health-care programs. Even unconditional cash transfers (UCTs) that impose no such demands on the poor are becoming increasingly common, especially in Africa.

Adoption of safety nets in general, and CCTs in particular, has accelerated markedly since 2000, especially since the food, fuel, and financial crises of 2008–9. Although the World Bank's CCT program had been established several years earlier, by 2009 it had expanded largely in response to the crises. In that year, World Bank lending for social safety nets (SSNs), including CCTs, had grown to US$3.4 billion, with Mexico's Oportunidades alone accounting for US$1.5 billion. By 2010, safety nets accounted for US$6.3 billion or 9 percent of World Bank disbursements (World Bank 2011a).

Since Mexico and Brazil introduced the first subnational CCT programs in the late 1990s, cash transfer schemes have become ubiquitous in Latin America and are expanding rapidly in Africa and Asia. The number of countries with CCT programs in Latin America, for example, grew from just one in 1995 to eighteen by 2011, benefiting over 130 million people (Stampini and Tornarolli 2012). Since 2000, Africa has seen no fewer than 123 cash transfer programs of various kinds in thirty-four of forty-seven countries, only one-quarter of which are conditional (World Bank 2012b).

As noted by Barrientos and Hulme (2008, 3), "social protection increasingly defines an agenda for social policy in developing countries." Within this general trend, CCTs occupy a more prominent place than ever. During the 1980s and 1990s, safety nets were introduced to mitigate the worst consequences of financial stabilization and structural adjustment programs. Once considered a relatively insignificant, even residual, approach to social policy designed to mop up the most uncomfortable and embarrassing consequences of poverty, cash transfers have taken on an altogether different image and role. They are rapidly becoming absorbed as core social policy initiatives, carrying a high economic, social, and especially political profile. They are no longer the "silent partner to development efforts" (Fiszbein, Kanbur, and Yemtsov 2013, 4).

This chapter focuses on the role of the World Bank in facilitating the expansion of conditional cash transfer programs across the world. It argues that the growing popularity of CCTs is due to a number of complementary and mutually reinforcing interests of both the World Bank and borrowers. Furthermore, it contends that this combined support for cash transfers as social policy is having a globalizing effect on the direction of social policy in the South.

The Rise of CCTs

There has been a general expansion of cash transfer programs since the late 1990s, and by 2008 they were present in over thirty developing countries (see Figure 7.1). Latin America has the widest coverage, while sub-Saharan Africa alone has over 120 conditional and (mainly) unconditional schemes (Garcia and Moore 2012). According to the latest survey, there are currently 52 CCT and 119 UCT programs underway in the South (World Bank 2014). Even New York City authorities, based on the Mexican Oportunidades experience, introduced the Opportunity NYC – Family Rewards scheme in 2007 to reduce poverty among six of the most deprived areas (Riccio et al. 2010).

Arguably, the most prominent institutional voice behind cash transfers and the dominant source of both technical and financial support for countries seeking to introduce CCTs as a major instrument of social protection has been the World Bank. From 2005 to 2011, World Bank–funded safety net programs benefited 266 million people, 95 million through CCTs and a further 78 million via other cash transfers (World Bank 2012c).

Figure 7.1
Conditional cash transfers in the world, 1997 and 2008

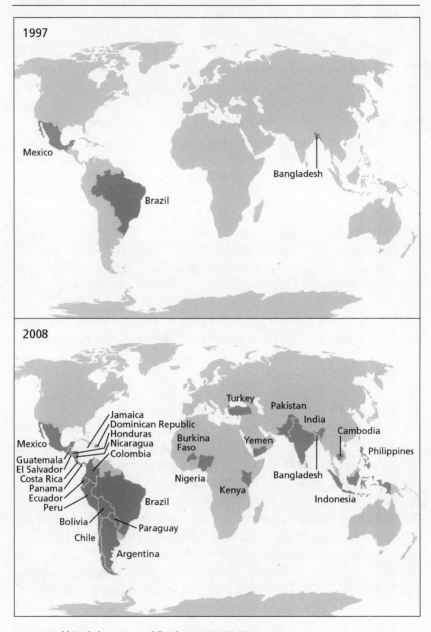

Source: World Bank, http://go.worldbank.org/RFYYFBQPU0.

Anthony Hall

Figure 7.2
Growth of CCTs and UCTs in World Bank operations, 2000–10

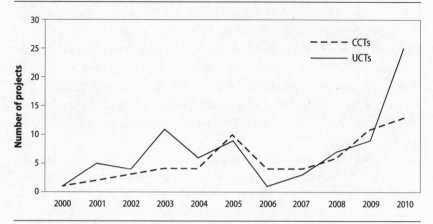

Source: World Bank (2011a, 159).

Figure 7.2 illustrates the growing presence of CCTs in the World Bank's safety net portfolio from 2000 to 2010, rising from one to thirteen major projects. In 2007, by dollar volume, CCTs accounted for one-third of its social protection portfolio, though by now this figure will have risen considerably (Milazzo and Grosh 2008). Unconditional cash transfers have become even more prominent, growing from a similar low base in 2000 but now accounting for twenty-five operations, double the number of CCTs. Until 2007, about 70 percent of CCTs in Africa were largely unconditional. This has been attributed to problems with enforcing compliance and poor implementation capacity in the education and health sectors (Garcia and Moore 2012).

As noted above, the increase in UCTs has been especially marked since 2009 following the financial crisis as assistance has been expanded to embrace low-income countries (LICs) in Africa and the Middle East in an apparent attempt to correct the middle-income country bias of the past. Conditional transfers now account for 27 percent of World Bank programs in middle-income countries and 12 percent in low-income countries (World Bank 2011a). The World Bank's influence on the spread of CCTs, however, is more substantial than these figures suggest because of its prominent role in providing analytical and advisory services to national governments, discussed below.

Middle-income countries (MICs) continue to account for the bulk of SSN lending by the World Bank, with almost 62 percent of its projects and 80 percent of its total lending. Over the decade, ten large borrowers accounted for 70 percent of World Bank lending for SSNs, though these countries contain just

15 percent of the poor in client countries (World Bank 2011a).[1] The World Bank itself attributes this bias to the higher borrowing and spending capabilities of MICs as well as their relatively stronger technical and institutional capacities.

Safety net programs in general, and CCTs in particular, have also become popular with other multilateral development institutions and bilateral donors. Along with the World Bank, the Inter-American Development Bank (IDB) helped to pioneer the spread of cash transfer programs in Latin America, which now account for 7 percent of its loan portfolio (IDB 2012). The IDB has been involved in supporting most of the region's eighteen national CCT programs. In a more modest fashion, the Asian Development Bank has funded key cash transfer programs such as that in the Philippines. The United Kingdom's Department for International Development has played a major role in providing direct support for social protection or "social transfers," particularly in Africa. During 2010–11, it provided £192 million in funding and has attempted to exercise strong policy influence (Davies 2009; Hickey et al. 2009; United Kingdom 2012).

Cash Transfers: A "Win-Win" Solution for Poverty?

Cash transfers as a form of social protection have become popular with both donors and national governments because they seem to offer a mutually attractive and beneficial solution for addressing extreme poverty. This is the case in terms of financial, technical, and political dimensions. Through its multidimensional support for CCTs, the World Bank in particular has been able to exercise an unprecedented level of influence within a growing area of social policy making in developing countries. This has coincided with the fact that adoption of cash transfers has also proven to be advantageous to national governments in many respects.

Anti-Poverty Effectiveness
A fundamental starting point is the relative effectiveness of cash transfers in reducing extreme poverty. Early programs often faced severe criticism on the ground that they represented a temporary, residual, almost Victorian approach to dealing with poverty. Yet their increasingly ubiquitous nature in countries such as Brazil, Mexico, and Colombia has placed them centre stage with a high political profile. This has made CCTs popular both with the World Bank and with client governments. Although the long-term development impacts of cash transfers await future evaluation given the relatively recent genesis of most such schemes, early evidence suggests that they have been effective in mitigating

Anthony Hall

poverty in the short term and even helping to reduce inequalities in some instances.

Clearly, such conclusions are bound to be highly context specific. Independent research on Brazil's Bolsa Família, for example, the world's largest and oldest CCT program after Mexico's Oportunidades, concluded that it has contributed significantly to a reduction of absolute poverty levels, especially in the poor northeast (IPEA 2010; Soares 2012). Together with factors such as the increase in legal minimum wages as well as other social assistance schemes targeted at the poor, elderly, and disabled, it has even been partially credited with a small but noticeable reduction in the GINI coefficient of income inequality.

The World Bank concluded in its internal evaluation of safety net projects that, judged by their relevance, efficacy, and efficiency, they perform better than the rest of its portfolio. The best-performing SSN schemes in terms of achieving their short-term, poverty-alleviating objectives were found to be conditional and unconditional cash transfers (World Bank 2011a). Researchers concluded that, "by and large, CCTs have had positive effects on household consumption and on poverty," with beneficial effects on food security (Fiszbein and Shady 2009, 12–16).

Research by the World Bank on a range of CCT programs, from the largest initiatives in Brazil, Mexico, and Colombia to smaller initiatives in Chile, Kenya, and Nicaragua, found that they have been effective in meeting their immediate education and health goals. Yet major constraints exist on their longer-run effectiveness. In education, for example, enrolments have increased, but there is little or no evidence that CCTs have improved learning quality or educational performance. This would require parallel investments to boost school infrastructure, strengthening the supply side of the equation. Yet, in general, the balance of opinion on CCT impacts seems to be cautiously (and sometimes enthusiastically) optimistic, not just in the World Bank but also more generally.[2]

Filling Funding Gaps

A second mutual advantage of cash transfer programs is that they attract donor funding, thus filling key financial gaps. Client countries short of money can turn either to the World Bank or the IDA for key financial assistance to get programs up and running. For the World Bank itself, CCT operations allow a substantial amount of funds to be rapidly disbursed, especially when packaged as part of sector-wide development policy loans (DPLs). In the decade to 2010, $11 billion was spent on safety nets, a major proportion of which went to funding CCTs. Annual commitments to SSNs rose from $1 billion in 2000 to almost $4 billion by 2009 (World Bank 2011a).

Furthermore, timely aid disbursement pays dividends. If they value their careers in the World Bank, task managers soon learn to respect the golden rule "use it or lose it." It is no secret that senior managers regard unspent budgets as an indicator of unsatisfactory performance: operations staff judged guilty of such parsimony might well find their career prospects compromised.

Research and Technical Assistance

If direct financial assistance from the World Bank for cash transfer programs has been growing significantly in recent years, the institution's support for disseminating research and providing technical expertise has arguably been even more critical. Analytical and advisory activities, comprising economic and sector work and non-lending technical assistance, form a major part of the World Bank's efforts. This ensures that the institution enjoys a high profile and level of credibility. Almost 300 instances of research and technical assistance activities in this area were supported from 2000 to 2010, costing over $60 million (World Bank 2011a). During the financial crisis, the proportion of funding for analytical and advisory activities supplied via trust funds, earmarked by bilateral donors, increased markedly to about one-third. Middle-income countries continue to enjoy the lion's share of support in this area.

According to one prominent World Bank spokesperson in the social protection field, it has played a strong role in exercising "technocratic leadership."[3] A major spinoff from World Bank involvement is thus the sheer technical expertise applied in the design and execution of cash transfer programs. Most developing countries lack such know-how and, initially at least, rely heavily on external inputs to assist in setting up and running programs. As noted above, the World Bank invests heavily in supporting targeted research and non-lending technical assistance, a trend especially pronounced in the field of social protection.

General research publications and global knowledge sharing enable the World Bank to exercise a continuing strong influence in this policy arena regardless of funding levels. For example, the World Bank has organized several major international CCT conferences[4] and study tours advertising the virtues of cash transfers. These contacts are reputed to have sparked government interest in cash transfer programs in the Philippines and Indonesia. The World Bank counts on its own Global Expert Team for Safety Nets. The Latin American and Caribbean CCT Learning Circle is reported to have had a "positive influence" on decision making among national representatives from Mexico, Chile, El Salvador, and Brazil (World Bank 2011a, 22).

Internal evaluations have shown that the social protection sector "was generally viewed by sector managers as one of the best with regard to global knowledge management," was strongly client focused, and was very supportive of regional operations (World Bank 2012d, 50). The World Bank's technical rigour and credibility have also been enhanced by the strong emphasis on impact evaluation of programs. Three-quarters of the ninety-two safety net studies carried out from 2000 to 2010 (67 percent involving CCTs) took place in Latin America.

There are many critical areas in which non-lending support for CCTs is vital and helps to explain the World Bank's emphasis on technical assistance. They include, for example, undertaking social research on identifying the poor and vulnerable groups to be targeted; designing interventions appropriate to the needs and characteristics of the population; deciding whether programs should be conditional or unconditional and the criteria to be adopted; establishing targeting and eligibility instruments; carrying out training and capacity building for national government staff and civil society participants; setting up a centralized database for potential beneficiaries; building up the relevant institutional infrastructure; and setting out procedures for impact evaluation studies. It would also include facilitating knowledge sharing and encouraging South-South dialogue through both face-to-face meetings and electronic media such as video links.

The evaluation role is highly important for the World Bank as an external actor, since impact evaluations are intended to generate lessons about the effectiveness of cash transfers that will influence future CCT policy design and implementation (World Bank 2011b). This is significant given the historical lack of independent evaluation exercises undertaken for aid projects more generally. Some 26 percent of lending projects in the Human Development sector of the World Bank have ongoing or planned impact evaluations facilitated by special bilateral trust funds.[5] In addition, the World Bank funds CCT evaluation studies undertaken by outside institutions and plays an active role in disseminating its research findings within the academic and policy-related development community.

The Political Dimension

Thus far, it is clear that CCTs are an appealing policy option for both the World Bank and its client governments on three grounds. First, cash transfers seem to be effective in alleviating poverty and possibly strengthening human capital, at least in the short term. Second, they fill key funding gaps for hard-pressed borrowers while allowing substantial sums to be disbursed and budgets to be spent in a timely fashion. Third, the World Bank's considerable research capacity and technical expertise are invaluable supports for inexperienced governments just entering this relatively new social policy field. Yet there is a fourth major aspect that receives relatively less attention but that is arguably at least as important as the other three: namely, the political benefits that accrue to both the World Bank and its clients from promoting CCTs.

From the point of view of the World Bank, support for cash transfers conveys several political advantages. Above all, CCTs are consistent with the current post–Washington Consensus development ideology. During the 1970s and 1980s, reducing poverty was seen as being dependent on promoting economic growth through trade and market liberalization, investing in physical infrastructure and providing basic social services for the poor to increase their human capital, complemented by "a program of well-targeted transfers and safety nets as an essential complement to the basic strategy" (World Bank 1990, 3). A decade later this had evolved into a three-pronged strategy around providing greater opportunities for people, promoting empowerment, and enhancing individuals' security. Poverty reduction would involve reducing the vulnerability of the poor and minimizing risks through a range of interventions, including cash transfers and other safety nets designed to support immediate consumption needs (World Bank 2001).

Since 2000, the role of targeted safety nets has been strengthened and expanded as the concept has evolved to combine reducing risks and vulnerabilities with strengthening human capital in order to boost productive capacities of the poor, providing a "springboard" for economic growth, boosting incomes and employment, and breaking the intergenerational cycle of poverty by investing in children (World Bank 2000). The introduction of education and health conditionalities is meant to guarantee this link through co-responsibility of governments and beneficiaries.

This strategy appears to have paid dividends. As evaluation studies have shown, there is evidence that cash transfers, both conditional and unconditional, have helped to alleviate poverty and create resilience to economic shocks, at least in the short run. High-profile cases such as that of Brazil allow the World Bank to claim that its social protection policies are effective and that it is taking major steps toward meeting its central mission of a "world without poverty." At the same time, however, its own Independent Evaluation Group (IEG) is critical of its claims, asserting that far more research needs to be done before firm conclusions can be reached (World Bank 2011b). The IEG argues that the longer-term challenge is how to create stronger links among social protection measures and encourage sustainable economic development.

From a wider perspective, another obvious political advantage of the CCT as an instrument of incremental change is that cash transfers do not rock the development boat. They avoid the need to seriously consider more deep-seated structural reforms or redistribution of assets as a prerequisite for promoting national economic progress. Consistent with the generally non-confrontational policy approach taken by the World Bank and other official agencies, CCTs are a safe option. In other words, "despite the numerous new policy initiatives launched by the Bank in the last decade, the normative and ideological foundation of its development assistance has not changed dramatically" (Stone and Wright 2007, 21).

The emergence of social protection as a strong part of the World Bank's development agenda has been facilitated, paradoxically, by the fact that the organization is more fluid and open than is generally imagined. Far from being a monolithic entity, it constantly adapts to evolving pressures and influences both from within and from external actors such as civil society and client governments. Various parts of the World Bank have been able to adopt CCTs on their specific agendas. Safety nets and CCTs come under the overall responsibility of human development, whereas the poverty reduction and economic management network often undertakes vital analytical work.

At the same time, the regional social protection department houses technical knowledge and investment projects on SSNs/CCTs while also carrying out its own studies. Multisectoral development policy loans are supported by the regional economic policy unit within the poverty reduction and economic management network. In fact, projects containing social protection components often involve all networks, and thirteen sector boards are responsible for approving projects (World Bank 2011a).

There is therefore no obvious central engine driving the growth of safety net and cash transfer policies but a coming together of initiatives across the World Bank within a strategy on which there is a large measure of agreement within the technocratic, apolitical approach referred to above. This has been somewhat undermined by the "matrix" management system introduced in 1997. It was intended to encourage cross-departmental collaboration and to help ensure the delivery of quality services by World Bank–wide networks of sector specialists.

According to one perspective, this has encouraged competition among staff, created new policy-generating space, and conceded more power to World Bank foot soldiers, making the sector boards less dominant. This contrasts with the IMF, for example, which is more centrally controlled. This flexibility has stimulated a certain openness and creativity within the World Bank, so that it "embraces many ideas, absorbing information, criticisms and people from outside" (Vetterlein 2007, 140). In this context, it could be argued, the organizational structure of the World Bank allows political and policy space for new ideas to be taken forward and appropriate support to be generated.

However, a downside of the matrix system has been the creation of internal organizational "silos" and disincentives for cross-sector collaboration (Hall 2007; World Bank 2012d). Thus, even if the broad ideology underlying social protection and adoption of CCTs is shared, its operationalization is rather fragmented. In mid-2013, at the time of writing, the World Bank's matrix organizational structure was being reviewed with the intention of introducing reforms.

Be that as it may, however, the World Bank's strong technical role in driving forward the CCT social policy agenda has given the institution a commanding political role in disseminating knowledge on cash transfer policies. As the World Bank/IMF Development Committee expressed it,

> the World Bank's value to client countries' work on safety nets rests in its distinctive ability to work with policymakers and practitioners in both the "architecture" and "engineering" of the agenda – from diagnostic analysis and evaluation, to strategy formulation, to the identification of policy options, to devising detailed policy and implementation measures, and finally assistance with financing technical assistance and capacity building. (World Bank 2012a, iii)

Even allowing for an element of hubris in this claim, technical dominance places the World Bank in a very strong position in dealings with client governments that are considering adopting cash transfers.

If the current emphasis on social protection measures for poverty alleviation, including cash transfers, makes perfect political sense from the World Bank's perspective, this is no less true of its client governments. National regimes stand to gain diverse political advantages from adopting CCTs, especially when backed by World Bank technical and financial assistance. The precise nature of such gains will depend on the specific country situation, but there is no mistaking the wave of political enthusiasm for the introduction of CCTs on social policy agendas in developing countries. At least four key political aspects can be highlighted: electoral, governance related, strategic social policy direction, and international influence.

The most obvious way in which CCTs serve the agendas of national politicians is electorally. Research from around the world demonstrates that political choices are highly responsive to government income transfers (Arnold, Conway, and Greenslade 2011). In Latin America, social assistance programs have clear effects on presidential voting, to the extent that more extreme critics label them as "legalized vote-buying schemes implemented with political expediency in mind" (Layton and Smith 2011, 1). Nowhere is this association better illustrated than in the case of Brazil, where the Bolsa Família (BF) benefits 13 million families or roughly one-quarter of the total population. Studies have demonstrated unequivocally that President Lula's strong backing for, and expansion of, the program were major factors in his re-election in 2006 (Hunter and Power 2007; Zucco 2010).

President Lula was also able to apply his populist and oratorical skills to good effect in portraying BF as his personal gift to the poor. Furthermore, so strong is the electorate's support for BF that it has created a policy lock-in that cuts across ideological or partisan differences. Politicians of all persuasions have bent over backward to pledge their undying support for BF and even promise to expand the program were they to be elected (Hall 2012, 2013).

In Latin America at least (if not necessarily in all other parts of the world), cash transfers were politically "sold" to the middle classes by conditioning payments to beneficiaries who met certain social obligations. In most cases, this involved guaranteeing minimum levels of school attendance and participation in health campaigns. This would justify CCTs as a boost to human capital to fuel economic growth and serve as evidence that the poor "deserved" to be helped for fear that such schemes might otherwise become charitable handouts used for clientelistic purposes. This move away from an image of paternalistic social assistance to one of co-responsibility was evident in the planning of the two largest CCT schemes in the region, in Brazil and Mexico (Britto 2008).

Another source of potential political appeal relates to the influence on national governance of introducing CCT schemes. The design and implementation of a large CCT program can allow the government to strengthen its political control even if execution of the scheme is decentralized to the local level. In the case of Brazil, for example, BF is controlled by the executive, which can execute it from the centre while devolving much operational responsibility to the municipalities, for example in terms of beneficiary selection and registration, targeting, monitoring of compliance with conditionalities, and distribution of payments. In so doing, the federal government has been able to bypass possible political interference by regional state administrations and to reduce governors' powers of patronage (Fenwick 2009).

Cash transfer programs might also hold a more subtle political attraction to the extent that they allow national governments to prioritize social assistance as a major (possibly mainstream) form of social policy. For cash-strapped governments, safety nets are relatively inexpensive, typically absorbing 1–2 percent of GDP at most and usually less. Brazil's Bolsa Família and Mexico's Oportunidades cost 0.5 percent of each country's respective GDP (World Bank 2011a, 2012a). This is an extremely affordable option, invariably dwarfed by the public sector pensions bill, for instance.[6] However, accepting substantial aid to set up and/or expand a CCT program can substantially increase the debt burden and create a political backlash in certain cases. In the Philippines, for example, the World Bank and the Asian Development Bank fund two-thirds of the country's $1.3 billion CCT program, provoking regular media protest (see de los Reyes 2011).

This immediate economic advantage can also be offset by longer-term political consequences. There is a danger that the affordability and short-term, politically expedient vision underpinning CCTs could encourage social policy makers to prioritize such schemes at the expense of deeper-seated social investments. Indeed, cash transfer programs themselves have been described as a form of "social investment" because of their focus on children and human capital strengthening (Jenson 2010). However, this seems to be questionable in the developing country context, in which the supply side is often neglected and basic services are often underfunded. Failure to invest in basic social infrastructure can undermine not just the potentially beneficial impacts of CCTs themselves but also the education and health foundations of economic development.

In Brazil, for example, as funding for BF advanced, a high "social deficit" was allegedly accompanied by a relative decline in federal funding for education, health, and sanitation (Costa 2009). If the example of Brazil is typical, then earmarking CCTs as social policy "for the poor" can induce a short termism that works against the introduction of more universal and equitable social investment as a basic citizenship right (Hall 2013). Further research is necessary to ascertain whether there is such a causal relationship and whether the principle of universality in social policy is likely to be undermined in the future. Worse still, in societies severely underprovided with public services, such as India, CCTs might prove to be highly inappropriate as a poverty solution since they are intended to complement rather than replace basic service provision (Drèze and Sen 2013). The latest Human Development Report also reminds us in no uncertain terms that CCTs are no substitute for systematic investment in social infrastructure as the foundation for development (UNDP 2013).

In the face of continued social underinvestment, however, it is possible that growing numbers of the deprived and excluded will increasingly view cash

benefits as an entitlement and apply political pressure for their greater univer-
salization to cover the poor population. This could apply especially in countries
hosting the largest CCT schemes that cover significant sections of their poor
populations, such as Brazil, Mexico, Colombia, and Ecuador, where people's
expectations have been significantly raised. There is a strong potential for
grassroots political protest for continuation of cash benefits and/or for greater
levels of investment in basic services, as witnessed in 2013 in Brazil (Hall 2013).

A fourth political dimension making CCT programs attractive to client
governments is the international influence that such programs can generate.
Brazil, with the world's largest CCT program, has applied the knowledge
acquired in this field as a tool of "soft foreign policy" through South-South
cooperation. Although the country is probably unique in this respect, social
protection is one area (along with agricultural research and treatment of
HIV/AIDS) in which Brazil has attempted to spread its expertise and dis-
seminate lessons learned in the context of global poverty challenges, its expanding commercial interests, and its growing technical cooperation program in
Africa (Cabral and Weinstock 2010; Hall 2013; Sotero 2010).

Conclusion

That CCTs are so attractive to both the World Bank and its client governments
makes it likely that they will become an increasingly popular anti-poverty tool
across the developing world. In extreme cases, given their political desirability,
income transfers can come to be incorporated as mainstream social policy rather
than just a complementary or temporary measure, as they were originally conceived. This leads us to the question of what might be the wider implications
for the World Bank's role in spreading cash transfers as a form of "globalized"
social policy.

A range of institutional players at domestic and supranational levels is increasingly shaping social policy. The World Bank has emerged since the 1990s
as a major new international player in this field, in which globalization is characterized by greater interconnectedness leading to a "shrinking of time and
space" among social policy actors (Deacon 2007, 8). Positions on the relative
roles and strengths of transnational and global institutions vary from the "strong"
globalization stance of some analysts to the "weak" interpretation of others.
Deacon, Hulse, and Stubbs (1997, 61), for example, contend that multilateral
agencies such as the World Bank play a prominent role and have become "*the*
locus of global social policy making." Others, such as Yeates (2009), caution
against crude suggestions that nation-states have lost much of their sovereignty

to international financial organizations. The case of CCTs and the World Bank's role in implementing them suggests that something of an intermediate position along this continuum would be apposite.

However, the exact nature and extent of any wider World Bank influence on global social policy will depend on how it casts its lot in with other agencies at this level and on the responses from client governments. To date, its support for CCTs has been consistent with the goal of building a general safety net policy designed to support targeted poverty reduction to strengthen efficiency and economic growth. However, the World Bank's "residual" approach contrasts with the ILO's policy of establishing a universal social protection floor (SPF), a form of "basic universalism" that aims to guarantee a minimum level of social security for all citizens and not just officially registered workers. The SPF "rights-based" approach aims to bring the entire population above the poverty line as an end in itself (Deacon 2013 and this volume).

Spearheaded by the ILO and WHO, consultations have been taking place for several years among UN agencies, involving the World Bank, over how much convergence is feasible between these two sets of ideas. The ILO adopted the SPF in 2012 as a reference point for further interagency negotiations. The World Bank's *Social Protection and Labor Strategy,* published the same year, appears to have made some concessions, shifting the emphasis from prevention, protection, and promotion to a "life cycle approach" concerned with resilience (insurance), equity (assistance), and opportunity (human capital development). However, Deacon (2013) questions how much overlap really exists between this approach and the ILO's four guarantees concerning universal access to basic minimum incomes, livelihoods, and services. In addition, he raises serious doubts about whether the UN system can operationalize the idea of a universal SPF and calls on other agents of civil society, such as trade unions, to fight for the cause.

The global context has thus matured since the earlier exclusive emphasis on targeted safety nets for the poorest, with countries such as Brazil and Mexico examining ways of integrating CCTs into wider anti-poverty and development strategies. Taking an optimistic stance, it can be argued that there has been growing agreement among major institutional players within the SPF debate on the need for a global SPF in the post-2008 crisis situation (Deacon 2009, 2013). This evolution is mirrored within funding organizations themselves. There is now some informal support, for example, among World Bank staff for a more rights-based (rather than a risk management) approach to social protection and CCTs.[7] Those in the World Bank engaged in the "human development" sector, for example, are reportedly more sympathetic toward the

ILO model, while those in the "poverty reduction and economic management" area favour the more traditional targeted model. Further research is needed to map out the extent and nature of such debates within the institution and the extent to which a shift in emphasis is likely in the longer term.

Notwithstanding the power of international organizations such as the World Bank to influence (even globalize) social policy, we should not forget that national governments, for the most part, retain decision-making powers. They should not be regarded as mere pawns in an international game of chess. Their rulers recognize the economic and political advantages of courting support from Washington for social protection, whether selective or more universal in flavour. What we have, therefore, is perhaps not so much a clear, unmitigated position of global hegemony for the World Bank in propagating conditional cash transfer programs as a central thrust of social policy in the global South. Rather, the emerging pattern is more likely to be characterized by a jockeying for influence both among international organizations and within their internal corridors of power as well as among these agencies and their client governments. In the quest for global social policy leadership after the Millennium Development Goals, it remains to be seen what *modus vivendi* will be reached as they tango across the ideological and political dance floor.

Acknowledgments
This paper was presented at the workshop on Global Crisis and the Changing Prospects for Social Policy, McMaster University, Hamilton, Canada, 27–28 September 2013. I would like to thank Steen Jorgensen and Arup Banerjee of the World Bank for their valuable assistance.

Notes
1 Indonesia, Pakistan, Ethiopia, Brazil, Philippines, Peru, Colombia, Mexico, and Argentina.
2 See, for example, Banerjee and Duflo (2011); Barrientos and Hulme (2008); Bastagli (2011); Hanlon, Barrientos, and Hulme (2010).
3 Steen Jorgensen, personal communication, World Bank, Washington, DC, 30 May 2013.
4 Mexico (2002), Brazil (2004), Istanbul (2006).
5 See World Bank (2011b). They include the Spanish Trust Fund for Impact Evaluation, the African Impact Evaluation Initiative, and the Development Impact Evaluation Initiative.
6 In Brazil, social insurance accounts for 47 percent of federal spending, with under 7 percent allocated to social assistance for the poorest.
7 Steen Jorgensen, personal communication, World Bank, Washington, DC, 30 May 2013.

References
Arnold, Catherine, Tim Conway, and Mathew Greenslade. 2011. "Cash Transfers: Evidence Paper." Department for International Development, London.
Banerjee, Abhijit, and Esther Duflo. 2011. *Poor Economics: A Radical Rethinking of the Way to Fight Global Poverty.* New York: Public Affairs.

Barrientos, Armando, and David Hulme, eds. 2008. *Social Protection for the Poor and Poorest: Concepts, Policies, and Politics.* Basingstoke: Palgrave Macmillan. http://dx.doi.org/10.1057/9780230583092.

Bastagli, Francesca. 2011. "Conditional Cash Transfers as a Tool of Social Policy." *Economic and Political Weekly* 46, 21: 61–66.

Britto, Tatania F. 2008. "The Emergence and Popularity of Conditional Cash Transfers in Latin America." In *Social Protection for the Poor and Poorest: Concepts, Policies, and Politics,* edited by Armando Barrientos and David Hulme, 181–93. Basingstoke: Palgrave Macmillan.

Cabral, Lídia, and Julia Weinstock. 2010. *Brazilian Technical Cooperation for Development: Drivers, Mechanics, and Future Prospects.* London: Overseas Development Institute.

Costa, Nilson do Rosário. 2009. "A proteção social no Brasil: universalismo e focalização nos governos FHC e Lula." *Ciencia & Saude Coletiva* 14, 3: 693–706.

Davies, Mark. 2009. "DFID Social Transfers Evaluation Summary Report." Working Paper 31, Department for International Development, London.

de los Reyes, Che. 2011. "CCT Debt Trap? Future of Pro-Poor Deal a Poser." Philippine Center for Investigative Journalism, 31 May.

Deacon, Bob. 2007. *Global Social Policy and Governance.* London: Sage.

–. 2009. "From 'Safety Nets' Back to 'Universal Social Provision': Is the Global Tide Turning?" In *The Global Social Policy Reader,* edited by Nicola Yeates and Chris Holden, 371–79. Bristol: Policy Press.

–. 2013. *Global Social Policy in the Making: The Foundations of the Social Protection Floor.* Bristol: Policy Press. http://dx.doi.org/10.1332/policypress/9781447312338.001.0001.

Deacon, Bob, Michelle Hulse, and Paul Stubbs. 1997. *Global Social Policy: International Organizations and the Future of Welfare.* London: Sage.

Drèze, Jean, and Amartya Sen. 2013. *An Uncertain Glory: India and Its Contradictions.* London: Allen Lane.

Fenwick, Tracy. 2009. "Avoiding Governors: The Success of Bolsa Família." *Latin American Research Review* 44, 1: 102–31. http://dx.doi.org/10.1353/lar.0.0073.

Fiszbein, Ariel, Ravi Kanbur, and Rusian Yemtsov. 2013. *Social Protection, Poverty, and the Post-2015 Agenda.* Washington, DC: World Bank. http://dx.doi.org/10.1596/1813-9450-6469.

Fiszbein, Ariel, and Norbert Shady. 2009. *Conditional Cash Transfers: Reducing Present and Future Poverty.* Washington, DC: World Bank. http://dx.doi.org/10.1596/978-0-8213-7352-1.

Garcia, Marito, and Charity M.T. Moore. 2012. *The Cash Dividend: The Rise of Cash Transfer Programs in Sub-Saharan Africa.* Washington, DC: World Bank. http://dx.doi.org/10.1596/978-0-8213-8897-6.

Hall, Anthony. 2007. "Social Policies in the World Bank: Paradigms and Challenges." *Global Social Policy* 7, 2: 151–75. http://dx.doi.org/10.1177/1468018107078160.

–. 2012. "The Last Shall Be First: Political Dimensions of Conditional Cash Transfers in Brazil." *Journal of Policy Practice* 11, 1–2: 25–41. http://dx.doi.org/10.1080/15588742.2012.624065.

–. 2013. "Political Dimensions of Social Protection in Brazil." In *Social Protection, Economic Growth, and Social Change,* edited by James Midgley and David Piachaud, 166-83. Cheltenham: Edward Elgar. http://dx.doi.org/10.4337/9781781953952.00021.

Hanlon, Joseph, Armando Barrientos, and David Hulme. 2010. *Just Give Money to the Poor: The Development Revolution from the Global South.* Stirling, VA: Kumarian Press.

Hickey, Sam, Rachel Sabates-Wheeler, Bruce Guenther, and Ian Macauslan. 2009. *Promoting Social Transfers: DFID and the Politics of Influencing*. London: Department for International Development.

Hunter, Wendy, and Timothy Power. 2007. "Rewarding Lula: Executive Power, Social Policy, and the Brazilian Elections of 2006." *Latin American Politics and Society* 49, 1: 1–30. http://dx.doi.org/10.1353/lap.2007.0005.

IDB. 2012. *CCTs: Overview and Outlook*. PowerPoint presentation, Inter-American Development Bank, Washington, DC.

IPEA. 2010. *Políticas sociais: Acompanhamento e análise. No. 18*. Brasília: IPEA.

Jenson, Jane. 2010. "Diffusing Ideas for after Neoliberalism: The Social Investment Perspective in Europe and Latin America." *Global Social Policy* 10, 1: 59–84. http://dx.doi.org/10.1177/1468018109354813.

Layton, Mathew, and Amy Smith. 2011. "Social Assistance Policies and the Presidential Vote in Latin America." Americas Barometer Insights No. 66, Vanderbilt University, Nashville, Tennessee.

Milazzo, Annamaria, and Margaret Grosh. 2008. "Social Safety Nets in World Bank Lending and Analytical Work: FY2002–2007." Social Protection Discussion Paper No. 0810, World Bank, Washington, DC.

Riccio, James, Nadine Dechausay, David Greenberg, Cynthia Miller, Zawadi Rucks, and Nandita Verma. 2010. *Towards Reduced Poverty across Generations: Early Findings from New York City's Conditional Cash Transfer Program*. New York: MDRC.

Soares, Sergei. 2012. "Bolsa Família: Its Design, Its Impacts, and Possibilities for the Future." Working Paper 89, International Policy Centre for Inclusive Growth, Brasília.

Sotero, Paulo. 2010. "Brazil's Rising Ambition in a Shifting Global Balance of Power." *Politics* 30, S1: 71–81. http://dx.doi.org/10.1111/j.1467-9256.2010.01394.x.

Stampini, Marco, and Leopoldo Tornarolli. 2012. "The Growth of Conditional Cash Transfers in Latin America: Have They Gone Too Far?" Policy Brief IDB-PB-185, Inter-American Development Bank, Washington, DC.

Stone, Diane, and Christopher Wright, eds. 2007. *The World Bank and Governance: A Decade of Reform and Reaction*. London: Routledge.

UNDP. 2013. *Human Development Report 2013: The Rise of the South: Human Progress in a Diverse World*. New York: UNDP.

United Kingdom. 2012. *Public Accounts Committee, 65th Report*. London, 23 January.

Vetterlein, Antje. 2007. "Change in International Organizations: Innovation or Adaptation? A Comparison of the World Bank and the International Monetary Fund." In *The World Bank and Governance: A Decade of Reform and Reaction*, edited by Diane Stone and Christopher Wright, 125–44. London: Routledge.

World Bank. 1990. *World Development Report 1990: Poverty*. Washington, DC: World Bank.

–. 2000. *Social Protection Strategy Paper: From Safety Nets to Springboard*. Washington, DC: World Bank.

–. 2001. *World Development Report 2000–2001: Attacking Poverty*. Washington, DC: World Bank.

–. 2011a. *Social Safety Nets: An Evaluation of World Bank Support*. Washington, DC: World Bank.

–. 2011b. *Evidence and Lessons Learned from Impact Evaluations on Social Safety Nets*. Washington, DC: World Bank.

– 2012a. *Safety Nets Work during Crisis and Prosperity*. Washington, DC: World Bank and IMF.

–. 2012b. *Managing Risk, Promoting Growth: Developing Systems for Social Protection in Africa*. Washington, DC: World Bank.

–. 2012c. *The World Bank Annual Report 2012*. Washington, DC: World Bank.

–. 2012d. *The Matrix System at Work: An Evaluation of the World Bank's Organizational Effectiveness*. Washington, DC: World Bank.

–. 2014. *The State of Social Safety Nets 2014*. Washington, DC: World Bank.

Yeates, Nicola. 2009. "Social Politics and Policy in an Era of Globalization: Critical Reflections." In *The Global Social Policy Reader,* edited by Nicola Yeates and Christopher Holden, 35–55. Bristol: Policy Press.

Zucco, Cesar. 2010. *Cash Transfers and Voting Behaviour: An Assessment of the Political Impacts of the Bolsa Família Program*. Princeton: Woodrow Wilson School and Department of Politics, Princeton University.

PART 3: EMERGING AREAS

8

Integrating the Social into CEPAL's Neo-Structuralist Discourse

RIANNE MAHON

This chapter focuses on a part of the world where the "global" financial crisis has been associated not with austerity and social policy cuts but with ongoing social policy development, especially in key countries. Latin America has moved in the opposite direction from most parts of the world, making visible progress in reducing inequality. As the *Economist* recently noted, "in most Latin American countries the GINI coefficient in 2010 was lower than in 2000."[1] Although insights can be gained from studying particular country examples, the near-continent-wide scale of change suggests that it is also worth shifting the focus to the regional scale. Accordingly, this chapter examines social policy ideas promoted by the Economic Commission for Latin America and the Caribbean (CEPAL),[2] which has rightly been described as "the hemisphere's most influential economic think tank" (Leiva 2008, xvii).

In the postwar period, CEPAL played an innovative role, developing the theoretical justification for the model of import-substituting industrialization (ISI) spreading throughout the region. The crisis of the ISI model threw into question CEPAL's structuralist discourse and opened the way for neo-liberal structural adjustment in the 1980s. Its neo-structuralism was in turn formed as a critical response to the latter's increasingly manifest failures in the region. Like the original structuralist discourse, CEPAL's neo-structuralist strategy initially focused on economic development, but over the past decade it has come to incorporate a strong social dimension into its discourse. This opening was made possible not only by shifts in the global universe of social policy discourse, such as those described by Deacon and Jenson in this volume, but also, and more importantly, by the failure of neo-liberal reforms to deliver the promised "trickle down" benefits, a failure underlined by popular protests and the electoral "pink tide" across the region and documented by CEPAL's Social Development Division.

The chapter begins by locating CEPAL as a particular node within complex sets of overlapping networks traversing multiple scales. It then outlines the contested process through which CEPAL developed its original structuralist alternative to the dominant economic model. The introduction of a social dimension into the latter came late – perhaps too late – as military dictatorships were moving to crush the left and open the way to neo-liberal structural adjustment. The final section of the chapter traces the incorporation of social policy ideas drawn from diverse sources – global, transregional, and national – into CEPAL's neo-structuralist strategy.

CEPAL as a Key Node in Overlapping Networks

CEPAL's potential influence on member states' policy horizons works primarily through the gathering, interpretation, and dissemination of information relating to the economic and social development of the region – that is, "governance through comparison" – and the organization of conferences, expert group meetings, and seminars – that is, the orchestration of dialogical encounters – through which CEPAL engages with national officials, experts, and civil society organizations. CEPAL is well positioned to do this as an important node linking the regional and global scales. Thus, as a creature of the United Nations, reporting through the Economic and Social Council (ECOSOC), it is well positioned to assist "in bringing a regional perspective to global problems and forums and introducing global concerns at the regional and sub-regional levels."[3] It also has important links with donors, including the European Commission.[4] Thus, even though CEPAL is located geographically in the Americas and, in the 1980s and 1990s, came under pressure to adopt a social policy model closer to the residualist American model, contemporary social policy thinking has also been influenced by European ideas. However, CEPAL has never functioned as a mere "switch point" facilitating the flow of ideas from global and extraregional sites to the region's governments and from the latter to the global. From the outset, it developed a coherent organizational discourse that served to "Latin Americanize" policy ideas. CEPAL became "a channel for the diffusion of a whole set of theses concerning the causes and

Rianne Mahon

conditions of development and the obstacles in its way, thus stamping a sort of hallmark on Latin American thinking in the realm of economics" (Cardoso 1977, 9).

The Secretariat, based in Santiago, Chile, consists of twelve divisions. Of particular interest here is the Social Development Division. There are also two subregional headquarters, one for Central America based in Mexico City and one for the Caribbean based in Port of Spain, Trinidad and Tobago, plus five regional offices. These subregional sites give CEPAL institutional access to local debates and concerns. CEPAL also has several subsidiary bodies, including the Regional Conference on Women in Latin America and the Caribbean.

In terms of key documents likely to reflect the development of CEPAL's organizational discourse, those produced for CEPAL's biennial meetings and the Regional Conferences on Women in Latin America and the Caribbean are clearly of central importance. In addition, the relevant flagship publications – in this case the annual *Social Panorama of Latin America and the Caribbean*, produced jointly by the Statistics and Social Development Divisions – offer insights into the development of CEPAL's organizational discourse and the outcomes of debates that it has engendered within the organization. *CEPAL Review* publishes academic works contributed by CEPAL staff and others within and beyond the region. As such, it offers insights into key theoretical debates that can presage development at the more practical, policy-oriented level. I analyze such documents in the section tracing development of the social component of CEPAL's neo-structuralist discourse. Before I examine CEPAL's contemporary organizational discourse, however, I look at its foundational moment and the original structuralist discourse for which it became famous.

CEPAL's Structuralist Discourse

CEPAL, and Raúl Prebisch, the Argentinean economist who played a critical role in its founding years, are noted for their original contribution to development theory – the centre-periphery thesis – which provided the intellectual underpinnings for the ISI model of development. Prebisch played a key role in establishing the core elements of CEPAL's structuralist discourse, beginning with the publication of *Introducción al primer estudio económico de América Latina* (1948) and then, for CEPAL's first session (in Havana in 1949), *El desarrollo económica de la América Latina y sus principales problemas* (Gabay 2008). These and subsequent documents produced by Prebisch and his team of economists[5] provided "a ringing critique of the international division of labour and the declining terms of trade for the producers of primary products" (Sikkink 1991, 58). During its first decade, CEPAL focused its critique on external constraints to peripheral development, with little attention to internal inequalities, and social and labour market policies needed to tackle them, beyond the assertion that policies geared to promoting industrialization "not be brought about through restriction of popular consumption, which was already too low" (Cardoso 1977, 25). Attention to the social would only come later.

Prebisch's ideas formed part of a broader reflection on the "contested failure" (Best 2014) of the 1930s Depression. As Prebisch later noted, "during the Great Depression, although I had been a neo-classical economist, I realized that, in light of the crisis, it was necessary to industrialize. I did this with misgiving, since all my ideas ran against it. But faced with the facts, faced with the intensity of the crises, I said there was no alternative" (interview with Sikkink 1991, 76). In this, of course, Prebisch was not alone. Keynesian theory had begun to challenge the classical economic paradigm in the 1930s, and this challenge helped to create space for other challengers. Although others – notably Hans Singer, Werner Sombart, and German Chilean economist Ernst Wagemann – also influenced Prebisch's thinking (Gabay 2008), this was not a case of the passive diffusion of ideas. Prebisch and the group of heterodox economists whom he helped to assemble at CEPAL headquarters "Latin Americanized" these ideas.

Not surprisingly, CEPAL came to be perceived as "a potential threat to the policies of the U.S. government, of the Bank and [the] Fund and GATT" (Pollock, Kerner, and Love 2001, 20), and Ivy League economists such as Jacob Viner sought to attack its core theses (Cardoso 1977, 18). In fact, CEPAL was founded against the opposition of both superpowers. As Prebisch would later note, "when Hernan Santa Cruz presented to the Economic and Social Council ... his project for the creation of ECLA, naturally he encountered much opposition from the great powers, and especially from the US" (interview with Pollock, Kerner, and Love 2001, 13). The United States then tried to fold the organization into the Organization of American States (OAS), in which it held sway, a move successfully resisted by Prebisch, with the support of key allies in the region (Pollock, Kerner, and Love 2001, 14). ECOSOC, through which CEPAL reported, clearly hoped to limit its role to the neutral provision of information on the region. Thus, it responded to Prebisch's introduction to the first *Economic Survey of Latin America* by stating that, though the report had "great content," "it speaks about development, industrialization, terms of trade, and many other matters ECLA is not supposed to deal with" (Pollock, Kerner, and Love 2001, 11).

Not content simply to challenge the Ricardian theory of comparative advantage that lay behind the dominant postwar paradigm, Prebisch's centre-periphery thesis also had a practical orientation. As Cardoso (1977, 40) argued in his classic essay, "the ideas formulated by CEPAL ... deal with questions which had to be faced in order to tackle the practical economic problems arising, and although they were based on analytical instruments fashioned in other settings, they had to recast these for the purposes of explaining an inequitable international trade situation and justifying policies favourable to the industrialization of the periphery." In thus providing theoretical justification for ISI on the agendas of many Latin American governments, CEPAL retained considerable support across the region. As a result, "ECLA went ahead, did things and influenced reality whether ECOSOC listened to it or not" (Pollock, Kerner, and Love 2001, 15).

Sikkink (1991) rightly cautions against seeing CEPAL as the centre of the diffusion of policy ideas simply picked up by national governments. Rather than seeing CEPAL as the centre from which such ideas emerged, it is more useful to think of it as an important site for the reception and development of ideas circulating within key intellectual and policy centres within the region. Nevertheless, Sikkink admits that

> noted Latin American economists like Prebisch infused CEPAL's work with originality and dynamism, while Latin American statesmen and diplomats contributed to the creation and continued existence of the organization. At the same time, CEPAL reports, theory, technical assistance teams, and training workshops gave information, evidence, and support to governments throughout the region. Economists who worked at CEPAL found their work enriched by the broader regional perspective that informed CEPAL analysis. (59)

CEPAL's influence was helped by the fact that, like Prebisch, many of the key figures bridged the divide between research and policy. Thus, Celso Furtado, a Brazilian economist involved in CEPAL from the outset, went on to become the head of Brazil's powerful development bank and then the minister of planning under the Goulart government (1961–64). Pedro Vuskovic, a professor at the University of Chile throughout his nearly two decades at CEPAL, went on to become Allende's minister of economic affairs.

Although the core elements of CEPAL's organizational discourse were forged in the 1950s, they were subject to contestation and change. In particular, during the 1960s and 1970s, the virtues of the ISI model with which CEPAL had come to be so closely associated were contested first from the left and then from the right. The Cuban revolution, which lent credence in the hemisphere to the socialist path to development, opened the way for left critiques of CEPAL's focus on external causes of underdevelopment at the expense of examining internal reasons, while the military coups in Brazil (1964), Argentina (1966), and Chile and Uruguay (1973) would pave the way for neo-liberal structural adjustment.

As Cardoso (1977, 30–31) later noted,

> it seems that the persistent leftist criticism (the 1957 theses of Baran[6] may be recalled) and the failure of industrialization policies to improve the population's level of living and to absorb the economically active population – in view of population growth, rural-urban migration and the initial impact of a capital-intensive style of industrialization – ended by shaking some of CEPAL's firmly founded convictions.

André Gunder Frank's *The Development of Underdevelopment* (1966), which highlighted the link between external inequality and the domestic power structure, was soon followed by critical contributions by intellectuals associated with CEPAL, including Furtado,[7] Cardoso, and Osvaldo Sunkel. The OAS-initiated Alliance for Progress, launched during the Kennedy administration as an attempt to counter the Cuban revolution's influence in the region, similarly focused attention on internal obstacles to development, while the newly established Inter-American Development Bank began to finance land reform as well as health and education projects.

In response, CEPAL began to turn its attention to the role played by internal inequality in blocking development. As Cardoso notes (1977, 31), "in the document which sums up CEPAL thinking in the early 1960s,[8] social aspects were for the first time explicitly discussed and introduced into the explanatory model." CEPAL's 1968 *Economic Survey of Latin America* referred to Vuskovic's work that offered statistical evidence of the failure of ISI to deliver "trickle down" benefits (Cardoso 1977, 34). Of particular importance for the future was the conceptual innovation introduced by the Chilean economist Aníbal Pinto. Pinto's concept of "structural heterogeneity" was used to highlight the negative impact of "a development style based on poles of modernization, which brings about a three-fold concentration of the fruits of technical progress, at the social level, at that of the economic 'strata' and at the regional level" (Cardoso 1977, 33). Poverty and inequality could thus be attributed to the underemployment

Rianne Mahon

generated by capital-intensive industrialization, often under the aegis of foreign capital, the low productivity in the domestic sector, and the abundant labour supply generated by rural-urban migration, compounded by international restrictions on the mobility of labour (Bielschowsky 2009, 186). This concept would reappear in CEPAL's neo-structuralist discourse but not until after the rupture associated with the "lost decade" of the 1980s.

Although in the early 1980s the left globally had an alternative to neo-liberalism – the "new international economic order" then championed by UNESCO – in Latin America the wave of military dictatorships combined with the new orthodoxy championed by the IMF and World Bank made neo-liberal structural adjustment the dominant solution. Initially, CEPAL seemed to be unable to formulate its response. Leiva (2008, 35–36) argues that "throughout the 1970s and early 1980s ... ECLAC was unable to articulate a coherent proposal capable of challenging the neoliberal policies supported by the World Bank and the IMF, which partly thanks to the repressive power of Latin America's military, imposed programs of structural reforms." Bielschowsky (2009, 17) suggests that in this period there was "less than full consensus among the institution's technical teams and leaders on how to approach the problem." Nevertheless, heterodox views were not entirely absent during this period. Of particular importance was the work of Fernando Fajnzylber, a Chilean economist associated with CEPAL. His 1983 *La industrialización trúnca de América Latina* drew on a mix of neo-Schumpeterian ideas and analyses of Northern European and Northeastern Asian experiences to reassert the role of the state in promoting industrialization through innovation.[9] These ideas would come to the fore as CEPAL began to challenge neo-liberalism.

CEPAL began to embrace a "neo-structuralist" alternative with the adoption of *Changing Production Patterns with Social Equity* at its twenty-sixth session. The document, penned by Fajnzylber and championed by the director, Gert Rosenthal, formulated a new set of foundational ideas centred on the concept of "systemic competitiveness." It rejected the "low road" (comparative advantage based on low wages and exports of raw materials) in favour of a "high road" (competitive advantage, to be achieved by the state's support for innovation and the spread of productivity increases throughout the economy). Although it embraced the idea of flexible labour markets so central to neo-liberal discourse, in CEPAL's version "functional" flexibility, via investment in the education and training of the population as a whole, was emphasized over numerical (hire and fire) flexibility celebrated in neo-liberal discourse. Equity figured in the equation too, and here Pinto's concept of "structural heterogeneity" would be rediscovered to shed light on the reasons for the region's high levels of poverty and inequality. Initially, however, CEPAL shared with the World Bank a preference for social policies targeting the very poor.

CEPAL accepted the neo-liberal argument for macroeconomic stability but also came to embrace improved fiscal capacity via increasing income taxes and/or eliminating tax avoidance. Although it accepted a role for the state in promoting development, the state was not to assume the central role that it had played under ISI; rather, it was to operate in partnership with civil society actors. As part of this reorientation, CEPAL argued for the negotiation of covenants that would bring the key actors – the state, business, labour, and civil society organization – together around a common plan of action. The failure of neo-liberal reforms to deliver global stability, underlined by the ripple effects of the Asian financial crisis and the Argentinean meltdown a few years later, led to further modifications of the neo-structuralist discourse during Ocampo's directorship. More importantly for this chapter, growing inequality linked to the lowering of wages, expansion of the informal economy, and associated reduction of social insurance coverage prompted CEPAL to develop the social and labour market policy aspects of the neo-structuralist discourse.

From "Equity" to "Equality" and a Rights-Based Model

Over the past decade, CEPAL has moved away from a limited concern with "equity" and toward a rights-based, universalist conception of social protection. It has done so against the backdrop of contested failures – locally, regionally, and globally – of the post-Washington Consensus. As successive issues of *Social Panorama* documented, the first wave (1980s) and second wave (1990s) of reforms not only failed to make significant headway against poverty and inequality in the region but also contributed to increasing insecurity that has reached well into the middle class. The "benefits" of neo-liberal globalization, moreover, were actively contested not only at the global scale (the "anti-globalization" movement of the 1990s; the World Social Forum, founded in Porto Alegre, Brazil, in 2001) but also in the region, most recently with the protests in Brazil and Chile. In addition, CEPAL's surveys in the late 1990s had revealed that 67 percent of those polled considered the distribution of wealth unfair (CEPAL 2004a, 4). Such widespread dissatisfaction contributed to a series of victories by governments of the left and centre-left, beginning in 1999.[10]

The development of CEPAL's discourse was also shaped by its location at the intersection of a diverse set of knowledge networks traversing multiple scales. As noted by a recent CEPAL report, *Inclusive Social Protection in Latin*

Rianne Mahon

America, CEPAL's conception of social protection has "emerged from a series of discussions, analyses, and concrete proposals on rights-based social protection by various academic circles in the region and by international organisations, rather than from a single source" (Cecchini and Mártinez 2012, 40). The extraregional networks on which CEPAL thinkers drew in developing its conception of social protection are diverse. They include the United Nations, with its rights-based discourse, and the ILO, with its Decent Work campaign (see Haworth and Hughes, this volume). Of particular importance are CEPAL's links with the European Commission and key European states,[11] connections strengthened through EurosociAL, a biregional partnership through which, since 2004, the European Commission has contributed over 70 million euros to promote "best practices" linked to concepts such as "social cohesion." As a result, EurosociAL claims that, "thanks to the program's support, the concept of social cohesion has become a frame of reference which is increasingly used in developing public policies in a region which continues to be the most unequal in the world."[12] As we shall see, however, CEPAL has contributed to the "Latin Americanization" of this and other "European" concepts, such as "flexicurity."

Ideas have not simply travelled from the global to the regional but also moved from the "bottom up." Thus, countries in the region, notably Mexico and Brazil, created the idea of conditional cash transfers (CCTs), which have become global exemplars of "social investment," the post-neo-liberal conception of social policy that appeared in the 1990s (Jenson 2010 and this volume). CEPAL has been less enthusiastic about CCTs than the World Bank. For CEPAL's Social Development Division, CCTs are best seen as part of a broader social protection matrix, while its Gender Affairs Division is particularly critical of their reinforcement of women's maternal role. CEPAL's social policy ideas have also been formed in the context of dialogue and debate among social policy experts in the region, which has contributed, among other things, the idea of basic universalism.[13]

Changing Production Patterns with Equity was primarily concerned with outlining an alternative model for economic development. In this version, greater equity can be achieved as a result of the long-run transformation of the basis for international competitiveness, from low wages and unprocessed natural resources to products based on sophisticated technology and skilled labour. This formulation, however, left open the question of what to do in the short and medium terms:

> No matter how intensive the effort to secure changes is, it will undoubtedly be a long time before it is possible to overcome the existing structural

heterogeneity through the absorption of all marginalized sectors into activities of greater productivity. It will therefore be necessary to think in terms of supplementary redistributive measures, including technical, financial and marketing services as well as mass training programmes for micro-entrepreneurs, self-employed workers and peasants; the reform of various kinds of regulations which hinder the establishment of micro-businesses; the adaptation of social services to the needs of the poorest sectors; the promotion of reciprocal ... arrangements and proper representation of the needs of the most under-privileged groups to the State authorities; and measures to take full advantage of the redistributive potential of fiscal policy, both on the income side and as regards the orientation of public spending. (CEPAL 1990, 7)

In other words, policies to promote the development and diffusion of technological innovations would need to be supplemented by education, training, and social programs targeting the "most underprivileged." Few details, however, were provided about what to do regarding poverty and inequality at this stage.

CEPAL (1998) began to flesh out its attack on one side of the problem – Latin American states' weak fiscal capacities – with publication of *The Fiscal Covenant: Strengths, Weaknesses, and Challenges.* Here CEPAL argued for the need for broad national agreements (covenants) to "legitimate the amount, composition and organization of public expenditures and the tax burden necessary to finance it" (9). This document also took a mildly Keynesian position to the extent that it suggested the need for countercyclical fiscal policies, designed to reduce the vulnerability of the population to external financial crises. State revenues to finance expanded social programs would also be enhanced by combatting tax evasion and avoidance and increasing direct taxation.[14] In this document, however, CEPAL's social policy conception reflected a combination of social investment (the injunction to spend more on primary education, health, and employment) and a residualist approach (targeting the poor while cutting back on "regressive" expenditures on social security and tertiary education).

CEPAL's social policy needs to be seen against the backdrop of existing social policy regimes in the region. The social policy regimes developed throughout Latin America in the postwar era were built largely along Bismarckian lines – that is, focused on the provision of social insurance for those (male bread-winners) employed in the formal work sector. In some countries where the formal work sector covered a large part of the labour market, these programs came close to universal coverage, whereas in others with substantial rural populations many were not included (Filgueira 2005). Expansion of the informal sector in the 1980s and 1990s, however, led to a drop in coverage in all countries.

Although CEPAL's initial acceptance of a residualist approach thus makes sense from a narrow redistributive standpoint, it ignored the growing vulnerability of the middle class, even while *Social Panorama* had begun to document the latter.[15] More broadly, residualist approaches fail to recognize what Korpi and Palme (1998) call the "paradox of redistribution": that is, residualist welfare regimes tend to be the least generous, whereas those built along classic universalist lines are typically more generous precisely because they secure middle-class buy-in. CEPAL's support for targeting at the expense of social security thus posed problems for its wider fiscal reform agenda. As Carroll and Palme would later point out, "combined with current problems in Latin American tax collection, the current Latin American social policy equilibrium is one of vicious rather than virtuous circles, between low quality social services and low middle- and upper-class willingness to pay more taxes – an equilibrium which it can be very hard to break" (2006, 55).

CEPAL's involvement in the UN system provided an occasion for critical reflection on its position. *Equity, Development, Citizenship,* prepared for its twenty-eighth session, thus proudly laid claim to the "global values" of human rights, social development, gender equity, and respect for ethnic and cultural diversity embodied in UN doctrines (CEPAL 2001, 10). In this document and the one prepared for the region's second follow-up conference to the 1995 UN-sponsored World Summit on Social Development, *The Equity Gap: A Second Assessment,* CEPAL articulated a set of core principles that seemed (but ultimately failed) to break with the residualist approach: universality, solidarity, and efficiency. Thus, in terms consistent with the concept of citizenship,[16] CEPAL now embraced the right of access by all to benefits considered necessary to participate fully in society, seen to necessitate the addition of non-contributory benefits (CEPAL 2000a, 282). In addition, such benefits were to be financed through the tax system. Nevertheless, at this point, CEPAL's conception of universality left the better off to rely on the market for enhanced levels of protection. "Efficiency" was also interpreted as requiring a reduced role for the state – a state beset not only by lack of competition, as the neo-liberals stressed, but also by strong vestiges of clientelism – and a correspondingly enhanced role for civil society actors to overcome government as well as market failures (CEPAL 2001, 11).

By the middle of the decade, however, evidence of the failure of previous reforms continued to mount. Thus, a special issue of *Social Panorama, A Decade of Social Development in Latin America 1990–1999* (CEPAL 2004a), pointed to the continued expansion of the informal sector, a growing wage gap between it and the formal sector, the proliferation of part-time and temporary work, the expansion of grounds for dismissal, reductions in severance pay, and restrictions on the right to strike, collective bargaining, and union membership. This critique was reiterated in the document prepared for CEPAL's thirtieth session, *Productive Development in Open Economies* (CEPAL 2004b). In addition to elevating "social cohesion" to new prominence in CEPAL's discourse by calling for a "social cohesion covenant,"[17] the document drew on two other concepts that had come to dominate European debates: "new social risks" and "flexicurity."

Thus, growth of the informal sector – and of precarity in the formal sector itself – was identified as a "new social risk"[18] arising out of the transformation of labour markets wrought by the rapid economic liberalization and privatization of the previous decades and intensified by the economic volatility associated with international financial flows and the contagion effects of international crises. In this context, "structural heterogeneity" came to be understood not simply as a legacy of the era of import-substituting industrialization but also of the very reforms that CEPAL had (partially) endorsed. Drawing on the Danish/Scandinavian examples of "flexicurity" (flexibility with security), the document argued that increased precarity was not a necessary feature of the contemporary economy. In Latin America as in Europe, flexicurity could be achieved through the reregulation of labour markets, with an eye to incorporating the informal sector, the introduction of portability to existing social insurance programs, and the replacement of severance pay with unemployment insurance.[19] In this document, too, CEPAL recommended balancing export-led growth with domestic demand: "Macroeconomic policies help to reduce instability when they favour demand, especially household demand, which results in a significant increase in the consumption of products from small national enterprises (which then generate employment), creating virtuous economic circles and easing difficult periods" (2004b, 290n24).

Shaping the Future of Social Protection (CEPAL 2006), prepared for CEPAL's thirty-first session, clearly located its argument within the neo-structuralist discourse: systemic competitiveness remains the "linchpin" of development and the key to the task of tackling structural heterogeneity by transforming the production structure to create decent jobs (the ILO demand) and investing in human capital formation. Its view of social protection, however, incorporated a more European, even Nordic, view.[20] Moreover, the gender bias of existing social insurance programs, from which many women were excluded or

Rianne Mahon

dependent on access through their spouses, also received new attention. Thus, *Shaping the Future* argued that CEPAL's long-term development strategy needs to be complemented by the adoption of a rights-based social covenant, extending to all citizens an equal right to social protection. This required the development of a comprehensive system, combining contributory and tax-financed benefits. The idea of targeting had not been abandoned, but, it was argued, it "cannot ... justify a policy under which the State would provide services and benefits to the poor alone, since such an approach would clearly be at odds with the universalistic nature of social rights" (CEPAL 2006, 14). The move toward classic universality was also reflected in its treatment of CCTs. Although not rejecting them, *Shaping the Future* argued that they should be treated as just one of the elements in an integrated social protection system. Moreover, though many CCT programs focused on the demand side (e.g., encouraging school attendance), *Shaping the Future* argued that this focus had to be balanced by investment in the supply side (i.e., in good-quality, universally accessible health care and education). It also noted that many CCT programs constituted a heavier workload for women and should instead be designed to help balance their paid and unpaid work. Although CEPAL continued to support the principle of mixed provision, *Shaping the Future* advocated a stronger role for the state: "The definition of which rights are guaranteed and which risks society is willing to assume as its collective responsibility, should lead to an explicit designation of public goods whose provision by the state – and only by the state – is indelegable, regardless of whether delivery of such goods is conducted by public or private institutions" (CEPAL 2006, 20).

The document for CEPAL's thirty-third session, *Time for Equality* (CEPAL 2010a), prepared in the wake of the 2008 financial crisis, also opened the way to more critical thinking within CEPAL.[21] As Bárcena, CEPAL's director, stated in the preface, "it might be possible to mitigate the financial repercussions, but the global awareness acquired over the past years regarding the arbitrary nature of the model will not easily be erased, nor will the indignation caused by its inequities" (13). Such indignation helped to create the space for CEPAL to move beyond the muted criticism of the global (dis)order offered in earlier documents. Thus, *Time for Equality* was explicitly critical of global finance capital's detachment from the real economy. For CEPAL, the crisis underlined not only the need for a new global architecture but also the importance of re-evaluating the export-led growth model. *Time for Equality,* moreover, openly called for a growth strategy that balanced exports and the expansion of aggregate domestic demand, especially in the wealthier countries of the region.

With regard to social protection, *Time for Equality* reinforced the earlier message that social protection was to be regarded as a right – but this time a right not only to equal opportunity but also to a certain equality of outcome. In addition, it offered a different rationale for combining universality and selectivity. Building on earlier thinking about the importance of recognizing the rights of "the other," it argued that "citizenship or equal rights, social justice or substantive equality, recognition for diversity or equality in difference: these are the three components of the concept of equality that cannot be subordinated to one another and that together form the concept of equality we are propounding" (CEPAL 2010a, 42).[22] In other words, CEPAL now argued that universal programs also had to accommodate diverse needs and ways of living in order to cultivate recognition of and respect for "the other."

Finally, *Time for Equality* did not shy away from incorporating the concepts of class and gender. Thus building on the earlier argument for "flexicurity," it emphasized the importance of "full respect for the rights and protection of workers *as the structurally weaker actors on the labour market*" (2010a, 151; emphasis added). Gender inequality was understood as a reflection of unequal power relations, which, by assigning women primary responsibility for unpaid work in the home, not only put them in a weaker position within the labour market but also entailed a double workday, especially for those in poorer households. The achievement of gender equality, it argued, requires a combination of equitable pay, public investment in childcare, and measures to encourage an equitable sharing of household tasks between men and women. The increasing incorporation of gender into CEPAL's discourse in turn reflects the progress made by feminists within the organization, with support at both the regional scale and the global scale.[23]

Conclusion

This chapter began with the modest objective of tracing how a series of "contested failures" paved the way for the incorporation of new social policy ideas into CEPAL's organizational discourse, first the structuralist discourse of the postwar era and then, more strongly, the neo-structuralist version. In both cases, the original focus was on developing the theoretical justification for the state's role in promoting domestic development in the face of external inequalities. The social came later as a result of "contested failures" first of ISI and then of neo-liberal reforms to "trickle down" to the masses. During the 1980s, the original discourse entered a deeper period of crisis in which, to paraphrase

Rianne Mahon

Gramsci, the old was dying but the new had yet to be born. Yet, even during this hiatus, CEPAL intellectuals – notably Fernando Fajnzylber – were sowing the seeds of renewal. While Fajnzylber developed a rationale for "changing production capacity with equity" and resuscitated Pinto's concept of "structural heterogeneity," the social remained underdeveloped until later, when popular demonstrations against neo-liberal failures and the resulting "pink tide" of electoral victories created a political opening. Within CEPAL, the Social Development Division contributed to this shift by documenting the spread of informality and the associated deepening of inequality and vulnerability that reached well into the middle class. In thinking through CEPAL's response thereto, the division was inspired by ideas flowing through its overlapping networks that operate across different scales, reaching "down" to national and subregional sites, "across" to other bodies in the region and the European Union, and "up" to the United Nations and other international organizations and agencies operating at the global scale.

Some of these ideas, such as "social cohesion," "flexicurity," and "care economy," trace their origins to sites beyond the region.[24] Yet, just as in the postwar era, the ability of CEPAL to forge a powerful organizational discourse allowed it to translate these ideas into concepts and policies designed to illuminate – and tackle – Latin American particularities. An examination of any of the key documents cited above would show that CEPAL has "remained on message" even while it has widened its bandwidth. Thus, systemic competitiveness has not been abandoned, but recent documents suggest a turn to balancing export-led and domestic demand–led growth. Structural heterogeneity remains the principal explanation for inequality within, but it is now understood not simply as a remnant of the "bad old (ISI) days" (and the brute neo-liberalism of the 1980s) but also as a reflection of deeply rooted class, gender, and racial-ethnic relations, which even the elections of governments of the left have failed to tackle.

Clearly, this chapter does not begin to explore the related but distinct question of whether and how CEPAL's ideas have been picked up at the national or subnational scale in the region. Certainly, recent initiatives taken by the Argentinean and Chilean governments fit with CEPAL's call for universal programs. The strongest parallel, however, is between CEPAL's discourse and Brazil's "neo-developmentalist" strategy.[25] Although it would be too much to attribute this to CEPAL's capacity to influence Brazilian policy – domestic forces, with their particular historical experiences and distinct institutional environments are clearly critical – there is evidence to suggest a connection to heterodox economists who have gained important positions within the Brazilian state since 2005. Thus, Morais and Saad-Filha (2012, 790–91) suggest that key heterodox economic advisers such as Bresser-Peirera and Sicsú have been influenced by CEPAL. Again, no more than in the past, the flow of ideas is probably best described as multidirectional, a flow facilitated, but not determined, by CEPAL's multiscalar networks of intellectuals and policy advisers.

Acknowledgments

I would like to thank Kathryn Hochstetler, Evelyne Huber, Juliana Martinez-Franzoni, Jose Nun, and Cristina Rojas for their comments on the first draft of this chapter. I assume full responsibility for any remaining weaknesses.

Notes

An earlier version of this chapter appeared in *Global Social Policy* 15, 1 (2015): 3–22.

1 www.economist.com/news/special-report/21564411-unequal-continent-becoming-less-so-gini-back-bottle.

2 CEPAL is the Spanish acronym for the Economic Commission for Latin America and the Caribbean to the English (ECLAC).

3 socinfo.eclac.org/en/mandato-y-mision. Accessed 2 March 2015.

4 In part, extra-hemispheric connections arise from its membership, which includes not only the eighteen Latin American countries and thirteen Caribbean countries but also donor countries such as Canada, France, Germany, Italy, Japan, the Netherlands, Portugal, Korea, Spain, the United Kingdom, and the United States. Donors, including the European Commission, also finance special projects. According to the report of the Twenty-Sixth Session of the Committee as a Whole (New York, 28 March 2012), though nearly three-quarters of its activities are financed from its core budget ($118.1 million of $164.3 million), just under a quarter are financed through extra-budgetary projects ($35.9 million).

5 The team included important Latin Americans such as Celso Furtado and Pedro Vuskovic and later Aníbal Pinto, Osvaldo Sunkel, and sociologist Fernando Cardoso.

6 Paul Baran had earlier sought to focus attention on the appropriation of any surplus by the upper class.

7 Furtado's left turn might have been influenced by his experience as director of the Goulart government's bold initiative for the impoverished northeast of Brazil, SUDENE.

8 The document to which he refers is Prebisch's "Towards a Dynamic Development Policy for Latin America" (1964).

9 The neo-Schumpeterian school was centred in the Science Policy Research Unit at Sussex and the Nordic countries, with the latter focusing on the concept of national innovation systems. One of the contributors, however, was Carlota Perez, a Venezuelan economist, who would subsequently publish a piece in *CEPAL Review* (see Perez 2001).

10 Chavez's 1999 victory in Venezuela launched his Bolivarian republic. In Chile, Lagos's centre-left government of 2000–6 was followed by that of Bachelet. The centre-left has governed in Brazil since Lula's victory in 2002, followed by that of Rousseff. Vázquez came to power in Uruguay in 2004 and Morales (the Pluri-National Republic of Bolivia) and Correa (Ecuador) in 2006.

11 The European states that seem to have been the most involved, largely through their aid agencies, are Germany, Spain, and Sweden.

12 ec.europa.eu/europeaid/regions/latin-america/eurosocial_en. Accessed 2 March 2015.

13 The concept of basic universalism was developed by a group of social policy intellectuals brought together by the Inter-American Development Bank's Instituto Interamericano para el Desarrollo Social in 2005 (email communication from Evelyne Huber, 30 April 2013). As Huber and Stephens (2012, 258) note, basic universalism is different from classic universalism in that it does not provide the same basic transfers to everyone in society, regardless of income, but it broadly – not narrowly – focuses on those who need the transfers. In many countries of the global South, this would include the growing, but still vulnerable, middle class.

14 Here, as in later documents, CEPAL pointed out that Latin American countries' low tax rates relative to OECD countries meant that these countries had considerable room to increase taxes without harming competitiveness. In the mid-1990s, the average tax take (minus social security contributions) in Latin America was only 13.6 percent of GDP compared with the OECD average of 29 percent. As Sanchez (2011) documents using recent Argentinean and Chilean efforts, fighting tax evasion will be no easy matter.

15 Thus, *Social Panorama 1999–2000,* in noting the turn to targeted social assistance in the region, noted that "many middle income and lower middle income households feeling the crunch of the crisis and the resulting decline of their incomes, have had to pay all or part of the costs of these services directly ... Depending on their ability to pay, these sectors have sometimes seen their coverage reduced and the quality of services deteriorate; some have even lost their benefits as their incomes have fallen in poorly performing economies" (CEPAL 2000b, 16).

16 Calderón, Hopenhayn, and Ottone's 1994 article in *CEPAL Review* introduced the concept of citizenship, while Hopenhayn (2001) compared traditional and contemporary views thereof.

17 The social cohesion covenant was to rest on four principles: a coherent fiscal and income policy; an active policy to create employment, including support for the "formalization" of the informal sector; generous but financially viable social protection policies; and a renewed emphasis on education and training.

18 In European debates, the new social risks also focused on the "care crisis" linked to women's growing labour force participation. Although the document provides evidence of women's increased labour force participation in Latin America, the lack of measures to deal with the care crisis was not elevated to an important position until later.

19 In Latin America, severance pay for formal sector workers had provided a functional equivalent to unemployment insurance. See Ozkan (2014).

20 CEPAL explicitly acknowledged German and Swedish contributions to the thinking that lay behind *Shaping the Future.* This influence included the paper by Carroll and Palme cited above, which formed the basis for a seminar organized by CEPAL's Social Development Division. The paper made a strong pitch for designing a social protection system that included the middle and upper classes.

21 See also *Inclusive Social Protection in Latin America: A Comprehensive Rights-Based Approach,* produced by Simone Cecchini and Rodrigo Mártinez (2012) for CEPAL, with funding from the German and Swedish aid agencies, for a further development of the theoretical and empirical underpinnings of this citizenship-based approach. This study also provides good insights into CEPAL debates with the ILO and World Bank as well as experts in the region.

22 For the earlier thinking, see Hopenhayn (2007). His interpretation of social cohesion accorded with the resurgence of Indigenous people's movements, notably in the Pluri-National Republic of Bolivia and Ecuador.

23 The earlier version of this chapter, "Travelling Policy Ideas: Integrating the Social into CEPAL's Neo-Structuralist Discourse," presented at the annual meetings of the International Studies Association, San Francisco, April 2013, included a section on this, cut to reduce the manuscript to a manageable length. I will develop it into a stand-alone paper in the near future.

24 I did not have space to include a discussion of the ways in which CEPAL has worked to translate social cohesion into terms that made sense in a region where the problem was not Europe's "two-thirds" society but a deeper one involving a majority of the population. For insight into some of this work, see *Social Cohesion in Latin America: Concepts, Frames of Reference, and Indicators* (CEPAL 2010b). Of particular interest, however, is the redefinition that appears in Hopenhayn (2007), cited earlier, which opened the way to talking about universality and (racial-ethnic) difference.

25 On the latter, see Ban (2013); Berg (2011); and Huber and Stephens (2012).

References

Ban, Cornel. 2013. "Brazil's Liberal Neo-Developmentalism: New Paradigm or Edited Orthodoxy?" *Review of International Political Economy* 20, 2: 298–331. http://dx.doi.org/10.1080/09692290.2012.660183.

Berg, Janine. 2011. "Laws or Luck? Understanding Rising Formality in Brazil in the 2000s." In *Regulating for Decent Work: New Directions in Labour Market Regulation,* edited by Sangheon Lee and Deirdre McCann, 123-47. New York: ILO and Palgrave Macmillan.

Best, Jacqueline. 2014. *Governing Failure: Provisional Expertise and the Transformation of Global Development Finance.* Cambridge, UK: Cambridge University Press.

Bielschowsky, Ricardo. 2009. "Sixty Years of ECLAC: Structuralism and Neo-Structuralism." *CEPAL Review* 97: 171–92.

Cardoso, Fernando. 1977. "The Originality of a Copy: CEPAL and the Idea of Development." *CEPAL Review* 4: 7–40.

Carroll, Eero, and Joakim Palme. 2006. "Inclusion of the European Nordic Model in the Debate: Concerning Social Protection Reform: The Long-Term Development of Nordic Welfare Systems (1890–2005) and Their Transferability to Latin America in the 21st Century." Special Studies Unit, Executive Secretary's Office, CEPAL.

Cecchini, Simone, and Rodrigo Mártinez. 2012. *Inclusive Social Protection in Latin America: A Comprehensive Rights-Based Approach.* UN LC/G.2488-P. Santiago: United Nations. http://dx.doi.org/10.2139/ssrn.2009321.

CEPAL. 1990. *Changing Production Patterns with Social Equity.* Santiago: United Nations.

–. 1998. *The Fiscal Covenant: Strengths, Weaknesses, Challenges* (summary). UN LC/G 2024. Santiago: United Nations.

–. 2000a. *The Equity Gap: A 2nd Assessment.* Second regional conference in follow-up to the World Summit for Social Development, Santiago, 15–17 May. UN LC/G 2096. Santiago: United Nations.

–. 2000b. *Social Panorama of Latin America and the Caribbean 1999–2000.* Santiago: United Nations.

–. 2001. *Equity, Development, and Citizenship.* Abridged ed. LC/G.2133-P. Santiago: United Nations.

–. 2004a. *Social Panorama of Latin America and the Caribbean: A Decade of Social Development in Latin America 1990–1999.* UN LC/G.2212-P. Santiago: United Nations.

–. 2004b. *Productive Development in Open Economies* (summary). UN LC/G.2247 (SES 30/4). Santiago: United Nations.

–. 2006. *Shaping the Future of Social Protection: Access, Financing, and Solidarity* (summary). UN LC/G2295 (SES 31/4). Santiago: United Nations.

–. 2010a. *Time for Equality: Closing Gaps, Opening Trails.* Prepared for the 33rd Session of ECLAC, Brasilia, 30 May–1 June. UN LC/G.2432 (SES 33/3). Santiago: United Nations.

–. 2010b. *Social Cohesion in Latin America: Concepts, Frames of Reference, and Indicators.* Santiago: United Nations.

Economist. "Latin America: GINI Back in the Bottle: An Unequal Continent Is Becoming Less So." *Economist,* 13 October 2012, www.economist.com/new/special-report/21564411-unequal-continent-becoming-less-so-gini-back-bottle.

Fajnzylber, Fernando. 1983. *La industrialización trunca de América Latina.* Mexico, FD: Editorial Nueva Imágen.

Filgueira, Fernando. 2005. *Welfare and Democracy in Latin America: The Development, Crises, and Aftermath of Universal, Dual, and Exclusionary Social States.* Geneva: UNRISD.

Frank, André Gunder. 1966. *The Development of Underdevelopment.* New York: Monthly Review Press.

Gabay, Ruth Eliana. 2008. "Revistando a Raúl Prebisch al paper de la CEPAL en las ciencas socials de América Latine." *Íconos (Quito)* 31: 103–13.

Hopenhayn, Martin. 2001. "Old and New Forms of Citizenship." *CEPAL Review* 73: 115-26.

–. 2007. "Cohesión social: Una perspective en proceso de elaboración." In *Cohesión social en América Latina y el Caribe: Una revisión perentoria de algunas dimensiones,* edited by Ana Sojo and Andreas Utoff, 37–47. Documentos de proyecto, CEPAL. Santiago, Chile: CEPAL.

Huber, Evelyne, and John D. Stephens. 2012. *Democracy and the Left: Social Policy and Inequality in Latin America.* Chicago: University of Chicago Press. http://dx.doi.org/10.7208/chicago/9780226356556.001.0001.

Jenson, Jane. 2010. "Diffusing Ideas after Neoliberalism: The Social Investment Perspective in Europe and Latin America." *Global Social Policy* 10, 1: 59–84. http://dx.doi.org/10.1177/1468018109354813.

Korpi, Walter, and Joakim Palme. 1998. "The Paradox of Redistribution and Strategies of Equality: Welfare State Institutions, Inequality, and Poverty in the Western Countries." *American Sociological Review* 63, 5: 661–87. http://dx.doi.org/10.2307/2657333.

Leiva, Fernando Ignacio. 2008. *Latin American NeoStructuralism: The Contradictions of Post-Neoliberal Development.* Minneapolis: University of Minnesota Press.

Morais, L., and A. Saad-Filha. 2012. "Neo-Developmentalism and the Challenge of Economic Policy Making under Dilma Rouseff." *Critical Sociology* 38, 6: 789–98. http://dx.doi.org/10.1177/0896920512441635.

Ozkan, Umut Riza. 2014. "Comparing Formal Unemployment Compensation Systems in 15 OECD Countries." *Journal of Social Policy and Administration* 48, 1: 44–60.

Perez, Carlota. 2001. "Technical Change and Opportunities for Development as a Moving Target." *CEPAL Review* 75: 109–30.

Pollock, David, Daniel Kerner, and Joseph L. Love. 2001. "Raúl Prebisch on ECLAC's Achievements and Deficiencies: An Unpublished Interview." *CEPAL Review* 75: 9–22.

Sanchez, Omar. 2011. "Fighting Tax Evasion in Latin America: Contrasting Strategies of Chile and Argentina." *Third World Quarterly* 32, 6: 1107–25. http://dx.doi.org/10.1080/01436597.2011.584724.

Sikkink, Kathryn. 1991. *Ideas and Institutions: Developmentalism in Brazil and Argentina.* Ithaca: Cornell University Press.

Rianne Mahon

9

The Impact of the Global Financial Crisis on Mexican Social Policy

LUCY LUCCISANO AND LAURA MACDONALD

After decades of social and political stability in the post-revolutionary period, Mexico has been rocked by multiple economic crises since the 1980s. The most prominent were the debt crisis of 1981, the peso crisis of 1995, and the most recent crisis precipitated by the global recession of 2008–9. Each crisis has been followed by fundamental shifts in social policy. Indeed, social policy can be seen as a key tool used by the Mexican state to promote social stability and to protect the interests of the political class in the face of recurrent crises. Nevertheless, successive attempts to re-engineer the social protection system have failed to make a real difference in addressing the entrenched levels of poverty and inequality that have accompanied the Mexican state's commitment to neo-liberal policies since the early 1980s.

Mexico was the Latin American country hardest hit by the most recent crisis, with a GDP of −6.2 percent in 2009 (compared with the much more manageable declines in growth in Brazil and Argentina). There was a subsequent bounce-back, with a growth rate of 5.5 percent in 2010 and Mexico outpacing growth in Brazil and Argentina in 2011 and 2012. Declarations that Mexico was roaring back to renewed levels of economic success (the country was labelled the "Aztec Tiger" by the *Financial Times*) have been belied by the subsequent sputtering of the economy. Since President Enrique Peña Nieto assumed power in January 2013, there has also been a renewed political crisis, with allegations of corruption and allegations of government complicity. The most well-known example is the September 26, 2014, kidnapping/disappearance of 43 students from the Ayotzinapa Normal School in Guerrero. In 2014, the

Ministry of Finance indicated that the growth rate for 2013 was 1.3 percent, the slowest rate of expansion since the 2009 recession (Harrup 2014). This was a significant contrast to the previous forecast of 3.1 percent (Flannery 2013). In response to the economic crisis, the president has adopted changes to the country's social policy model, launching the "Crusade against Hunger" program shortly after taking office.

The key turning point for Mexican social policy occurred after the debt crisis of the early 1980s, which led to a shift away from the model of social spending that had characterized Mexico since the 1940s. In that system, relatively generous benefits were tied to employment in the formal sector and to support for the dominant political party, the Partido Revolucionario Institucional (PRI). Since the crisis, successive Mexican administrations have experimented with various methods of alleviating extreme poverty while maintaining orthodox neo-liberal macroeconomic policies. After a period of experimentation with a highly politicized form of social spending under President Carlos Salinas (1988–1994), his successor, President Ernesto Zedillo (1994–2000), implemented the much-touted conditional cash transfer (CCT) program Progresa (renamed Oportunidades in 2002 and Prospera in 2014). This program was devised as much to break the model of clientelistic social policy that the PRI had perfected in previous decades as to break the intergenerational cycle of poverty. The former goal was to be achieved through careful objective measurement and identification of people living in extreme poverty, whereas the latter goal reflected the social investment paradigm (Jenson and Saint-Martin 2006) and was to be achieved through guaranteeing school attendance, health care, and nutrition for the children of the very poor.

What does Mexico's experience of social policy reform since the financial crisis tell us about middle-income developing states? First, the Mexican case confirms the fact (discussed in the introduction to this volume) that there have been multiple financial crises and that the 2008 crisis was not necessarily the most important in the recent evolution of social policies in the developing world. Second, it confirms the diversity of ways in which states have been affected, even within Latin America. Mexico was hit harder by the crisis than other states in the region and responded in different ways. Third, the heavy impact of the crisis in Mexico highlights the problems with neo-liberal economic and social policies. Mexico was particularly affected by the 2008 crisis partly because of its high levels of integration with the United States that resulted from signing the neo-liberal North American Free Trade Agreement (NAFTA) in 1994. The Mexican case also calls into question neo-liberal social policies based on targeting, since CCTs are fundamentally designed to address the causes of poverty over the long term and lack a mechanism to respond to short-term economic crises.

We begin this chapter by describing the impact of the global financial crisis on Mexico and explore the reasons for its severity there. Next we outline the evolution of Mexican social policy since 1988, and we review changes in social policy since the return to power of the PRI, led by Peña Nieto. We conclude by revisiting some of the questions raised in this volume regarding the relationship between welfare states and crisis in a developing country context.

Impact of the 2008 Global Financial Crisis in Mexico

As discussed above, the most important financial crisis in recent Mexican history was the 1980s debt crisis, which fundamentally reshaped economic and social policies based on import-substituting industrialization (ISI). Mexico was the first country to face crisis in the 1980s as a result of its inability to service its debt, and it was one of the first developing countries to adopt neo-liberal solutions to the crisis, in return for renewed financial support from the United States Treasury and the International Monetary Fund (IMF). In the aftermath of the debt crisis of the 1980s, Mexico experienced the "roll-back" stage of neo-liberalization (Peck and Tickell 2002), with significant cuts in social spending and dramatic increases in poverty and dispossession undertaken by the PRI, which had been the architect of state-sponsored industrialization.[1] Mexico also went through a deep economic crisis in 1995, shortly after President Zedillo assumed power, leading to a fundamental rethinking of social provision.

The impact of the 2008–9 global financial crisis varied widely across Latin America, with some countries experiencing severe declines in annual GDP in the year that the crisis hit (Mexico, −6.0 percent; Paraguay, −4.9 percent; Venezuela, −3.2 percent) and others sustaining positive growth (Colombia, +1.7 percent; Bolivia, +3.45 percent; Panama, +3.85 percent) (Freije-Rodriguez and Facchini 2013, 7). Unemployment and informal employment increased rapidly after the onset of the crisis in late 2008: open unemployment peaked at 6.4 percent by September 2009, a level twice as high as that in May 2008 (Moreno-Brid 2010, 5). Several reasons both external and internal to Mexico account for why the crisis was so intense in Mexico compared with other countries in the region.

First, particularly since the signing of NAFTA in 1994, the Mexican economy has been closely tied to the US economy and thus much more vulnerable to its economic fluctuations. Mexico's level of export dependence has increased dramatically in recent years, with exports representing 26 percent of the Mexican

GDP in 2009 and 80 percent of those exports destined for the United States (Villareal 2010, 2). Exports soared in the years after NAFTA was signed, but imports increased at a higher rate, while the decline of internal forward and backward linkages undermined the capacity of export growth to sustain high levels of growth (Moreno-Brid 2010, 4).

The downturn in the US economy thus hit Mexican exports hard: total exports declined by 21.5 percent and foreign direct investment contracted by 42.5 percent in 2009 (Villareal 2010, 7–10). The biggest impact was on the manufacturing sector on the US-Mexican border, with automobile production, construction, and tourism hardest hit (*Economist* 2009). Oil exports also declined dramatically (with quarterly rates of −50.3 percent in the fourth quarter of 2008 and 25.7 percent in the first quarter of 2009). The decline in oil revenues had a negative effect on Mexico's balance of payments and reduced the revenue available for public spending, since oil revenues finance about 40 percent of Mexico's public sector revenues. Total public sector revenues represented 22.4 percent of GDP in 2009, compared with 23.6 percent in 2008 (Moreno-Brid 2010, 5–6). Even several years after the crisis, Mexico continues to suffer from the lack of sustained recovery in the United States. An impressive recovery occurred between 2010 and 2012, and both the Mexican government and the IMF issued confident statements about the country's capacity to weather the global economic crisis (IMF 2010). At the beginning of 2013, however, just after President Peña Nieto assumed power, sluggish sales to the United States contributed to a reduction of growth rates to just 0.8 percent compared with the same period in 2012 (*Economist* 2013).

Another important cause of the strong impact of the Mexican crisis is the country's financial dependence on remittances sent home by migrants to the United States. Remittances are the second most important source of Mexican income after oil. Mexican and Central American immigrants to the United States suffered higher levels of unemployment than other foreign-born and native-born workers after the recession hit (Orozco 2009, 8; also see Villareal 2010, 12–13). As a result, the amount of remittances sent to Mexico declined 20 percent from the second quarter of 2008 to the first quarter of 2009, and the percentage of Mexican families receiving remittances fell from 4.3 percent to 3.4 percent. Remittances represent approximately 38 percent of the total income of these families (Alcarez, Chiquiar, and Salcedo 2012).

Second, it has been argued that domestic Mexican policies have exacerbated the crisis. Orthodox neo-liberal policies meant that the country has been slow to adopt countercyclical policies that would reduce the impact of the crisis and contribute to recovery. Vidal, Marshall, and Correa (2011) argue that the

Mexican government responded to the crisis by attempting to protect the country's elite by maintaining low levels of taxation, promoting privatization and deregulation of the banking sector, and making cuts in spending, policies that are pro-cyclical in their impacts. Mexico's research director for the United Nations Economic Commission for Latin America and the Caribbean (ECLAC), Juan Carlos Moreno-Brid, also points to the country's devotion to neo-liberal orthodoxy as a key factor in explaining the severity of the crisis. In March 2006, for example, the Mexican Congress approved the Law for Fiscal Responsibility, which required the government to maintain a zero fiscal balance. The Mexican Central Bank was also granted autonomy, with the central mandate of maintaining low and stable levels of inflation (Moreno-Brid 2010, 3). The combination of a volatile exchange rate and stock market and uncertainty regarding US recovery led the private sector to postpone or cancel various investment projects. According to Moreno-Brid (2010, 6), total investment declined by 10 percent in real terms in 2009. As this critical evaluation by an ECLAC analyst shows, Mexico's policies deviate substantially from the type of policy advocated by ECLAC, as discussed in the chapter by Rianne Mahon in this volume.

The Mexican government only slowly and moderately turned to modest countercyclical policies. The government's initial response to the crisis was to argue that Mexico's "solid macroeconomic fundamentals" would shield the country from the potentially destabilizing effects of the US economic downturn. In 2009, however, the Mexican Congress modified the Law of Fiscal Responsibility to permit moderately expansionary fiscal policies as well as to permit investment in the expansion and modernization of the oil industry (Moreno-Brid 2010, 11). Stimulus measures adopted in the aftermath of the crisis included creation of a National Infrastructure Fund; creation of the Program of Support to the Economy, Investment, and Employment in March 2008; support for small and micro-enterprise development; support for the state-owned oil company PEMEX; reduced gasoline and electricity prices; and expansion of a temporary employment program (ILO 2010).

Low levels of taxation also limited the country's capacity to respond to the crisis. Mexico traditionally has had one of the lowest levels of taxation in Latin America. Whereas Brazil collected taxes equivalent to 26.7 percent of GDP in 2008, Mexico collected 8.1 percent, lower than the amounts of many Central American states. The country's largest companies contribute less than 2 percent of their earnings to taxation (Vidal, Marshall, and Correa 2011, 429). According to a *Forbes* report, Carlos Slim, who earned the title of the world's richest man for the fourth consecutive year in 2013, increased his net worth by $4 billion over the previous year (Flannery 2013). Meanwhile, the country's security crisis continues to restrict foreign direct investment while leading to enormous costs in military and police spending on fighting drug trafficking, estimated at $60 billion by the end of President Calderón's term (Castañeda 2012, 2). According to Amnesty International (2013, 177), during the Calderón period, 60,000 people were killed and 150,000 displaced as a result of drug-related violence.

Social Impacts of the Financial Crisis

The 2008 global financial crisis had severe effects on levels of poverty and inequality in Mexico, though recovery has been quicker than during earlier crises, and there has not been as dramatic an impact on the design of social policy. Poverty levels spiked alarmingly after the 2008 crisis from 48.8 million people to 52.0 million people living in poverty in 2010. In 2004, the Mexican government established the National Council for the Evaluation of Social Development Policy (CONEVAL) to evaluate the country's social programs and progress on alleviating poverty. Although it is located in the Ministry of Social Development, it was granted significant autonomy from the government. CONEVAL data indicate that, between 2010 and 2012, Mexico's poverty rate dropped slightly, by 0.6 percent, from 46.1 percent to 45.5 percent. Nevertheless, though this was a period of apparent economic recovery, the absolute number of people living in poverty actually increased, from 52.8 million to 53.3 million, because of the increase in the population (CONEVAL 2012).

Mexican federal policies clearly have helped to mitigate the effects of globalization and the recent global financial crisis for the poorest members of society. For example, the increase in the levels of poverty in the post-2008 period was less than the dramatic decline in growth in 2009 (CONEVAL 2012, 188), partly because of the increases in social spending and the admission of new beneficiaries into the Seguro Popular (health insurance) and the Seventy and More pension program before 2008. In the past ten years, social spending has increased slightly above the level of GDP growth. However, according to an evaluation of the Mexican social protection system commissioned by ECLAC, the increase in social spending related to GDP in 2009 was mainly due to the large fall in GDP in that year (–6.1 percent) rather than to a significant increase in social spending (Lomelí, Rodríguez, and Weber 2011, 29–30).

A disturbing aspect of the new CONEVAL data is that they show that, though there has been a long-term decline in levels of extreme poverty and a recovery from the 2009 recession, poverty as measured solely by income continues to increase. That is, though poor Mexicans have increased access to social services such as education, housing, and health care (albeit often of very low quality), their incomes have not been rising as quickly as prices (see CONEVAL 2012, 23).

A 2012 report from CONEVAL states that, despite the efforts of the federal government to address the social crisis discussed below, these actions were not able to contain the increase in levels of poverty because of several aspects of the crisis: increasing food prices, declining wages, and diminishing remittances (54–55). CONEVAL notes the lack of instruments available to protect the most vulnerable from short-term economic fluctuations. Particularly problematic is the lack of unemployment insurance programs (55). As the report points out, Oportunidades, Mexico's most important anti-poverty program, was designed to break the intergenerational cycle of poverty over the long term and is mostly directed at residents of rural areas, whereas the recent crisis affected mostly citizens in urban areas and in the border region with the United States.

Wilson and Silva (2013) argue that the poor have not benefited as much as the wealthy from the modest recovery that has occurred since the crisis for two main reasons. First, food prices have been rising much faster than overall inflation, and the poor tend to spend a larger percentage of their earnings on food than the rich. Second, the modest growth of income, which averaged 1.5 percent between 2010 and 2012, has been unequally distributed. In fact, the income of the poorest decile of the population experienced the highest rates of growth, but the income of the poor in deciles 3, 4, and 5 declined while food prices rose. Although the income of the middle class has declined, the income of the wealthy has risen (Wilson and Silva 2013, 5) (see Table 9.1).

These figures suggest that the innovations in social policy in Mexico in recent decades have acted to protect the extreme poor from the worst effects of the crisis and that the effects of the most recent crisis on poverty levels were much less extreme than those experienced after the 1995 crisis. Nevertheless, reforms need to be undertaken in fiscal and labour market policy, including raising the minimum wage, in order to address the situation of citizens experiencing moderate poverty and the growth of the informal sector.

Crisis and Reform in Mexico's Social Protection System

As discussed above, Mexico's social protection system has undergone many changes since the onset of the debt crisis of 1981–82. The Mexican state adopted a system of social protection after the revolution of 1910–20 that was a compromise between state actors and organized labour. The IMSS (Mexican Social Security Institute) was created in 1943 for private sector workers, and in 1959

Table 9.1

Total household income by deciles of the Mexican population (pesos, average quarterly income)

Household decile	National total			Percent change	
	2008	2010	2012	2008–10	2010–12
Total	42,865	37,574	38,125	−12.3	1.5
1	7,136	6,633	6,997	−7.0	5.5
2	12,460	11,673	11,794	−6.3	1.0
3	16,792	15,611	15,734	−7.0	0.8
4	20,986	19,650	19,513	−6.4	−0.7
5	25,628	23,973	23,914	−6.5	−0.2
6	31,501	29,059	28,862	−7.8	−0.7
7	39,381	35,605	35,570	−9.6	−0.1
8	50,084	45,089	44,849	−10.0	−0.5
9	69,159	61,133	61,014	−11.6	−0.2
10	155,525	127,313	133,003	−18.1	4.5

Note: Income deciles result from ranking all households in the population in ascending order according to income and then dividing the population into ten equal groups, each comprising approximately 10 percent of the total population. The first decile contains the poorest 10 percent, and the tenth decile contains the richest 10 percent.

Source: Wilson and Silva (2013, 7).

the ISSSTE (Institute for Social Security and Services for State Workers) was established for state employees. The post-revolutionary social protection system in Mexico shared much in common with welfare regimes in other Latin American countries, such as Argentina, Chile, and Uruguay. This system protected the (male) breadwinner through occupationally stratified social insurance schemes and job protection. Benefits provided included only old age and disability pensions, health care, work-related injury compensation, and illness insurance and did not include unemployment insurance or family allowance (Dion 2005, 61). Also, in contrast with the European Bismarckian regimes, these benefits rarely reached workers in the informal sector. Barrientos (2004) called this system "conservative-informal" (also see Lopreite and Macdonald 2014). Carmelo Mesa-Lago (1989, 154) documents that in 1983 "forty percent of the total population and sixty percent of the economically active population (EAP) were not covered by social security." In 2009, IMSS covered about 40 percent of the Mexican population, and ISSSTE provided coverage for 6 percent (Aguila and Kapteyn 2012).

Social policies had a strong political logic and were designed to entrench in power the dominant party (the PRI) by delivering benefits to selected sectors of the population organized into corporatist organizations (labour, peasants, and the middle class) in return for political support. These policies reached only a small segment of the population; at their highest point in 1980, they included only 27 percent of the wage-earning population (de la Garza, Melgoza, and Compillo 1999, 249). Also, import substituting industrialization (ISI) programs were designed to reduce poverty gradually through high levels of growth. Non-contributory social insurance assistance benefits were provided to the rural poor in 1973 under IMSS-COPLAMAR (National Program for Depressed Areas and Marginal Groups). The benefits included pensions and health care. The IMSS-COPLAMAR program was mainly funded through the IMSS pension reserves (Dion 2008, 436). Beginning with PIDER (the Rural Development Investment Program) in 1970, COPLAMAR and later SAM (Mexican Food System) in 1980–82, these programs were designed to channel government resources to rural areas to increase the production of staple grains to support domestic consumption.

The post-revolutionary system of social protection underwent dramatic reform, however, with the adoption of neo-liberal economic policies in the 1980s and 1990s that maintained some aspects of the post-revolutionary system of social provision but moved closer to what Barrientos (2004) calls a liberal-informal regime. Structural adjustment programs adopted under IMF and World Bank tutelage initially promoted deep cuts in existing social programs aimed at the poor, though organized workers who did not lose their jobs maintained relatively high levels of benefits through the IMSS and ISSSTE systems. These cuts led to a rapid increase in levels of poverty and inequality and threatened to undermine the control of the dominant party.

Subsequently, PRI governments experimented with a series of different social programs designed to guarantee social peace while maintaining a strong commitment to neo-liberalism. These experiments were based on a shift away from a social insurance model that provided coverage to all formal sector workers and toward social assistance–type programs targeted to the poor. According to Dion (2008, 435), the shift also reflected the increased infor-malization of the labour market: "Rather than try to incorporate more workers into the formal labour market and universalize social insurance coverage, the new emphasis on social assistance provides residual, means-tested benefits to those at the margins of the formal labour market."

The first such program, the National Solidarity Program (PRONASOL), was introduced by President Salinas in an effort to win popular support and defuse tensions emerging from the neo-liberal reforms. PRONASOL supported public works and social welfare projects such as school repairs, road paving, electricity, water, sewage, and health, theoretically designed to improve poor communities' living standards without requiring ongoing subsidies like those delivered during the populist era (Bruhn 1996). This program was designed to improve the efficiency of social spending by replacing universal benefits with targeted programs. Nevertheless, the program quickly became subject to widespread criticism because the projects were often wasteful and funds were directed to foster PRI political support rather than on the basis of community need (Grimes and Wängnerud 2009).

The next crisis, which erupted shortly after Salinas left power, led to a more technocratic approach to poverty alleviation. The government of Ernesto Zedillo launched a new program, Progresa, in 1997, designed to avoid the pitfalls of PRONASOL while maintaining the emphasis on targeting and introducing a focus on human capital development. Progresa was a CCT program designed to promote human capital development by delivering cash stipends to mothers in carefully identified extremely poor families. In return for this support, mothers had to ensure that their children were attending school and health clinics regularly (Luccisano 2006; also see Molyneux 2006). This program represented a step toward the depoliticization of social policy, since beneficiaries were selected through an elaborate social census rather than through their affiliation with the governing party. The program was viewed as being so successful that it was maintained and rebranded Oportunidades by the new government of Vicente Fox after the PRI was displaced by the National Action Party (PAN) in the 2000 elections and maintained by the subsequent PAN government of Felipe Calderón (2006–12). In 2014, Peña Nieto renamed the program Prospera.

After the global financial crisis erupted in 2008, the Calderón government's first response was to expand Oportunidades. Under Calderón's administration, three new components were added to the program, which diluted the initial social investment logic: cash transfers to seniors in 2006, an energy subsidy in 2007 (in response to rising oil prices), and a Food Assistance Program (PAL) that began in 2010. PAL provides cash transfers for food purchases to 700,000 poor families in remote locations that did not qualify for Oportunidades benefits. The budget for Oportunidades for 2010 was almost US$5 billion, representing a 23.3 percent increase from the 2009 budget (Enciso 2010, 14). The 2010 budget for PAL was US$4 million. Oportunidades and PAL supported a total of 6.5 million families or 32.5 million Mexicans (Enciso 2010, 14). These budgetary increases were a response, in part, to the international financial crisis but also took place during an important election year in Mexico, in which elections took place at the subnational level across the country, providing incentives for a return to political manipulation of social policies (Luccisano and Macdonald 2012).

The tendency toward proliferation and repoliticization of social programs has apparently multiplied since the return to power of the PRI with the election of Enrique Peña Nieto in July 2012. A scandal early in his term appears to confirm the fears of many that the return of the PRI would lead to the resurgence of corrupt and clientelistic practices. The minister of the Secretariat of Social Development (SEDESOL), Rosario Robles, fired six employees in the state of Veracruz, governed by the PRI, and suspended her department's chief representative in the state after the media revealed taped discussions by SEDESOL officials about how to use anti-poverty programs, including Oportunidades, to promote the PRI's prospects in upcoming local elections (Stevenson 2013).

In January 2013, Peña Nieto launched what he called the most important social program of his government, the National Crusade Against Hunger. The program, expected to cost 3 billion pesos or $250 million, seems to have removed Oportunidades from the media spotlight, even though Oportunidades remains in place. The program is designed to eliminate hunger through adequate nutrition for those in extreme poverty who lack access to food, eliminate infant malnutrition and improve weight and height indicators among children, increase food production and the income of farmers and small-scale producers, minimize loss of crops, and promote community participation (México 2013).

The National Crusade Against Hunger program claims that it will reconnect the farmer with the urban food system, and multinational companies such as Nestlé, Coca-Cola, PepsiCo, Walmart, and Bimbo have been invited to participate. The program thus represents an attempt to introduce public-private partnership into the campaign to reduce hunger.

The program aims to reach 7.4 million Mexicans in the 400 municipalities with the highest levels of hunger and poverty. Some observers have charged, however, that the program displays a return to the PRI's clientelistic past, since many of the 400 municipalities would not qualify as being among the poorest in the country, including cities in the state of Baja California, where the poverty rate is only 3.5 percent, compared with some municipalities in the south of the country, where almost the whole population would qualify as being poor. Baja California at this time was the site, however, of a closely contested gubernatorial election in which the PRI was hoping to displace the PAN government.[2] Mexico City, a PRD (Party of the Democratic Revolution) stronghold, was also included even though levels of extreme poverty are low there ("La Cruzada" 2013).

The involvement of food multinationals such as PepsiCo and Nestlé has also resulted in considerable criticism since the program is being launched at a time when there are serious concerns over morbid obesity and diabetes in Mexico (Carlsen 2011). Basic dependence on food imports is very high – 80 percent in rice, 95 percent in soybeans, 33 percent in beans, and 56 percent in wheat – and Mexico is the top importer of powdered milk (Carlsen 2011). Former PRD deputy Yazmin Copete Zapot charged that these companies "in the last 25 years destroyed the bases of food security and destroyed the production of white corn." Las Abejas, a civil society organization of Tzotzil Maya, has stated that "the Crusade is supported by transnationals that carry off our riches, the same transnationals that are the cause of our country's hunger." In addition, Las Abejas said, "with the Crusade the preferred weapon of the current government has shifted from 'lead bullets' to 'sugar bullets'" (Hershaw 2013).

The government intends to finance expanded social policies through fiscal reforms. Changes to the tax system include the elimination of many exemptions that favour the richest Mexicans; new taxes on capital gains, carbon emissions, and soft drinks; and increased income taxes for those making over US$39,000 a year. The government suggests that the revenue generated would pay for a new universal pension for all Mexicans over sixty-five, a new unemployment insurance scheme, and more spending on schools and infrastructure (Malkin 2013).

In some ways, Peña Nieto's social policy reforms signal a return to the old way of doing social politics in Mexico. The National Crusade Against Hunger has been suspected of permitting a renewed politicization of social policy since it moves away from targeting extremely poor individuals and toward focusing on communities and since the criteria for the selection of communities are vague and apparently open to manipulation to benefit the governing party. The program also appears to represent a return to a focus on agricultural production, similar to some of the rural development programs of the pre–debt crisis period. However, the fact that Oportunidades continues to exist and has received a new injection of funds from the Inter-American Development Bank (IDB) indicates that these very different social policy logics will coexist for some time (IDB 2013).

Peña Nieto's fiscal reform was only one of the dozen reform bills passed in the Mexican Congress in 2013, including bills on energy, telecommunications, and education. There has been mixed reaction to the reforms. The international edition of *Time* (February 2014) featured Peña Nieto on the front cover with the caption "Saving Mexico," and Moody's upgraded Mexico to an A grade sovereign rating. However, within Mexico, there was immediate criticism in the social media circuit, and alternative slogans such as "Slaying Mexico" and "Sinking Mexico" reflected widespread cynicism about Peña Nieto's reforms.

Conclusion

This review of the impact of the global financial crisis of 2008–9 on social policy in Mexico points to some important lessons. The Mexican case is distinct from most of the countries in Latin America, and Mexico was hit harder by the crisis than other countries in the region. This was partly a result of Mexico's proximity to the United States and its high level of dependence on US trade and investment and remittances from Mexicans working there. However, the harsh impact of the crisis also relates to the Mexican state's enthusiastic maintenance of Washington Consensus–type policies, even in a supposedly post–Washington Consensus period. Orthodox macroeconomic policies, privatization, and the failure of fiscal reform left the country particularly vulnerable to the economic downturn.

The impact of the crisis was felt most directly by the moderately poor since social policy reform that had taken place since 1997 was able to mitigate the harsh effects of the crisis for the extremely poor. This reform instituted a new CCT approach to social policy based on the delivery of benefits to the very poor after their acceptance of several conditions. The impact of the crisis highlighted, however, some of the weaknesses of the CCT approach. Oportunidades was designed to reduce poverty over the long term through support for human capital development and had no countercyclical mechanism built into it. Mexico, like other Latin American states, was able to expand its CCT program in response to the crisis, but this response had clear limitations. As Robert Zoellick, president of the World Bank, boasted to the Inter-American Dialogue's Thirtieth Anniversary dinner, "these [CCTs] are safety net programs that appeal to a fiscal conservative. They cost only about half a percent of GDP" (2012, 3). In order to achieve more stable and long-term reductions of poverty and inequality, Mexico needs to move toward less cheap forms of social policy and labour market reform. As discussed in the chapter by Cook and Lam on China, this failure also has implications for the country's long-term social stability.

The existing model of social protection in Mexico is a hybrid version, based on the coexistence of older and newer styles of policy. The old corporatist social insurance programs based on the conservative informal model persist, providing expensive social benefits to workers in the formal sector. Onto this old system has been grafted more liberal forms of social benefits to the very poor, who were previously excluded, in the form of conditional cash transfers. And, since the most recent financial crisis, Peña Nieto has created a new social policy initiative that in some ways represents a return to some aspects of the post-revolutionary system by moving away from targeting extremely poor individuals and toward support for farmers and communities and to more politicized and clientelistic forms of social policy. Overall, the global financial crisis appears to have resulted in greater policy incoherence than any clear movement toward a new model of social provision that will address the persistence of high levels of poverty in Mexico.

Acknowledgments

We thank Leanne MacDonald and Sophie O'Manique for their research assistance on this chapter and the Social Sciences and Humanities Research Council of Canada and Carleton University for their financial assistance. We thank Wilfrid Laurier University for its financial assistance through the Undergraduate Research Assistantship. We also thank Stephen McBride and the participants in the McMaster University workshop The Crisis and Global Social Policy for their helpful comments on an earlier draft of this chapter.

Notes

1 Peck and Tickell (2002) argue that the "roll-back" stage of destruction and cutbacks during the 1980s was followed by a more creative "roll-out" phase during the 1990s and beyond, a period of creation and invention of new forms of neo-liberalized governance. The invention of CCTs in Mexico in the 1990s discussed below corresponds to this second phase.
2 The PRI's bid was ultimately unsuccessful, and the outcome was the election of a PAN-PRD coalition government.

References

Aguila, Emma, and Arie Kapteyn. 2012. "Chance of a Generation." *Rand Review* 36, 1. http://www.rand.org/pubs/periodicals/rand-review/issues/2012/spring.html.

Alcaraz, Carlo, Daniel Chiquiar, and Alejandrina Salcedo. 2012. "Remittances, Schooling, and Child Labor in Mexico." *Journal of Development Economics* 97, 1: 156–65. http://dx.doi.org/10.1016/j.jdeveco.2010.11.004.

Amnesty International. 2013. "Amnesty International Report 2013: The State of the World's Human Rights." https://docs.google.com/viewer?url=http://www.amnesty.ca/sites/default/files/air2013_english_embargoed_until_2301gmtwed22may2013_1.pdf.

"La Cruzada: Lo que se temía es realidad." 2013. *Sin Embargo*, 18 April. http://www.sinembargo.mx/opinion/18-04-2013/13838.

Barrientos, Armando. 2004. "Latin America: Towards a Liberal-Informal Welfare Regime." In *Insecurity and Welfare Regimes in Asia, Africa, and Latin America*, edited by Ian Gough, 121–68. Cambridge: Cambridge University Press.

Bruhn, K. 1996. "Social Spending and Political Support: The 'Lessons' of the National Solidarity Program in Mexico." *Comparative Politics* 28, 2: 151–77. http://dx.doi.org/10.2307/421979.

Carlsen, Laura. 2011. "NAFTA Is Starving Mexico." Americas Program. http://www.cipamericas.org/archives/5617.

Castañeda, Jorge. 2012. "Time for an Alternative to Mexico's Drug War." *Economic Development Bulletin* 16, 24 September. http://www.cato.org/publications/economic-development-bulletin/time-alternative-mexicos-drug-war.

Lucy Luccisano and Laura Macdonald

CONEVAL. 2012. *Informe de evaluación de la política de desarrollo social in México.* http://www.coneval.gob.mx/Informes/Evaluacion/IEPDS2012/Pages-IEPDSMex2012-12nov-VFinal_lowres6.pdf.

de la Garza, Enrique, Javier Melgoza, and Marcia Compillo. 1999. "Unions, Corporations, and the Industrial Relations System in Mexico." In *The State and Globalization: Comparative Studies of Labour and Capital in National Economies,* edited by Martin Upchurch, 248–68. London: Mansell Publishing.

Dion, Michelle L. 2005. "The Political Origins of Social Security in Mexico during the Cárdenas and Ávila Camacho Administrations." *Mexican Studies/Estudios Mexicanos* 21, 1: 59–95.

–. 2008. "Retrenchment, Expansion, and the Transformation of Mexican Social Protection Policies." *Social Policy and Administration* 42, 4: 434–50. http://dx.doi.org/10.1111/j.1467-9515.2008.00613.x.

Economist. 2009. "A Different Kind of Recession." 19 November. http://www.economist.com/node/14917758.

–. 2013. "Reality Bites." 25 May. http://www.economist.com/news/americas/21578440-lacklustre-growth-shows-need-reform-reality-bites.

Enciso, L. Angélica. 2010. "Sedeso anuncia programa de blindaje electoral." *La Jornada,* 22 April. http://www.jornada.unam.mx/2010/04/22/index.php?section=politica&article=014n3pol.

Flannery, Nathaniel Parish. 2013. "Mexico: Is the Aztec Tiger Starting to Whimper?" *Forbes,* 27 August. http://www.forbes.com/sites/nathanielparishflannery/2013/08/27/mexico-is-the-aztec-tiger-starting-to-whimper/.

Freije-Rodriguez, Samuel, and Gabriel Facchini. 2013. "Changes in Poverty and Inequality in Latin America during the Great Recession." Paper presented at the IZA Workshop on the Future of Labour, Bonn, Germany, February. http://www.iza.org/conference_files/FutureOfLabor_2013/freije-rodriguez_s4090.pdf.

Grimes, M., and L. Wängnerud. 2009. "Curbing Corruption through Social Welfare Reform? The Effects of Mexico's Conditional Cash Transfer Program on Good Government." Paper presented at the International Studies Association meeting, New York, 15–18 February.

Harrup, Anthony. 2014. "Mexico Says Economy Likely Grew 1.3% in 2013." *Wall Street Journal* http://www.wsj.com/news/articles/SB10001424052702303743604579353773863237480.

Hershaw, Eva. 2013. "Politics, Sugar Bullets, and Mexico's National Crusade Against Hunger." *Americas Program,* 6 July. http://www.cipamericas.org/archives/5617.

ILO. 2010. "Mexico's Response to the Crisis. G20 Country Briefs. G20 Meeting of Labour and Employment Ministers 20–21 April." http://www.ilo.org/public/libdoc/jobcrisis/download/g20_mexico_countrybrief.pdf.

IMF. 2010. "Mexico Recovering, but Crisis Spotlights Challenges, Says IMF." *IMF Survey,* 16 March. http://www.imf.org/external/pubs/ft/survey/so/2010/new031610a.htm.

Inter-American Development Bank (IDB). 2013. "News Release: Mexico to Receive $600 Million in IDB Financing for Oportunidades Program." 5 September. http://www.iadb.org/en/news/news-releases/2013-09-05/oportunidades-program-for-mexico,10557.html#.UkRtT2TF2UQ.

Jenson, Jane, and Denis Saint-Martin. 2006. "Building Blocks for a New Social Architecture: the Lego™ Paradigm of an Active Society." *Policy and Politics* 34, 3: 429–51. http://dx.doi.org/10.1332/030557306777695325.

Lomelí, E., D. Rodríguez, and D. Weber. 2011. "Sistema de protección social en México a inicios del siglo XXI: CEPAL." http://www.cepal.org/cgi-bin/getProd.asp?xml=%2F publicaciones%2Fsinsigla%2Fxml%2F8%2F43778%2FP43778.xml&xsl=%2F publicaciones%2Fficha.xsl&base=%2Fpublicaciones%2Ftop_publicaciones.xsl.

Lopreite, Débora, and Laura Macdonald. 2014. "Gender and Latin American Welfare Regimes: Early Childhood Education and Care Policies in Argentina and Mexico." *Social Politics* 21, 1: 80–102.

Luccisano, Lucy. 2006. "The Mexican Oportunidades Program: Questioning the Linking of Security to Conditional Social Investments for Mothers and Children." *Canadian Journal of Latin American and Caribbean Studies* 31, 62: 53–85. http://dx.doi.org/10. 1080/08263663.2006.10816902.

Luccisano, Lucy, and Laura Macdonald. 2012. "Neo-Liberalism, Semi-Clientelism, and the Politics of Scale in Mexican Anti-Poverty Policies." *World Political Science Review* 8, 1: 1–27. http://dx.doi.org/10.1515/wpsr-2012-0006.

Malkin, Elisabeth. 2013. "President of Mexico Proposes Tax Overhaul." *New York Times,* 8 September. http://www.nytimes.com/2013/09/09/world/americas/president-of-mexico -proposes-tax-overhaul.html?_r=0.

Mesa-Lago, Carmelo. 1989. *Ascent to Bankruptcy.* Pittsburgh: University of Pittsburgh Press.

México. Gobierno de la República. 2013. Sinhambre Cruzada Nacional. http://sinhambre. gob.mx/.

Molyneux, M. 2006. "Mothers at the Service of the New Poverty Agenda: Progresa/ Oportunidades, Mexico's Conditional Transfer Programme." *Social Policy and Administration* 40, 4: 425–49. http://dx.doi.org/10.1111/j.1467-9515.2006.00497.x.

Moreno-Brid, Juan Carlos. 2010. "The Mexican Economy and the International Financial Crisis." ECLAC. http://wiego.org/sites/wiego.org/files/publications/files/Moreno -Brid_Mexican.Economy.and_.Financial.Crisis.pdf.

Orozco, Manuel. 2009. "Migration and Remittances in Times of Recession: Effects on Latin American and Caribbean Economies." http://www.oecd.org/dev/americas/42753222. pdf.

Peck, Jamie, and Adam Tickell. 2002. "Neoliberalizing Space." *Antipode* 34, 3: 380–404. http://dx.doi.org/10.1111/1467-8330.00247.

Stevenson, M. 2013. "Mexico Fires Seven Officials in Alleged PRI Vote-Influence Scandal." *Huffington Post,* 18 April. http://www.huffingtonpost.com/2013/04/19/mexico-voting -scandal-seven-fired_n_3117311.html.

Vidal, Gregorio, Wesley C. Marshall, and Eugenia Correa. 2011. "Differing Effects of the Global Financial Crisis: Why Mexico Has Been Harder Hit than Other Large Latin American Countries." *Bulletin of Latin American Research* 30, 4: 419–35. http://dx.doi. org/10.1111/j.1470-9856.2010.00501.x.

Villareal, M. Angeles. 2010. "The Mexican Economy after the Global Financial Crisis." Congressional Research Service, 16 September. http://www.fas.org/sgp/crs/row/R41402. pdf.

Wilson, Christopher, and Gerardo Silva. 2013. "Mexico's Latest Poverty Stats." 12 August. http://www.wilsoncenter.org/article/mexicos-latest-poverty-stats.

Zoellick, Robert B. 2012. "Globalization: Made in the Americas." 7 June. http://www. worldbank.org/en/news/speech/2012/06/07/globalization-made-in-the-americas.

10

Social Policy in South Africa
Cushioning the Blow of the Recession?

MARLEA CLARKE

During the 2008 budget speech, the minister of finance, Trevor Manuel, warned South Africa to brace for a storm but indicated that the country was well positioned to weather the global economic crisis. Despite government predictions of positive economic growth, the economy shrank by 1.8 percent in the final quarter of 2008, officially plunging the economy into its first recession in twenty years. This chapter explores the global economic recession's impact on South Africa by exploring the links between social policy and labour markets. It suggests that social protection, especially the Child Support Grant, helped to mediate the effects of the crisis on poverty. However, though the current employment crisis in South Africa existed long before the 2008–9 global economic crisis, the recession has put the social security system under strain and exacerbated longstanding structural problems in the economy. Unemployment, already excessive by international standards, increased in the years following the crisis, and both unemployment (currently about 34.9 percent of the labour force, including "discouraged job seekers") and precarious, unprotected forms of employment have grown as a result of the recession. Unless the government responds to this crisis with a broader package of reforms, as in the late 1980s, the recession's long-term impact will be to escalate poverty and inequality – with major implications for consolidation of the country's democracy. Indeed, the wave of strikes throughout South Africa in 2012, beginning with the Marikana miners' strike, is one indication of growing social and political discontent. In addition to employment generating economic growth, this chapter argues that a new employment and social security framework is needed, one that understands risk, vulnerability, and insecurity along a continuum between formal and precarious employment.

The chapter is organized into four main sections, beginning with an overview of effects of the global economic crisis on South Africa and the government's response to the crisis. The next section explores the early development of social policy in South Africa and reforms introduced during the last decade of apartheid aimed at eliminating racial discrimination in welfare and social policies. The third section discusses contemporary social policies, followed by a section that examines the strengths and limitations of social protection by looking at the relationship between social protection and the labour market. It points to two key lessons that South Africa offers: social supports can be a critical buffer against increased poverty during periods of recession, but social policy alone – especially in the context of chronic unemployment – can do little to address inequality and systemic poverty.

The Global Economic Crisis and South Africa

South Africa has been resilient to the global financial crisis, in contrast to many countries, but it has been much harder hit than the rest of sub-Saharan Africa. South Africa's economy had been performing well in the years leading up to the 2008 economic crisis because of rising global prices of precious metals, iron ore, coal, and diamonds – some of the country's most important exports – but also because of increased investment. After several years of sluggish growth, the economy had picked up substantially by 2004 (though still trailing well behind the most dynamic emerging economies in the world, such as India and China; see Cook and Lam, this volume), and growth averaged about 5 percent annually through to 2007 (OECD 2008, 20–21). By early 2007, the economy was performing so well that Minister of Finance Manuel projected another year of increased public spending on social services and infrastructure, and, for the first time since 1994, the national government budgeted for a modest surplus (Steytler and Powell 2010). The economic situation and outlook changed dramatically with the global economic crisis in 2008. The economy shrank by 1.8 percent in the final quarter of 2008 and by 6.4 percent in the first three months of 2009, officially plunging it into a recession (Bell 2009).

The government responded by introducing a stimulus plan largely based on fiscal measures and an expansionary budget in 2009 that included funds aimed at infrastructure development (public transport, road and rail networks, schools, and various provincial infrastructure projects). Although the government's commitment to infrastructure projects predated the crisis and was largely

Marlea Clarke

linked to the FIFA World Cup, additional funds for infrastructure programs and a National Jobs Initiative were introduced to help save jobs in the mining and auto industries and other sectors already hard hit by the crisis. As discussed below, reforms were introduced to the Child Support Grant and the Old Age Pension in order to expand support to some of the most vulnerable groups. However, limited progress has been made in implementing new initiatives outlined in the government's Framework Agreement for dealing with the economic crisis, such as the new Social Relief of Distress Fund and other food security strategies, the Training Layoff Scheme for workers, or improvements to the Unemployment Insurance Fund.

Although the crisis was not too severe or long, recovery has been slower than anticipated, and the economy lagged behind those of other emerging markets. Real GDP has recovered from −1.7 percent in 2009 to 2.8 percent in 2010, more similar to the OECD average than the more dynamic Brazil, Russia, India, Indonesia, and China (BRIIC) group (OECD 2013). Real GDP growth averaged 3.3 percent in 2010–11, falling to 2.5 percent in 2012. A continued slow and modest recovery was expected for 2013 and 2014, mostly fuelled by increased demand for exports from southern African countries and China. However, low rates of economic growth (GDP growth was only 0.9 percent during the first quarter of 2013) led some economists to conclude that the economy had lost momentum, and the dreaded *recession* word started to be used again.

South Africa's vulnerability to the global economic downturn and its continued slow recovery are attributable to sudden stops of short-term financial inflows as investors react to potential risk, weak demand for exports (manufactured goods and primary commodities such as platinum and gold), and a sharp reduction in consumer demand and private investment (Devarajan and Kasekende 2011; OECD 2013). Some sectors were especially hard hit. The mining and manufacturing sectors recorded negative growth: −22 percent annualized growth for manufacturing in the first quarter of 2009 and −33 percent annualized growth for mining in the same quarter (Kahn 2009, 23). The manufacturing sector's decline was largely due to lower export demand. Similar contractions were apparent in the retail and wholesale trade.

Despite this, the recession in South Africa was not nearly as deep as elsewhere, partly because the country did not experience any major bank failures and partly because the decline was offset by lower oil prices and strong growth in the construction industry in preparation for the FIFA World Cup. In addition, intra-African investment and trade have been rising substantially, led by South African firms (Bassett 2013, 6). These links might have helped to buffer

South Africa from the worst effects of the crisis. Still, the global financial crisis deeply affected the labour market and resulted in massive job losses and rising unemployment. Of course, the South African labour market was already characterized by persistent high rates of long-term unemployment and discouraged job seekers.[1] However, unemployment had fallen between 2002 and 2007 as economic conditions had improved. The official unemployment rate (the "narrow definition" that excludes discouraged job seekers) had dropped to 25.0 percent in 2007 from 31.2 percent in 2003 (Government of South Africa 2008) and to 22.9 percent in 2008 (Verick 2011). This trend came to an end with the 2008 recession, after which average yearly unemployment continued to rise (peaking at 4.7 million, or 25.6 percent, or 34.9 percent using the expanded definition in June 2013) (Government of South Africa 2013). Almost a million jobs were lost over 2009 and 2010 alone, driven especially by employment losses in the manufacturing, wholesale and retail trade, and construction sectors (Verick 2011, 1).

Although these unemployment rates are high, they tell only part of the story. The crisis contributed to a dramatic rise in discouraged job seekers – those who have stopped looking for work – from an average of 1.12 million in 2008 to 1.98 million in 2010. "In comparison, narrowly-defined unemployment increased over the same period by only 214,000 (from 4.08 to 4.29 million)" (Verick 2011, 4). Youth (aged fifteen to twenty-four) unemployment is especially high and has increased since the economic crisis. Narrowly defined youth unemployment increased by 5 percentage points, from 45.5 percent in 2008 to 50.5 percent in 2010. Using the broad definition, the annual average youth unemployment was 51.5 percent in 2008 and "has since skyrocketed to 60.3 percent in 2010, representing an increase of 8.8 percentage points" (Verick 2011, 7).

Unemployment has increased more for non-whites, lower-skilled workers, and those with less formal education. Furthermore, provinces with a high proportion of former "homelands" (the "reservations" for blacks created by the apartheid regime) are the poorest in the country and have the highest rates of discouraged unemployed workers. Households in these regions are highly dependent on social transfers, especially the Old Age Pension and Child Support Grant. Even before the economic crisis, unemployment was a chronic, not a temporary, problem for many people. The economic crisis exacerbated this situation: these individuals lack present or future access to employment (especially formal sector employment with benefits), have no access to training or education to increase their skills or to other employment, are unable to generate sufficient income to escape from poverty, yet are not eligible for unemployment

Marlea Clarke

assistance or other social grants. These individuals make up the core of post-apartheid's chronic poor.

Inequality is also tightly bound up with labour market outcomes. Income from paid work contributed 85 percent of income inequality in 2008 (Leib-brandt et al. 2010). Much of that was driven by the large number of individuals without work income. However, inequality among households with labour market earnings is also high, as real earnings in the bottom deciles have not risen in the post-apartheid period and have fallen markedly relative to earnings in the top deciles (OECD 2013, 18).

Emergence and Development of the Welfare State

The origins of South Africa's welfare state lie in the mid-1920s, when the government first introduced a range of employment and welfare measures. Benefits were mostly limited to white people (though sometimes "coloured" people received them). Demands for major welfare reforms came in the early 1940s from various parliamentary committees and from diverse groups in society, ranging from (white) Afrikaans nationalist organizations and Afrikaner churches to black trade unions and "socialist" politicians (Duncan 1993; Seekings 2000a). Disenchantment with the existing system, combined with clear social need and growing public pressure, resulted in the introduction of new welfare measures and the deracialization of large parts of the system (Seekings 2000a, 2000b).

Rapid growth in primary and secondary industries after the Second World War meant that the state could afford to reform and universalize the system. Thus, the nascent welfare state began to evolve into a multiracial welfare system by the mid-1940s, with the adoption of a universal Old Age Pension program and Unemployment Insurance (Seekings 2000b). However, though influenced by developments in other countries, such as the United States, New Zealand, and especially Britain, the South African "government's commitment to meaningful provisions was never more than lukewarm" (Duncan 1993, 106–7). Indeed, legislation passed between 1945 and 1948 fell far short of expectations. For instance, almost all African people were excluded from the family allowances introduced in 1947, and, even when programs were extended to Africans, benefit rates were discriminatory.

Election of the National Party in 1948 and introduction of apartheid policies meant that any progress made toward the development of an inclusive and expansive welfare state was halted. The new government amended existing legislation to exclude Africans from coverage. Expenditure from general government revenue on African education was frozen (Seekings 2000b), and earlier progress made in several other social policy areas was reversed. Reforms to existing policies and the introduction of new social and employment policies over the next several decades were designed to protect whites against various contingencies. Blacks were provided with lower rates of coverage, partly excluded from coverage because of various exemptions in the policies (e.g., based on job classification), or completely disqualified from protection because of racial exclusions.

In general, welfare provisions during the first two decades of apartheid were aimed at protecting poor whites who did not benefit from their preferential treatment in the labour market or households that did not have a male wage earner because of temporary unemployment, age, sickness, or disability (Seekings 2000a). State welfare expenditure helped to maintain white support for the apartheid government by securing jobs for white workers and ensuring that distribution and redistribution benefited white working-class families (Patel 1992). The system was designed to protect only certain vulnerable groups of people (the white "deserving poor"), families without a male breadwinner, or people temporarily unable to earn an income through no fault of their own (Barchiesi 2007; Sevenhuijsen et al. 2003).

Major welfare reforms were undertaken in the 1970s and especially 1980s, largely as a result of the economic and political crisis facing the country, calls by business to reform the system, and growing militancy among black workers and unions for inclusion in the labour relations and social welfare system. Far-reaching reforms were introduced as the National Party moved toward eliminating racial discrimination in welfare and social policies. These reforms meant that exclusions and differential benefit rates were gradually removed and that more black workers were slowly incorporated into the system. Even though legislative reforms resulted in the partial dismantling of legislated racism in social policies and the labour market, labour market segmentation and extreme levels of inequality persisted.

Post-Apartheid Social Protection

The African National Congress (ANC) election platform in 1994, South Africa's first democratic election, focused on the need to address poverty and reduce overall levels of inequality, captured in its election slogan, "A Better Life for All." Since then, the country has been governed by the ANC, a party committed, at least rhetorically, to addressing the legacies of apartheid, specifically to reducing poverty and inequality. Revamping the country's labour laws and social security system has been central to this aim. The government's 1997 white paper on social development outlined its strategy for such reforms.

Marlea Clarke

The current social security system is a product of reforms introduced in stages since 1994, largely by adapting and revising existing policies and programs. Similar to the inherited model, the system is made up of three main pillars: contributory social (occupational) insurance, non-contributory social assistance, and a voluntary private system. The first category consists of retirement benefits, workers' compensation, and health insurance for some workers (generally skilled workers). Within this category, the Unemployment Insurance Act (UIA) is the main statute that offers benefits to workers permanently or temporarily out of work. Although the primary beneficiaries are unemployed workers, contributors can also claim benefits for absence from work because of illness, maternity, or adoption. Reforms to the UIA resulted in far more extensive coverage, especially with the inclusion of domestic and farm workers in April 2003. However, significant exemptions remain: only formal sector workers in a formal employer-employee relationship are covered; many groups of workers, such as most self-employed, informal, temporary, and casual workers (those working less than twenty-four hours a month for an employer), are excluded from Unemployment Insurance Fund (UIF) coverage, and domestic workers' four-month maternity leave is unpaid.

South Africa's contributory workplace pension system is anomalous compared with the systems in many other countries, especially those after which the South African system was modelled. Instead of a mandatory public system, it is a private system made up of pension and provident funds. Most full-time, formal sector employees can belong to either a pension or a provident fund, and employers deduct a percentage (generally up to 10 percent) of employees' wages to contribute to the fund. Pension and provident funds operate in a similar manner, the main difference being how workers receive their benefits. Similar to exclusions in the UIF, casual, temporary, self-employed, and informal sector workers are not covered.

The second pillar comprises six types of social grants aimed at supporting vulnerable groups through monthly income transfers: Older Persons Grant, Disability Grant, Child Support Grant, Care Dependency Grant, Foster Child Grant, and War Veterans Grant. A seventh, the Grant-in-Aid, is given to those already in receipt of the Disability, Older Persons, or War Veterans Grant (Government of South Africa 2010). The three core social grants covering disability, old age pensions, and children and families are means-tested (van der Berg 1997, 484). The Older Persons Grant (formerly called the Old Age Pension) provides important supports to older persons, especially those in rural areas. Reforms introduced in 2010, partly in response to the economic crisis, equalized men's age of eligibility with women's age at sixty (instead of sixty-five for men).

The Child Support Grant (CSG) currently reaches children from birth to eighteen years of age and pays ZAR 300 (approximately thirty-two dollars Canadian) per month per child (to a maximum of six children) via the primary caregiver of the child. Until 2008, the CSG was available only to children aged from birth to thirteen years; in 2009, it was extended to include children aged fourteen; in 2010, the age of eligibility was increased to eighteen years. The marked expansion of the grant was both a direct reaction to the economic crisis and a response to ongoing pressure to increase eligibility. Although the benefits of the CSG have increased over the past several years, the Older Persons Grant is the most generous grant and currently the biggest driver of social assistance expenditure (ILO 2012).

The main area of policy reform in the post-apartheid period has been child support. Although the new CSG falls far short of a universal benefit, it marked a significant shift from the previous grant, which had such stringent conditions that it resulted in extremely poor coverage, especially among African children (McEwen and Woolard 2012). The amounts paid have increased in real terms since 2001, and access to the grant has improved, largely because the age of eligibility was increased, from below seven years (when the grant was first introduced) to eighteen years. As a result, the CSG is the largest program in terms of beneficiaries, with about 11 million children, approximately two-thirds of the total number of social assistance beneficiaries (ILO 2012).

Social Security and the Changing Labour Market

In the global South context, South Africa is seen to have an extensive, generous, and progressively targeted social security system: "The South African state redistributes approximately 3.5% of GDP through non-contributory social assistance programs, paying out more than 13 million grants every month, in a country whose total population is less than 50 million. No other country in the global South spends as much on social assistance or reaches as high a proportion of the population" (Seekings and Matisonn 2010, 1). The system is perceived to have played an important role in addressing poverty and inequality in the post-apartheid period. South Africa is one of the few countries in the global South to have an extensive non-contributory, non-employment-based pension for elderly people (the Older Persons Grant).[2] The grant has wide coverage and is viewed as generous; more than 90 percent of older black South Africans access this grant, and the monthly cash transfers play an important role in sustaining households affected by poverty (Ferreira 2006; Schatz et al. 2012). Significant progress has also been made in addressing child poverty as a result

Marlea Clarke

of the increased age eligibility and wider coverage among the population (e.g., to those in harder-to-reach areas of the country, such as rural areas). According to a UNICEF study, in April 2001 "approximately one million people received the CSG; this had increased more than eight-fold by April 2008" (UNICEF and the Financial and Fiscal Commission of South Africa 2010, 9).

Introduction of the CSG and expansion of other social grants have resulted in growing numbers of the poor and vulnerable receiving social grants: beneficiaries increased from 2,889,443 in April 1997 to 13,114,033 in April 2009 (Potts 2012, 75). By 2011, 14.4 million people were receiving social assistance of some kind in South Africa, more than a quarter of the population and more than six times the number of grant beneficiaries in 1998 (ILO 2011, 11). Expansions to the system and increases in real benefit levels combined with a range of administrative reforms aimed at improving delivery have had a positive effect on poverty. Indeed, there is growing evidence that poverty has been declining since 2000, and this decline has been attributed to the expansion of social grants (see, e.g., Leibbrandt, Woolard, and Woolard 2009; van der Berg, Louw, and Yu 2008). As the ILO (2012) contends, "income support makes a tangible difference to households with little or no income, along with in-kind transfers, fee waivers, subsidies and other social wage benefits." Social grants provided a measure of protection against effects of the economic recession in 2009 triggered by the global economic crisis.

However, despite this success, poverty and inequality remain exceptionally high, especially "within group inequality." South Africa's GINI coefficient – a commonly used measure of inequality – was reported by the UNDP to be .63 in 2013, one of the highest in the world. Despite the important role of income supports for those living in poverty and those without work, calls to increase levels of social spending have been met with hesitation. Indeed, some policy analysts and economists note that spending on social grants is already high by international standards and worry that the ratio of taxpayers to grant recipients is unsustainable (UNICEF and the Financial and Fiscal Commission of South Africa 2010, 13). Affordability of the current system is certainly an issue, not just because the government's fiscal position has worsened as a result of the global economic crisis, but also because the path of growth pursued since independence has been leading to chronic and structural unemployment and precariousness in the labour market. Most unemployed South Africans and those in precarious employment fall outside the social security net. Although the existing social security system effectively acts as a buffer for those eligible for social assistance, it offers little support to the unemployed and precarious workers and exacerbates their marginalization.

Next I briefly outline some of the key factors shaping social exclusion and inequality in South Africa. Although work-centred discourses of citizenship continue to dominate policy making in the country (Barchiesi 2011), high levels of unemployment alongside loopholes, exemptions in legislative protection, and the expansion of precarious employment have limited the reach of South Africa's welfare state. That state was structured on the "visibility" of work and wages, a system that favoured those employed in formal labour markets (Esping-Andersen 1990). Under apartheid, visibility was largely based on "race." Today's system formally incorporates all workers, but failures and limitations of the labour market mean that work is increasingly precarious, informal, or excluded from protection, thus "invisible" to the state. In OECD countries, workers in the formal sector and "regular" jobs are privileged welfare state "insiders," whereas those informally employed are marginalized "outsiders" (Emmenegger et al. 2011; Rueda 2007). This is increasingly the case in South Africa. These problems were exposed by the global economic crisis, but the government has not introduced policy changes to address the situation.

Major reforms are needed to improve social security protection, especially with regard to social assistance for the working-age population, including workers in a wide range of employment relationships. Perhaps what is most needed is a broader, long-term strategy to create jobs alongside the adoption of a Basic Income Grant or some other form of basic income not tied to formal sector employment. Without such a strategy, the entire system is likely to come under extreme pressure as unemployment and precarious forms of work continue to rise and as more people – such as the elderly, poor children, and those affected with HIV/AIDS and other serious illnesses – remain dependent on existing supports (Lund 2002, 199-200).

The introduction of a longer-term strategy to create and sustain jobs would require the restructuring of the South African economy – a significant change in government economic strategy. Soon after coming to office, the ANC replaced its more people-centred socio-economic development plan, the Reconstruction and Development Programme (RDP), which focused on state-led development and redistribution, with Growth, Employment, and Redistribution (GEAR), a neo-liberal macroeconomic program. GEAR focused on trade and market liberalization, debt reduction, stringent fiscal deficit reduction targets, and the privatization of state assets and public utilities. It also called for wage restraints for public sector and other organized workers and the relaxation of labour regulations, especially for unskilled workers (Clarke and Bassett 2008). The consequences of this macroeconomic policy shift for social security were that reforms to child benefits broadened coverage, but monthly stipends were

Marlea Clarke

cut; the value of the Old Age Pension declined by one-fifth in real terms between 1994 and 2000; and, despite an increased number of beneficiaries, social grants fell as a percentage of GDP between 1997 and 2002, in line with the government's commitment to restrain public spending (Bassett and Clarke 2008; Seekings 2002, 3). Furthermore, the government's commitment to fiscal conservatism by emphasizing debt reduction led to reduced access to health-care delivery, diminished water and other municipal services for millions because of privatization and contracting out of public services, and parallel expansion of the private health insurance system. Bond and Dugard (2008, 7) argue that Africa's worst recorded cholera outbreak can be traced to an August 2000 decision to cut water to people who were not paying a KwaZulu-Natal regional water board.

There are few social benefits available to working-age, able-bodied adults, and access to these benefits hinges on a defined employer-employee relationship and on employees being in full-time, permanent work in the formal sector. The main provision for social assistance to unemployed workers is the UIF, but informal, seasonal, temporary, and casual workers and those who work less than twenty-four hours a month are excluded. Other labour laws, such as the Basic Conditions of Employment Act (BCEA) and the Labour Relations Act (LRA), have similar exemptions. These new laws exclude independent contractors (self-employed individuals and those working under a "contract for service" rather than an employment contract) and precarious workers as well as those working in cooperatives. Most workers in various forms of precarious employment are not covered, or only weakly protected, by legislation governing working conditions, collective bargaining, unfair dismissal, and other labour relations issues and employment benefits. In short, precarious workers generally are not protected in employment, nor do they have access to social assistance during times of unemployment. Such a system leaves them continually vulnerable, especially in a labour market with chronic and structural unemployment and high levels of precarious employment.

By the mid-1990s, unemployment and precarious forms of work were already high and growing – reversing the trend toward more stable and full-time hours of work that had shaped the labour market in the 1960s and 1970s.[3] Labour legislation, social assistance for workers, and the entire bargaining council system reformed and reinforced under the ANC were predicated on a particular labour market that no longer existed. Furthermore, the model (similar to models elsewhere) presumed a particular family structure, one that might never have existed for the majority of South Africans, who typically lived in extended, multigenerational families or had been destroyed by the migrant labour system and other apartheid laws decades earlier.

The sharp rise in unemployment and precarious employment in the 1990s and 2000s, and the lack of protection for these workers, reveal the weaknesses of the existing system. Initially, the growth in unemployment was driven by the rapid rise in labour supply in the post-1994 period because of an increase in the working-age population and a rise in labour force participation rates among less-skilled youth, women, and African workers – the last group's entry into the labour market was especially important given their low participation rates during apartheid (Leibbrandt et al. 2010, 4). Similarly, skills-based technological changes and the structural shift in the economy away from the primary sector and toward tertiary and service sectors contributed to the demand for higher-skilled labour and a parallel decline in employment in manufacturing and lower-skilled jobs. These initial conditions contributed to rising unemployment in the 1990s and were compounded by retrenchments of workers in sectors such as clothing and agriculture hard hit by trade liberalization over two decades. Workplace-restructuring initiatives, including outsourcing, subcontracting, and other strategies aimed at reducing labour costs by placing workers outside the ambit of new labour laws, exacerbated the problem.

By the early 2000s, it was clear that labour demand lagged behind labour supply. The government responded with various job creation strategies, such as a Public Works Program. In 2010, it released the country's new economic strategy, the New Growth Path or NGP (the second since GEAR was introduced in 1996), aimed at enhancing growth, creating employment, and ensuring equity. This strategy, with its focus on employment creation in six priority areas – including agriculture, manufacturing, and the "green" economy – represented a departure from the goals of trade and market liberalization contained in GEAR, but it provided little detail about how such ambitious job creation targets would be met. And, in the context of sluggish growth in 2012 and 2013, such initiatives have made little dent in unemployment. The manufacturing sector shed 18,000 jobs in the first quarter of 2013 alone, while the agricultural and services sectors shed 26,000 and 22,000 jobs, respectively (Martinez and Mbatha 2013).

Various forms of precarious work increased alongside unemployment. The proportion of workers with casual jobs in the formal sector (seasonal, temporary, casual, or temporary part-time work) rose from 16 percent to 20 percent between September 2001 and September 2005 (Statistics South Africa 2002; 2006). The proportion of informal work also increased between 2002 and 2005, especially in some sectors, such as agriculture, clothing and retail. Unemployment levels have fluctuated in certain quarters of each year, but overall unemployment has risen since the recession. Based on the narrow definition (excluding discouraged job seekers), unemployment rose from 21.9 percent in 2008 to a high of

Marlea Clarke

25 percent by early 2013 (36 percent including discouraged job seekers). Yet only a fraction of these workers are eligible for unemployment insurance, either because they have never been in formal employment or because they have been unemployed for longer than a year and have exhausted any benefits for which they were eligible. In addition, the slow pace of job creation alongside retrenchments in some sectors has resulted in more people becoming unemployed for longer periods. In 2010, 628,595 people received unemployment subsidies, which amounted to only 15 percent of the 4.1 million unemployed (ILO 2012). Most unemployed youth – the largest group of unemployed workers – are not eligible for UIF because they have never been in formal sector jobs that contributed to the fund.

Trends in the agricultural sector provide a good example of these dynamics and the ways in which other policies and processes of exclusion intersect and reinforce labour market trends. The adoption of agricultural policies that favour large-scale, commercial, industrial agriculture and neglect small farmers has contributed to a decline both in the total number of commercial farms and in employment in the sector (du Toit and Neves 2008, 2–3). Farmers have responded to the incorporation of farm workers into new labour legislation and resulting increases in labour costs by replacing full-time workers with seasonal/part-time labourers; evicting workers and their families living on the farms; increasing the number of temporary and contract workers by using temporary employment agencies ("labour brokers"); and introducing new technologies or making other workplace changes to increase the productivity of existing labour, even when output was expanding (Clarke and Greenberg 2003; Tregurtha, Vink, and Kirsten 2009, 46). Employment on commercial farms declined by more than 40 percent between 1993 and 2006 (Tregurtha, Vink, and Kirsten 2009, 20), "fueling farm evictions that have dumped the rural poor in informal settlements around small towns" (du Toit and Neves 2008, 2). The 2008 economic crisis placed further strain on agriculture, and widespread retrenchments continued to take place in 2010 and 2011. Although recovery was quite strong in 2012 and 2013 – restoring 114,000 jobs – agricultural employment is still reported to be 80,000 jobs below pre-crisis levels (Reddy 2013). These conditions, combined with food price increases that outstripped official inflation rates, led to the wave of strikes and protests through the agricultural sector in late 2012 and early 2013 (interviews, May 2013).

In the agricultural industry and all other sectors, workplace restructuring and retrenchment, conditions that have escalated in many sectors since the 2008 crisis, mean that a growing number of workers, the majority in many workplaces, are in precarious employment. A growing percentage of the working population has either limited or no access to employment-related benefits (e.g., pension, medical aid) and minimum wage rates or is unemployed and has no access to social assistance at all. Post-apartheid initiatives have expanded and reformed social assistance, largely by removing the racial basis of this system, but in many ways have perpetuated its key exclusionary trends (Seekings and Nattrass 2005). There is no social protection for the "able-bodied" poor and no effective state support for poor households without pensioners or children. Consequently, in the early 2000s there were 1.2 million "workerless" households (some 3.9 million people) with no access to either wage income, pensions, or any form of remittances (Samson 2002, 73). This is the core group of the "chronic poor" in South Africa: a large and growing group of able-bodied individuals who lack present or future access to employment that provides social benefits and protection and generates sufficient income to escape from poverty. And, though the country has an extensive non-contributory grant for elderly people, there is a clear need for workplace pension reform. The private system of workplace retirement schemes is accessible only to formal sector workers, and benefits received are low for many who have access to the system because their wages are so low, meaning that they cannot be financially stable or keep themselves out of poverty in retirement. In short, the existing system of unemployment insurance cannot address the major unemployment risks associated with structural rather than cyclical unemployment (van der Berg 1997, 484). Although unemployment, adverse incorporation, and inequality are legacies of apartheid, they have been "exacerbated by a policy mix that undermines sustainable livelihoods at the bottom of the economy," thus creating a particular dynamic of social exclusion and adverse incorporation (du Toit and Neves 2008, 2).

Partly in response to the limitations of the system and high poverty levels, South Africa has considered broadening social protection by introducing a universal Basic Income Grant (BIG) to be financed from an increase in the Value-Added Tax (VAT) and other indirect taxes. This proposal has been endorsed by a growing alliance of civil society organizations. A number of research studies, including a commissioned study by the ILO (Samson et al. 2002, 4), concluded that the grant "is feasible, affordable, and supportive of poverty reduction, economic growth and job creation. A universal basic income grant has the potential to fortify the ability of the poor to manage risk while directly improving their livelihoods." Despite evidence of its feasibility and potential benefits, alongside widespread support for its introduction, the government has not moved forward on this proposal, nor has it introduced any policy directly aimed at addressing the unemployment crisis facing the country. Indeed, debates

Marlea Clarke

within the government about the potential benefits and feasibility of BIG have exposed some of the contradictory views of the ANC on social assistance. For instance, as Barchiesi (2006, 16) notes, despite the context of mass unemployment, the government has continued to argue that "South Africans must rely for their livelihood on normal participation in the economy" rather than depend on the government for social grants, and Minister of Finance Trevor Manuel has lambasted BIG as an "unsustainable" and "populist" idea. Even as the effects of the economic crisis were being felt across the country, the government and ANC remained strongly opposed to the grant, insisting, as they had before, that "South Africa does not and should not have a 'welfare state.'" (Barchiesi 2006, 16)

Conclusion

South Africa has quite a generous social grant system, one that was initially based on social security principles in industrialized countries but under apartheid developed into a racially based system that either excluded blacks or entitled them to inferior benefit levels. This system was reformed and extended under the ANC, which now boasts of an extensive and generous social grant system. This system did buffer the poor from some of the effects of the global economic crisis of 2008 and lessened its impact on child poverty (UNICEF 2010). However, though it offers important supports to social sectors of the population, it is ill equipped to provide protection to the growing group of able-bodied, unemployed, or precariously employed individuals. There are few avenues of assistance for working-age people, and those that are in place are restrictive (largely based on employment status) and short term. As Lund (2002, 192) argues, "social security policies in the future need to move away from the creation of 'special programmes' … as if they are atypical minorities with temporary special needs. There is a need for systematic reform of the whole system of social protection, which takes into account the fact that many people may work for their whole lives, and yet remain poor."

In contrast to the multiple economic crises of the 1980s in South Africa that led to extensive political, social, and economic reforms (and eventually political negotiations to "end" apartheid), this recent recession has not yet led to any major change in social or economic policy. Instead, the 2008 crisis exacerbated problems and gaps in the existing system without inducing significant policy changes. At the same time, the recession has contributed to rising social unrest in South Africa, demonstrated by the wave of "wildcat" strikes and protests that spread across the country in 2012. Extensive reform of South Africa's social assistance system is needed. But such reforms are needed within an overall context of broader policy change that would involve massive reforms to the country's poor education system, the development of training programs (especially for low-skilled workers and youth), and the introduction of concrete initiatives to create permanent jobs. However, South Africa currently has few options to "create jobs" within a liberalized economic model. The 2008 crisis exposed the gaps in and limitations of the social assistance system in the country and the serious problems with the national economic program. Systemic reform is needed but likely impossible within the country's current economic model.

Notes

1 In South Africa, unemployment is reported using both the official definition and what is called the "expanded" definition. The former includes only those unemployed individuals who reported that they had taken active steps to look for work or to start some form of self-employment in the four weeks prior to the interview. The expanded definition drops the criterion of "work-seeking activity," thus including discouraged job seekers.

2 Non-employment-based pensions are becoming more common in the global South. Namibia, Nepal, and Mauritius have similar systems.

3 For a full discussion of the history of labour laws and employment trends, see, for example, Clarke, Godfrey, and Theron (2002).

References

Barchiesi, Franco. 2006. "The Debate on the Basic Income Grant in South Africa: Social Citizenship, Wage Labour, and the Reconstruction of Working-Class Politics." Paper presented at the Harold Wolpe Memorial Trust's Tenth Anniversary Colloquium Engaging Silences and Unresolved Issues in the Political Economy of South Africa, Cape Town.

–. 2007. "'Schooling Bodies to Hard Work': The South African State's Policy Discourse and Its Moral Constructions of Welfare." Paper presented at the North Eastern Workshop on Southern Africa (NEWSA), Burlington, Vermont.

–. 2011. *Precarious Liberation: Workers, the State, and Contested Social Citizenship in Post-apartheid South Africa*. Albany, NY: SUNY Press and University of KwaZulu-Natal Press.

Bassett, Carolyn. 2013. "Incorporation, Empowerment or More Exploitation? The Significance of Africa's Recent Global Economic Experiences." Paper presented at International Studies Association Annual Meeting, San Francisco.

Bassett, Carolyn, and Marlea Clarke. 2008. "The Zuma Affair, Labour, and the Future of Democracy in South Africa." *Third World Quarterly* 29, 4: 787–803. http://dx.doi.org/10.1080/01436590802052763.

Bell, Gordon. 2009. "Contracts Most since 1984: GDP Fell Annualised 6.4%". Reuters, 26/V/2009 http://lists.fahamu.org/pipermail/debate-list/2009-May/022746.html.

Bond, Patrick, and Jackie Dugard. 2008. "Water, Human Rights and Social Conflict: South African Experiences." *Law, Social Justice & Global Development Journal (LGD)* 1: 1-21. http://www.go.warwick.ac.uk/elj/lgd/2008_1/bond_dugard.

Clarke, Marlea, and Carolyn Bassett. 2008. "South African Trade Unions and Globalisation: Going for the 'High Road,' Getting Stuck on the 'Low Road.'" *Work Organisation, Labour, and Globalisation* 2, 1: 133–51.

Clarke, Marlea, Stephen Godfrey, and Jan Theron. 2002. *Workers' Protection: An Update on the Situation in South Africa, Commission Research Report for the International Labour Organisation (ILO)*. Cape Town: Labour and Enterprise Project Research Unit.

Clarke, Marlea, and Stephen Greenberg. 2003. *Global Influences on Macro-Economic Policy and Practice in Post-Apartheid South Africa*. Cape Town: Women on Farms Project.

Devarajan, Shantayanan, and Louis A. Kasekende. 2011. "Africa and the Global Economic Crisis: Impacts, Policy Responses, and Political Economy." *African Development Review* 23, 4: 421–38. http://dx.doi.org/10.1111/j.1467-8268.2011.00296.x.

du Toit, Andries, and David Neves. 2008. *Chronic and Structural Poverty in South Africa: An Overview*. Report for the Chronic Poverty Research Centre, Institute for Poverty, Land, and Agrarian Studies (PLAAS), Cape Town.

Duncan, David. 1993. "The Origins of the Welfare State in Pre-Apartheid South Africa." In *Collected Seminar Papers 45*: 106–19. London: Institute of Commonwealth Studies.

Emmenegger, Patrick, Silja Häusermann, Bruno Palier, and Martin Seeleib-Kaiser, eds. 2011. *The Age of Dualization: The Changing Face of Inequality in Deindustrializing Societies*. Oxford: Oxford University Press.

Esping-Andersen, Gosta. 1990. *The Three Worlds of Welfare Capitalism*. Princeton: Princeton University Press.

Ferreira, Monica. 2006. "The Differential Impact of Social-Pension Income on Household Poverty Alleviation in Three South African Ethnic Groups." *Ageing and Society* 26, 3: 337–54. http://dx.doi.org/10.1017/S0144686X0600482X.

Government of South Africa. 2008. *Labour Force Survey, Historical Revision March Series 2001 to 2007. Labour Force Survey, Statistical Release PO210*. Pretoria: Statistics South Africa.

–. 2010. *An Overview of South Africa's Social Security System*. Pretoria: Department of Social Development.

–. 2013. *Quarterly Labour Force Survey, Quarter 3. Statistical Release PO211*. Pretoria: Statistics South Africa.

ILO. 2011. *Social Protection Floor in South Africa: Draft Version Geneva, International Labour Organisation*. Geneva: ILO.

–. 2012. "Global Extension of Social Security (GESS)." http://www.socialsecurityextension.org/gimi/gess/ShowWiki.action?wiki.wikiId=854.

Kahn, Brian. 2009. "South Africa's Policy May Offset the Financial Downturn." *Development Outreach* 11, 3: 22–24. http://dx.doi.org/10.1596/1020-797X_11_3_22.

Leibbrandt, Murray, Ingrid Woolard, Hayley McEwen, and Charlotte Koep. 2010. "Employment and Inequality Outcomes in South Africa: What Role for Labour Market and Social Policies?" Southern Africa Labour and Development Research Unit, School of Economics, University of Cape Town.

Leibbrandt, Murray, Ingrid Woolard, and Christopher Woolard. 2009. "Poverty and Inequality Dynamics in South Africa: Post-Apartheid Developments in the Light of the Long-Run Legacy." In *South African Economic Policy under Democracy*, edited by Brian Kahn, Ingrid Woolard, Janine Aron, and Geeta Kingdon, 270–299. Oxford: Oxford University Press. http://dx.doi.org/10.1093/acprof:oso/9780199551460.003.0010.

Lund, Francie. 2002. "Social Security and the Changing Labour Market: Access for Non-Standard and Informal Workers in South Africa." *Social Dynamics: A Journal of African Studies* 28, 2: 177–206, DOI: 10.1080/02533950208458737.

Martinez, Andres, and Amogelang Mbatha. 2013. "South African Second-Quarter Jobless Rate Rises to 25.6%." *Bloomberg Businessweek,* 30 July, http://www.bloomberg.com/news/articles/2013-07-30/s-africa-second-quarter-jobless-rate-increases-to-25-6-.

McEwen, Hayley, and Ingrid Woolard. 2012. "The Fiscal Cost of Child Grants in the Context of High Adult Mortality in South Africa: A Simulation to 2015." *Development Southern Africa* 29, 1: 141–56. http://dx.doi.org/10.1080/0376835X.2012.645648.

OECD. 2008. *OECD Economic Surveys: South Africa Economic Assessment.* Paris: OECD.

–. 2013. *OECD Economic Surveys: South Africa, March 2013.* Paris: OECD.

Patel, Leila. 1992. *Restructuring Social Welfare: Options for South Africa.* Johannesburg: Raven Press.

Potts, Rebecca. 2012. "Social Welfare in South Africa: Curing or Causing Poverty?" *Penn State Journal of International Affairs* 1, 2: 72–90.

Reddy, Niall. 2013. *Not All Peachy on the Farm Jobs Front.* Johannesburg: Mail and Guardian.

Rueda, David. 2007. *Social Democracy Inside Out: Government Partisanship, Insiders, and Outsiders in Industrialized Democracies.* Oxford: Oxford University Press. http://dx.doi.org/10.1093/acprof:oso/9780199216352.001.0001.

Samson, Michael. 2002. "The Social, Economic and Fiscal Impact of Comprehensive Social Security Reform for South Africa." *Social Dynamics* 28, 2: 69–97.

Samson, Michael, Claudia Haarmann, Dirk Haarmann, Kenneth MacQuene, Ingrid van Niekerk, Gilbert Khathi, and Oliver Babson. 2002. "Research Review on Social Security Reform and the Basic Income Grant for South Africa." EPRI Policy Report 31, Economic Policy Research Institute (EPRI), Cape Town.

Schatz, Enid, Xavier Gómez-Olivé, Margaret Ralston, Jane Menken, and Stephen Tollman. 2012. "The Impact of Pensions on Health and Wellbeing in Rural South Africa: Does Gender Matter?" *Social Science and Medicine* 75, 10: 1864–73. http://dx.doi.org/10.1016/j.socscimed.2012.07.004.

Seekings, Jeremy. 2000a. "Apartheid Revisited: Analysing Apartheid as a Distributional Regime." Centre for African Studies Seminar, Cape Town.

–. 2000b. "The Origins of Social Citizenship in Pre-Apartheid South Africa." *South African Journal of Philosophy* 19, 4: 386–404.

–. 2002. "The Broader Importance of Welfare Reform in South Africa." *Social Dynamics* 28, 2: 1–38. http://dx.doi.org/10.1080/02533950208458731.

Seekings, Jeremy, and Heidi Matisonn. 2010. "The Continuing Politics of Basic Income in South Africa." Centre for Social Science Research (CSSR) Working Paper No. 286, University of Cape Town.

Seekings, Jeremy, and Nicoli Nattrass. 2005. *Class, Race, and Inequality in South Africa.* New Haven and London: Yale University Press.

Sevenhuijsen, Selma, Vivienne Bozalek, Amanda Gouws, and Marie Minnaar-McDonald. 2003. "South African Social Welfare Policy: An Analysis Using the Ethic of Care." *Critical Social Policy* 23, 3: 299–321. http://dx.doi.org/10.1177/02610183030233001.

Statistics South Africa. 2002. Labour Force Survey: September 2001, Statistical Release P0210, Pretoria, South Africa.

–. 2006. Labour Force Survey March 2006, Statistical Release P0210, Pretoria, South Africa.

Steytler, Nico, and Derek Powell. 2010. "The Impact of the Global Financial Crisis on Decentralized Government in South Africa." *L'Europe en formation* 358, 4: 149–72. http://dx.doi.org/10.3917/eufor.358.0149.

Tregurtha, Norma, Nick Vink, and Johann Kirsten. 2009. "Presidency Fifteen Year Review Project: Review of Agricultural Policies and Support Instruments in South Africa 1994–2007." Paper presented at the Workshop on the Fifteen Year Review of Government Performance for Economic and Social Sectors, Pretoria.

UNICEF. 2010. "Vulnerability of Children and Poor Families to the Economic Recession of 2008-2009." The Department of Social Development, South Africa, and the United Nations Children's Fund (UNICEF).

UNICEF and the Financial and Fiscal Commission of South Africa. 2010. *The Impact of the International Financial Crisis on Child Poverty in South Africa*. Pretoria: UNICEF and the Financial and Fiscal Commission of South Africa.

van der Berg, Servaas. 1997. "South African Social Security under Apartheid and Beyond." *Development Southern Africa* 14, 4: 481–503. http://dx.doi.org/10.1080/037683597 08439982.

van der Berg, Servaas, Megan Louw, and Derek Yu. 2008. "Post-Transition Poverty Trends Based on an Alternative Data Source." *South African Journal of Economics* 76, 1: 58–76. http://dx.doi.org/10.1111/j.1813-6982.2008.00161.x.

Verick, Sher. 2011. "Giving Up Job Search during a Recession: The Impact of the Global Financial Crisis on the South African Labour Market." Discussion Paper Series, IZA and ILO, Bonn.

11

In the Shadow of Crisis
Change and Continuity in China's
Post-Crisis Social Policy

SARAH COOK AND WING LAM

Welfare states at the epicentre of the financial crisis are still grappling with the direct ramifications of crisis and ongoing fiscal austerity, with significant implications for social policy and provision. China, in contrast, has continued to expand its welfare provisions in the post-crisis period. Total central government social spending more than doubled between 2008 and 2012 (from 575 to 1,423 billion yuan), while the total, including subnational expenditures, rose from 1,456 to 4,566 billion yuan (Ministry of Finance, various years). The share of national fiscal spending on social programs rose from 29.2 percent in 2007 to 36.2 percent in 2012. The deeper question of concern here is whether the crisis has shifted in any meaningful way the nature, direction, or logic of social policy or welfare regime development in China.

Although partially insulated from the worst ravages of the crisis, China did not escape from the fallout of acute financial failure in the West. Impacts swiftly arrived in the real economy through channels of trade, foreign investment, and (more gradually) shifting demand. China was one of the first major economies to respond decisively to the crisis, with a massive 4 trillion yuan (US$586 billion) fiscal stimulus package introduced in November 2008. It was supplemented by a range of measures designed to reduce the negative impacts on the real economy, with the overall objective being to stabilize struggling enterprises, maintain employment, and boost domestic consumption in order to sustain growth. Critical elements of this package were a range of social policy interventions aimed at protecting the vulnerable and socially oriented investment programs, such as social housing.

Such use by the Chinese government of social policy instruments in economic crisis management was recognized at the time as unprecedented (Wen 2010b; Xinhuanet 2011b). In earlier work (Cook 2012; Cook and Lam 2011), we explored how the Chinese state used such policies to manage the consequences of crisis and promote recovery and whether the crisis served as a catalyst to expedite the process of welfare restructuring or to lay the foundations for more sustainable, inclusive, domestic, demand-driven growth. Here we further examine whether the crisis is having longer-term impacts on the evolution of China's welfare system.

The chapter is organized as follows. The following section discusses the nature of the welfare system emerging in China. The third and fourth sections look at the impacts of and responses to the crisis, both direct and indirect, as a basis for assessing the implications for longer-term welfare reform. The fifth section examines other drivers of welfare reform in China to understand the relative significance of the crisis. The concluding section considers the broader implications of China's reform path: in the context of an apparent crisis in Western welfare states, do new pathways to better welfare pursued by countries such as China offer more robust alternative models, particularly for developing countries?

What Type of "Welfare Regime" Is Emerging in China?

China's evolving "welfare" or "social policy regime" does not fit easily into standard welfare state typologies. It is a work in progress and, like the proverbial elephant, appears to be a very different beast depending on where one starts to explore it. Thus, some studies emphasize varying dimensions of state capitalism, corporatism, Confucianism, developmentalism, productivism, fragmentation, incrementalism, and residualism. Shi (2012a) distinguishes among scholars who identify problems associated with social change and then examine social policy responses to those problems (e.g., Guan 2005; Leung 2003; Saunders and Shang 2001); those who examine the trends of social policy in the transition from socialist to pluralist welfare production (Leung and Nann 1995; Wong 1998; Wong and Flynn 2001); and those who focus on the cultural and "familial" dimensions underlying welfare reforms (Chan and Chow 1992; Chang 1993; Chen 1996). More recently, a number of scholars have focused on the role of social policy in legitimating the party state (Chan 2010; Cook 2012; Frazier 2010; Li 2012) or tried to understand whether China's model conforms to the productivist "welfare developmentalism" of East Asian states (Cook and Kwon 2008; Goodman, White, and Kwon 1998; Kwon 2005) typified by South Korea.

Apparent throughout all of these studies is that the system of the 2010s is vastly different from that of the late 1990s (the period of state sector restructuring), let alone the late 1970s, when "reform and opening" began. A clearer structure of welfare provision is now emerging that rests on the three pillars of social assistance, social insurance, and welfare services (Zheng 2008). However, the coverage, access, quality, and benefits remain uneven, often extended incrementally on a group or regional basis and at times reinforcing old or creating new forms of inequality and exclusion. Given the core *redistributive* function of any social policy system, many studies focus on inequalities and dimensions of variation: Duckett and Carrillo (2011) on local variation, particularly at the level of implementation (see also Solinger and Hu 2012); Shi (2012b) on emerging regional variations; Ringen and Ngok (2013) on system fragmentation; Gao, Yang, and Li (2013) on the size, structure, and redistributive effects of China's "state capitalist" welfare state, particularly through the lens of rural/urban difference.

Clearly, China's social policy reform process has not followed any blueprint. Throughout the recent period, consistent drivers of social policies have been the dual pillars of social stability and economic growth – "a 'safety net' underpinning social stability and a 'shock absorber' supporting the sound operation of the economy" (Leading Party Members' Group of the Ministry of Human Resources and Social Security 2013, 1). New social initiatives tend to be a response to specific challenges, often reflecting the social tensions inherent in rapid transformation. The Chinese state has capacities that enable it to respond to (selective) social problems as they arise (as demonstrated by responses to SARS, natural disaster, crisis, and unrest); these responses can then be locked in to shape further system and institutional development.

International ideas have also influenced the reform process. China's integration into the global economy started just as Western countries were questioning the Keynesian foundations of liberal welfare states and cutting back on welfare provisions, supported by a neo-liberal ideology that emphasized the supremacy of markets and a minimal role for the government. In this ideological climate, China's early reform decades (marked by state withdrawal from, or neglect of, many aspects of social provisioning as market mechanisms emerged) have been interpreted at times as state acceptance of neo-liberalism (Mok and Wong 2011). Although its emphasis on growth and a greater reliance on markets resonated with the dominant international ideology, in reality China moved less intentionally in this direction than is sometimes claimed. Despite processes of decollectivization and decentralization, the Chinese state has consistently resisted privatization or a reduction of its role in many areas of the economy. Chinese proponents of more radical privatization are met by strong countervailing forces for maintaining a strong state role alongside growing concerns about equality and social justice. The withdrawal of the state has thus been highly variable but (consistent with neo-liberalism) is most apparent in areas that affect the livelihoods and security of the most vulnerable, as opposed to those supporting wealth creation (Cook 2011).

By the late 1990s, state enterprise restructuring brought the social costs of reform home to the better protected urban population but also provided an impetus for more fundamental reform of the social security system.[1] Incremental shifts toward employment-based and contributory social insurance programs took place as replacements for the state-sponsored, enterprise-based welfare regime (the iron rice bowl) of the Mao era. Social assistance programs, previously residual and ad hoc, were massively expanded and systematized, particularly with the establishment of the minimum living standard program (*dibao*).[2] Major initiatives introduced at key moments early in the twenty-first century cleared a path toward social insurance as the core of the system, underpinned by an expanded basic social assistance system. In October 2006, the Chinese government openly committed to building a universal social security system by 2020, a commitment restated by the current leadership (CPC 2006; State Council 2012a). In 2010, the National People's Congress adopted the first national Social Insurance Law (State Council 2010; Wen 2010a), which lays the foundation for a social insurance–based comprehensive social security system aimed at universal coverage. The twelfth Five-Year Plan (2011–15) has further prioritized strengthening of the social security system as part of a second generation of economic reforms to achieve more sustainable and inclusive development.

As the Chinese state has negotiated its path of reform, it has also developed its own distinctive discourses to justify its policies – from market socialism to the "harmonious society" of Hu Jintao that helped to elevate social policy on the national policy agenda. Despite its increasing prominence, however, social policy has not emerged as an autonomous sphere with intrinsic goals representing societal values; rather, it remains principally a dependent instrument for achieving other objectives. It is unclear which core *values* might form the basis of a lasting social contract underlying the emerging welfare system in China – beyond the commitment to maintain stability and growth as the bedrock of regime legitimacy. Nor is it clear what kind of politics will be needed to maintain party-state legitimacy as social issues become more acute, protests more frequent, and interests more divergent in the market economy, while spaces for reconciliation of interests remain limited and fragile (Cook 2012; Fewsmith 2010).

Given these developments, initiatives following the 2008 crisis must be seen as part of a longer process of welfare reform and reconstruction that has accompanied China's major economic and social transformations of the past three decades. Although largely insulated from the Asian financial crisis in the late 1990s, China did get some impetus from it to strengthen social protection mechanisms. By the time of the 2008 crisis, China had in place the instruments as well as the resources to rapidly respond to it through fiscal and social policies. Its welfare model was already moving toward an insurance-based system, with the state limiting its role in direct provision.[3] An expansion of social programs to groups not initially among the "core" beneficiaries (urban workers) has continued, with major programs now covering the rural population and other urban residents and with signs that integrating migrants will be a priority for the current leadership. In all of these developments, while stability and growth remain fundamental priorities, more attention is being paid to reducing inequality and promoting inclusive and sustainable development.

The response to the crisis does not, therefore, mark a major departure from the productivist and developmental orientation of pre-crisis social policies. It did, however, clearly reinforce the need for China to rebalance its economy away from both investment- and export-led growth and toward consumption-led growth and the development of higher value-added sectors. These economic transformations remain ongoing priorities for the new leadership – and social policies are recognized as a critical instrument for achieving them.

Direct Impacts: Crisis Response and the Role of Social Policy

The impacts of the crisis, and China's swift response and recovery, are discussed elsewhere (Cook and Lam 2011). In response to a dramatic decline in exports, soaring bankruptcies, and a massive rise in unemployment, the government introduced a huge stimulus package (4 trillion yuan) co-funded by central and local governments, aiming to stimulate the economy and restore jobs and growth; reduce the economic burden on enterprises; minimize job losses or withdrawals from social insurance funds; boost domestic consumption; and maintain social stability through improved social protection (Cook and Lam 2011, 145). The social policy investments planned as part of the package, including interventions aimed at boosting consumption and protecting the vulnerable, were particularly noteworthy – as was the fact that resources allocated to social programs were increased when the allocations were revised in March 2009 (see

Sarah Cook and Wing Lam

Table 11.1

Investment portfolio of the stimulus package (investment amount in billion yuan and share of the total investment in percent)

Components of the stimulus package	November 2008 N	(%)	March 2009 (revised) N	(%)	Change
Social welfare (health care, education, etc.)	40	(1)	150	(3.75)	110
Technical upgrading and R&D	160	(4)	370	(6.25)	210
Public housing	280	(7)	400	(10.0)	120
Energy conservation and environment	350	(8.75)	210	(5.25)	−140
Rural infrastructure	370	(9.25)	370	(9.25)	0
Post-earthquake reconstruction	1,000	(25)	1,000	(25)	0
Transport and power infrastructure	1,800	(45)	1,500	(37.5)	−300
Total	4,000		4,000		

Note: Social initiatives were defined as including social welfare, public housing, rural infrastructure, and post-earthquake reconstruction.

Source: Caijing.com (2009).

Table 11.2

Contribution to growth, 2008–12

		Share of growth rate contributed by ...		
	Economic growth (%)	Consumption (government and household)	Fixed capital formation	Net exports
2008	9.6	4.2	4.5	0.9
2009	9.2	4.6	8.1	−3.5
2010	10.4	4.5	5.5	0.4
2011	9.3	5.3	4.4	−0.4
2012	7.8	4.1	3.9	−0.2

Source: NBSC Statistical Database (National Bureau of Statistics of China, n.d)

Table 11.1). This was the first time that the Chinese government had used such social policy instruments so prominently in economic crisis management (Wen 2010b; Xinhuanet 2010).

The stimulus program succeeded in restoring growth; it also played a role in saving an estimated 8.53 million jobs (Xinhuanet 2011b). As can be seen in Table 11.2, fixed capital formation accounted for 87.6 percent of total GDP growth in 2009, while final consumption contributed half of economic growth, compensating for negative growth in net exports during the year. Thus, the stimulus program had a positive impact on the economy in the midst of global financial turmoil; however, its longer-term economic impacts remain disputed. As concerns over side effects of the largely government investment–led stimulus package intensified – including rising local government debt, inflation, and overcapacity in many industries – the Chinese government recognized the need to reduce the growth target to a more modest level and was thus cautious about launching another round of economic stimulus in 2011–12.

Nevertheless, it appears that the crisis provided the momentum and political will, and possibly the political space, to further policy efforts on the social policy front. It highlighted the urgency of addressing structural problems in China's economy, translating into a slower but more sustainable and balanced growth target in the years ahead.

Post-Crisis Social Policy

Post-crisis trends in social policy show a continuing rapid expansion (see Table 11.3). Expenditures on social insurance (both individual and government fiscal contributions) and social protection schemes, and the coverage of these programs,

Table 11.3
Changes in social policy coverage and expenditures

	2007		2012	
	Enrolment (million people)	Expenditure (billion yuan)	Enrolment (million people)	Expenditure (billion yuan)
Urban residents				
"Five insurance" schemes				
• Pensions	201.4	596.5	304.3	1,821.0
• Medical	223.1	156.2	536.4	554.4
• Unemployment	116.4	21.8	152.3	45.1
• Work injury	121.7	8.8	190.1	40.6
• Maternity	77.8	5.6	154.3	21.9
Urban *dibao*	22.7	27.7	21.4	67.4
Rural residents				
Rural pensions*	51.7	4.0	462.7	58.8
Rural medical	730.0	34.7	805.0	240.8
Rural *dibao*	35.7	10.9	53.4	71.8
Rural *wubao*	5.3	n.a.	5.5	14.5

* The figure for 2007 refers to the old rural pension program, whereas the figure for 2012 refers to the new rural pension program introduced in 2011.[4]

Sources: Data reported by the Ministry of Human Resources and Social Security (see http://www.mohrss.gov.cn/SYrlzyhshbzb/zwgk/szrs/), Ministry of Civil Affairs (http://www.mca.gov.cn/article/zwgk/tjsj/), and National Health and Family Planning Commission (http://www.nhfpc.gov.cn/zwgkzt/pwstj/list.shtml).

Sarah Cook and Wing Lam

increased sharply between 2007 and 2012. The most notable increase is seen in the rural pensions scheme, launched in 2009. Government commitment to maintaining living standards of the poorest is seen in rises in the *dibao* subsidy: whereas the beneficiaries of the urban *dibao* program decreased slightly, the expenditures tripled.

Overall, total national social spending increased by an annual average of 25.8 percent between 2008 and 2012; as a share of GDP, this was an increase from 4.2 percent in 2003 to 8.8 percent in 2012. Although still far below international trends for welfare states or developed economies (e.g., Denmark at 31 percent or Japan at 22 percent), it is catching up with the level of South Korea (9.3 percent).[5] The share of central government expenditure has also steadily increased to about one-third of total government expenditures, of which a significant increase has occurred on social expenditures. Central government spending on social security programs, including *dibao,* pensions, and social insurance subsidies, rose between 2007 and 2012 from 42 percent to 45 percent. On education, the central government's share increased from 14.4 percent in 2007 to 18.0 percent in 2012.[6] In 2007, central government transfer payments to local governments for social security and employment accounted for approximately 38 percent of the local government's total expenditure on this item. According to the Ministry of Finance, 517 billion yuan (or 43 percent of local government spending in this area) was disbursed in 2012 from the central government to local governments for employment and social security. These expenditure increases reflect both new and expanded programs and increased standards, as illustrated by the following examples.

Pensions

Pension expenditures have increased rapidly, now accounting for almost one-third of total government social security spending. The fiscal subsidy more than doubled from 160 billion yuan in 2008 to 375 billion yuan in 2012. Pension payments per year to urban workers increased from an average of about 700 yuan in 2005 to 1,721 yuan in 2012 (China.com 2013). This was mainly the result of a steady increase of approximately 10 percent per year since 2008 in the basic pension, financed from the fiscal budget.

In rural areas, a new rural pension program was piloted in 2008 and rapidly rolled out in 2009. By 2012, it had been implemented in almost all rural areas, with an enrolment of 462.7 million residents, triple the 143 million of 2010. The government's fiscal subsidy to the new rural pension fund rose from 24.0 billion to 93.3 billion yuan between 2010 and 2012, particularly to enable the rural elderly above sixty to enrol and claim a basic pension (i.e., the portion funded

Table 11.4

Pension programs for rural and urban residents

	Enrolment (in million people)		Number who claim benefits (in million people)		Expenditures (billion yuan) on benefits (individual account + government finance)	
	New rural pension	Urban residents pension	New rural pension	Urban residents pension	New rural pension	Urban residents pension
2007	51.71	n.a.	3.92	n.a.	4.0	n.a.
2008	55.95	n.a.	5.12	n.a.	5.68	n.a.
2009	86.91	n.a.	15.56	n.a.	7.6	n.a.
2010	143.0	n.a.	42.43	n.a.	20.0	n.a.
2011	358.0	5.39	89.22	2.35	58.8	1.1
2012		483.70		130.75		115.0

Note: 2007–8 data are likely to refer to the old rural pension scheme, whereas 2009 might include the new rural pension scheme.
Source: Ministry of Human Resources and Social Security Annual Statistical Report, various years, http://www.mohrss.gov.cn/SYrlzyhshbzb/zwgk/szrs/.

by the government) without having paid contributions to the scheme. In 2010 (the second year of implementation), 42 million elderly Chinese claimed pension benefits (see Table 11.4).

Pensions were also expanded to urban residents who were not part of the urban workers program on a contributory basis. The urban resident basic old age pension scheme also allows the elderly already at retirement age to enrol and claim a basic pension. Official data show that 5.4 million urban residents enrolled in the scheme in 2011, with about half claiming benefits. The benefits and mechanisms of the urban resident basic old age pension program are aligned with those of the new rural pension program, making it possible to unify the two programs. This has been occurring since 2012, referred to in official documents as the urban-rural resident pension program. Such steps toward integration will enhance the coordination of financing for the basic pension as funding responsibility moves from the county level to the better-resourced provincial government. These steps toward integration are important in facilitating the coverage of migrants as well as the rapid urbanization process set as a goal of the current leadership (*21st Century Business Herald* 2013).

Social Assistance

China's basic social assistance program – the minimum living standard or *dibao* – also saw rapid increases in coverage and spending (see Table 11.5). The number of rural *dibao* beneficiaries increased about sevenfold between 2007 (when it

Sarah Cook and Wing Lam

Table 11.5

Overview of *dibao* standard and average subsidy levels in rural and urban areas

	Urban *dibao* (yuan per month)				Rural *dibao* (yuan per month)			
	Standard (ppl/mth)	y-o-y (%)	Subsidy	y-o-y (%)	Standard (ppl/mth)	y-o-y (%)	Subsidy	y-o-y (%)
2005	156.0	n.a.	72.3	11.2	n.a.	n.a.	n.a.	n.a.
2006	169.6	8.7	83.6	15.6	n.a.	n.a.	n.a.	n.a.
2007	182.4	7.5	102.7	22.8	70.0	n.a.	38.8	12.5
2008	205.3	12.6	143.7	39.9	82.3	17.6	50.4	29.9
2009	227.8	10.9	172.0	19.7	100.8	22.5	68.0	34.9
2010	251.2	10.3	189.0	9.9	117.0	16.1	74.0	8.8
2011*	287.6	14.5	240.3	27.1	143.2	22.4	106.1	43.4
2012	330.1	14.8	239.1	−0.5	172.3	20.3	104.0	−2.0

* "Subsidy" is the amount actually paid to bring low-income households up to the "standard." In 2011, this included a special one-off subsidy for all *dibao* beneficiaries.

Source: Annual Statistical Report on Social Services Development, Ministry of Civil Affairs, various years, http://www.mca.gov.cn/article/zwgk/tjsj/.

was rolled out nationwide) and 2012, while public funding also rose rapidly. The trend for urban *dibao* has been steadier, given that the program was already well established and more comprehensive. The central government did increase its funding, however, to raise *dibao* between 2008 and 2011, including several one-off subsidies to beneficiaries to compensate them for food price inflation. Central and local government financial support to the programs in both rural and urban areas rose from 38.6 billion yuan in 2007 to 139.2 billion yuan in 2012, representing a share of total government spending on employment and social security of 6 percent in 2007 and 11 percent in 2012.

Increases in the *dibao* standard reflect wider efforts by the government to raise minimum living standards, also seen in a rapid rise in the minimum wage and in wages overall. Following the temporary suspension of the minimum wage adjustment in the crisis years (2008–9), the subsequent increase has been two- to threefold: according to provincial data, the monthly minimum wage (in yuan) in 2008 ranged from 315 (Jiangxi) to 750 (Shanghai); in 2013, the range was from 1,030 (Guizhou) to 1,620 (Shanghai) (ACFTU 2006; *People's Daily* 2013). This striking increase reflects the government's stated intention of raising employment income and boosting domestic demand, with a target of raising minimum wage standards on average 13 percent per year during the twelfth Five-Year Plan (2011–15) (State Council 2012b).

Affordable housing also received a major boost through the stimulus package, accounting for 10 percent of the total package. Public spending on affordable housing initiatives increased from 72.6 billion yuan in 2009 to 448 billion yuan in 2013. In total, during this period, the government committed 1.1 trillion yuan, or 8 percent of total social spending, of which over half came from the central government. The program gained further momentum in 2011 after the former premier, Wen, announced the goal of building 36 million affordable housing units by 2015, to reach the target set in the twelfth Five-Year Plan (*Nanfang Daily* 2012). Questions remain, however, about the allocation of housing units and their social impacts (Xinhuanet 2011a; Zhang 2012).

Indirect Impacts, Lessons, Consequences, and Policy Choices

The evidence presented above suggests that (a) the crisis provided an impetus for China to expand its social policies and provisions; (b) this expansion showed continuities with prior policies and has moved in a consistent direction post-crisis; and (c) the use of social policy before, during, and after the crisis was consistent with the government's continued prioritization of growth and social stability. Two further questions need to be addressed, however, to understand the longer-term consequences or significance of the crisis for social policy in China. First, what are the indirect ways in which the crisis might affect social policy through its impact more broadly on other aspects of the economy or society? Second, what other factors determine China's social policy trajectory?

The financial crisis provided a critical backdrop to the twelfth Five-Year Plan, while its repercussions continue to reverberate through the global economy. Slow recovery and austerity elsewhere reinforce the need for China to continue its own economic restructuring in order to reduce reliance on its major export markets and products. Its own commodity dependence, while currently boosting growth in many less developed economies, also exposes areas of vulnerability that affect longer-term economic policy making. The potential impacts of shifting policies elsewhere – such as uncertainty over further quantitative easing in the United States – create new instabilities in and concerns for emerging market economies (with feedback again into global markets).

Domestically, China faces a set of challenges associated with the transformation of its economy, at unprecedented speed, in an era when (in contrast even to "late liberalizers" of the twentieth century) there is much less space to negotiate its development path on a purely domestic basis (Tsai and Cook 2005). Structural weaknesses in the economy have been exacerbated by the highly expansionary credit policies of the stimulus program, reflected, for example, in the poor quality of investments, an overheated property market, and hugely unsustainable levels of local government debt. Weaning China off the stimulus package, and managing the consequences of scaling back investment, pose both economic and political challenges (Naughton 2010). Between 2005 and 2010, the overall growth in central government revenues was twice the rate of GDP or 21.5 percent per year (Fewsmith 2010), thus creating space for expansionary fiscal and social policies. These revenues will shrink as growth slows, while China's export surpluses are also declining. As revenues shrink, policy choices become more difficult, while interests (between elites and others, rich and poor, rural and urban, region and region) also become more contentious and will require different mechanisms for their reconciliation.

Among the major priorities of the Chinese leadership in the current phase of structural transformation are urbanization, migration, and employment; population aging; and environmental issues, including the crises in water and air pollution. Issues of scale and pace, multiple levels of governance, and the nature of the political system are among the factors adding to complexity of policy choices in the context of a more difficult and uncertain external environment. A further task, which calls for creativity and innovation, particularly for large industrializing and urbanizing economies, is to manage this transformation in an environmentally sustainable manner. There are inherent tensions among these goals: promoting domestic demand in part through a massive urbanization project will have huge implications for sustainable resource use while increasing the risk of social tension.

An area in which the crisis might be having less direct but still significant impacts is in attitudes toward risk and risk management and their extension to the social sphere. The rising concern with social management or "stability preservation" (Yu 2010), reflected in considerable shrinking of the space for social activism and social media, might be connected with the need to manage risks, particularly when party-state legitimacy is questioned. This is also reflected in the fear of social protests that swept the world (from the Arab Spring to the Occupy movement) following the crisis. Such indirect reverberations are reflected in the wider political and policy-making context in China.

For many in China, the key issue remains maintaining growth in order to meet the basic needs of a large low-income population with high levels of poverty; issues of the environment or redistribution are secondary. For others, the pattern of growth – in terms of inclusiveness and environmental sustainability – has become more prominent. In either case, to ensure the continued economic transformation, the inclusion of groups currently living at the margins – the remaining rural poor and western regions and migrants – will require continued major public sector spending, particularly from the central government. Thus, a commitment to continued high levels of spending and redistribution will be necessary to avoid a slowdown or even regression in recent progress.

Although some of the challenges and disparities noted above have received greater attention in the policy agenda in recent years – particularly in the expansion of programs to rural and migrant populations and the elderly – others remain barely visible. Ethnicity is one. Another is gender. Women have benefited from many aspects of China's economic reforms and social policies, but there has been significant retrogression in terms of the provision of services for care – whether of children, the sick, or the elderly – with serious implications for women's labour force attachment, employment status, and thus access to formal social insurance benefits through employment (Cook and Dong 2011). The reinforcing of traditional gender roles through neglect of accessible and affordable service provision in these areas will have long-term consequences for future welfare needs and provision, particularly in a context of rapid population aging.

A still more fundamental challenge might be the politics of welfare construction in a one-party state. Again, parallels with the transformation of the East Asian developmental states are pertinent: the rise of social protest and expansion of social policies in response to crisis were contributing factors to the pressures ultimately leading to political openings and democratic transitions (Kwon 2005). The delicate task for the Chinese government remains the maintenance of its legitimate authority: initially it was achieved through the delivery of improved living standards to the majority of the population, but this option is becoming increasingly complex. Globally integrated elites, middle-class consumers, transnational capital, and multiple forms of deprivation create social tensions that can be eased but not resolved through the better distribution of welfare alone.

The Chinese state has used its increasing fiscal resources to further its redistributive and social peace–building agenda but lacks many effective levers of control over local governments and their economies. The central state has limited capacity to manage competing local, regional, and bureaucratic interests or to set incentives and create monitoring mechanisms that ensure compliance. In response to dissatisfaction, and without adequate mechanisms for resolution, increasing numbers of citizens turn to forms of protest and social activism – some of which can be seen as legitimate and lead to demands being met, but in many cases the government's response is pressure, including on local governments to maintain stability and harmony. The result is often a closing down of

Sarah Cook and Wing Lam

space for expressions of social citizenship even as the mechanisms of state and citizenship building associated with welfare regimes are being massively expanded.

Citizens who have been incorporated into the state through their access to social benefits and legitimate entitlements are increasingly aware of their rights and the responsibilities of local governments and the state, and increasingly they assert their claims. Whether China can turn its expansionary social policies toward a form of developmental inclusion is not obvious. What is clear from policy in recent years and from statements of the current leadership is that the risks of relaxing the pressure on social expression are considered too high, creating a potentially unstable form of welfare authoritarianism to which new responses will need to be found. However this process unfolds, it is clear that the new disparities that have emerged along different lines, and that are being shaped by changing social policies, will continue in turn to "shape the future contours of social policy and social citizenship in China" (Shi 2012b).

Ultimately, domestic factors, particularly associated with structural transformation, the threat of instability, and the ability of the central state to negotiate its policies and ensure their implementation, are the main drivers of China's choice of policies with respect to social welfare. Unlike in the developed economies, China's social welfare system was far from being a stable system rocked by a crisis. It is a system in the process of construction, developing without a blueprint but with overarching criteria and priorities and with capacities to respond pragmatically to issues as they arise. Thus, the logic of China's social policy development remains primarily a domestic issue, even as the constraints arising from the external environment impinge on it. In turn, the social policy choices made at critical moments play a role in shaping its future development trajectory and structural transformation: in other words, social policy itself helps to constitute the path of development.

Conclusion

In this chapter, we have argued that the crisis has not fundamentally shifted the direction of China's social policy, but nonetheless it has provided some impetus to the rate of expansion while changing some of the conditions within which new social policies are being negotiated. The crisis was a vivid illustration of the risks to China itself of failing to push forward with its own economic restructuring – in which social policies will again play a major role. How it will build institutions or pursue policies that can balance increasingly divergent and often conflictual interests in this process remains to be seen.

The process of welfare system building under these conditions calls for innovation. China (like many emerging economies) faces a unique situation in this new phase of development. Although large and rapidly growing economies have more autonomy in the integrated global economy than smaller or poorer developing countries, they are constructing their social policies with less domestic autonomy than any of their predecessors. And their new social policy regimes have to address sets of risks and changing conditions that were not central concerns during most earlier welfare state–building processes. They are doing so in a context dominated by neo-liberal policies; high levels of informality, particularly in labour; financialization and the risks that it implies (including for the funds that they need to amass for their future elderly); unprecedented mobility and communication necessary for a knowledge economy; and environmental crisis. For China in particular, its rise as a new power in a multipolar world adds complexity to many of its policy choices.

China, along with other large emerging economies, is negotiating these new challenges and constructing a social policy system that will need to be more resilient to this expanded set of risks and crises. These countries will need to build capabilities among societies and individuals to meet the demands of a different economy, working life, family structure, care needs, and a changing environment. Their experiences (both successful and otherwise) should ultimately help not only their own populations but also those of other developing countries entering similar territory: perhaps they will also provide new inspiration to former welfare states emerging from austerity measures.

Notes

1 Note that many earlier initiatives, pilots, false starts, and studies also took place during this period on issues such as health and pension reform.
2 These reforms coincided with the Asian financial crisis of 1997–98; although China was not directly affected by this crisis, the lessons of not having a safety net in place were clear.
3 This was noted in Cook and Lam (2011) and is reinforced by current discussions in China about increasing the role of non-governmental, non-profit, and social organizations in the delivery of welfare services.
4 The new program was rolled out as a pilot initiative in 2008, and many areas gradually merged the old and new schemes. However, progress of the merger varies. There is no information on expenditure on the new program in 2012.
5 Data taken from the OECD Social Expenditure Database (OECD n.d.). According to the ADB's social protection index, the share of total social protection expenditure in 2009 as a percentage of GDP was 5.4 (up from 4.9 in 2005), compared with India (1.5 from 0.4 in 2004) and Vietnam (2.4 from 2.1 in 2003) (ADB 2013).
6 Lack of itemized local government transfer payments pre-2006 means that we cannot compare the trend in central government total social spending before 2007.

References

All-China Federation of Trade Unions (ACFTU). 2006. "An Overview of Minimum Wage Standard and All Other Categories of Social Protection Standard across the Country in 2006 [in Chinese: 2006 nian ge di zui di gong zi biao zhun ji ge lei bao zhang xian tiao zheng qing kuang]." http://bzgzb.acftu.org/template/10002/file.jsp?aid=247.

Asia Development Bank (ADB). 2013. *Social Protection Index: Assessing Results for Asia and the Pacific*. Manila: ADB.

Caijing.com. 2009. "Facelift for China's Economic Stimulus Plan." Caijing.com.cn, 6 March. http://english.caijing.com.cn/2009-03-06/110114405.html.

Chan, Cecilia L., and Nelson W. Chow. 1992. *More Welfare after Economic Reform? Welfare Development in the People's Republic of China*. Hong Kong: University of Hong Kong.

Chan, Chak-kwan. 2010. "Rethinking the Incrementalist Thesis in China: A Reflection on the Development of the Minimum Standard of Living Scheme in Urban and Rural Areas." *Journal of Social Policy* 39, 04: 627–45. http://dx.doi.org/10.1017/S0047279410000322.

Chang, Kyung-sup. 1993. "The Confucian Family Instead of the Welfare State? Reform and Peasant Welfare in Post-Mao China." *Asian Perspective* 17, 3: 169–200.

Chen, Sheying. 1996. *Social Policy of the Economic State and Community Care in Chinese Culture: Aging, Family, Urban Change, and the Socialist Welfare Pluralism*. Aldershot: Avebury.

–. 2013. "State Council Decides to Raise Basic Pensions of Urban Worker Retirees by 10% This Year [in Chinese: Guo wu yuan jue ding jin nian qi ye tui xiu ren yuan ji ben yang lao jin ti gao 10%]." China.com.cn, 10 January. http://finance.china.com.cn/money/insurance/bxyw/20130110/1228996.shtml.

Communist Party of China (CPC). 2006. "Communiqué of the Sixth Plenum of the 16th CPC Central Committee." *People's Daily*, 12 October. http://en.people.cn/200610/12/eng20061012_310923.html.

Cook, Sarah. 2011. "Global Discourses, National Policies, Local Outcomes: Reflections on China's Welfare Reforms." In *China's Changing Welfare Mix: Local Perspectives*, edited by Jane Duckett and Beatriz Carrillo, 211–22. London: Routledge.

–. 2012. "Rebounding from Crisis: The Role and Limits of Social Policy in China's Recovery." In *The Global Crisis and Transformative Social Change*, edited by Peter Utting, Shahra Razavi, and Rebecca Varghese Buchholz, 141–60. Basingstoke: Palgrave Macmillan and UNRISD. http://dx.doi.org/10.1057/9781137002501.0014.

Cook, Sarah, and Huck-ju Kwon. 2008. "Revisiting Welfare Developmentalism: Economic Reforms and Trajectories of Social Policy in East Asia." *Italian Journal of Social Policy* 1: 511–29.

Cook, Sarah, and Xiao-yuan Dong. 2011. "Harsh Choices: Chinese Women's Paid Work and Unpaid Care Responsibilities under Economic Reform." *Development and Change* 42, 4: 947–65. http://dx.doi.org/10.1111/j.1467-7660.2011.01721.x.

Cook, Sarah, and Wing Lam. 2011. "China's Response to Crisis: What Role for Social Policy?" In *Social Policy in Challenging Times: Economic Crisis and Welfare Systems*, edited by Kevin Farnsworth and Zoe Irving, 139–58. Bristol: Policy Press. http://dx.doi.org/10.1332/policypress/9781847428288.003.0008.

Duckett, Jane, and Beatriz Carrillo, eds. 2011. *China's Changing Welfare Mix: Local Perspectives*. London: Routledge.

Fewsmith, Joseph. 2010. "Now for the Hard Part: Into the Next Decade." *Global Asia* 5, 2: 16–21.

Frazier, Mark W. 2010. *Socialist Insecurity: Pensions and the Politics of Uneven Development in China*. Ithaca: Cornell University Press.

Gao, Qin, Sui Yang, and Shi Li. 2013. "The Chinese Welfare State in Transition: 1988–2007." *Journal of Social Policy* 42, 4: 743–62. http://dx.doi.org/10.1017/S0047279413000329.

Goodman, Roger, Gordon White, and Huck-ju Kwon, eds. 1998. *The East Asian Welfare Model: Welfare Orientalism and the State*. London: Routledge.

Guan, Xinping. 2005. "China's Social Policy: Reform and Development in the Context of Marketisation and Globalisation." In *Transforming the Developmental Welfare State in East Asia*, edited by Kwon Huck-ju, 231–56. London: Palgrave Macmillan.

Kwon, Huck-ju. 2005. *Transforming the Developmental Welfare State in East Asia*. London: Palgrave Macmillan.

Leading Party Members' Group of the Ministry of Human Resources and Social Security. 2013. "A Social Safety Net for Urban and Rural Residents Has Taken Shape in China." *Qishi* 5, 1. http://english.qstheory.cn/society/201302/t20130227_213711.htm.

Leung, Joe C.B. 2003. "Social Security Reforms in China: Issues and Prospects." *International Journal of Social Welfare* 12, 2: 73–85. http://dx.doi.org/10.1111/1468-2397.t01-1 -00246.

Leung, Joe C.B., and Richard C. Nann. 1995. *Authority and Benevolence: Social Welfare in China*. Hong Kong: Chinese University of Hong Kong Press.

Li, Bingqin. 2012. "Social Welfare and Protection for Economic Growth and Social Stability: China's Experience." In *A Changing China: Emerging Governance, Economic and Social Trends*, edited by Civil Service College, Singapore, 39–60. Singapore: Civil Service College.

Ministry of Finance. PRC. Various years. "Report on Final Accounts of National Public Finance [*Quan guo cai zheng jue suan*]." Fiscal Statistics, Ministry of Finance, PRC. http://yss.mof.gov.cn/zhengwuxinxi/caizhengshuju/.

Mok, Ka Ho, and Yu Cheung Wong. 2011. "Regional Disparities and Educational Inequalities: City Responses and Coping Strategies." In *China's Changing Welfare Mix: Local Perspectives*, edited by Jane Duckett and Beatriz Carrillo, 126–50. London: Routledge.

Nanfang Daily. 2012. "MOHURD: Purchase Restriction to Continue Next Year [in Chinese: Zhu jian bu: Ming nian ji xu shi xing xian gou]." *Nanfang Daily*, 26 December. http://epaper.southcn.com/nfdaily/html/2012-12/26/content_7154876.htm.

National Bureau of Statistics of China (NBSC). N.d. *NBSC Statistical Database*. http://www.stats.gov.cn.

Naughton, Barry. 2010. "Policy Challenges of Post-Stimulus Growth." *Global Asia* 5, 2: 22–27.

OECD. N.d. Social Expenditure Database (SOCX). OECD Social Policies and Data. http://www.oecd.org/social/expenditure.htm.

People's Daily. 2013. "An Overview of Minimum Wage Standard in 20 Provinces and Cities and Guangdong Ranks Third at 1,550 Yuan Per Month [in Chinese: 20 sheng shi zui di gong zi biao zhun yi lan Guangdong 1550 yuan pan di san wei]." *People's Daily*, 11 July. http://www.51labour.com/show/187311.html.

Ringen, Stein, and Kinglun Ngok. 2013. "What Kind of Welfare State Is Emerging in China?" UNRISD Working Paper.

Saunders, Peter, and Xiaoyuan Shang. 2001. "Social Security Reform in China's Transition to a Market Economy." *Social Policy and Administration: An International Journal of Policy and Research* 35, 3: 274–89. http://dx.doi.org/10.1111/1467-9515.00233.

Shi, Shih-Jiunn. 2012a. "Towards Inclusive Social Citizenship? Rethinking China's Social Security in the Trend towards Urban-Rural Harmonisation." *Journal of Social Policy* 41, 4: 789–810. http://dx.doi.org/10.1017/S0047279412000517.

–. 2012b. "Social Policy Learning and Diffusion in China: The Rise of Welfare Regions?" *Policy and Politics* 40, 3: 367–85. http://dx.doi.org/10.1332/147084411X581899.

Solinger, Dorothy J., and Yiyang Hu. 2012. "Welfare, Wealth, and Poverty in Urban China: The Dibao and Its Differential Disbursement." *China Quarterly* 211: 741–64. http://dx. doi.org/10.1017/S0305741012000835.

State Council. 2010. "The Medium and Long Term Plan for Education Reform and Development (2010–2020). [*Quo jia zhong chang qi jian yu gai ge he fa zhan gui hua gang yao* (2010-2020)]. *People's Daily*, 30 July. http://politics.people.com.cn/GB/1026/12292564.html.

–. 2012a. "Outline of 12th Five-Year Plan for Social Security [in Chinese: She hui bao zhang shi er wu gui hua gang yao]." State Council Order (2012) No. 17. http://www.gov.cn/zwgk/2012-06/27/content_2171218.htm.

–. 2012b. "Employment Promotion Plan (2011–2015) [in Chinese: Cu jin jiu ye gui hua]." State Council Order (2012) No. 6. http://business.sohu.com/20120208/n334118154.shtml.

Tsai, Kellee, and Sarah Cook. 2005. "Developmental Dilemmas in China: Socialist Transition and Late Liberalization." In *Japan and China in the World Political Economy*, edited by Saadia Pekkannen and Kellee Tsai, 45–66. London: Routledge.

21st Century Business Herald. 2013. "Li Keqiang: A People-Based Approach to Promote New Urbanization [in Chinese: Li ke qiang: Yi ren wei ben lai tui jinx in xing cheng zhen hua]." *21st Century Business Herald*, 19 March. http://finance.qq.com/a/20130319/001198.htm.

Wen, Jiabao. 2010a. "The Government's Work Report 2010 – Full Text [in Chinese: 2010 nian zheng fu gong zuo gao (quan wen)]." Speech presented at the Third Plenary Meeting of the Eleventh NPC, 5 March, Beijing). China.com.cn, 15 March. http://www.china.com.cn/policy/txt/2010-03/15/content_19612372.htm.

–. 2010b. "Several Questions Regarding Social Development Affairs and the Improvement of People's Livelihoods [in Chinese: Quan yu fa zhan she hui shi ye he gai shan min sheng de jig e wen ti]." *Qiushi* 7. http://www.qstheory.cn/zxdk/2010/201007/201003/t20100326_25272.htm.

Wong, Linda. 1998. *Marginalisation and Social Welfare in China*. London: Routledge.

Wong, Linda, and Norman Flynn, eds. 2001. *The Market in Chinese Social Policy*. Basingstoke: Palgrave Macmillan. http://dx.doi.org/10.1057/9781403919939.

Xinhuanet. 2010. "More Affordable Housing Urged in China." Xinhuanet.com, 20 May. http://news.xinhuanet.com/english2010/china/2010-05/20/c_13304913.htm.

–. 2011a. "Inequality in the Allocation of Affordable Housing Required Attention [in Chinese: Bao zhang fang fen pei bu gong xian xiang yan zhong zhi de zhong shi]." Xinhuanet.com, 4 August. http://news.xinhuanet.com/2011-08/04/c_121814657.htm.

–. 2011b. "China's Massive Stimulus Creates Side Effects, Economic Development Adjustments Needed: Economist." Xinhuanet.com, 2 December. http://news.xinhuanet.com/english/indepth/2011-12/02/c_131285242.htm.

Yu, Jianrong. 2010. "Social Issues: The Mechanisms of 'Rigid Stability.'" *Global Asia* 5, 2: 28–39.

Zhang, Min. 2012. "Examining the Equality in the Allocation Mechanism of Affording Housing [in Chinese: Bao zhang xing zhu fang gong ping fen pei ji zhi tan xi wen ti]." *China Economic and Trade Herald*, 27 March. http://thesis.cei.gov.cn/modules/ShowDoc. aspx?DocGUID=30ff330b77e947b98a318afeae4677f6.

Zheng, Gong-cheng. 2008. *China's Social Security in Thirty Years* [in Chinese: *Zhong guo she hui bao zhang san shi nian*]. Beijing: People's Press.

PART 4: GLOBAL NORTH

12

Global Crisis and Social Policy in Peripheral Europe
Comparing Ireland, Portugal, and Greece

BERKAY AYHAN AND STEPHEN McBRIDE

By 2008, the sub-prime mortgage credit crunch in the United States triggered imbalances inherent in the European Union, and by 2010 the recession turned into a major sovereign debt crisis that raised serious doubts about the future of the eurozone.

Some states experienced very large increases in unemployment and debt, whereas others weathered the storm with relatively little impact. The peripheral countries of the eurozone – Greece, Ireland, and Portugal – were among the worst affected (see Table 12.1). As members of the eurozone, these countries had lost policy capacity in a number of areas, notably the ability to devalue their currency. As a result, "internal devaluation" by reducing wages and living standards seemed the only available alternative to achieve greater competitiveness. This "option" was imposed on them by what became known as the troika – the European Commission (EC), European Central Bank (ECB), and International Monetary Fund (IMF) – in the form of harsh austerity conditions attached to loans. The turn to austerity clearly had impacts on social policy through major cutbacks in social welfare spending as well as labour market flexibility reforms.

In this chapter, we explore the political economy of the global crisis as it affected the peripheral countries of the eurozone. We argue that the *core-periphery relationship in the eurozone* is the central dynamic that explains pre- as well as post-crisis political economy and social policy reforms of the peripheral European countries. The crisis exposed and exacerbated imbalances between the core and peripheral states within the European Union as well as weaknesses

Table 12.1

Impact of the crisis: Labour markets and public finances

Variable (unit) Year	Greece	Ireland	Portugal	Eurozone average	OECD average
Unemployment rate (% of labour force)					
2007	8.39	4.67	7.97	7.46	5.60
2010	12.71	13.85	10.79	9.97	8.29
2014	26.49	11.26	13.90	11.54	7.32
Youth unemployment (%, aged 15–24)					
2007	22.7	9.10	16.70	15.10	11.90
2010	33.0	27.60	22.80	20.90	16.70
2014	52.4	23.90	34.80	23.80	15.10
Employment rate (%, aged 15–64)					
2007	60.9	69.20	67.60	65.50	66.40
2010	59.1	59.70	65.30	64.00	64.50
2014	49.4	61.70	62.60	63.80	65.70
Budget balance (% of GDP)					
2007	−6.74	0.27	−3.00	−0.61	−1.54
2010	−11.07	−32.55	−11.17	−6.14	−7.90
2014	−3.55	−4.11	−4.45	−2.43	−3.66
Gross public debt (% of GDP)					
2007	102.76	23.96	68.43	65.24	–
2010	145.31	87.47	96.18	84.26	–
2014	177.44	109.69	130.18	94.62	–
Private sector debt (% of GDP)					
2007	113.09	257.34	278.78	–	–
2010	139.87	362.14	301.51	–	–
2013	148.56	377.30	305.66	–	–

Sources: OECD Economic Outlook No. 97 June 2015; OECD Short-Term Labour Market Statistics; OECD Financial Indicators – Stocks.

in the constitution of the eurozone. Our analysis highlights the necessity of exploring the broader political economy dynamics within the eurozone to gain a comprehensive understanding of when, why, and how social policy reforms are initiated within peripheral states. We begin by reviewing the institutional structure of the Economic and Monetary Union and then explore the political economy of core-periphery dynamics, locating the peripheral countries within the pre-crisis context. This provides a backdrop for an analysis of post-crisis social policy reforms in Ireland, Portugal, and Greece, respectively.

Political Economy of the Eurozone and Pre-Crisis Dynamics

Formed in 1991, the Economic and Monetary Union (EMU) brought about the close coordination of economic policy making, fiscal policy coordination, and single monetary policy with the common currency euro (European Commission 2014). Within this framework, monetary policy is governed by the European Central Bank, a supranational institution that has been granted independence from elected governments and the mandate to maintain price stability. Fiscal policy coordination is maintained with the Stability and Growth Pact principles supposed to limit budget deficits of member states to 3 percent of GDP and public debt to 60 percent of GDP.

The institutional framework of European economic integration has sparked serious criticisms of the way in which it is pursued within the neo-liberal understanding that entails "flexibilization of the labour markets, monetarist monetary policy, financial market liberalization, [and] free movement for capital across Europe" (Becker and Jager 2011, 6). Arguably, this framework is beneficial for capital while detrimental to the working class because it provides "means to undermine national social regulations and promote wage restraint," hence a "race to the bottom" (Macartney 2013, 6; Lapavitsas et al. 2010, 1). Pursuit of such a neo-liberal agenda is removed from popular accountability through depoliticized supranational economic policy-making bodies (Gill 1998, 5; McBride 2010). National governments are thus protected from effective criticism because the tight fiscal and monetary policy is imposed by the EU institutions. An important consequence of a single monetary policy is that states cannot pursue an independent monetary policy and use the tool of "external devaluation." Moreover, unlike a conventional central bank, the ECB is not allowed to manage the public debt of its members (Lapavitsas et al. 2010, 5). This problematic design of the EMU structure played a major role prior to and throughout the crisis.

In addition to the structure of the EMU, the relationship between core and peripheral states within the eurozone is the key to explaining pre- as well as post-crisis political economy dynamics. Of the eighteen member states that have entered into the eurozone, four – Germany, France, Netherlands, and Belgium – belong to the core, whereas five – Italy, Spain, Ireland, Greece, and Portugal – can be described as peripheral (Lapavitsas et al. 2010, 2).[1] Of central importance here is the relationship between the "export-led growth in the core and mounting deficits and productivity imbalances in the periphery" (Macartney 2013, 7). Germany, the prominent core country within the eurozone, has "structural strength" derived from its prominence in the capital goods and technology sectors (Bellofiore and Halevi 2010, 20). In addition, Germany pursued a deflationary policy that allowed it to suppress wages effectively. As labour's share in German output declined over the past two decades, "German competitiveness has thus risen further within the Eurozone. The result has been a structural current account surplus for Germany, mirrored by current account deficits for peripheral countries" (Lapavitsas et al. 2010, 6).[2] The European periphery provided the crucial demand for the core countries' export products. Introduction of the EMU perpetuated the superiority of the core countries because the peripheral countries were no longer able to devalue their currencies. When the euro was launched, Germany had a balanced current account, but by 2007 it had achieved a surplus of 7.7 percent of GDP (Becker and Jager 2011, 8). These current account surpluses were "recycled through foreign direct investment and German bank lending to peripheral countries" (Lapavitsas et al. 2010, 4). In other words, "Germany was exporting credit dependence to others: German banks lending to the 'PIGS' created demand for its own exports" (Featherstone 2011, 200). This overaccumulated capital constituted the basis of unhealthy growth and sustained imbalances in the peripheral countries up until the crisis.

From the perspective of peripheral countries, entrance to the eurozone implied low interest rates and hence easy access to cheap credit, while the competitiveness gap between core and periphery led to the weakening of the productive sectors and deindustrialization in the peripheral countries (Becker and Jager 2011, 9). Growth in peripheral countries became financialized and dependent on capital inflows from the core: "Growth has come from expansion of consumption financed by expanding household debt, or from investment bubbles characterized by real estate speculation. There has been a general rise of indebtedness, whether of households or corporations" (Lapavitsas et al. 2010, 5). In general terms, property bubbles in Ireland and Spain as well as high personal indebtedness in Greece are direct reflections of this trend of the financialized regime of accumulation (Becker and Jager 2011, 9). The financialization dynamic, though it took different forms, is thus visible in each of the peripheral countries that we examine here.

Ireland had become a hub for multinational corporations in the field of information technology from the 1990s on. The "Celtic Tiger" was viewed as a *flexible developmental state*, "defined by its ability to nurture post-Fordist networks of production and innovation, to attract international investment, and to link these local and global technology and business networks together in ways that promote development"' (O'Riain 2000, 158). An alternative account

Berkay Ayhan and Stephen McBride

conceptualized Ireland as a *competition state* that "prioritises goals of economic competitiveness over those of social cohesion and welfare" (Kirby and Murphy 2011, 20). Both terms refer, however, to Ireland's reliance on neo-liberal prescriptions of deregulating financial markets and seeking to attract foreign capital by providing a business-friendly environment with low taxation (Allen 2012, 424; Kirby and Murphy 2011, 34). This growth model was supplemented by a welfare regime that had many liberal features (Esping-Andersen 1990) but some hybrid elements to the extent that it included a corporatist wage-bargaining structure from the mid-1980s on (Cousins 1997, 226).[3]

Although Ireland's economic record had appeared successful on macro-economic indicators, the underlying financialized accumulation regime and property bubble were highly dependent on capital flows from the core. Until the collapse of Lehman Brothers in September 2008, the Irish economy had adequate rates of economic growth, low public debt, and a very low unemployment rate. Lehman's collapse set off a domestic crisis as Ireland's housing bubble burst and its banks became insolvent. Overaccumulated credit from the core had been "channeled into a poorly regulated domestic financial market which, in turn, channeled the cheap credit into real estate" (Regan 2012, 472).[4] Irish banks had changed their sources of capital by relying not only on deposits but also on international investors' bonds (Whelan 2011, 8). During the housing boom, prices quadrupled in Ireland, and "construction accounted for 13.3 percent of all employment, the highest share in the OECD" (Whelan 2011, 5).

Greece and Portugal had a Southern European welfare regime. Sometimes considered as a sub-category of the state-corporatist model (Katrougalos and Lazaridis 2003), these countries share a common past of "late industrialization, a right-wing dictatorship in the 20th century and a strong role played by the church in promoting traditional family-oriented values" (Tavora 2012, 63). There is segmentation and fragmentation in the labour market as well as in welfare provision, resulting in generous protection of men (especially in the public sector) at the expense of women, young people, and migrants (Karamessini 2008, 47). Commentators criticized the "lack of an efficient, rational, Weberian type administration" in these states (Katrougalos and Lazaridis 2003, 7) and clientelism and patronage in the distribution of welfare benefits (Ferrera 1996, 17).

In Portugal's case, there was neither a property bubble nor a banking crisis but the gradual erosion of competitiveness because of core-periphery dynamics. Both the economic boom of the 1990s and the poor performance of the 2000s stemmed from Portugal's relationship with the European Union. Throughout the 1990s, Portugal benefited significantly from transfers from the European

Union for renewing its infrastructure, while positive expectations of the benefits of joining the monetary union created a demand-led growth (Torres 2009, 57). As Soares (2007, 467) notes, "in 1986, the Portuguese GDP was just 54% of the average European GDP of 15 member states; in 2001, Portuguese GDP was 75% of the average European GDP of 15 member states." It did not solve, however, the basic loss of competiveness (Lopes 2003, 284–85). With entrance into the eurozone by the early 2000s, the Portuguese economy regressed, and mainstream commentators declared Portugal the "new sick man of Europe," noting that, in terms of GDP growth, it was the last among all of the European countries by 2006 (*Economist* 2007). Greece's sovereign debt crisis has been attributed to inefficient public administration, lack of a meritocratic bureaucracy, prevalence of clientelism and rent seeking, widespread tax evasion, and public debt problems leading to fiscal difficulties (Featherstone 2011, 196; Katsimi and Moutos 2010, 570; Pagoulatos and Triantopoulos 2009, 36; Tsarouhas 2012, 86–88). Although these issues contributed to the severity of the crisis, the mainstream discourses of Greece as "rent seeking" and a "society living beyond its means" have been instrumental in legitimating harsh austerity reforms (Markantonatou 2013, 62; on Greece, see also Haworth and Hughes, this volume).

The austerity approach misdiagnoses the crisis as stemming from public debt, which supposedly could be cured by austerity (Hay and Wincott 2012, 217). We argue that the crisis is better viewed in the European context as resting on fundamental problems of accumulation regimes and growth as well as core-periphery dynamics. Indeed, the productive capacity of Greece significantly deteriorated, and the pre-crisis growth was "artificially maintained" by "a construction boom fuelled by the 2004 Olympic Games" (Tsarouhas 2012, 88). The core-periphery relationship in terms of overaccumulated capital flows manifested itself in the bailout process of Greece. By 2008, "gross cross-border claims from core to periphery reached €1.5 trillion" (Lapavitsas et al. 2010, 2). These financial claims became crucial in the decision to bail out Greece by core countries, especially Germany, since the latter faced the "stark choice of bailing out Greece or bailing out its own banking system" (Featherstone 2011, 203). In sum, the pre-crisis political economy of Greece reveals the dynamics of power at play in the core-periphery relationship.

Post-Crisis Policy Responses of Ireland, Portugal, and Greece

The starting points of EU member countries were varied, and the same is true of the impacts of the crisis. The employment-related and public finance data in

Table 12.1 illustrate the performance of these countries in relation to the OECD average and to the eurozone countries in particular. In each case, the three peripheral countries diverged not only from their own pre-crisis positions but also from their positions relative to broader European averages. Since the specifics of the three cases vary, this suggests that structural forces connected to their relative positions within the European political economy were at work.

The financial collapse in the core countries rendered the Irish banks vulnerable to collapse. To avoid this, the Irish government "provided a guarantee to cover the debts and deposits of the six domestic banks. The guarantee extended over assets and liabilities to the volume of €440 billion" by September 2008 (Allen 2012, 423). This decision placed a huge burden on public finances (Kirby and Murphy 2011, 35),[5] such that Ireland turned to the IMF and the European Union for a bailout plan. A shared €85 billion bailout agreement with the troika was concluded in December 2010. The three-year program included banking system reform, fiscal consolidation, and structural reform. Banking system reform aimed at reaching "a robust, smaller, and better capitalized banking system" (IMF 2010b, 1). In fiscal policy, Ireland resorted not to Keynesian-style stimulus programs but to unprecedented austerity measures right from the beginning (Dukelow 2011, 409), amounting to "the equivalent of 13 percent of … GDP, or €4,600 per person[,] and represent[ing] the largest budgetary adjustments seen anywhere in the advanced economic world in modern times" (Whelan 2011, 7). Tax increases were also implemented, though not the 12.5 percent corporation rate (Government of Ireland 2011, 12). This is illustrative of the class dimension of tax increases: workers, specifically "low and middle income earners," carried the burden of extra taxation (Allen 2012, 430). Structural reform also involved the reduction of labour costs through wage cuts, which function as an internal devaluation measure. Although public sector pay cuts were legitimized through attacks on a "bloated public sector" and "overpaid civil servants," this characterization did not reflect the reality since "the share of GDP spent on public sector pay and pensions in Ireland ha[s] consistently remained below [the] EU15 average" (Whelan 2010, 247; Allen 2012, 428). The unilateral implementation of this pay cut revealed the weakness of corporatist bargaining (Regan 2012, 466).

The adoption of an austerity agenda held clear implications for social policy since it resulted in significant cuts in social policy expenditures, already low compared with European Union and OECD figures (Dukelow 2011, 411). In 2006, Ireland spent 28.6 percent of its expenditure on social protection, compared with the EU-19 average of 37.7 percent and the OECD-26 average of 34.2 percent (OECD 2009a, 1). The *National Recovery Plan 2011–2014*

(Government of Ireland 2011, 11–12) called for social expenditure reductions of €7 billion by 2014, 41 percent from social welfare expenditures and 17 percent from public sector paycuts. The reductions meant lower basic welfare rates and child benefits and increased poverty rates (interview, think tank economist, Dublin, February 2013). Some reductions were direct and universal; others were achieved by tightening eligibility thresholds, means testing, adjustments to supplementary benefits such as the fuel allowance, or targeting certain types of recipients, such as lone parents. Cuts to programs meant fewer home helps, fewer public beds in nursing homes, and fewer special needs and language needs assistants in schools, all of which have gendered effects in a society in which women remain the primary caregivers. Other targeted cuts included disability benefits, allowances for those on jobseeker benefits, and travellers' education (Barry and Conroy 2012). The Think Tank for Action on Social Change (TASC 2011) concluded that those with low incomes were hardest hit by austerity measures, and, since women were overrepresented in that group, they suffered disproportionately.

The structural reform agenda was presented as "a strategy to remove remaining structural impediments to competitiveness and employment creation" (IMF 2010b, 8). The minister for enterprise, trade, and innovation revealed the government's thinking: "Let us be clear: labour market reform is a prerequisite for Ireland's long-term economic recovery. Unless steps are taken now to address labour market inflexibility, it is likely to inhibit job growth in Ireland and lead to a loss of competitiveness in coming years" (O'Keeffe 2010). It is important to note, however, that Ireland's labour market regulations were already flexible. Indeed, by 2008, Ireland already ranked seventh among twenty-nine OECD countries on labour market regulations that encourage flexibility (OECD 2009b, 84). An important piece of that regulatory structure, Joint Labour Committees and Employment Regulation Orders, however, came under fire as part of the structural reforms, with the result that regulation is even lighter than before. The institutional home of social partnership, the National Economic and Social Council (NESC), has survived the crisis but finds its budget and staff much reduced and now functions largely as a research centre providing background papers. Members of the policy community in Ireland (interviews, Dublin, February 2012) concurred in viewing social partnership as largely abandoned in the crisis period, with descriptors ranging from "dormant" to "in mothballs" to "dead."

Meanwhile, the links between the labour market and social policy have been tightened, and greater emphasis has been placed on activation of the unemployed. Outlined in *Pathways to Work* (Government of Ireland 2012), the

Berkay Ayhan and Stephen McBride

new approach involves closer management of the unemployed, including regular meetings with case workers, profiling the unemployed in terms of the likelihood of their finding employment, signing "contracts" spelling out the rights and responsibilities of the unemployed, applying sanctions to those who do not fulfill them, and focusing on employability assistance. Consideration was given to using private service providers to handle case management, job matching, and other functions and to relying on payment by results to private providers.

With the removal of a social partnership and the nature of policies pursued under the rubric of austerity, it seems reasonable to concur with Dukelow (2012) that neo-liberalism has been intensified in Ireland since the crisis. Ireland's policy responses to the global crisis reveal the resonance of neo-liberal paradigm and austerity measures. The state effectively socialized the losses of private banks in property speculation and made the working classes pay the bill. In terms of social policy, this meant reductions in social welfare expenditures and significant reductions in real wages of workers as well as rises in indirect taxes and income taxes.

The Portuguese response to the global crisis can be explored in three phases: financial, economic, and fiscal (Caldas 2012). In the last quarter of 2008, the majority socialist government put forward a financial stability package, the Initiative to Strengthen Financial Stability. This package brought reforms in "transparency of financial institutions, guarantees on bank deposits, the granting of state guarantees, up to a maximum value of €20 billion and strengthening the financial soundness of credit institutions" (Torres 2009, 60). By the end of the year, the government had nationalized Banco Portugues de Negocios and provided Banco Privado Portugues with a state guarantee in order to avoid a rush to withdraw deposits from the banking system.

In the next stage of the crisis (December 2008 to February 2010), Portugal resorted to some short-term Keynesian stimulus measures in various areas, including social policy. These measures included the modernization of schools and technological infrastructure, poverty reduction, protection of families, support for small and medium-sized enterprises, and programs to increase support and benefits for children, the elderly, and disabled people (Caldas 2012, 4–5). The Initiative for Investment and Employment, launched in January 2009, promoted social protection by supporting businesses that hired "young people, the long-term unemployed and the unemployed over-55s" (Caldas 2012, 5). Training programs were launched to target the unemployed and youth.

The Europe-wide focus on fiscal discipline came to Portugal with the launch of the Stability and Growth Program by March 2010. Labelled PEC I, this austerity program actually became the first of a series of fiscal measures, followed by PEC II in May 2010, PEC III in September 2010, and finally PEC IV in March 2011. The fourth austerity package was rejected by the parliament, which led to the government's resignation. Borrowing in international markets became more difficult, with increasingly punitive interest rates. Eventually, Portugal turned to the troika and struck a three-year, €78 billion bailout agreement in May 2011 focused on controlling the fiscal balance and public debt (Caldas 2012, 6–7).

These austerity measures hit wages and benefits and resulted in reductions in social welfare programs. On the revenue generation side, the austerity programs involved reductions in tax allowances and increases in personal and corporate income taxes as well as value-added taxes, and increases in employee contributions to public employees' pension system. Privatizations were also envisaged in the "energy sector, naval and defence construction, air transport, rail, financial communications, paper distribution and mining" (Caldas 2012, 6–7). On the expenditure side, public sector salary reductions, freezes on pensions and promotions, and strict control of recruitments were put forward. In addition, as Caldas (2012, 6–7) documents, "reductions of expenditure on social benefits (social security and social protection scheme for state employees)" and "reduction of expenditure on the national health service" were implemented.

These reforms, however, were but the beginning. Under a stand-by agreement with the troika, Portugal agreed to "(i) deep structural reforms to boost potential growth, create jobs and improve competitiveness, (ii) a credible and balanced fiscal consolidation strategy, [and] (iii) efforts to safeguard the financial sector" (IMF 2011, 1). Structural reform included the neo-liberal flexibility paradigm – "a reduction in severance payments, more flexible individual dismissals and working time arrangements, reduction of overtime pay, and some more scope for firm-level wage negotiations" (OECD 2012, 6) – as well as fiscal devaluation by reducing employer social security contributions, reforms in the judiciary with the aim of increasing efficiency, and enhancing competition by limiting the state's role in the private sector (IMF 2011, 14–16). Fiscal consolidation meant comprehensive actions in the following areas: expenditure cuts (reductions in the wage and pension bills as well as reductions in public employment), revenue increases (rises in consumption taxes and reductions in tax privileges), efficiency and transparency measures in public financial management, cost reductions in state-owned enterprises, acceleration of privatizations, capacity and efficiency improvements in revenue administration, and cost-cutting measures in public administration (IMF 2011, 3–10).

Overall, the troika's economic program for Portugal was prepared to further institute neo-liberal reforms to the labour market, social policy, fiscal policy,

Berkay Ayhan and Stephen McBride

and public administration. The troika's latest review of program implementation noted "positive" developments in meeting performance targets, banking sector recapitalization, and Portugal's return to international markets for borrowing (IMF 2013a, 4). However, this involved a contraction of real GDP (−1.3 percent in 2011, −3.2 percent in 2012, and −1.4 percent in 2013) and a high unemployment rate of 16.3 percent for 2013 (IMF 2014, 36). Youth are especially hard hit with an unemployment rate of 40 percent (IMF 2013a, 6). In April 2013, however, Portugal's Constitutional Court ruled that cuts in public sector wages and pensions were unconstitutional since they violated the principle of trust between pensioners and the state. These cancelled measures amounted to 20 percent of the total €5 billion austerity package envisaged in 2013 and raised the question of whether Portugal would resort to a new bailout (Tayfur 2013, 212).

In October 2009, a new Greek government aiming at transparency declared that the preceding conservative government had "misreported" the budget deficit. The difference from previously reported figures was startling. The budget deficit for 2009 moved to 12.5 percent, and later 15.8 percent, of GDP from 3.7 percent. And the debt-to-GDP ratio was similarly affected (Matsaganis 2012, 407). This revision of budget figures led the American credit-rating agencies to reduce the credit rating of Greece, making the cost of borrowing extremely high, prompting the government to turn to the troika for a €110 billion bailout, with €80 billion coming from the eurozone states and €30 billion from the IMF.[6] As the IMF intoned, "it is an extraordinary international support for what needs to be an extraordinary Greek adjustment effort" (2010a, 1).

The troika program subordinated incomes and social security programs to fiscal austerity and brought reductions in wages and benefits, especially for public sector workers. From 2009 to 2011, public sector wages declined 19.6 percent (Matsaganis 2012, 410). Other parts of the program emphasized freezing pensions, enhancing labour market flexibility, and creating a business-friendly environment. The austerity program also involved the reorganization of the Greek state through privatization, reduction in the number of local administrations, introduction of a three-year budget strategy, and reform of the statistics system (IMF 2010a, 17). Labour market flexibility was to be secured through "increased dismissals limit, shorter notice period, smaller severance pay, [and] loose regulations about 'unfair dismissal'" (Markantonatou 2013, 69).

In late 2011, the troika "informed the government that the sixth tranche of the Greek loan (needed to pay next month's salaries and pensions) would not be made available unless the main political parties reached consensus for fiscal consolidation and structural reforms" (Matsaganis 2012, 408). Prime Minister Papandreou resigned, and an interim coalition government, led by a former vice-president of the European Central Bank, was formed to handle the bailout agreement. The country's debt ratio to GDP rose from 116 percent in 2009 to over 150 percent by 2012 and had become unsustainable. "In March 2012, the Greek government successfully negotiated a debt write-down worth €105 billion, a 53 percent reduction of its debt to private creditors" (Tsarouhas 2012, 85). At the same time, the government signed a new four-year standby agreement amounting to €144.7 billion. This new agreement recognized the detrimental effects of fiscal consolidation and eased the terms somewhat. Nevertheless, the revised program involved further reductions in the public wage bill, reduced public sector employment, and decreased social spending, along with other reforms. Indeed, cuts in social spending on pensions, health, and social security were envisaged (IMF 2012, 6–9). The new agreement also continued to push labour market flexibilization, extending it to the private sector, "including deregulation of collective labour agreements, flexibility of dismissals, reduced compensation, wage flexibility and reduction of the national minimum wage" (Markantonatou 2013, 71; see also Haworth and Hughes, this volume).

In 2013, the troika's review of the program outlined deteriorating economic conditions: "The economy is in the sixth year of recession. Output has fallen by nearly 25 percent since its peak in 2007. The unemployment rate is about 27 percent, and youth unemployment exceeds 57 percent" (IMF 2013b, 4). Austerity failed to secure economic growth. Instead, it was detrimental to wages, benefits, and social welfare programs, all of which are essential for workers, the unemployed, and the poor. There are severe social consequences of this insistence on austerity in Greece, including "strangling of the lower middle class, migration of younger highly educated people, rising homelessness, [and] suicides hit[ting] record levels" (Markantonatou 2013, 74).

Conclusion

Within the eurozone, the global crisis resulted in varied outcomes. We have explored the social and labour market implications of the crisis for the worst-affected peripheral countries Ireland, Portugal, and Greece. We have argued that pre-crisis as well as post-crisis dynamics can be best explained by reference to core-periphery relations in the eurozone. The peripheral countries of the eurozone were deeply dependent on the core for sustaining unhealthy growth rates and financialized accumulation. Competitive pressures from the powerful eurozone core had already undermined the productive capacity of the periphery. When the global recession led to economic stagnation, these peripheral states had limited policy options. Through the eurozone's institutional structure, they were deprived of monetary policy autonomy and could not resort to external devaluation. Furthermore, while the European Central Bank actively bailed out the fragile banking system, its mandate prevented it from managing state debt, which resulted in ineffectiveness in the face of financial speculations against countries. Indeed, after being declared risky by a credit-rating agency, Greece effectively lost its ability to borrow from international markets. Eventually, Greece, Ireland, and Portugal resorted to the troika for bailout packages, which imposed harsh conditionalities.

The troika packages aimed to achieve internal devaluation, transferring the burden of adjustment onto workers by cutting wages and welfare benefits. This was "intended to reduce the demand for imports and improve the current account in order to sustain short term ability to pay" (Becker and Jager 2011, 15). The troika programs thus have meant convergence toward austerity in all three cases: widespread fiscal austerity, including reductions in public sector wages, benefits, and pensions, cuts in social welfare spending, increases in income and indirect taxation, and emphasis on flexibility in labour markets. Initiation of these reforms resulted in the deepening of recession, the persistence of high unemployment, especially among youth, and rising discontent, as seen in waves of protests, that fuelled radical left and right parties. Greece, Ireland, and Portugal have experienced a deepening of the neo-liberal social and labour market policy agenda, with a huge social and economic "cost" attached to it. The ways in which these troika programs are imposed and managed by technocratic governments are indicative of another casualty: namely, democratic accountability (Bozkurt 2013). The arguments of enhancing competitiveness, eliminating rent seeking and corruption, and securing efficiency are frequently circulated to derive support for these reforms.

Although there are many similarities, we can also identify country-relevant differences in the content, magnitude, or timing of these reforms. That said, the pre-crisis macroeconomic success on indicators was not a major factor in explaining the convergence toward austerity (see Farnsworth and Irving, this volume). Regarding country-specific items, reform in the statistics system of Greece was a unique demand that stemmed from misrepresentation of public debt. In terms of overall content, Ireland's already institutionalized liberal political economy implied limited reforms in areas such as privatization and public sector management, whereas the latter had more marked impacts on Portugal and Greece. In addition, though Portugal did begin by launching significant stimulus programs, Ireland was determined to pursue austerity from the beginning. In terms of the magnitude of the crisis, Greece faced a particularly severe debt problem, whereas Ireland's banking system proved to be especially vulnerable.

We have highlighted the need to look to the broader system of the eurozone, with its power dynamics, crisis in the regime of accumulation, and growth models, to find the underlying causes of the crisis. The dominant view that blames peripheral Europe's sovereign debt crisis proposes to solve the crisis with a harsh version of austerity. This austerity agenda can be considered a political project that aims to secure class interests related to disciplinary neo-liberalism. However, to the extent that the fundamental causes of the crisis are not addressed, austerity is likely to create more social and economic problems than solutions.

Notes

1 The referent "peripheral Europe" has changed over time. Although the "old" peripheral Europe comprises Portugal, Italy, Ireland, Greece, and Spain, the "new" periphery refers to Central and Eastern Europe. In this chapter, we focus only on the three worst affected countries of the old periphery (Stockhammer 2011, 4).

2 Whereas Germany was certainly the leading core country in trade surpluses, other core countries also benefited from their superiority in terms of competitiveness: "Spain, Portugal and Greece run permanent trade deficits and provide a net export area for Germany, France and Italy by absorbing 7, 10, and 9 percent, respectively, of their total exports" (Bellofiore and Halevi 2010, 22).

3 Some commentators argued that this corporatist mechanism functioned to promote neo-liberalism and flexible labour markets (Taylor 2005). Others characterized it as "a form of embedded liberalism" or "a strategy of the state to generate the domestic capacity to manage distributional tensions in a neoliberal economy" (Regan 2012, 468).

4 To demonstrate the magnitude of the financialization and property bubble, "in 2007, at the high point of the boom, Irish banks lent out €342 billion to the Irish private sector, the bulk of it for property speculation. That was three times the size of the Irish economy and was far higher than the €166 billion they held in deposits" (Allen 2012, 423).

5 This was a controversial decision. Whelan (2011, 9) points out that the "government appears to have taken seriously the assurances of the Irish Central Bank that the banks were fundamentally sound and were merely suffering from a short-term liquidity problem. Thus, the government appears to have believed that the guarantee would not have consequences for the state finances."

6 Acceptance of this deal led to outrage in Greece. The general strike and demonstrations of 5 May 2010 are considered as the most significant protests of the labour movement since the end of the dictatorship.

References

Allen, K. 2012. "The Model Pupil Who Faked the Test: Social Policy in the Irish Crisis." *Critical Social Policy* 32, 3: 422–39. http://dx.doi.org/10.1177/0261018312444418.

Barry, U., and P. Conroy. 2012. *Ireland 2008–2012: Untold Story of the Crisis – Gender, Equality, and Inequalities.* Dublin: TASC.

Becker, J., and J. Jager. 2011. "From an Economic Crisis to a Crisis of European Integration." Paper presented at the IIPPE Conference on Neoliberalism and Crisis of Economic Science, Istanbul.

Bellofiore, R., and J. Halevi. 2010. "'Could Be Raining': The European Crisis after the Great Recession." *Journal of International Political Economy* 39, 4: 5–30. http://dx.doi.org/10.2753/IJP0891-1916390401.

Bozkurt, S. 2013. "'Politically Sensitive' Labour Market Reforms and Technocratic Crisis Management Strategies in Greece and Italy." Paper presented at the 14th Mediterranean Research Meeting, Mersin, Turkey.

Caldas, J.C. 2012. "The Impact of 'Anti-Crisis' Measures, and the Social and Employment Situation." European Economic and Social Committee Workers' Group.

Cousins, M. 1997. "Ireland's Place in the Worlds of Welfare Capitalism." *Journal of European Social Policy* 7, 3: 223–35. http://dx.doi.org/10.1177/095892879700700304.

Dukelow, F. 2011. "Economic Crisis and Welfare Retrenchment: Comparing Irish Policy Responses in the 1970s and 1980s with the Present." *Social Policy and Administration* 45, 4: 408–29. http://dx.doi.org/10.1111/j.1467-9515.2011.00782.x.

–. 2012. "Financial Crisis and the Path of Retrenchment and Reform in the Irish Welfare State." Paper presented at the EPSAnet Annual Conference, Edinburgh.

Economist. 2007. "The Portuguese Economy: A New Sick Man of Europe." *Economist*, 12 April. http://www.economist.com/node/9009032.

Esping-Andersen, G. 1990. *The Three Worlds of Welfare Capitalism.* Princeton: Princeton University Press.

European Commission. 2014. "Economic and Monetary Union." http://ec.europa.eu/economy_finance/euro/emu/index_en.htm.

Featherstone, K. 2011. "The Greek Sovereign Debt Crisis and EMU: A Failing State in a Skewed Regime." *Journal of Common Market Studies* 49, 2: 193–217. http://dx.doi.org/10.1111/j.1468-5965.2010.02139.x.

Ferrera, M. 1996. "The 'Southern Model' of Welfare in Social Europe." *Journal of European Social Policy* 6, 1: 17–37. http://dx.doi.org/10.1177/095892879600600102.

Gill, S. 1998. "European Governance and New Constitutionalism: Economic and Monetary Union and Alternatives to Disciplinary Neoliberalism in Europe." *New Political Economy* 3, 1: 5–26. http://dx.doi.org/10.1080/13563469808406330.

Government of Ireland. 2011. *National Recovery Plan 2011–2014.* Dublin: Government Publications.

–. 2012. *Pathways to Work.* Dublin: Government Publications.

Hay, C., and D. Wincott. 2012. *The Political Economy of European Welfare Capitalism.* New York: Palgrave Macmillan.

IMF. 2010a. *Greece: Staff Report on Request for Stand-By Arrangement.* http://www.imf.org/external/pubs/ft/scr/2010/cr10111.pdf.

–. 2010b. *Ireland: Letter of Intent, Memorandum of Economic and Financial Policies, and Technical Memorandum of Understanding.* http://www.imf.org/external/np/loi/2010/irl/120310.pdf.

–. 2011. *Portugal: Letter of Intent, Memorandum of Economic and Financial Policies, and Technical Memorandum of Understanding.* http://www.imf.org/external/np/loi/2011/prt/051711.pdf.

–. 2012. *Greece: Letter of Intent, Memorandum of Economic and Financial Policies, and Technical Memorandum of Understanding.* http://www.imf.org/external/np/loi/2012/grc/030912.pdf.

–. 2013a. *Portugal: Seventh Review under the Extended Arrangement and Request for Modification of End-June Performance Criteria.* http://www.imf.org/external/pubs/ft/scr/2013/cr13160.pdf.

–. 2013b. *Greece: Fourth Review under the Extended Arrangement under the Extended Fund Facility, and Request for Waivers of Applicability and Modification of Performance Criterion.* http://www.imf.org/external/pubs/ft/scr/2013/cr13241.pdf.

–. 2014. *Portugal: Eleventh Review under the Extended Arrangement, and Request for Extension of the Arrangement and Waivers of Applicability of End-March Performance Criteria.* http://www.imf.org/external/pubs/ft/scr/2014/cr14102.pdf.

Karamessini, M. 2008. "Still a Distinctive Southern European Employment Model?" *Industrial Relations Journal* 39, 6: 510–31. http://dx.doi.org/10.1111/j.1468-2338.2008.00503.x.

Katrougalos, G., and M. Lazaridis. 2003. *Southern European Welfare States: Problems, Challenges, and Prospects.* New York: Palgrave Macmillan.

Katsimi, M., and T. Moutos. 2010. "EMU and the Greek Crisis: The Political-Economy Perspective." *European Journal of Political Economy* 26, 4: 568–76. http://dx.doi.org/10.1016/j.ejpoleco.2010.08.002.

Kirby, P., and M. Murphy. 2011. "Globalisation and Models of State: Debates and Evidence from Ireland." *New Political Economy* 16, 1: 19–39. http://dx.doi.org/10.1080/1356346 1003789795.

Lapavitsas, C., A. Kaltenbrunner, D. Lindo, J. Michell, J.M. Painceira, E. Pires, J. Powell, A. Stenfors, and N. Teles. 2010. "Eurozone Crisis: Beggar Thyself and Thy Neighbour." Research on Money and Finance Occasional Report.

Lopes, J. 2003. "The Role of the State in the Labour Market: Its Impact on Employment and Wages in Portugal as Compared with Spain." *South European Society and Politics* 8, 1–2: 269–86. http://dx.doi.org/10.1080/13608740808539651.

Macartney, H. 2013. "The Paradox of Integration? European Democracy and the Debt Crisis." Working paper.

Markantonatou, M. 2013. "Fiscal Discipline through Internal Devaluation and Discourses of Rent-Seeking: The Case of the Crisis in Greece." *Studies in Political Economy* 91: 59–83.

–. 2012. "Social Policy in Hard Times: The Case of Greece." *Critical Social Policy* 32, 3: 406–21. http://dx.doi.org/10.1177/0261018312444417.

Matsaganis, M. 2012. "Social Policy in Hard Times: The Case of Greece." *Critical Social Policy* 32, 3: 406-21. http://dx.doi.org/10.1177/0261018312444417.

McBride, S. 2010. "The New Constitutionalism: International and Private Rule in the New Global Order." In *Relations of Global Power: Neoliberal Order and Disorder,* edited by G. Teeple and S. McBride, 19–40. Toronto: University of Toronto Press.

OECD. 2009a. *Government at a Glance 2009. Country Note: Ireland.* http://www.oecd.org/gov/44212694.pdf.

–. 2009b. *Economic Surveys: Ireland.* doi: 10.1787/eco_surveys-irl-2009-en.

–. 2012. *Economic Surveys: Portugal.* doi: 10.1787/eco_surveys-prt-2012-en.

O'Keeffe, B. 2010. Speech by the Minister of Enterprise, Trade, and Innovation, 14 December. http://www.djei.ie/press/2010/20101214.htm.

O'Riain, S. 2000. "The Flexible Developmental State: Globalization, Information Technology, and the 'Celtic Tiger.'" *Politics and Society* 28, 2: 157–93. http://dx.doi.org/10.1177/003 2329200028002002.

Pagoulatos, G., and C. Triantopoulos. 2009. "The Return of the Greek Patient: Greece and the 2008 Global Financial Crisis." *South European Society and Politics* 14, 1: 35–54. http://dx.doi.org/10.1080/13608740902995844.

Regan, A. 2012. "The Political Economy of Social Pacts in the EMU: Irish Liberal Market Corporatism in Crisis." *New Political Economy* 17, 4: 465–91. http://dx.doi.org/10.1080/13563467.2011.613456.

Soares, A.G. 2007. "Portugal and the European Union: The Ups and Downs in 20 Years of Membership." *Perspectives on European Politics and Society* 8, 4: 460–75. http://dx.doi.org/10.1080/15705850701640835.

Stockhammer, E. 2011. "Peripheral Europe's Debt and German Wages: The Role of Wage Policy in the Euro Area." Research on Money and Finance Discussion Paper 29.

TASC. 2011. *Submission to Budget 2011*. Dublin: TASC.

Tavora, I. 2012. "The Southern European Social Model: Familialism and the High Rates of Female Employment in Portugal." *Journal of European Social Policy* 22, 1: 63–76. http://dx.doi.org/10.1177/0958928711425269.

Tayfur, M.F. 2013. "Debt Crisis of Southern Europe in Historical Context: Greece, Spain, and Portugal." In *Global Crisis and New Economic Order*, edited by F. Senses, Z. Onis, and C. Bakir, 187-219. Istanbul: Iletisim.

Taylor, G. 2005. *Negotiated Governance and Public Policy in Ireland*. Manchester: Manchester University Press.

Torres, F. 2009. "Back to External Pressure: Policy Responses to the Financial Crisis in Portugal." *South European Society and Politics* 14, 1: 55–70. http://dx.doi.org/10.1080/13608740902995851.

Tsarouhas, D. 2012. "The Political Origins of the Greek Crisis: Domestic Failures and the EU Factor." *Insight Turkey* 14, 2: 83–98.

Whelan, K. 2010. "Policy Lessons from Ireland's Latest Depression." *Economic and Social Review* 41, 2: 225–54.

–. 2011. "Ireland's Sovereign Debt Crisis." University College Dublin Centre for Economic Research Working Paper Series WP11/09. http://www.ucd.ie/t4cms/WP11_09.pdf.

13

Austerity Budgets and Public Sector Retrenchment
Crisis Era Policy Making in Canada, the United Kingdom, and Australia

HEATHER WHITESIDE

Austerity budgets, in the most straightforward sense, are those that reduce the cyclically adjusted fiscal deficit. Doing so often requires spending cuts to be made to social programs. The nature of austerity-induced cuts that accompany fiscal deficit reduction will be referred to here as the "politics" of austerity. Whereas the technical attributes of public sector budgeting incorporate projections and estimations of future government revenue (taxation and transfer payments), economic activity (anticipated growth and inflation), and future projected costs (of public services, programs, and infrastructure), the politics of austerity extend beyond mere accounting procedures because in practice changes in fiscal policy can lead to a restructuring of state-society relations. Alterations to social policy, necessary to accommodate austerity, often involve the commodification of public services and the dispossession of rights and benefits won through past struggles. Commodification and dispossession ("privatization") in turn alter the production, distribution, and consumption/enjoyment of goods and services, affecting power and well-being throughout society.

Austerity and privatization, of course, are nothing new. Mark Blyth has traced the "love of parsimony over prodigality" in economic thought back to Adam Smith, and austerity policies have existed in various forms for at least a century (2013a; see also 2013b). Instances of privatization too can be found throughout the history of the modern state. Austerity politics today are no cutting-edge solution to macroeconomic woes either; they mainly involve repackaging and re-employing pre-existing (pre-2008 crisis) neo-classical strategies initially aimed at resolving stagflation in the 1970s. In many ways, the past thirty years of neo-liberalism can be defined as an "age of austerity," and this historical context is crucial for understanding the current dimensions of the phenomenon given that austerity today follows three decades of public sector retrenchment.

In this vein, critical accounts of fiscal austerity often focus on how it is used to punish labour and/or public service recipients for the follies of capital (e.g., Callinicos 2012). The profligacy of government was seldom the underlying cause of public sector deficit and debt accumulated since 2008 – they were instead the by-products of the global financial crisis and subsequent bailouts (auto and finance sectors), stimulus spending, and a period of protracted low growth/recession. Budget cuts and privatization are thus tools for controlling labour – or, as Sam Gindin (2013) writes, for creating a state more autonomous from popular pressure – and the costs associated with the recent/ongoing capitalist crisis are being socialized in the process.

The three countries examined here – the United Kingdom, Canada, and Australia – support this critical interpretation yet also provide for a more nuanced understanding of how the politics of austerity unfold within distinct national contexts. Together they contrast with the experiences of several eurozone countries (e.g., Greece and Cyprus) where sovereign debt crises are leading drivers of budget imbalances and where austerity measures have been imposed through bailout packages by the IMF, European Central Bank, and European Commission (Ayhan and McBride, this volume; see also Lapavitsas 2012). Austerity is largely voluntary in the three countries examined here, indicating that it is an increasingly common-sense practice in certain countries of the global North that lack any overwhelming structural imperative urging such changes. This is reminiscent of Gramsci's description of how a common-sense worldview or set of beliefs can become deeply embedded and widely held in society despite being the product of narrow, particular interests (1971, 323–26). However, austerity also remains contested in some circles – popular discontent and resistance being mirrored in the fracturing of global policy advice, with many international organizations and economists cautioning against deep cuts – making austerity widespread but non-hegemonic since this status quo policy position has yet to enjoy the full consent of the governed.

Austerity measures in the United Kingdom are relatively severe since Britain has "led the way in voluntary deficit reduction" (Giles and Bounds 2012), and the social and economic costs continue to mount. Martin Wolf (2013) argues that fiscal austerity measures implemented from 2010 to 2013 have "turned a nascent recovery into stagnation." Not only has growth failed to materialize, but also, over the course of its now seven-year austerity plan (in 2010, it was introduced as a five-year plan), public sector employment will decrease dramatically: one in seven is estimated to lose his or her job by 2017 (Stewart 2012). According to projections by the Office for Budget Responsibility, by the end of the austerity period, the British public sector will be at its lowest level since the end of the Second World War (Stewart 2012), and the capacity for non-marketized public service provision will shrink accordingly.

In Canada, the politics of austerity are not strictly fiscal in nature given that the federal government aims to balance the budget "without raising taxes, cutting transfers to persons, including those for seniors, children and the unemployed, or cutting transfers to other levels of government that support health care and social services" (Government of Canada 2011), and overall government spending indeed increased in 2013. Instead, the overarching climate of austerity is used to justify neo-liberal intensification through, for example, the privatization of public infrastructure and services (which Labonté and Ruckert, this volume, argue constitutes a form of "austerity lite").

Austerity came relatively late to Australia, providing additional insight into the increasingly normalized, though highly political, nature of public sector budget cuts today. Despite mounting empirical evidence that austerity is hurting economic growth and producing social dislocation elsewhere, and policy advice favouring borrowing and deficits, in mid-2012 the federal government enacted its first austerity budget. Core elements of social policy were targeted for roll-back, shifting the burden of social reproduction in these areas for years to come. Austerity was also a prominent topic in the lead-up to the September 2013 federal election, with the opposition in favour of greater thrift. The resulting change in government indicates that austerity will likely be a feature of the policy landscape for years to come.

Two sections form this discussion. First, austerity is analyzed as a "solution" to capitalist crisis; second, its current policy attributes and how it has recently unfolded are described. The interrelation between changes in fiscal policy (from stimulus to austerity) and changes in social policy is considered through an analysis of the rhetoric, timing, and magnitude of budgetary reforms in Canada, the United Kingdom, and Australia. The argument made here is that, despite the erosion of empirical support for deep cuts to government spending, the politics of austerity nonetheless render it an increasingly common-sense mode of governing. This encourages privatization and is leading to an intensification of neo-liberalism in the post-2008 crisis period.[1]

Heather Whiteside

Austerity: New and Old

The resurgence of fiscal austerity is but the most recent episode of public sector belt tightening over the past three decades. In contrast to postwar, Keynesian era, countercyclical fiscal policy, in which government spending was thought to be an important tool of aggregate demand stimulation during economic downturns, austerity during the neo-liberal period is touted as a driver of economic growth and social prosperity. It gained prominence in the late 1970s/early 1980s as a solution to the problem of stagflation, which vexed the established Philips curve–derived policy orthodoxy at the time. Austerity provided a simple explanation: government spending on the welfare state in the global North was hurting growth by "crowding out" private spending and creating inflation through excess government borrowing in order to finance budget deficits. Austerity was similarly adopted by the IMF and World Bank and came to play a key role in the conditionality imposed on structural adjustment loans offered to developing world debtors in the 1980s and beyond.

In the 1990s, the rationale was further refined by neo-classical economists. Under the "expansionary fiscal consolidation thesis," it was argued that austerity was not only a solution to macroeconomic problems but also had a positive impact on expectations that generated its own virtuous cycle. The elimination of public sector deficits, though potentially painful in the short run, would boost investor confidence, reduce borrowing costs, stimulate private sector growth, and lead to lower unemployment (e.g., Alesina and Perotti 1995; Giavazzi and Pagano 1990). This hypothesis has also been referred to as "expansionary austerity" (Guajardo, Leigh, and Pescatori 2011). It was within the context of this received wisdom that a 2010 study by Harvard economists Carmen Reinhart and Kenneth Rogoff was marshalled as a common-sense rationale for terminating a widespread but short-lived experiment with quasi-Keynesian stimulus spending.[2] Using a forty-country, 200-year dataset, Reinhart and Rogoff (2010) found that, where government debt exceeds 90 percent of GDP, the average rate of economic growth is adversely affected.

The June 2010 G20 meeting in Toronto, Canada, stands out as a watershed moment, squashing calls for structural reform (e.g., bank tax) and further stimulus and signalling a near-global onset of fiscal austerity. The incipient rise of austerity as common-sense policy making was epitomized by the communiqué issued following that meeting that urged an "unwinding" of "extraordinary" (stimulus) measures.[3] A scan of the G20 policy commitments made at the 2012 Los Cabos Summit reveals that all members – with the exception of Indonesia, Mexico,[4] Russia, and Saudi Arabia – have committed to fiscal consolidation (debt reduction and deficit elimination) as a priority to take precedence well into the current decade (see G20 2012).

Despite adopting the mantle of a common-sense mode of governing, austerity is somewhat paradoxically becoming non-hegemonic. Aside from the obvious popular malcontent expressed through riots targeting austerity and privatization across Europe, the politics of austerity-induced restructuring are also losing ground ideologically and empirically. Three interrelated developments stand out: macroeconomic researchers are increasingly reporting not only on the lack of short-run benefits but also that fiscal consolidation is stunting longer-term prospects for economic recovery; "New Keynesian" thinking is growing in prominence in academic and popular press circles guided by influential economists such as Paul Krugman (see Krugman 2007, 2008, 2012); and equally influential policy advisers within leading international organizations and institutions (who are not necessarily New Keynesians) have begun to openly question the use of austerity in places such as the United Kingdom given the series of recessions experienced between 2010 and 2013.

Recent studies showing that austerity can hinder recovery include Roemer (2012, 10), who finds that "there is no correlation between austerity and the change in the debt situation over the relatively near term. The negative effects through lower growth appear to counteract the direct positive impact of the consolidation." Likewise, King et al. (2012, 6) argue that "the historical record provides very little evidence that austerity measures [are] effective, particularly in the context of a recession." A key problem arising from austerity efforts today (particularly in the United Kingdom and eurozone) is that unemployment is exacerbated, worsening the recession and harming social well-being (Roemer 2012, 19). Finally, a May 2013 study by Herndon, Ash, and Pollin uncovered that the once-lauded Reinhart and Rogoff study contains several errors, small and large, that seriously erode the veracity of its findings.[5] When Herndon and colleagues attempted to reproduce the study's results, they found that the study had selectively excluded years of high debt and average growth, contained problems with the methodology used to weight particular countries, and involved other spreadsheet-related errors.[6]

The current austerity debate among economists is not mere academic squabbling; the generosity, robustness, and future of national social policies pertaining to health, welfare, labour, and education are all at stake. Even after decades of neo-liberal roll-back, the state (whether "welfare" or "workfare") remains the leading source of support for labour and households during times of economic uncertainty or recession. Deleterious change in social policy as a result of austerity not only dampens prospects for economic growth but also threatens the well-being of individuals, households, and society more broadly. Recognizing this, in 2012 economists and policy advisers at institutions such as the IMF, World Bank, World Trade Organization, and OECD issued a warning against austerity and a "call to action" in favour of policies that promote economic growth and greater social cohesion (Elliot 2012a).[7] Martin Wolf, the chief economics commentator at the *Financial Times,* has also come to blame austerity for economic stagnation and social malaise (e.g., Wolf 2013).

The context for national-level austerity measures today is therefore one in which the intellectual and empirical underpinnings of fiscal consolidation have been eroded yet policy makers in much of the global North continue its voluntary pursuit, albeit at different tempos and with different programmatic features. It is to a discussion of the politics of austerity in Canada, the United Kingdom, and Australia that I now turn.

Austerity and Social Policy

The central way in which fiscal consolidation is felt by the public at large is through associated changes in social policy, and thus, in some sense, fiscal policy *is* social policy. As Schumpeter (1954, 6) argued in *Crisis of the Tax State,*

> the budget is the skeleton of the state stripped of all misleading ideologies
> … The fiscal history of a people is above all an essential part of its general
> history … The spirit of a people, its cultural level, its social structure, the
> deeds its policy may prepare – all this and more is written in its fiscal
> history … He who knows how to listen to its message here discerns the
> thunder of world history more clearly than anywhere else.

Social programs and services all require significant financing and long-term predictability in funding schedules in order to function properly. Changes in fiscal policy therefore indicate *who* (now) *gets what, when, and how* (to borrow from Harold Lasswell). The "how" of austerity politics tends to be answered through greater household burdens and the market provision of goods and services once collectively provided by the state. Fiscal austerity and spending cuts often result in the privatization of public sector programs, layoffs and/or more precarious employment, greater market dependence, and an enhancement of the structural power of capital – particularly finance capital through the growing reliance of the government on international bond markets (McBride and Whiteside 2011b). We must take seriously the possibility that austerity today is not a one-off reaction to crisis or budgetary deficits but a governance strategy (be it novel or recycled). In other words, as Peck (2012) suggests, there is "a prevailing politics of restructuring" occurring with fiscal consolidation.

As indicated by the following snapshots, fiscal consolidation in 2010 and beyond has often been adopted rather than imposed. The onset of fiscal consolidation in the three countries examined here was triggered by national elections (their results providing either the opportunity or the incentive to enact austerity), and the unrolling of austerity measures bears little correlation to intractable structural deficit and debt. The major caveat, and an issue highlighted by Farnsworth and Irving (this volume), is that the United Kingdom was hit harder and earlier by the economic crisis than either Canada or Australia. As small open economies, Canada and Australia were affected by the ensuing global recession and fluctuations in trade but, unlike the United Kingdom, managed to avoid the ravages of the 2008 financial meltdown. Nevertheless, cyclical deficits produced by poor economic growth, bailouts, and quasi-Keynesian pump priming are being used to renormalize neo-liberal restructuring in all three states.

Not only is austerity itself far from imperative, but also in each country the politics of deficit reduction display distinct policy *choices*. In the United Kingdom, this involves favouring deep spending cuts (affecting programs, services, and public sector employment) as opposed to raising revenue through other means, such as corporate taxation and longer-term growth stimulation strategies. In Canada, without macroeconomic conditions driving cuts, austerity was chosen as a way of disciplining labour through cuts to civil service employment and benefits in the lead-up to public sector bargaining in 2014 and in order to channel government funds toward privatized infrastructure projects. Australian austerity involves turning to fiscal consolidation as a common-sense governing position – and, like elsewhere, choosing to return to surplus through spending cuts and more miserly social programs – despite government deficits being cyclical rather than structural in nature.

The United Kingdom

The British government initiated its stimulus spending in 2008. By March 2009, this amounted to just under 1.9 percent of GDP (or roughly US$38 million) (OECD 2009a). The stimulus package was almost entirely revenue based – nearly all funds were committed to tax cuts rather than spending measures. Leading examples include a cut in the value-added tax (VAT) (a levy on sales temporarily reduced from 17.5 percent to 15.0 percent) and a sizable reduction in rates of personal income tax. Since the United Kingdom was at the epicentre of the global financial meltdown, the government also pursued "aggressive

Heather Whiteside

policy measures" to support the financial sector, such as injecting public capital into weak banks, providing liquidity for the banking sector, and insuring troubled assets (Iakova 2009). Northern Rock provides an instructive example. It was first bailed out in 2007, then nationalized in 2008, and subsequently privatized in 2011 (sales included only "good bank" assets, liabilities remain held in a "bad bank"), and taxpayers lost an estimated £0.5 billion in the process (BBC 2011a).[8]

The May 2010 election produced a Conservative-Liberal coalition that, in its first budget, announced major cuts in public spending, with most departmental budgets reduced by 25 percent (with cuts totalling £83 billion) (Reuters 2010). The aim was to balance the current account deficit by 2015-16. Whereas the stimulus package had favoured revenue measures over direct spending, austerity spending cuts were favoured far more than tax increases: balancing the budget would come from roughly 23 percent tax increases and 77 percent spending decreases. Tax hikes included increasing the VAT to 20 percent, raising payroll taxes 1 percent, and introducing a bank balance sheet levy. Changes in spending included freezing child benefits from 2011 to 2014, cutting £11 billion from welfare spending, imposing a two-year wage freeze on all but the lowest paid public sector workers, tripling university fees, and abolishing the Educational Maintenance Allowance, which encouraged youth in low-income households to remain in school (Reuters 2010). Such austerity measures constitute a particular form of privatization, one in which "policies shift responsibility for education, skill development and support of young adults back on to the individual or family and away from the state" (Grimshaw and Rubery 2012, 115).

Three departmental budgets were "ring-fenced," sparing them from the worst of the austerity measures: health, education, and foreign aid. However, ring-fencing is a deceptive label since previous commitments to annual increases for health and education were reversed and many "voluntary" cuts have since been made. Under pressure by Whitehall to come up with billions in savings, nearly 5,000 nursing positions were eliminated between April 2010 and August 2013 (Mason 2013). Greater job-related stress and poorer patient care have resulted. As reported in a 2013 *BMJ Quality and Safety* study looking at forty-six hospitals, nine out of ten nurses say that they are unable to perform all necessary basic care tasks in a given shift because of understaffing (tasks such as documenting care, changing a patient's position in bed to prevent bed sores, patient surveillance, and proper administration of medication) (Ball et al. 2013). Austerity-induced cuts are also being used to justify the ever-growing privatization of the National Health Service, with an estimated £5 billion in private for-profit contracts to be awarded in the near future (*Guardian* 2013).

Budget 2013 continues the austerity agenda, with departmental spending set to drop by £1.1 billion in 2013–14 and £1.2 billion in 2014–15, though again health, education, and foreign aid remain ring-fenced. The corporate tax rate was reduced to 20 percent, now making it the lowest in the G20 and further threatening government revenue should growth remain stalled.

Canada

Given the long-standing nature of budget freezes, cuts, and spending reforms first introduced in the 1980s, the austerity measures enacted in recent Canadian budgets have not been aimed at rolling back the Keynesian welfare state, as early neo-liberal advocates intended. Instead, austerity today addresses the fiscal deficits produced by a combination of poor economic growth and/or recession since 2007–8, stimulus spending initiated in 2009 following the global financial crisis of 2008, and bailout packages for the auto and banking sectors in 2009–10. Neither the profligacy of the government nor the profit squeeze of an emboldened working class can be blamed this time around. When the Conservatives took office in 2006, the federal government enjoyed a surplus of $8 billion; by 2010–11, the deficit was $33.4 billion (Stoney and Krawchenko 2013, 48).[9] Furthermore, as Labonté and Ruckert (this volume) indicate, austerity budgeting has been a long-standing element of the neo-liberal era in Canada – at least since the 1990s. Focusing here on federal budgets from 2009 to 2013, I show how the recent saga of timid, temporary, and targeted stimulus was enacted and how the return to austerity began in earnest.

Stimulus spending in reaction to the 2008 global financial crisis began in 2009, amounting to $47 billion federally and $14 billion provincially, and a $200 billion fund was created to support the banking sector should the need arise.[10] The 2010 federal budget extended some of the deficit-financed stimulus measures outlined in the previous budget but mainly concerned itself with tax cuts for business, spending cuts to federal departments, and freezes placed on public sector operating budgets. Altogether it sought to save $17.6 billion over five years by "streamlining and reducing the operating and administrative costs of government departments" (Evans 2010). Auto sector bailouts committed to in the same year (rescuing General Motors and Chrysler) amounted to $8.1 billion, with Canadian governments (federal and Ontario) covering roughly 20 percent and the United States financing the balance.

Despite the lack of economic recovery, Budget 2011 would introduce neither new spending nor tax cuts. It would, however, see the election of a majority Conservative government in May of that year, providing the government with the freedom to craft another austerity budget in 2012. Budget 2012 introduced

Heather Whiteside

cuts totalling $5.2 billion, targeting the federal public service in particular through the elimination of roughly 19,000 jobs. Program reforms were also implemented, the most prominent being an increase in the age of eligibility for Old Age Security. Budget 2013, in contrast, devoted $900 million to new spending and did not implement any additional tax cuts or increases. In its 2014 budget, the federal government announced that it would seek to save $7.4 billion over six years by reducing public sector benefits (May 2014), and by late 2014/early 2015, this had become a major feature of collective bargaining with seventeen federal unions pledging to fight sick leave benefit clawbacks in particular. A new funding formula determining federal transfer payments to the provinces for health and social programs has also been implemented, reducing the growth of future federal spending in these areas (see Labonté and Ruckert, this volume, for more details).

Notwithstanding the overarching focus here on the national scale, certain key elements of social policy (e.g., health and education) in Canada are managed by the provinces. Ontario, faced with a deficit of $15.3 billion, also implemented an austerity budget in 2012.[11] Public sector wage freezes were introduced with the aim of reducing program spending by $17.7 billion over three years and increasing revenue by $4.4 billion (Howlett 2012). Other (purportedly short-term) cost-cutting measures were introduced, such as freezing hospital funding, cancelling billions of dollars worth of infrastructure projects, and cancelling planned corporate tax cuts (Radwanski 2012). The substantial size of the deficit has been used as a justification for austerity, but a report by the Canadian Centre for Policy Alternatives (Hennessy and Stanford 2013) demonstrates the misleading nature of the assumptions and methods that underpin this projection. Within a few short months, the official estimate of the 2012–13 deficit had dropped by over $3 billion to $11.9 billion – still a significant amount but one that Hennessy and Stanford (2013) estimate could be eliminated by 2017–18 through economic recovery alone. The financial dimension of austerity is thus accompanied by underlying ideology and rhetoric that reinforce the long-standing climate of public sector thrift.

A common refrain heard from the federal and Ontario governments is that austerity measures are strategic, with spending increases doled out to certain areas and cuts/freezes applied to others. This is not merely political spin: health-care spending has been relatively protected (predictable given the strong public support for this program), but so has infrastructure spending, which incorporates the private for-profit sector via use of public-private partnerships (P3s). Federal Budget 2013, for example, increased spending on infrastructure by creating a new $14.4 billion infrastructure fund starting in 2014. A sizable portion of that fund, $1.25 billion, has been dedicated to P3 Canada, a federal crown corporation devoted to supporting municipal, First Nations, and provincial infrastructure developed as P3s. Infrastructure Ontario plays a somewhat similar role provincially, and it too benefits from austerity. Ontario's 2012 austerity budget stated that "the government will continue its investments in more than 30 new major hospital projects, in addition to the 25 major projects currently under construction ... [This will be achieved] through expanded use of Infrastructure Ontario's expertise, and a wider range of projects and sectors that use the Alternative Financing and Procurement (AFP) model of project delivery" (Ontario Ministry of Finance 2012, 40).[12] Thus, while austerity measures take aim at public pensions, jobs, and services outside politically privileged categories, privatization via P3s thrives.

Australia

Despite avoiding the worst of the global financial meltdown and ensuing recession, the Australian federal government enacted one of the comparatively largest stimulus packages. In early 2009, a $42 billion plan was unrolled, amounting to 5.4 percent of GDP, the third largest in the OECD (Colebatch 2009).[13] This followed a 2008 $10.4 billion stimulus injection. Altogether – including bank deposit guarantees, investment in residential-backed mortgage securities, and support for the auto industry – the government spent nearly $89 billion over 2008 and 2009 (*Daily Telegraph* 2009). The OECD (2009b) praised the stimulus package since it increased the employment rate by more than double the amount achieved elsewhere, and it estimated that unemployment would have been 2 percent higher without the stimulus.

From 2009 to 2012, the Australian economy performed relatively well, buoyed in large part by trade with China and a mining sector boom in 2010–11. Yet, in the May 2012 budget speech, Treasurer Wayne Swan promised that austerity was on the horizon, stating that "the deficit years of the global recession are behind us. The surplus years are here" (Swan 2012). This stance was duly reflected in the 2012 budget, which cut government spending by $33.6 billion and marked the first austerity budget for Australia since stimulus began in 2009 (Willingham 2012). Public sector departments were to find savings of 4 percent for 2012–13 (leading to roughly 3,000 jobs lost), means testing for health insurance was introduced, and welfare cuts of $700 million were imposed (ABC News 2012; Benson 2012). The May 2012 budget forecasted a federal surplus of $1.5 billion by mid-2013, though in October this amount was revised to $1.1 billion (Cullen 2012).

Heather Whiteside

Swan argued that surplus budgets would buffer against global economic turmoil witnessed at that time, stating that "conditions demand a surplus" and that economic uncertainty abroad called for a "clear and credible fiscal policy" (quoted in Coopes 2012). But the return to surplus was opposed by some noteworthy groups. The OECD (2012, 15) warned that "authorities should let automatic stabilisers work in case of a sharper-than-expected cyclical weakening, *even if this postpones the return to a budgetary surplus*" (emphasis added). This opinion was echoed by the Institute of Chartered Accountants, which stated that Australia's "revenue-raising position and expenditure commitments are robust: the case for seeking to return the budget to surplus in 2012/13 appears to have very little, therefore, to do with economic or financial motivations" (quoted in *Sydney Morning Herald* 2012). In other words, austerity measures were a political choice rather than a fiscal imperative.

By late 2012, economic conditions began to shift. Unemployment was on the rise, the strong Australian dollar was cutting into exports, and economic growth had slowed, which upset deficit-cutting projections. In response, the May 2013 budget cut an additional $580 million from public service spending over four years (ABC News 2013). An August 2013 economic update forecast that the deficit would rise to $30 billion and that a return to surplus would be achieved only in 2016–17. The update was released during the lead-up to the September 2013 federal election, and business leaders and the coalition opposition party accused the government of years of reckless spending, wasting the proceeds of a mining boom, and, despite the 2012 and 2013 austerity budgets, having no credible deficit management plan (Hepworth and Kitney 2013). On the other hand, Cameron Clyne, the chief executive of the National Australia Bank, argued in favour of deficit expansion in light of the country's AAA credit rating, stating that "Australia has a debt problem: we don't have enough" (quoted in Hutchens 2013).

Contradictions and Concluding Remarks

Faced with a worsening recession in 2011, the British chancellor, George Osborne, refused to consider alternatives to austerity, stating that he would not be "blown off course" (quoted in BBC 2011b). Perhaps part hubris, this sentiment also indicates the power of a common-sense position. Notwithstanding the mounting evidence that austerity was leading not to prosperity but to stagnation, if the United Kingdom had changed its stance, its credibility with bond markets would likely have been compromised. Confidence and expectations are core to neo-classical arguments for the benefits of fiscal consolidation, and whether or not one accepts these normative assumptions they can become self-fulfilling. The three countries examined here indicate that staying the course (the United Kingdom), going with the flow (Australia), and engaging in opportunism (Canada) are all features of the politics of austerity today. Austerity politics are thus widespread at the national scale but unfold within unique political circumstances. Traditional champions of austerity – including the OECD and IMF – are not nearly as fervent, and economists are divided on the benefits of austerity. Thus, policy advice at the global scale lacks uniformity, and austerity measures are often the result of a voluntary favouring of increasingly non-hegemonic neo-classical reasoning.

It is far from obvious who specifically is benefiting from fiscal consolidation. Examples supporting the critical position that capital benefits at the expense of labour can be readily found, and privatization clearly helps private contractors and those operating in P3 markets, but the politics of austerity are also undermining two primary roles held by the capitalist state: support for accumulation and legitimation. Consumption has been curtailed, expectations have not improved significantly, little change has been made to the casino-like nature of the global financial system, social unrest and democratic malaise are widespread, unemployment remains high, and growth is stalled – none of which gives an advantage to most fractions of capital or any other group.

Opportunities for structural economic change have been squandered in other ways as well. Although not a specific focus of this chapter, a tally of the problems generated by austerity would also include the relationship between fiscal policy and monetary policy. Quantitative easing, in which the central bank buys government bonds and/or highly rated private sector securities en masse, is another policy tool currently favoured in the United Kingdom, leading to very low long-term interest rates. The hope with quantitative easing is that greater borrowing and spending by households will help to stimulate growth and investment. Its effects on growth have yet to be definitively established (rock bottom interest rates could equally lead to inflation and low rates of saving), but it has provided the opportunity for historically cheap public investment through government borrowing and direct spending. This opportunity has been ignored in the United Kingdom and austerity chosen instead. The lost potential for green or other forms of innovative and transformative economic development must be factored into any analysis of the effects of austerity. To some extent, quantitative easing has helped to dampen the effects of austerity on household consumption; thus, if/when it is brought to an end, the impact of austerity will certainly deepen.[14]

Heather Whiteside

Clarifying the political dimensions of austerity helps to demystify this governance strategy. The neo-liberal state is neither hollow nor in retreat. The April 2013 death of Margaret Thatcher recalled the early neo-liberal mantra of less state and more market, yet now, some three decades later, this governance strategy has meant instead a different kind of state – one that is miserly and thoroughly market oriented. Austerity today is both symptomatic of neo-liberal intensification following a period of temporary quasi-Keynesian revival and a contradictory strategy whose success thus far can be measured only by the depth of its failure.

Notes

1 Neo-liberalism is conceptualized here as an ideology and a set of policies that privilege market-led social and economic development and are informed at least in part by neo-classical economics. Although this chapter argues that austerity is increasingly non-hegemonic, its implications nonetheless support McBride's (this volume) contention that the hegemony of neo-liberalism remains intact.

2 Use of the term "quasi-Keynesian" here indicates the lack of a robust Keynesian policy focus given that stimulus spending was designed to be temporary and shallow; alternatively, Peck, Theodore, and Brenner (2012, 276) call this 2008–9 moment "bastard Keynesianism."

3 Even among groups historically in favour of austerity, some ambiguity remained. Later that year, for example, the IMF (2010, Chapter 3) argued that fiscal consolidation would prove to be helpful only in the long run; in the short run, it could reduce economic output and increase unemployment. However, the overall tenor of this report supported an end to stimulus and a reduction in national deficits (Chapter 4).

4 Mexico first announced plans for fiscal austerity in 2009 and maintains it as a long-run objective but was also committed to stimulus spending at the 2012 G20 meeting.

5 Herndon, Ash, and Pollin (2013) aside, the conclusion that high debt *causes* low levels of growth has always been dubious given that the reverse could equally be true: poor growth might instead cause high levels of public debt. Furthermore, finding that public debt hurts economic growth should never have been conflated with the argument that austerity will lead to prosperity.

6 In response, Reinhart and Rogoff (2013) admitted to having made calculation errors but remained firm on their underlying argument: at a particular threshold, whether 90 percent as their study shows or 95 percent as an IMF study indicates, public sector debt can stifle economic growth.

7 Of course, as McBride (this volume) argues, the goal of fiscal consolidation remains ever present even if the speed and size of austerity measures are openly questioned by leading international organizations.

8 See Whiteside (2012) for more detail.

9 Canadian dollars are used throughout this section on Canada.

10 Recounted in greater detail in McBride and Whiteside (2011a). See also Auditor General of Canada (2010); CCPA (2009); Macdonald (2009).

11 In its 2013 provincial budget, British Columbia took a different approach: it committed to increasing annual average spending by 1.5 percent for the next three fiscal years, targeting

health program spending in particular (this is set to increase by $2.4 billion over three years). However, there are tradeoffs even within health-care-related spending. Premiums for British Columbia's Medical Services Plan (MSP) will increase by 4 percent. Given that enrolment in MSP is necessary for accessing provincial health-care coverage (with only the poorest exempt), this constitutes a regressive tax, hurting those who can least afford it. According to analysis by the Hospital Employees Union (HEU 2013), the increase in premiums will translate into an additional tax on BC families' incomes amounting to $2.39 billion by 2015–16.

12   Branding aside, AFP projects are P3 projects (Whiteside 2013).

13   Australian dollars are used throughout this section on Australia.

14   Furthermore, as the Bank of England reports, the benefits of quantitative easing have been disproportionately captured by wealthy households: the richest 5 percent enjoy 40 percent of the gains (Elliot 2012b).

References

ABC News. 2012. "Budget Winners and Losers." *ABC News*, 8 May. http://www.abc.net.au/news/2012-05-08/budgets-winners-and-losers/3998972.

–. 2013. "Government to Cut $580M from Public Service." *ABC News*, 12 May. http://www.abc.net.au/news/2013-05-12/government-to-cut-580m-from-public-service/4684404.

Alesina, A., and R. Perotti. 1995. "Fiscal Expansions and Adjustments in OECD Countries." *Economic Policy*. 21: 207–47.

Auditor General of Canada. 2010. "Chapter 1: Canada's Economic Action Plan." In *Fall Report of the Auditor General of Canada*. http://www.oag-bvg.gc.ca/internet/English/parl_oag_201010_01_e_34284.html.

Ball, J., T. Murrells, A.M. Rafferty, E. Morrow, and P. Griffiths. 2013. "'Care Left Undone' during Nursing Shifts: Associations with Workload and Perceived Quality of Care." *BMJ Quality and Safety* July: 116–25.

BBC. 2011a. "Osborne Plans to Sell Northern Rock to a Single Buyer." *BBC News*, 15 June. http://www.bbc.co.uk/news/business-13783724.

–. 2011b. "Osborne: We Won't Be Blown Off Course by Bad Weather." *BBC News*, 25 January. http://www.bbc.com/news/uk-12275973.

Benson, S. 2012. "Tough Love: Budget Targets Single Parents to Save $700M." *Daily Telegraph*, 3 May. http://www.adelaidenow.com.au/remote/check_cookie.html?url=http%3a%2f%2fwww.adelaidenow.com.au%2fmoney%2ftough-love-budget-targets-single-parents-to-save-700m%2fstory-fn84geaj-1226346302653.

Blyth, M. 2013a. "Why Austerity Is a Dangerous Idea." *Time*, 18 April. http://ideas.time.com/2013/04/18/why-austerity-is-a-dangerous-idea/.

–. 2013b. *Austerity: The History of a Dangerous Idea*. Oxford: Oxford University Press.

Callinicos, A. 2012. "Contradictions of Austerity." *Cambridge Journal of Economics* 36: 65–77.

Canadian Centre for Policy Alternatives (CCPA). 2009. *Federal Budget 2009: CCPA Analysis*. Ottawa: CCPA.

Colebatch, T. 2009. "OECD Praise for Canberra's Stimulus Package." *Age*, 17 September. http://www.theage.com.au/business/oecd-praise-for-canberras-stimulus-package-20090916-froi.html.

Coopes, A. 2012. "Savage Cuts Return Australia to Surplus." *Agence French Presse (AFP)*, 8 May. https://au.finance.yahoo.com/news/savage-cuts-return-australia-surplus-0042 04677.html.

Cullen, S. 2012. "OECD Delivers Snapshot of Aussie Economy." *ABC News*, 14 December. http://www.abc.net.au/news/2012-12-14/oecd-calls-for-flexibility-on-surplus-pledge/ 4427998.

Daily Telegraph. 2009. "Kevin Rudd Announces Economic Stimulus Package." *Daily Telegraph*, 3 February. http://www.dailytelegraph.com.au/remote/check_cookie.html?url= http%3a%2f%2fwww.dailytelegraph.com.au%2fkevin-rudd-announces-economic -stimulus-package%2fstory-e6freuy9-1111118741737.

Elliot, L. 2012a. "IMF Warns of Threat to Global Economies Posed by Austerity Drives." *Guardian*, 20 January. http://www.theguardian.com/business/2012/jan/20/austerity -warning-international-monetary-fund.

–. 2012b. "Britain's Richest 5% Gained Most from Quantitative Easing – Bank of England." *Guardian*, 23 August. http://www.theguardian.com/business/2012/aug/23/britains -richest-gained-quantative-easing-bank.

Evans, P. 2010. "Stead Budget Offers Few Surprises." *CBC News*, 4 March. http://www.cbc. ca/m/touch/news/story/1.867436.

G20. 2012. *Policy Commitments by G20 Members.* Los Cabos Summit, 18–19 June. http:// www.g20.utoronto.ca/summits/2012loscabos.html.

Giavazzi, F., and M. Pagano. 1990. "Can Severe Fiscal Contractions Be Expansionary? Tales of Two Small European Countries." In *NBER Macroeconomics Annual.* Edited by O. Blanchard and S. Fischer, 75-111. Cambridge, MA: MIT Press. http://dx.doi.org/10. 2307/3585133.

Giles, C., and A. Bounds. 2012. "Brutal for Britain." *Financial Times*, 15 January. http:// www.ft.com/cms/s/0/5cc73ea0-3e04-11e1-91ba-00144feabdc0.html?siteedition =intl.

Gindin, S. 2013. "Beyond the Economic Crisis: The Crisis in Trade Unionism." *Bullet*, 16 September. http://www.socialistproject.ca/bullet/878.php#continue.

Government of Canada. 2011. *Budget in Brief.* 6 June. http://www.budget.gc.ca/2011/ glance-apercu/brief-bref-eng.html.

Gramsci, A. 1971. *Selections from the Prison Notebooks of Antonio Gramsci*, edited and translated by Q. Hoare and G.N. Smith. New York: International Publishers.

Grimshaw, D., and J. Rubery. 2012. "The End of the UK's Liberal Collectivist Social Model? The Implications of the Coalition Government's Policy during the Austerity Crisis." *Cambridge Journal of Economics* 36, 1: 105–26. http://dx.doi.org/10.1093/cje/ber033.

Guajardo, J., D. Leigh, and A. Pescatori. 2011. "Expansionary Austerity: New International Evidence." IMF Working Paper, July. http://www.imf.org/external/pubs/ft/wp/2011/ wp11158.pdf.

Guardian. 2013. "NHS Privatisation: Land Grab." *Guardian*, 31July. http://www.theguardian. com/commentisfree/2013/jul/31/nhs-privatisation-land-grab.

Hennessy, T., and J. Stanford. 2013. *More Harm than Good.* Toronto: CCPA.

Hepworth, A., and D. Kitney. 2013. "Call to Tackle Deficit as Business Blasts Budget." *Australian*, 6 August. http://www.theaustralian.com.au/remote/check_cookie.html?url= http%3a%2f%2fwww.theaustralian.com.au%2fnational-affairs%2fcall-to-tackle -deficit-as-business-blasts-budget%2fstory-fn59niix-1226691734659.

Herndon, T., M. Ash, and R. Pollin. 2013. "Does High Public Debt Consistently Stifle Economic Growth? A Critique of Reinhart and Rogoff." Political Economy Research Institute, 15 April. http://www.peri.umass.edu/236/hash/31e2ff374b6377b2ddec04dea a6388b1/publication/566/ http://dx.doi.org/10.1093/cje/bet075.

Hospital Employees Union (HEU). 2013. "BC Liberals Balance Election Budget by Cutting Planned Health Spending; MSP Revenues to Outpace Corporate Tax Revenues by 2015." News release, 19 February.

Howlett, K. 2012. "Ontario's Austerity Budget Sets Up Public-Sector Showdown." Globe and Mail, 27 March. http://www.theglobeandmail.com/news/politics/ontarios-austerity -budget-sets-up-public-sector-showdown/article4096195/.

Hutchens, G. 2013. "We Have a Debt Problem, Says NAB Chief." Sydney Morning Herald, 2 August. http://www.smh.com.au/business/we-have-a-debt-problem-says-nab-chief -20130801-2r29e.html.

Iakova, D. 2009. "United Kingdom: From Rescue to Recovery." IMF Survey Magazine: Countries and Regions, 16 July. http://www.imf.org/external/pubs/ft/survey/so/2009/ car071609a.htm.

IMF. 2010. "World Economic Outlook: Recovery, Risk, and Rebalancing." IMF, Washington, DC, 10 October. http://www.imf.org/external/pubs/ft/weo/2010/02/pdf/text.pdf.

King, L., M. Kitson, S. Konzelmann, and F. Wilkinson. 2012. "Making the Same Mistake Again – or Is This Time Different?" Cambridge Journal of Economics. 36: 1–15.

Krugman, P. 2007. The Conscience of a Liberal. New York: W.W. Norton.

–. 2008. The Return of Depression Economics and the Crisis of 2008. New York: W.W. Norton.

–. 2012. End This Depression Now! New York: W.W. Norton.

Lapavitsas, C. 2012. Crisis in the Eurozone. London: Verso.

Macdonald, D. 2009. Too Little Too Late. Ottawa: Canadian Centre for Policy Alternatives.

Mason, R. 2013. "NHS Hospital Waiting Lists Reach Five-Year High of 2.9M People." Guardian, 15 August. http://www.theguardian.com/society/2013/aug/15/nhs-hospital -waiting-lists.

May, K. 2014. "Canada Budget 2014 Looks to Slash Public Servants' Benefits in Effort to Save Billions." National Post, 11 February. http://news.nationalpost.com/2014/02/11/ canada-budget-2014-looks-to-slash-public-servants-benefits-in-effort-to-save-billions/.

McBride, S., and H. Whiteside. 2011a. Private Affluence, Public Austerity: Economic Crisis and Democratic Malaise in Canada. Halifax: Fernwood.

–. 2011b. "Austerity for Whom?" Socialist Studies 7, 1–2: 42–64.

OECD. 2009a. "Policy Responses to the Economic Crisis." OECD, Paris, 11 May.

–. 2009b. Employment Outlook 2009 – How Does Australia Compare? Paris: OECD. http:// www.oecd.org/els/43707206.pdf.

–. 2012. OECD Economic Surveys – Australia. December 2012. Paris: OECD.

Ontario Ministry of Finance. 2012. 2012 Ontario Budget. http://www.fin.gov.on.ca/en/ budget/ontariobudgets/2012/ch1.html#c1_infrastructure.

Peck, J. 2012. "Austerity Urbanism." City 16, 6: 626–55. http://dx.doi.org/10.1080/136048 13.2012.734071.

Peck, J., N. Theodore, and N. Brenner. 2012. "Neoliberalism Resurgent? Market Rule after the Great Recession." South Atlantic Quarterly 111, 2: 265–88. http://dx.doi.org/10.1215/ 00382876-1548212.

Radwanski, A. 2012. "In Ontario, an Austerity Agenda That May Never Be Realized." Globe and Mail, 27 March. http://www.theglobeandmail.com/news/politics/in-ontario-an -austerity-agenda-that-may-never-be-realized/article627510/.

Reinhart, C., and K. Rogoff. 2010. "Growth in a Time of Debt." National Bureau of Economic Research, Working Paper No. 15639, January. http://www.nber.org/papers/w15639.

–. 2013. "Reinhart and Rogoff: Responding to Our Critics." *New York Times*, 25 April. http://www.nytimes.com/glogin?URI=http://www.nytimes.com/2013/04/26/opinion/reinhart-and-rogoff-responding-to-our-critics.html&OQ=pagewantedQ3DallQ26_rQ3D1Q26&OP=23b474efQ2FTY5Q5DTzvQ5DTPPPTQ7EQ5D.ITQ26YUj_YYQ5D6T6Q51V4TQ51Q3BT6wTY5-z-YzT_J-zQ7E3_Q5D23zQ262_YQ3AYNN2_Jj5YzQ26-zQ3A2Q5DY2YQ20_2U_-Q5D-UjMQ7EQ5D.I.

Reuters. 2010. *Factbox – British Austerity Measures*. 15 October. http://www.reuters.com/article/2010/10/15/britain-government-reform-spending-idUSLDE69D1S820101015.

Roemer, C.D. 2012. "Fiscal Policy in the Crisis: Lessons and Policy Implications." University of California, Berkeley, 16 April. http://eml.berkeley.edu/~cromer/Lessons%20for%20Fiscal%20Policy.pdf.

Schumpeter, J.A. 1954 [1918]. "The Crisis of the Tax State." *International Economic Papers* 4: 5–38.

Stewart, H. 2012. "Public Sector Workforce 'Will Shrink to Record Low by 2017.'" *Guardian*, 25 March. http://www.theguardian.com/society/2012/mar/25/public-sector-workforce-shrink-record-low-2017.

Stoney, C., and T. Krawchenko. 2013. "Crisis and Opportunism: Public Finance Trends from Stimulus to Austerity in Canada." *Alternate Routes* 24: 33–58.

Swan, W. 2012. *Budget Speech 2012–13*. 8 May. http://www.budget.gov.au/2012-13/content/speech/html/speech.htm.

Sydney Morning Herald. 2012. "Support Economy Not Surplus: Accountants." *Sydney Morning Herald*, 1 May. http://news.smh.com.au/breaking-news-national/support-economy-not-surplus-accountants-20120501-1xwar.html.

Whiteside, H. 2012. "Crises of Capital and the Logic of Dispossession and Repossession." *Studies in Political Economy* 89: 59–78.

–. 2013. "Stabilizing Privatization: Crisis, Enabling Fields, and Public-Private Partnerships in Canada." *Alternate Routes* 24: 85–108.

Willingham, R. 2012. "Budget 2012: Winners and Losers." *Sydney Morning Herald*, 8 May. http://www.smh.com.au/business/federal-budget/budget-2012-winners-and-losers-20120508-1ybbz.html.

Wolf, M. 2013. "Austerity in the Eurozone and the UK: Kill or Cure?" *Financial Times*, 23 May. http://registration.ft.com/registration/barrier?location=http%3A%2F%2Fblogs.ft.com%2Fmartin-wolf-exchange%2F2013%2F05%2F23%2Fausterity-in-the-eurozone-and-the-uk-kill-or-cure%2F&referer=?

14

Austerity Lite
Social Determinants of Health under
Canada's Neo-Liberal Capture

RONALD LABONTÉ AND ARNE RUCKERT

The austerity agenda, with its European birthplace in Greece, is sweeping across the continent, leaping to the Americas, and entrenching itself in much of the developing world. We argue, however, that the politics of austerity as practised in Canada do not represent a radical departure but reinforce neo-liberal trends already existent before the onset of the global financial crisis (GFC). The crisis simply provided newfound justification for the continuing and deepening of neo-liberal reforms in the area of social policy that have long been embraced by both Liberal and Conservative governments in Canada, at least since the mid-1990s. We focus in particular on the impacts of such policy choices on existing health inequities, which will undermine important social determinants of health (SDH) pathways in Canada, with the potential to inflict significant harm on people's health, especially the health of vulnerable populations.[1]

The chapter proceeds in three stages. First, we briefly review the global historical trajectory of neo-liberalism and its impact on the social policy and SDH scene in Canada before the onset of the GFC. Second, we present a generic conceptual framework that links the GFC to SDH and health equity. And third, we examine in more detail some of the SDH pathways identified in the conceptual framework. In this discussion, we focus on the reshaping of public finances in the aftermath of the GFC with cutbacks in social policy areas critical to SDH, such as housing, education, and social assistance, and the acceleration in the qualitative transformation of labour markets, with precarious forms of employment becoming increasingly common in Canada. In conclusion, we situate our analysis within a growing body of academic literature that assesses the impacts of the GFC on health, and discuss alternatives to the politics of austerity, by highlighting the potential for raising additional revenues to address fiscal imbalances and related social policy challenges. We end with a call to abandon the self-defeating politics of austerity and suggest that now is the right time to make large social and infrastructural investments that could nurture the Canadian economy back to health and positively contribute to reducing the inequitable distribution of SDH and persistent health inequities in Canada (Bryant et al. 2011).

From Neo-Liberalism 1.0 to 3.0: What's in It for Health?

Neo-liberalism's prevailing political narrative owes its genesis to the early 1970s: a period of economic recession, oil embargoes, and price hikes; the writing off of America's Vietnam War debts by unpegging the US dollar from the gold standard, setting financial exchanges adrift to allow money to be made through currency speculation; and the military coup in Chile, which gave Friedman's disciples their first neo-liberal experimental lab. Neo-liberalism 1.0 was an internationally inspired but not yet globally dominant world order that considered any form of state enterprise or service provision as "second best" to private markets. The 1980s developing world oil-shocked debt crisis and the collapse of the Soviet Union cemented the foundation of what later became known as the Washington Consensus: privatization, deregulation, tax reform (lower corporate and marginal rates), deficit reduction, and trade and financial liberalization. Structural adjustment was the globalizing tool wielded by the World Bank and IMF to coerce developing countries into alignment. The General Agreement on Tariffs and Trade did the same for wealthier countries, and by 1995 the World Trade Organization, with its "behind the border" creep into trade-related national policy space, further morphed the welfare state into the competitive state (Bond 2008; Koivusalo, Schrecker, and Labonté 2008; Lee 2006).

The erosion of national capitalisms with the deepening of internationalized trade and financial markets gradually brought us neo-liberalism 2.0. The 1970s declining profit rate, a result of capitalism's inherent and cyclical crisis tendency toward overproduction and underconsumption, was met by what Bond (2008) called "shifting and displacing." Corporations adopted strategies that allowed continual capital accumulation by lowering production costs (technology and outsourcing), opening new markets (reduced tariff and non-tariff barriers to goods and investment), and increasing financialization of the economy (digital technologies, bank deregulation, and removal of capital controls). The US banking crisis that began in 2007, precipitating the global financial crisis of 2008, is the still-evolving nadir of neo-liberalism 2.0, whose inevitability was cautioned by many economists at least a decade before it occurred (Deverakonda 2012). Outsourcing of production led to massive investment flows to low-wage countries. Export-oriented developing countries (especially China) accumulated huge reserves of US dollars and banked them in low-interest-paying treasury bills while borrowing on international markets from high-income country banks at substantially higher rates. This meant that developing countries, since the early 1990s, were transferring more capital each year to the United States and other wealthy nations than they received in investments or foreign aid, reaching an all-time high of US\$890 billion in 2008 (UNDESA 2010). Financial institutions leveraged much of this new capital to bet on currencies, stocks, and real estate, discovering that it was easier and faster to make money from money than by lending it to the "real economy" of production and consumption (Wade 2009).

The response to the 2008 crisis marks the advent of neo-liberalism 3.0 (Hendrikse and Sidaway 2010). One effect of neo-liberalism's two earlier versions was unravelling the postwar social contract, which had helped to flatten gross inequities in income distribution, even among the Anglo-American liberal nations. The Occupy movement had its basis in the extent to which a small group of people were able to capture most of the gains of the past several decades of economic growth, reaching or exceeding that which preceded the 1929 crash and Great Depression, which Wade (2009) suggests was actually the intent of neo-liberalism's early architects. While the 2008 GFC wiped out trillions of dollars in paper wealth, affecting the pensions and savings of many of the world's middle and working classes, the 24 million whom investment banks refer to as "high and ultra-high net worth individuals" saw their balance sheets decline for a year or two but then increase by over 20 percent (Baxter 2011), a remarkable feat that the pre-1929 oligarchs never accomplished. Billionaire wealth rose 20 percent alone in 2012 over 2011, in what *Forbes* (2013) described as "a very good year for billionaires." The stunning failure of the 2008 crisis to "starve the beast" of neo-liberalism (whose tax cuts for wealthy individuals and corporations were meant to "starve the beast" of government spending) reveals the depth of public/private isomorphism. Neo-liberalism was never about eliminating the state: it was about occupying it, "a reconfiguring of both (state and market) so that they become thoroughly enmeshed" (Hendrikse and Sidaway 2010, 2039), of which the austerity agenda is the most recent example. The key tenets of the austerity agenda differ little from earlier structural adjustment, with the entire neo-liberal era best described as an "age of austerity" (see

Ronald Labonté and Arne Ruckert

Figure 14.1
Total government tax revenue and government spending as percentage
of GDP in Canada

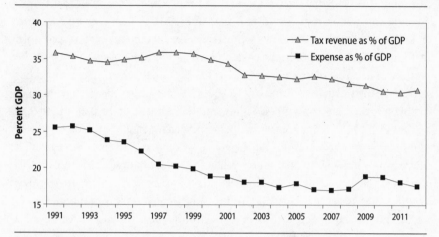

Sources: World Bank Expense Statistics 2012 and OECD Revenue Statistics 2012.

Whiteside, this volume). The global neo-liberal trajectory also left a strong
mark on the Canadian social policy scene before the onset of the GFC, with
deep implications for health, in particular through a deterioration of SDH. Like
other liberal welfare states, Canada began to undergo a sustained retrenchment
well before the GFC (Bryant et al. 2011; see also Whiteside, this volume). This
was partly related to shrinking government revenues linked to a variety of tax
cuts, with the average tax load of large corporations dropping from 49.1 percent
of profits in 2004 to 26.9 percent in 2010 (Simms 2013); marginal tax rates for
high-income earners falling from 43 percent in 1983 to 29 percent in 2010; and
the capital gains inclusion rate declining from 75 percent in 1990 to 50 percent
in 2006 (OECD 2011; Simms 2013). Tax revenue as a percentage of GDP in
Canada declined from 36 percent in 1990 to 31 percent in 2012 (see Figure 14.1),
a thirty-year low, ranking Canada twenty-fourth of thirty-four OECD member
nations and well below the EU15 average of 40 percent. This trend was accompanied by a steep decline in overall government spending, from 25 percent of
GDP in 1993 to 17 percent in 2012, with a short-lived uptick between 2008 and
2010 in response to the GFC (see Figure 14.1). Between 1980 and 1995, the
Canadian tax benefit system offset more than 70 percent of the rise in market
income inequality, declining to only 40 percent offset since (OECD 2011).

Canada's downward trend in redistribution has been driven largely by the
reduction in means-tested transfers (Kneebone and White 2009). Much of this

can be traced to the federal government's limiting the amount of financial transfers to the provinces for health and social programs (Bryant et al. 2011). Although the Canadian states' (federal and provincial) slow withdrawal from income and wealth redistribution is part of the reason for growing social inequalities, rising disparities in (pre-tax) market income are also responsible. Although income inequalities have increased in most OECD countries over the past three decades, disparities in Canada have widened faster than in any other OECD country over this period (OECD 2011). For example, the GINI coefficient (using adjusted after-tax income) has trended upward, from 0.28 in 1989 to 0.32 in 2010. More disaggregated statistics paint a much gloomier picture, with the income gap between the top 1 percent of earners and the rest becoming increasingly skewed. In 2010, the median income of the richest 1 percent was ten times the median income of the rest of income earners, up from seven times in 1982 (Statistics Canada 2013a). At the same time, the share of income going to the bottom four deciles has been declining over the past three decades (Schrecker and Yalnizyan 2010).

Deteriorating income inequalities have also had adverse impacts on other key SDH, through rising poverty and food insecurity levels and declining housing affordability. Poverty in Canada is generally measured through use of the Low-Income Measure (LIM), a relative measure of poverty that defines the poverty line as 50 percent of median income after adjusting for family size. Since 1990, the LIM has trended upward, reaching 13.0 percent by 2010, up from 11.7 percent in 1990 (Raphael 2011). The proportion of Canadians experiencing housing affordability issues also increased over this period, with the proportion of citizens spending more than 30 percent of their income on housing in large cities reaching alarming levels even before the GFC (43 percent in Vancouver, 42 percent in Toronto, and 36 percent in Montreal) and rental costs far outpacing income increases, especially for low-income earners (Bryant et al. 2011). Similarly, food insecurity in Canada has been increasing, with food bank use spiking in the late 2000s and reaching an all-time high in 2011 (Food Banks Canada 2012). Such developments are being reinforced by the GFC's impacts on health relevant pathways.

The GFC and Health Equity: Conceptual Connections

There is a growing body of literature that aims to connect macrostructural phenomena, such as the GFC, to health outcomes in regional and local settings by studying the impacts of such phenomena on different SDH relevant pathways

Ronald Labonté and Arne Ruckert

Figure 14.2
Health equity relevant pathways of the GFC

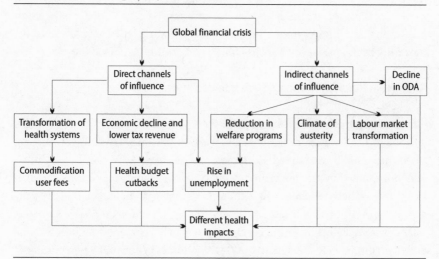

Source: Ruckert and Labonté (2012).

(e.g., Labonté and Schrecker 2007). A recent study in this regard is Therborn's (2013) *The Killing Fields of Inequality,* which, through empirical and statistical analysis, documents how growing social polarization and inequality have detrimental effects on the health of individuals. In the case of the GFC, our generic conceptual framework highlights both direct and indirect pathways linking it to health outcomes (see Figure 14.2). It is clear that some of the pathways, such as a decline in official development assistance, do not apply to Canada. Because of space constraints, our discussion will focus on the climate of austerity and budget decisions linked to SDH relevant pathways and the impact of the GFC on labour market performance. Such a focus is justified because of the central role that employment and budget decisions play as determinants of health in the Canadian context (Ruckert 2012). Employment and income are widely acknowledged as key social determinants of health, especially in social contexts in which fewer goods and services are provided by the state as a result of welfare retrenchment. A higher income gives one more economic resources and thus access to healthier nutrition, housing, or neighbourhood conditions, and it reduces stress because of the availability of more resources to cope with daily challenges (Pamuk et al. 1998). Budgetary decisions and their impacts on social programming are another area of high concern to proponents of the SDH approach because of the importance of government transfers for vulnerable populations and the likely negative health and health equity consequences of the withdrawal of support. Recent empirical evidence reinforces the view that more accessible social protection measures are associated with better population health, including lower excess mortality levels among older people and lower mortality rates among socially disadvantaged groups (CSDH 2008).

Austerity Lite? SDH in the Canadian Experience

Canada has largely been cast as having escaped the worst of both the GFC and the Great Recession that came in its wake. In Canada, where the banking sector has more prudent regulatory measures than in the United States, United Kingdom, and Europe, government quantitative easing rescue for Canadian banks ranged between $50 and $70 billion of a total $114 billion offered in emergency relief, all of which has since been repaid (Macdonald 2013). Canada's post-crisis GDP decline was fairly modest, with a 3.6 percent drop in economic activity from 2008 to 2009, compared with a total decline of 3.8 percent in the United States during 2008–9 and even larger declines in Europe and Japan (see Farnsworth and Irving, this volume). The recession lasted only three quarters (Cross 2010), with GDP moving slowly, if unspectacularly, forward since then. Adjusting for population growth, however, neither Canada's GDP nor its employment have recovered to pre-GFC levels, with employment lagging far behind (Stanford 2013a). Since 2007, after adjusting for population, Canada's GDP and employment recovery ranked sixteenth of thirty-four and seventeenth of thirty-three OECD countries, respectively.

The GFC and the Politics of Austerity

In direct response to the sudden drop in GDP, the federal government engaged in an economic stimulus program of further tax cuts and infrastructure spending (Stoney and Krawchenko 2013; see also Whiteside, this volume). Overall, Canada's stimulus package, comprising federal tax cuts of $6.2 billion, federal stimulus spending of $39.1 billion, and provincial stimulus spending of $18.4 billion, has been estimated at $63.7 billion, about 1.3 percent of GDP annually from 2008 to 2010 (Government of Canada 2012; Gup 2010). But stimulus rapidly gave way to a strong federal commitment to return to a balanced budget by fiscal year 2015, despite very low budget deficits since 2008 (between 1 percent and 3 percent of GDP). In 2012, the Conservative administration, with its first parliamentary majority, tabled a long-anticipated austerity budget, which the 2013 budget continued.

Ronald Labonté and Arne Ruckert

Although the 2012 budget contained no additional cuts to the federal corporate tax rate on general income, foregone revenue because of tax cuts (the federal corporate tax rate was reduced from 21 percent in 2005 to 15 percent in 2012) amounted to $13 billion in fiscal year 2012–13 alone (Jackson 2012), representing almost 10 percent of annual public sector health expenditure in Canada (CIHI 2012). This continued a recent trend that has seen about $220 billion of foregone revenue since 2006 because of tax cuts (Fanelli and Lefebvre 2012). Instead of reversing this decline in revenue, the 2013 budget addressed revenue shortfalls through further reductions in federal program spending and by limiting social and health transfers to the provinces, putting additional stress on provincial finances (as discussed in more detail below). The main focus of federal expenditure restraint has been on cutting the size of the public service, with the termination of an estimated 19,000 positions within the federal civil service. Total federal government spending on programs in 2015–16 is projected to be only 12.9 percent of GDP, compared with 14.1 percent in 2011–12, with spending cuts now outpacing new spending by a factor of 7:1 (CCPA 2012). Health and social transfers from the federal government to provincial governments will be maintained, but at a reduced level based on a new transfer formula, putting pressure on provinces to make further cuts to health and social services.[2] In health care alone, total spending as a percentage of GDP has fallen in each year since the GFC, with adjusted dollar increases in private spending rising more rapidly than in public spending (CIHI 2012).

As in the United States (Boychuk, this volume), one area of initially progressive social policy change was the (temporary) extension of employment insurance (EI) benefits in the direct aftermath of the GFC. However, the five-week extension of EI regular benefit measures (from forty-five to fifty weeks) was rather short lived and expired in September 2010, even before the wider fiscal austerity agenda was unleashed in 2012. As part of the 2012 austerity budget, EI eligibility was tightened, especially for part-time workers. The new regime puts EI claimants into three categories: long-tenured workers, frequent claimants, and occasional claimants. In each case, the requirements for staying on EI have been tightened, with workers forced to be less selective about acceptable forms of employment, including accepting a job paying 70 percent of previous wage levels (Whittington and Campion-Smith 2012). Even before these reforms, fewer than 40 percent of unemployed Canadians were able to qualify for EI in 2012, well below the pre-GFC level and the lowest level in EI history (Hennessy and Stanford 2013). Moreover, Canada lags far behind other OECD countries in EI benefits, with the lowest benefit replacement rate (i.e., the ratio of unemployment benefits to employment earnings) in the entire OECD realm (Osberg 2009).

Ontario's Austerity Drive and Social Program Cutbacks

Given the prominent role of provinces in the delivery and management of social policy and programs (e.g., health, education, housing, social protection), budget decisions at the provincial level have strong impacts on SDH relevant pathways in Canada. We will focus here on the largest province in Canada, Ontario, the most strongly affected by the GFC because of its close trade links with the United States. Like the federal government, Ontario has experienced post-GFC budget deficits, reaching more than 6 percent of provincial GDP in 2009 before dropping to 3 percent by 2012 (CCPA 2012). Part of Ontario's deficit was the result of its $27.5 billion stimulus spending package (Conference Board of Canada 2009), but as at the federal level the underlying driver is an inadequate level of taxation. Since the beginning of the crisis, the Ontario government has repeatedly stated that it will not increase taxes, even though corporate and individual taxes have fallen over the past thirty years, especially for high-income earners and large corporations. The top marginal tax rate decreased from close to 80 percent in 1970 to 49 percent by 2013, while corporate taxes fell from 15.5 percent in 1997 to 11.5 percent in 2013 (Cahill 2007). Since 2000, Ontario's "own source" revenues – from provincial taxes and fees rather than federal government transfers – declined from close to 16.0 percent to 13.6 percent of provincial GDP as a result of further cuts in provincial corporate tax rates (CROPS 2012). A government-initiated report to assess the province's finances post-GFC noted that, under an alternative fiscal scenario, with revenue collection returned to the level of 2000, the budget deficit would have been completely wiped out by 2010, with $22 billion left over to invest in social programs and services (CROPS 2012). Yet the only option put on the table by the Ontario government was to cut program spending in a wide variety of areas relevant to SDH.

In consequence, Ontario's 2012 austerity budget outlined $17.7 billion worth of program cuts over three years (2012–15) (CCPA 2012). Facing progressive political opposition, the provincial government introduced a small (2 percent) surtax for those earning more than $500,000 a year until the budget is balanced, allowing it to implement four dollars in spending cuts for every dollar in revenue increases. As with the federal government, most of the savings are expected to originate from a public sector wage freeze and the elimination of 1,500 positions from the provincial public workforce (Whiteside, this volume). Health care has also been affected, with hospital budgets frozen at 2012 levels. Given a growing population, such a freeze implies real cutbacks in service delivery and quality over time. The austerity budget also slightly reduces social

Ronald Labonté and Arne Ruckert

assistance rates (in real terms, with a 1 percent increase to rates, but with inflation running at about 2 percent), despite the Commission for the Review of Social Assistance recommendation to immediately raise welfare rates by at least $100 on a monthly basis (roughly a 15 percent increase for singles) (CRSAO 2012). Although inadequate social assistance rates are a problem, accessibility of social assistance is another concern, especially since the percentage of Ontarians relying on social assistance has not increased significantly since the onset of the GFC and Great Recession. Although social assistance uptake topped out at about 15.0 percent of the population during previous deep recessions (both in the 1930s and in the 1990s), it peaked at only 6.6 percent in 2012 (Hennessy and Stanford 2013). This implies that, because of changes to eligibility criteria associated with the workfare approach introduced under the Conservative Harris government in the mid-1990s, many families in need were not able to access social assistance. Combined with historically low rates of EI uptake, this clearly shows that income security programs have failed to protect many vulnerable Ontarians from the painful effects of the GFC, with potentially dire health consequences.

Additional provincial benefits that have positive impacts on health and quality of life for social assistance recipients have also been trimmed, such as the special dietary allowance that enables people suffering from chronic illnesses to have healthy diets. A recent report shows that, in 2011, 450,000 more Canadians were affected by food insecurity than in 2008, raising the number of those affected to 3.9 million (Tarasuk, Mitchell, and Dachner 2011). This is equivalent to one in eight households in Canada, with one in six children now experiencing chronic food insecurity. This has led to the increased use of food banks. During March 2012, 882,188 people (just under 3 percent of the total population) received food from a food bank in Canada, 31 percent higher than in 2008 (FBC 2012). Importantly, working people and home owners are increasingly seeking food bank assistance, leading the UN special rapporteur on the right to food to criticize Canada for lacking a proper food security strategy for people living in vulnerable conditions (De Schutter 2012). Finally, two critical provincial housing benefits for persons receiving social assistance were also put on the chopping block, while the provincial housing ministry in 2012 saw its budget drop 12 percent from its 2009 allocation (Ruckert 2012). This followed the federal government's decision in its 2012 budget to slash national housing repair and improvement programs by 94 percent – from $674 million in 2011, partly reflecting stimulus spending for private and some public housing repairs, to just $37 million in 2012 (CCPA 2012). Such policy choices are particularly dangerous in light of the federal funding freeze for the national homelessness initiative (frozen at 1999 levels) and given Canada's long-standing lack of adequate investment in new affordable housing. This has pushed wait lists for affordable housing to new records, with the Ontario wait list reaching 152,077 households in 2011 – up 17.7 percent from 2009. At the national level, a recent study found that a record 3 million Canadian households (of a total of about 12 million) faced challenges with housing affordability in 2010 (Conference Board of Canada 2010).

Precarious Canadian Labour Markets before and after the GFC

Canadian labour markets have undergone a dramatic transformation in recent decades through technological innovation and the offshoring of investment and manufacturing jobs to emerging economies. Employment in the latter, generally unionized and better paid, fell from over 20 percent of the workforce in the late 1970s to 11 percent in 2012 (Statistics Canada 2013b). Trade (wholesale and retail) and health care are now the two largest sectors of employment in the Canadian economy, with the former commonly associated with low wages and limited benefits. Many Canadians are resorting to multiple part-time jobs to supplement their low incomes: in 2012, 748,200 workers held multiple jobs, compared with 386,300 in 1987 (Statistics Canada 2013c). An upward trend in Canadian part-time employment has followed each of the past three recessions (Figure 14.3), accounting for much of the easing in post-recession unemployment rates. The rise of different forms of precarious employment in Canada is most obvious in temporary employment. Between 1989 and 2007, temporary employees as a proportion of all employees in Canada rose from 7 percent to 11 percent (Vosko and Clark 2009), while the incidence of newly hired employees in temporary positions rose from 11 percent in 1984 to 21 percent in 2004 (Morissette and Johnson n.d.), and the number of workers in the Greater Toronto Area who describe their work as temporary increased by 40 percent since 1997 (UWT 2013). Temporary employment has been singled out in the population health literature as a particularly health-damaging form of precarious employment, with workers reporting that such employment is leading to anxiety, with immediate consequences for their personal relationships and a decreased sense of well-being (UWT 2013).

The Great Recession has intensified this trend. Historically, economic downturns resulted in changes in job type, intensifying employment precariousness. This was confirmed by the 2008 GFC as the occupations that experienced the greatest amount of job loss during the subsequent recession were

Ronald Labonté and Arne Ruckert

Figure 14.3
Part-time work and unemployment rate in Canada, 1976–2012

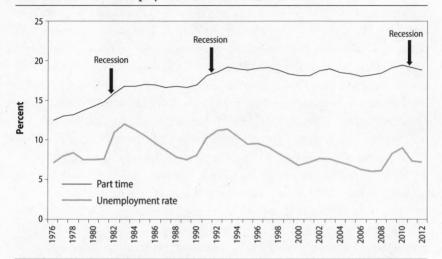

Source: Statistics Canada, Table 282–0008, Annual Labour Force Survey Estimates, CANSIM (database). Using E-Stat (distributor). Last updated 25 January 2012.

largely related to Ontario's well-paying manufacturing sector, with large companies (with more than 300 employees) shedding almost 30 percent of their workforces. At the same time, job gains in Ontario were concentrated in the less-well-paying service sector: between 2006 and 2012, close to 150,000 new positions were created in Ontario's sales and service sector (Hennessy and Stanford 2013). Many of these jobs were based on contract, short-term, part-time, and shift work arrangements, with below average levels of pay (Hennessy and Stanford 2013). Similarly, in Canada as a whole, between 2008 and 2011, the majority of job growth consisted of temporary (222,000) and part-time positions, whereas permanent positions actually decreased by 50,000 (CLC 2011; Corak 2013). Of particular concern is that the number of people working part time but wanting to work full time (involuntary part-time workers) grew during the recession, and has hardly declined since the end of the recession, still hovering at about 400,000 in Ontario alone (Hennessy and Stanford 2013).

Even with a strong year of growth in permanent work in 2012, Canada has still not reached pre-recessionary job output, with employment gains again slowing and part-time work rising, notably for older Canadian workers (Grant 2013). As Stanford (2013a, 25) notes, "jobs in lower-wage sectors account for more than 100 percent of all net new jobs created since the pre-recession peak,

... reinforc[ing] the continuing longer-run decline in the average quality of jobs in the Canadian labour market." In addition, workers at the low end of the pay and tenure scale – youth, recent immigrants, lone mothers, and workers with little skills training and education; that is, those most vulnerable and insecure – have been disproportionately affected by the economic downturn (LaRochelle-Coté and Gilmore 2009). Since 2008, the youth employment rate has decreased from 60 percent to 55 percent, and the proportion of recent immigrants working at least thirty hours a week has declined from 86.1 percent to 82.9 percent (Keung 2011). Self-employment, commonly associated with reduced social protection and income instability and adverse health effects, has also increased significantly following the GFC (LaRochelle-Coté and Gilmore 2009). At the same time, seniors are increasingly forced to return to the labour market, a process that has been intensified by the GFC and subsequent austerity. By 2012, Ontario's working seniors had tripled in number, with an estimated 240,000 Ontario seniors over sixty-five in the workforce today, about 12.5 percent of the total senior population (Hennessy and Stanford 2013).

Employment insecurity can be alleviated directly through active labour market policies (ALMP) or indirectly by increasing social protection. In Canada, neither approach has been given substantial attention in the aftermath of the GFC, with the exception of the temporary enhancement of EI benefits phased out in 2010. The 2013 federal budget gave greater emphasis to active labour market programs to address current unmet skill shortages, though the decision to renegotiate current labour market agreements with the provinces rather than to inject additional funding will most likely render the programs inconsequential, given the small size of ALMP in Canada (0.33 percent of GDP compared with above 1.0 percent for the Nordic countries) (OECD 2012). As noted above, many temporary, part-time, and self-employed workers are unlikely to qualify for EI benefits because of insufficient hours worked. The shift toward greater employment flexibility without complementary support to mitigate the ensuing insecurity can be seen as another example of health and social protection risks that increasingly are being transferred to individual workers.

Finally, the federal government has set out explicitly to reduce upward pressure on wages in both public and private sectors (Sanger 2013). Among its 2012 austerity budget measures for doing so are allowing employers to hire temporary foreign workers at 15 percent below the prevailing rate; eliminating EI benefits for claimants who refuse to accept jobs at up to 30 percent below their previous wages; and allowing contractors on federal construction jobs to pay workers as little as the legal minimum wage, undermining unionized rates for skilled labourers (Sanger 2013). The net effect will be deteriorating income levels for

Ronald Labonté and Arne Ruckert

parts of the Canadian labour force. Yet income trends are already worrying, to say the least. Post-GFC, from 2007 to 2010, the bottom fifth of all families in Ontario experienced a steep drop of 23 percent in real average market income (Government of Ontario 2012), and on average wages have barely kept up with inflation since the onset of the GFC in Canada (Tencer 2013). The reduction in public sector employment, estimated federally to be well over 100,000 from 2012–14 (including permanent and contract positions), will further weaken workers' collective bargaining power (given the higher proportion of union-ization in the public sector), undermine healthy wage growth, and have dis-proportionate and inequitable gender effects (with women in the public sector earning 4.5 percent more than women in comparable jobs in the private sector and men in the public sector earning 5.3 percent less than men in comparable jobs in the private sector) (Block 2013).

Conclusion: A Matter of Fair Taxation?

The austerity agenda arrived later on the radar screen of Canada's political elite than in many other countries discussed in this book. In contrast to social policy innovation and change outlined by Boychuk, and Luccisano and Macdonald, in this volume, Canada's social policy response to the GFC does not represent a clear departure from, but rather a deepening of, existing neo-liberal trends, reinforced through further tax cuts and targeted but limited cutbacks in SDH relevant programming areas. This chapter has focused on two pathways that link the GFC to SDH in Canada: the politics of austerity and associated program cutbacks and qualitative labour market transformations. Areas that are outside the remit of this chapter but deserve increased attention include the qualita-tive transformation of health systems, with early indications that public-private partnerships are becoming more widely used in the Canadian health-care system (Whiteside 2013); increases in the costs (co-payments) of publicly financed services (e.g., public transportation, higher education, recreation facilities); and the specific effects of public sector retrenchments given the evidence that in-creasing such employment during a recession has greater economic multiplier impacts than tax cuts to the private sector.

Canada is not the only country where the politics of austerity have clear health implications. The unhealthy and potentially lethal effects of fiscal aus-terity and further welfare retrenchment in the wake of the GFC are becoming the subject of a growing body of academic literature. David Stuckler and Sanjay Basu's (2013) recent contribution to this debate highlights the dangers of fiscal austerity through a statistical analysis of both past (Great Depression and post-communist transition) and present (Greece) experiments with fiscal austerity. They argue that even small changes in government budgets can have large – and possibly unintended – effects on population health, and they document in great detail the health costs of austerity. For example, in the European countries most affected by austerity, suicides and outbreaks of infectious diseases are becoming more common as budget cuts restrict access to health care and as welfare cuts undermine key SDH (see also Karanikolos et al. 2013). They conclude that austerity's advocates have ignored evidence of its health consequences and failed to grasp how fiscal retrenchment undermines economic performance, leading to a downward spiral of economic decline that then necessitates further austerity. This negative feedback loop has now been acknowledged by many leading international think tanks and organizations, including the IMF and OECD, both of which have been warning of austerity overkill. Yet neo-liberal prescriptions and austerity remain hegemonic in most parts of the world.

There are many reasons for neo-liberal perseverance in times of crisis. As McBride (this volume) suggests, cognitive lock-in by decision makers can partly explain the persistence of austerity in the face of evidence that it is neither working nor necessary and has potentially damaging effects on the wider population. Political leaders had no alternative playbooks to draw from and no organized civil society opposition sufficiently strong to force a different script. This hypothesis at least holds some optimism for the development of a clearer set of policy alternatives and a more organized civil society ready to proclaim when the next big crisis (financial or ecological) emerges. If economic wealth continues to accumulate disproportionately to capital rather than labour and within labour to elites rather than the majority, then we will continue to face financial crises; if we fail to deal with post-market redistribution both nationally and globally, then we will only accelerate environmental catastrophe. Yet there is also the problem of the predominance of neo-liberal discourse in public media, so that even more nuanced commentators accept as truisms that "more income redistribution inevitably dampens economic growth in a society like Canada's" and that "advocates of more government intervention must spell out all these costs, and demonstrate they are exceeded by the benefits from more equality" (Cross and Lee 2013), even as opinion polls indicate that a majority of Canadians are willing to pay more taxes to fund important health and social programs (Broadbent Institute 2012) and as the issue of inequality (and not simply poverty) assumes greater media attention.

This returns us to a discussion of the failure of Canadian taxation policy to support the social interventions known to be effective in buffering increasing social inequalities. A first consideration is whether expansionary deficit spending

Ronald Labonté and Arne Ruckert

(rather than contractionary spending cuts) is fiscally imprudent or economically unwarranted, as claimed by proponents of austerity. In economic terms, it is now generally accepted that public spending has a large GDP multiplier effect, roughly 1.6: for every dollar of public spending, GDP grows by $1.60 by generating more economic activity (Stanford 2013b). There is a growing econometric literature on this "crowding in" effect of public spending on private sector investment and spending. Stanford (2013b) examined this in light of federal corporate tax reductions post-GFC, estimated to cost public revenue $6 billion annually. The rationale for such reductions is that companies will invest, though this has not been the case with reinvestments of profits falling in step with declines in taxes (Sanger 2013; Stanford 2013b). At best, Canadian corporate reinvestment is estimated to be no more than 10 percent of the savings generated by tax cuts (Stanford 2013b). Using the 2011 promised federal corporate tax cuts of $6 billion, this would amount to $600 million in new productive investment. Applying the GDP multiplier effect of $6 billion in new public spending, this would generate almost $10 billion in new GDP growth and an additional $520 million in new corporate investment (Stanford 2013b). Even in terms of the rationale for corporate tax cuts (to stimulate investment and growth in the economy), retained public revenue and spending, with the additional $520 million in new corporate investment that this would create, outperform tax cut reinvestments by almost 10:1 ($6.53 billion versus $600 million). The net effects of such tax cuts, then, are a substantial redistribution of capital from public to private and a further "starving" of the redistributive welfare state, thus justifying austerity cuts to restrain deficits. But such deficits would not even be necessary were it not for the erosion of the Canadian tax base that began in the mid-1990s and accelerated immediately pre- and post-GFC.

Notes

1 SDH include the distribution of resources, income, goods, and services and the everyday circumstances of people's lives (e.g., neighbourhood characteristics, working conditions, physical environment, education, housing, availability of social assistance, etc.). The more unequal the distribution of these factors among different population groups, the greater the level of health inequities, broadly defined as unnecessary, avoidable, and unfair differences in health status among different population groups related to processes of social stratification (CSDH 2008).

2 This formula stipulates that transfers will grow annually by a maximum of 3 percent (or above but only if the rate of GDP growth surpasses 3 percent) after 2013–14, compared with the current maximum 6 percent annual escalator. Provinces already struggling with larger deficits than the federal government will likely have to make further cuts to health and social protection spending to absorb federal cutbacks.

References

Baxter, Joan. 2011. "The Glossary of Greed." *Pambazuka News* 523. http://www.pambazuka. net/en/category/features/72112.

Block, Sheila. 2013. "Austerity Is Bad for Our Health: Gender and Distributional Impacts of Ontario's 2012 Budget." *Alternate Routes: A Journal of Critical Social Research* 24: 199–206.

Bond, Patrick. 2008. "Global Political Economic and Geopolitical Trends, Structures, and Implications for Public Health." Globalization Knowledge Network; World Health Organization Commission on the Social Determinants of Health. http://www.global healthequity.ca/electronic%20library/Globalization%20Global%20polictical%20 economic%20and%20geopolitical%20trends.pdf.

Broadbent Institute. 2012. "Towards a More Equal Canada: A Report on Canada's Economic and Social Inequality." http://www.broadbentinstitute.ca/sites/default/files/documents/ towards_a_more_equal_canada.pdf.

Bryant, Toba, Dennis Raphael, Ted Schrecker, and Ronald Labonté. 2011. "Canada: A Land of Missed Opportunity for Addressing the Social Determinants of Health." *Health Policy (Amsterdam)* 101, 1: 44–58. http://dx.doi.org/10.1016/j.healthpol.2010.08.022.

Cahill, Sean A. 2007. "Corporate Income Tax Rate Database: Canada and the Provinces, 1960–2005." http://www4.agr.gc.ca/resources/prod/doc/pol/pub/itdat60-05/pdf/tax_e. pdf.

Canadian Centre for Policy Alternatives (CCPA). 2012. "A Budget for the Rest of Us: Alternative Federal Budget 2012." http://www.policyalternatives.ca/sites/default/files/ uploads/publications/National%20Office/2012/03/AFB2012%20Budget%20Document. pdf.

Canadian Institute for Health Information (CIHI). 2012. "National Health Expenditure Trends, 1975 to 2012." https://secure.cihi.ca/free_products/NHEXTrendsReport2012EN. pdf.

Canadian Labour Congress (CLC). 2011. "Recession Watch Bulletin: Issue 5 – Spring 2011." Canadian Labour Congress, Ottawa.

Commission for the Review of Social Assistance in Ontario (CRSAO). 2012. "Brighter Prospects: Transforming Social Assistance in Ontario." http://www.mcss.gov.on.ca/ documents/en/mcss/social/publications/social_assistance_review_final_report.pdf.

Commission on the Reform of Ontario's Public Services (CROPS). 2012. *Public Services for Ontarions: A Path to Sustainability and Excellence.* Toronto: Government of Ontario; Queen's Printer for Ontario.

Commission on Social Determinants of Health (CSDH). 2008. *Closing the Gap in a Generation: Health Equity through Action on the Social Determinants of Health.* Geneva: World Health Organization.

Conference Board of Canada. 2009. "Ontario Budget Deficit: Big Stimulus, Big Deficits." http://www.conferenceboard.ca/topics/economics/budgets/on_2009_budget.aspx.

–. 2010. "Building from the Ground Up: Affordable Housing in Canada." Conference Board of Canada, Ottawa.

Corak, Miles. 2013. "Secure Jobs on the Rise in Canada, but the Young Are Still Shut Out of the Job Market." http://milescorak.com/2013/01/04/secure-jobs-on-the-rise-in -canada-but-the-young-are-still-shut-out-of-the-jobs-market/.

Cross, Philip. 2010. *Year End Review of 2009.* Statistics Canada. http://www.statcan.gc.ca/ pub/11-010-x/2010004/part-partie3-eng.htm.

Cross, Philip, and Ian Lee. 2013. "Is Inequality a Problem Worth Fixing?" *Globe and Mail*, 6 August 2013. http://www.theglobeandmail.com/globe-debate/is-inequality-a-problem-worth-fixing/article13608880/.

De Schutter, Olivier. 2012. "Report of the Special Rapporteur on the Right to Food: Mission to Canada." http://www.ohchr.org/Documents/HRBodies/HRCouncil/Regular Session/Session22/AHRC2250Add.1_English.PDF.

Deverakonda, Ravi Kanth. 2012. "The Battle over Development-Led Globalization." Terraviva. http://www.ipsnews.net/2012/04/the-battle-over-development-led -globalisation/.

Fanelli, Carlo, and Priscillia Lefebvre. 2012. "The Ottawa and Gatineau Museum Workers' Strike: Precarious Employment and the Public Sector Squeeze." *Alternate Routes: A Journal of Critical Social Research* 23: 121–46.

Food Banks Canada (FBC). 2012. "Hungercount 2012: A Comprehensive Report on Hunger and Food Bank Use in Canada." http://foodbankscanada.ca/getmedia/ 3b946e67-fbe2-490e-90dc-4a313dfb97e5/HungerCount2012.pdf.aspx.

Forbes. 2013. "Inside the Billionaires List: Facts and Figures." *Forbes*, 4 March. http://www. forbes.com/sites/luisakroll/2013/03/04/inside-the-2013-billionaires-list-facts -and-figures/.

Government of Canada. 2012. "Budget 2012." http://www.budget.gc.ca/2012/plan/anx2 -eng.html.

Government of Ontario. 2012. *Breaking the Cycle: The Fourth Progress Report*. Toronto: Ministry of Children and Youth Services.

Grant, Tavia. 2013. "Economy Adds Jobs but Growth Still Slow." *Globe and Mail*, 6 September 2013. http://www.theglobeandmail.com/report-on-business/economy/jobs/canada -jobs/article14157765/.

Gup, B.E. 2010. *The Financial and Economic Crises: An International Perspective*. Northampton: Edgar Elgar Publishing. http://dx.doi.org/10.4337/9781849806763.

Hendrikse, Reijer P., and James D. Sidaway. 2010. "Neoliberalism 3.0." *Environment and Planning* 42, 9: 2037–42. http://dx.doi.org/10.1068/a43361.

Hennessy, Trish, and Jim Stanford. 2013. "More Harm than Good: Austerity's Impact in Ontario." http://www.policyalternatives.ca/sites/default/files/uploads/publications/ Ontario%20Office/2013/03/More%20Harm%20Than%20Good_0.pdf.

Jackson, Andrew. 2012. "CLC Analysis of the Federal Budget 2012." Canadian Labour Congress. http://behindthenumbers.ca/2012/03/29/clc-analysis-of-the-2012 -federal-budget/.

Karanikolos, Marina, Philipa Mladovsky, Jonathan Cylus, Sarah Thomson, Sanjay Basu, David Stuckler, Johan P. Mackenbach, and Martin McKee. 2013. "Financial Crisis, Austerity, and Health in Europe." *Lancet* 381, 9874: 1323–31. http://dx.doi.org/10. 1016/S0140-6736(13)60102-6.

Keung, Nicholas. 2011. "Immigrants Hardest Hit by Recession, Study Says." *Toronto Star*, 15 July. http://www.thestar.com/news/gta/2011/07/15/immigrants_hardest_hit_by_ recent_recession_study_says.html.

Kneebone, Ronal D., and Katherine G. White. 2009. "Fiscal Retrenchment and Social Assistance in Canada." *Canadian Public Policy* 35, 1: 21–40. http://dx.doi.org/10.3138/ cpp.35.1.21.

Koivusalo, Meri, Ted Schrecker, and Ron Labonté. 2008. "Globalization and Policy Space for Health and Social Determinants of Health." Globalization Knowledge Network;

World Health Organization Commission on the Social Determinants of Health. http:// www.globalhealthequity.ca/content/presentations-and-publications-2.

Labonté, Ron, and Ted Schrecker. 2007. "Globalization and Social Determinants of Health: Introduction and Methodological Background." *Globalization and Health* 3, 5.

LaRochelle-Coté, Sebastien, and Jason Gilmore. 2009. "Canada's Employment Downturn." Statistics Canada Report No. 75-001-X. http://www.statcan.gc.ca/pub/75-001-x/2009112/pdf/11048-eng.pdf.

Lee, Yong-Shik. 2006. *Reclaiming Development in the World Trading System.* New York: Cambridge University Press. http://dx.doi.org/10.1017/CBO9780511511349.

Macdonald, David. 2013. *The Big Banks' Big Secret: Estimating Government Support for Canadian Banks during the Financial Crisis.* Ottawa: Canadian Centre for Policy Alternatives.

Morissette, R., and A. Johnson. N.d. "Are Good Jobs Disappearing in Canada?" Analytical Studies Branch, Statistics Canada, Research Paper Series No. 239.

Organization for Economic Cooperation and Development (OECD). 2011. *Why Inequality Keeps Rising.* Paris: OECD Publishing.

–. 2012. "Public Expenditure on Active Labour Market Policies." Employment and Labour Markets: Key Tables from OECD (No. 9). doi: 10.1787/lmpxp-table-2012-1-en.

Osberg, Lars. 2009. "Canada's Declining Social Safety Net: The Case for EI Reform." Canadian Centre for Policy Alternatives. http://www.policyalternatives.ca/sites/default/files/uploads/publications/National_Office_Pubs/2009/Canadas_Declining_Safety_Net.pdf.

Pamuk, Elise, Diane M. Makuc, Katherine E. Heck, Cynthia Reuban, and Kimberley Lochner. 1998. *Socioeconomic Status and Health Chartbook.* Atlanta: National Center for Health Statistics.

Raphael, Dennis. 2011. *Poverty in Canada: Implications for Health and Quality of Life.* Toronto: Canadian Scholars Press.

Ruckert, Arne. 2012. "The Federal and Ontario Budgets of 2012: What's in It for Health Equity?" *Canadian Journal of Public Health* 103, 5: 373–75.

Ruckert, Arne, and Ron Labonté. 2012. "The Global Financial Crisis and Health Equity: Toward a Conceptual Framework." *Critical Public Health* 22, 3: 267–79. http://dx.doi.org/10.1080/09581596.2012.685053.

Sanger, Toby. 2013. "Canada's Conservative Class War: Using Austerity to Squeeze Labor at the Expense of Economic Growth." *Alternate Routes: A Journal of Critical Social Research* 24: 59–84.

Schrecker, Ted, and Armine Yalnizyan. 2010. "The Growing Economic Gap: What It Means for Canadian Families and the Canadian Future." Institute of Population Health. http:// www.academia.edu/250999/The_Growing_Economic_Gap_What_it_means_for_Canadian_families_and_the_Canadian_future.

Simms, David. 2013. "Canada Best Place in G8 to Pay Business Taxes." CBC News. http:// www.cbc.ca/news/business/taxes/canada-best-place-in-g8-to-pay-business-taxes-1.1380380.

Stanford, Jim. 2013a. "The Myth of Canadian Exceptionalism: Crisis, Non-Recovery, and Austerity." *Alternate Routes: A Journal of Critical Social Research* 24: 19–32.

–. 2013b. "The Failure of Corporate Tax Cuts to Stimulate Business Investment." In *The Great Revenue Robbery,* edited by R. Swift. Ottawa: Canadians for Tax Fairness.

Statistics Canada. 2013a. "High-Income Trends among Canadian Taxfilers, 1982 to 2010." Statistics Canada. http://www.statcan.gc.ca/daily-quotidien/130128/dq130128a-eng.htm.

–. 2013b. "Labour Force Survey Estimates, by North American Industry Classification System, Sex, and Age Group, Persons (Annual)." http://www5.statcan.gc.ca/cansim/a05?lang=eng&id=282003.

–. 2013c. "Labour Force Survey Estimates, Multiple Job Holders by National Occupation Classification for Statistics, Sex, and Age Group, Persons (Annual)." http://www5.statcan.gc.ca/cansim/a05?lang=eng&id=2820034.

Stoney, Christopher, and Tamara Krawchenko. 2013. "Crisis and Opportunism: Public Finance Trends from Stimulus to Austerity in Canada." *Alternate Routes: A Journal of Critical Social Research* 24: 33–58.

Stuckler, David, and Sanjay Basu. 2013. *The Body Economic: Why Austerity Kills*. New York: Basic Books.

Tarasuk, Valerie, Andy Mitchell, and Naomi Dachner. 2011. "Household Food Insecurity in Canada 2011." http://nutritionalsciences.lamp.utoronto.ca/wp-content/uploads/2014/01/foodinsecurity2011_final.pdf.

Tencer, Daniel. 2013. "Canada's Inflation Rate Is Low, but Still Eating Your Pathetically Small Wage Gain." *Huffington Post*, 24 August. http://www.huffingtonpost.ca/2013/08/24/inflation-wage-gains-canada_n_3806352.html.

Therborn, Göran. 2013. *The Killing Fields of Inequality*. London: Polity Press.

United Nations Department of Economic and Social Affairs (UNDESA). 2010. "World Economic Situations and Prospects." United Nations. http://www.un.org/en/development/desa/policy/wesp/wesp_archive/2010wesp.pdf.

United Way Toronto (UWT). 2013. *It's More than Poverty: Employment Precarity and Household Wellbeing*. Toronto: United Way Toronto.

Vosko, Leah, and Lisa Clark. 2009. "Canada: Gendered Precariousness and Social Reproduction." In *Gender and the Contours of Precarious Employment*, edited by L. Vosko, M. Macdonald, and I. Campbell, 26–42. Abingdon: Routledge.

Wade, Robert. 2009. "From Global Imbalances to Global Reorganizations." *Cambridge Journal of Economics* 33, 4: 539–62. http://dx.doi.org/10.1093/cje/bep032.

Whiteside, Heather. 2013. "The Pathology of Profitable Partnerships: Dispossession, Marketization, and Canadian P3 Hospitals." PhD diss., Simon Fraser University.

Whittington, Les, and Bruce Campion-Smith. 2012. "EI Reform: Unemployed Canadians Face Crackdown under Federal Changes." *Toronto Star*, 24 May. http://www.thestar.com/news/canada/2012/05/24/ei_reform_unemployed_canadians_face_crackdown_under_federal_changes.html.

15

US Incremental Social Policy Expansionism in Response to Crisis

GERARD W. BOYCHUK

The United States was the epicentre of the global financial crisis of 2008, and its policy response to the crisis has received considerable attention. In terms of social policy, there are significantly divergent assessments of the US response to the Great Recession – in terms of both the adequacy of the initial response and its significance for the overall trajectory of American social policy into the future. On the one hand, portrayals of the response as inadequate confront those arguing that it was a generous effort to raise the national social safety net. On the other, in terms of longer-term implications, depictions of the crisis as having little effect on political or ideological realignment confront those arguing that the response set a new direction in American social policy.

The first section of this chapter argues that US fiscal expansionism in response to the Great Recession developed increasingly in a direction toward "social Keynesianism" and away from its initial orientation toward liberal (or market-conforming) Keynesianism.[1] Income tax reductions – the central focus of the individual transfer component of the original stimulus bill – simply expired. In stark contrast, unemployment insurance benefit enrichments and expansions – much less clearly "market conforming" than tax cuts – extended across a five-year period following the crisis. Using Canada as a comparative reference point, the chapter argues that the cumulative result was significant. The US response shifted the overall US system of unemployment insurance benefits, at least temporarily, to a higher level of generosity than the Canadian unemployment insurance system. In fact, for some categories of households, the overall US income transfer system, in the wake of the crisis, became more generous than the Canadian income transfer system – a remarkable fact for many, especially Canadian, observers.

The second section of the chapter provides some initial discussion regarding the long-term political implications of social policy expansionism in response to the fiscal crisis. It argues that the social policy response to the crisis in the United States did not appear as a radical rupture from the existing policy equilibrium; however, undertaken via a strategy of social policy expansionism through stealth, it would not have been expected to appear as such. The section examines the degree to which the social policy response to the Great Recession might have indicated ideational shifts, entailed incidental institutional shifts, and suggested the potential for future political coalitions that could underpin a shift in US social policy.

Divergent Portrayals of the US Social Policy Response

There are starkly divergent assessments of the immediate significance of the US social policy response to the financial crisis. In terms of its immediate effects, the social policy element of the stimulus package has been described as "grossly inadequate" both in terms of its overall magnitude and in terms of its emphasis on tax benefits (Kregel 2011, 24). In this vision, political deadlock has precluded any significant policy response except for "monetary stimulus through quantitative easing" (McBride, this volume). Similarly, according to Kregel (2011, 25), the US political environment has "eviscerated fiscal policy," and "political paralysis has meant that fiscal policy is no longer a counter cyclical policy tool, since it can never achieve Congressional support." The conventional narrative is that a combination of institutional fragmentation in a context of political polarization has significantly limited the ability of the US government to respond (Ashbee 2014; McCarty 2012). This view of the US social policy response remains contested. Other observers, such as Daguerre (2011, 402), note that "the Recovery Act, however insufficient according to many liberals, remained an exceptionally generous financial effort to raise the nation's safety net and to alleviate the plight of low-income families." According to Alter (2011, 131), the stimulus bill of 2009 was a "generous and compassionate bill" that represented "a tremendous boon to the working poor."

There are also starkly divergent assessments of the potential longer-term political effects of the crisis response on social policy in the United States. Various observers conclude that the stimulus package did not represent a significant shift in social policy. Ashbee (2014, 94) highlights the "limited character of institutional change in the US ... and the degree to which the period was characterized by institutional extension rather than displacement." McCarty (2012, 226) asserts that, "rather than restructure the American political economy, the financial crisis highlighted its dominant features." More generally, Kahler and Lake (2013, 2) conclude that "the economic crisis has provided few signs of fundamental political realignment, policy experimentation ... or mobilization by new political actors in any of the most seriously affected economies." They crisply note "the disjuncture between a deep economic crisis and its relatively slender effects to date on political realignment and ideational reorientation." Bermeo and Pontusson (2012, 28) conclude that "those who hoped that the Great Recession might provide the opportunity for the forging of new coalitions to lessen economic inequality must be sorely disappointed."

Yet other observers argue that the US response to the financial crisis "set a new direction in American social policy" (Alter 2011, 132). Somewhat more guardedly, Jonsson and Stefansson (2013, 17) note that "the first two years of the Obama administration saw the adoption of potentially substantive change in US social policy." According to Philip (2014, 200), the primary effect of the financial crisis of 2008 was its "role in reshaping political attitudes": "Political institutions in the US have not changed by much since 2008, but the mentality of its policy makers has indeed."

The US Social Policy Response in the Immediate Term

The primary US response to the financial crisis was embodied in the American Recovery and Reinvestment Act (ARRA) passed by the Obama administration in January 2009 – popularly known as the "stimulus bill." Although the document was more than 400 pages long, the basic formula was relatively simple: one-third of expenditures for transfers to individuals, one-third for state stabilization, and one-third for infrastructure (Alter 2011, 81–82). Thus, the stimulus package represented a relative balance among transfers to individuals, transfers to other governments, and direct spending. In terms of transfers to individuals, it also represented a relative balance between tax cuts (reduced tax revenues) and spending (increased government cash outlays). Benefits to individuals comprised between one-third and just under one-half of the stimulus package (see Figure 15.1).[2]

The "middle-class tax cut" entitled Make Work Pay was the centrepiece of the package of benefits to individuals. It is difficult to overstate the symbolic import of the significance of this element of expenditure in the overall package of benefits to individuals. The title clearly signified that the tax credit, though

Figure 15.1
ARRA, 2009, estimated expenditures for transfers to individuals and all other stimulus (direct spending, transfers to states, tax expenditures)

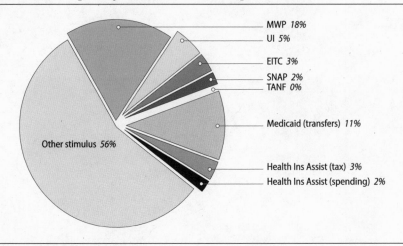

MWP *18%*
UI *5%*

EITC *3%*
SNAP *2%*
TANF *0%*

Medicaid (transfers) *11%*

Other stimulus *56%*

Health Ins Assist (tax) *3%*
Health Ins Assist (spending) *2%*

Source: Congressional Budget Office.

refundable, was intended for those who were working, and it was widely referred to as constituting middle-class tax cuts (see Alter 2011). The policy problem at which the Make Work Pay tax credit was obviously aimed was the weakness of work incentives – hence the need to "make work pay." Although its genesis lay in the general election campaign of 2008, this construction of the policy challenge appears to have been starkly at odds with other imagery invoked by the stimulus bill – that major dimensions of the problem were lowered demand across the economy (hence the need for stimulus) and associated high levels of unemployment (the latter most directly invoked by the proposal to expand and extend emergency unemployment benefits).

After the Make Work Pay tax cut/credit, this latter component was the second most significant expansion of benefits provided directly to individuals. The extension of unemployment insurance in the stimulus bill built on an earlier expansion of unemployment insurance in 2008. Despite attempts in the Senate, an extension of unemployment insurance was not ultimately included in the first stimulus package proposed under President Bush in January 2008 (McCarty 2012, 213). However, a bill extending unemployment insurance was passed in the middle of 2008, increasing direct spending on unemployment benefits by $11.7 billion over a ten-year period. The program extended eligibility for beneficiaries by providing full federal funding for an additional thirteen weeks of

Table 15.1
ARRA benefits to individuals and post-ARRA expansions

Program	ARRA provision	ARRA period	Value of ARRA	Extensions (post-ARRA)	End date (most recent extension)	Value of extensions
Make Work Pay	Refundable tax credit ($500 per taxfiler) phased out above threshold	2009, 2010	$45B outlays $99B reduced revenues $144B total	n/a	n/a	n/a
TANF	Emergency fund for transfers to states with TANF spending (2009–10) above (2007–8)	Expires end 2010	$2.3B estimated ($5B authorized)	n/a	n/a	n/a
SNAP	Increase maximum benefits	5 years (to end of Oct 2013)	$20B	n/a	n/a	n/a
EITC ACTC	Eliminate limitation on amount used to calculate refundable portion of the $1,000 child tax credit; increase EITC for families with three or more children	2009, 2010	$23B outlays $3B reduced revenues $25B total*	Dec 2010 Jan 2013	Dec 2017	unavailable** • est. $62.5B to end 2013 • est. $112.5B to end of 2017

| EUC08 | Emergency unemployment benefits; full federal funding of extended benefits; benefit increase | EUC eligibility cutoff (Dec 2009) | $38B | Nov 2009
Dec 2009
Mar 2010
Apr 2010
Jul 2010
Dec 2010
Dec 2011
Feb 2012
Jan 2013 | 31 Dec 2013 | $177.1B |

Notes:

TANF – Temporary Assistance for Needy Families

SNAP – Supplemental Nutrition Assistance Plan

EITC – Earned Income Tax Credit

ACTC – Additional Child Tax Credit

EUC08 – Emergency Unemployment Compensation 2008 (and extensions)

* CBO estimates do not provide a breakdown for each of these changes.

** US Congress Joint Committee on Taxation for expansions only provides cost estimates of total amounts for the full child tax credit rather than increased expenditures because of changes.

Source: For MWP, TANF, SNAP, and EUC08 ARRA-extension – Congressional Budget Office, Cost Estimate H.R. 1 American Recovery and Reinvestment Act of 2009, 26 January 2009; For EITC/ACTC, ARRA provisions – Joint Committee on Taxation, Estimated Revenue Effects of the House Amendment to the Senate Amendment to HR 4853, 2 December 2010; For EUC08 extensions – Congressional Budget Office, Cost Estimate, H.R. 3548 Worker, Homeownership and Business Act of 2009, 25 November 2009; Congressional Budget Office, Cost Estimate Temporary Extension Act of 2010, 24 February 2010; Congressional Budget Office, Budgetary Effects of Senate Amendment 4425, the Unemployment Compensation Extension Act of 2010, 30 June 2010; Congressional Budget Office, Estimate of the Statutory Pay-as-You-Go Effects for HR 6419, Emergency Unemployment Compensation Continuation Act, 18 November 2010; Congressional Budget Office, Budgetary Effects of the Temporary Payroll Tax Cut Continuation Act of 2011, 22 December 2011; Congressional Budget Office, Budgetary Effects of HR 3630, the Middle Class Tax Relief and Job Creation Act of 2011, 6 January 2012; Congressional Budget Office, Estimate of the Budgetary Effects of H.R. 8, the American Taxpayer Relief Act of 2012, 1 January 2013; For EITC/ACTC post-ARRA extensions, Joint Committee on Taxation, Estimated Revenue Effects of H.R. 8, the American Taxpayer Relieve Act of 2012, 1 January 2013.

benefits in all states and an additional thirteen weeks of benefits in states that reached a specified unemployment threshold and would be available to the end of April of the following year.[3] In December 2008, the program was further enhanced, with the number of weeks for the first tier of emergency benefits (all states) increased to twenty for a maximum extension of thirty-three weeks – an expansion with an estimated cost of $5.7 billion.[4] The stimulus bill of 2009 included an even more significant expansion of benefits. Including extending the duration of benefits and including a slight enhancement of benefits of twenty-five dollars per week, the ARRA unemployment insurance component had an estimated value of $38 billion – roughly double the estimated costs of the expansions of 2008.[5] Nevertheless, the Make Work Pay tax cut/credit remained more than three and a half times the magnitude of the unemployment insurance extension included in ARRA.

However, after this point, the political fates of the two programs were to diverge radically. The Make Work Pay tax cut/credit had generated very little public recognition – much less political capital for the Obama administration (Alter 2011, 87; Cooper 2010). The Make Work Pay tax cut/credit was applied to tax withholding for 2009 and 2010 in relative obscurity, and there were no evident public discussions on extension of the credit. In stark contrast, following the ARRA expansion in early 2009, unemployment insurance benefits were expanded or extended on nine separate occasions (see Table 15.1).

The cumulative results of these expansions were staggering. In terms of program size, the new programs (emergency benefits as well as federal additional compensation) quickly rivalled existing unemployment insurance benefits. As early as 2010, expenditures on expanded benefits roughly equalled total spending on existing regular and extended benefits. By the end of 2013, the emergency unemployment benefits program (and other minor expansions) had a total estimated cost of $230 billion – more than one and a half times the value of the entire stimulus package proposed by President Obama in the 2008 election campaign (Alter 2011, 88). As a simple counterfactual, Figure 15.2 depicts the stimulus package had the estimated value of the unemployment insurance expansions been included in the original package. In this rendering, the expansion was the largest element of benefits to individuals. It was also fully three-quarters the size of all other stimulus.

The incremental pattern, key to the program's overall expansion, is most clearly highlighted in Figure 15.3, which outlines the cumulative fiscal impact of each program extension and expansion. The most recent extension, in January 2013, brought the estimated total cost of post-ARRA expansions to just under

Gerard W. Boychuk

Figure 15.2
ARRA, benefits, expansions, and other stimulus, 2009–19 (direct spending, transfers to states, tax expenditures, including post-ARRA UI expansions to February 2013)

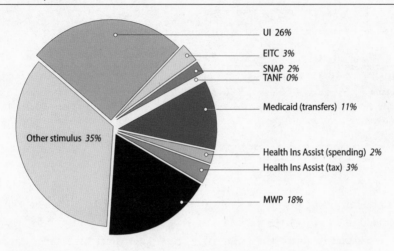

UI 26%
EITC 3%
SNAP 2%
TANF 0%
Medicaid (transfers) 11%
Other stimulus 35%
Health Ins Assist (spending) 2%
Health Ins Assist (tax) 3%
MWP 18%

Source: Congressional Budget Office, Cost Estimate H.R. 1 American Recovery and Reinvestment Act of 2009, 26 January 2009.

Figure 15.3
Estimated expenditures, emergency unemployment compensation and federal additional compensation, extensions, and expansions, 2008–13

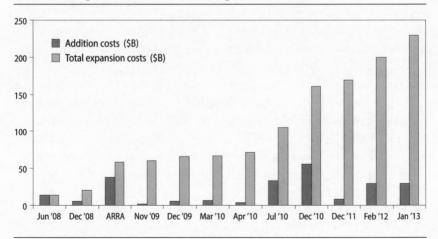

Source: See Table 15.1.

Table 15.2

Change in unemployment rates and passive labour market expenditures, 2006–9 (OECD liberal market economies)

| | Unemployment rates | | | | PLMP expenditures | | | |
| | Rates | | Difference | | % of GDP | | Difference | |
	Low (2007–8)	High (2009–10)	Points	%	Low (2006–7)	High (2008–9)	Points	%
Australia	4.20	5.60	1.40	33.3	0.09	0.11	0.02	22.2
Canada	6.00	8.30	2.30	38.3	0.09	0.12	0.03	33.3
Japan	3.90	5.10	1.20	30.8	0.07	0.08	0.01	14.3
United Kingdom	5.30	7.80	2.50	47.2	0.03	0.04	0.01	33.3
United States	4.60	9.60	5.00	108.7	0.05	0.14	0.09	180.0

Source: Rueda (2012, Tables 12.7 and 12.8).

$210 billion– more than five and a half times the value of the initial expansion included in the ARRA legislation.

The expansion was also significant in cross-national terms. In an examination of active and passive labour market policies pre- and post-crisis across OECD countries, Rueda (2012, 385) concluded that "it is not clear that there has been any reaction to the crisis in these countries." However, in contrast, he crisply noted that "the only exception is the United States." As outlined in Table 15.2, though it is debatable that there was no response in other countries, it is clear that the response in the United States was significant.

Policy Outputs: Comparing the United States and Canada

The Canadian social policy response to the financial crisis was relatively muted in comparison with that of the United States (see Table 15.2). However, a comparison helps to put the US changes in perspective and highlights the significance of the US response. The most striking shift has been in terms of unemployment insurance generosity for those eligible for such benefits in the United States. Whereas net replacement rates (cumulative across time) in the United States had been lower than those in Canada prior to the financial crisis, US unemployment benefits became more generous than replacement rates in Canada after 2008 (see Figure 15.4.) In fact, the relative positions of the two countries flipped. Net replacement rates were more than one and a half times more generous in Canada than in the United States in 2007. By 2011, net replacement rates in the United States were one and two-thirds times more generous than those in Canada.

Gerard W. Boychuk

Figure 15.4

Unemployment benefits, US and Canada, 2005-11, net average earnings replacement rates, across 60 months (no social assistance, housing, or child benefits)

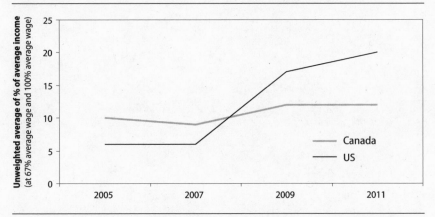

Source: OECD, Benefit Generosity: Net Replacement Rates Over a Five Year Period Following Unemployment. 2001-2011. Benefits and Wages: Statistics online database. http://www.oecd.org/els/benefits-and-wages-statistics.htm.

As noted above by Alter (2011), transfers to low-wage earners and minimum-wage earners were also significantly improved in the United States as a result of the enrichments of the Earned Income Tax Credit and Child Tax Credit.[6] The effects of these enrichments in comparison with Canada are also significant (see Figures 15.5 and 15.6). Net transfers to low-wage earners in the United

Figure 15.5

Net transfers to low-wage earners, United States and Canada, 2005–11, by family type

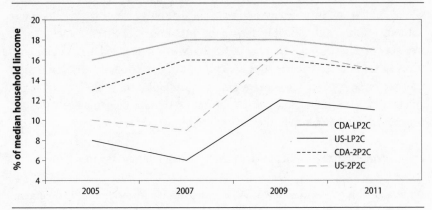

Source: OECD, Incomes of Workers in Other Low Paid Jobs, 2005-11. Benefits and Wages: Statistics. http://www.oecd.org/els/benefits-and-wages-statistics.htm.

Figure 15.6

Net transfers to minimum-wage earners, United States and Canada, 2005–11, for families with children, by type

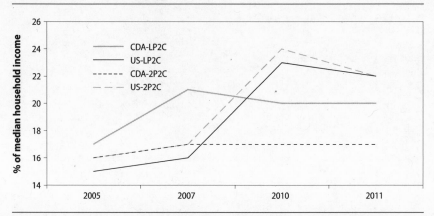

Source: OECD, Incomes of full-time minimum wage earners, 2005-11. Benefits and Wages: Statistics. http://www.oecd.org/els/benefits-and-wages-statistics.htm. Net transfers calculated by author.

States converged significantly with the level of net transfers to low-wage earners in Canada. A similar pattern of relative improvement in US net replacement rates is also evident in regard to transfers to minimum-wage earners, though, because of differences in minimum wages, this is somewhat more difficult to interpret.

In contrast to the increased value of cumulative unemployment insurance benefits over time as well as net transfers to those with low-income or minimum-wage jobs, there has been virtually no change in the United States for those reliant wholly on transfer income (see Figure 15.7).[7] The only change in benefits at the national level for these recipients was the enrichment of SNAP benefits for a five-year period (through October 2013) that was not renewed, with minor cuts to SNAP announced in early 2014 with passing of the farm bill.[8] Minimum cash transfer income for this category remains considerably more generous in Canada than in the United States, and there are no signs of convergence and little prospect for convergence in the near or medium-term future.

Long-Term Political Implications of the US Social Policy Response

It is reasonable to wonder how various observers can draw as starkly divergent conclusions regarding the US social policy response, as outlined at the outset of this chapter, and the degree to which these distinct portrayals can be reconciled.

Gerard W. Boychuk

Figure 15.7

Minimum cash transfer income, United States and Canada, 2005–11 for families
with children, by type

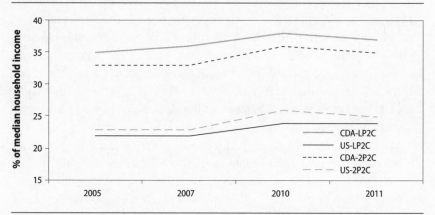

Source: OECD, Incomes of families relying on minimum-income safety-net benefits, 2005-11.
Benefits and Wages: Statistics. http://www.oecd.org/els/benefits-and-wages-statistics.htm.

In examining responses to the crisis, the existing literature on US social policy
as well as the US response more broadly appears to focus on looking for evidence
of a critical juncture, a path-breaking change, a point punctuating the existing
policy equilibrium. In fact, this appears to be the central question underlying
comparisons of the Great Recession with the Great Depression and comparisons
of the response of the Obama administration with that of the Roosevelt administration. Perhaps not surprisingly, very few of these contemporary comparisons
find evidence of the path-breaking changes for which they are looking, and
different authors offer different explanations for this. Evidence of such a direct
and obvious shift is indeed elusive.

However, a somewhat earlier strand of literature – less in evidence in
considerations of social policy responses to the financial crisis – stresses the
potential importance of incremental change occurring in forms such as conversion, layering, and drift (Hacker 2004). In response to an earlier generation of
welfare state literature arguing that "remarkably few welfare states have experienced fundamental shifts," Hacker (2004, 243) compellingly outlines significant incremental change occurring through layering, conversion, and drift
by which risk, in the United States, had become increasingly privatized. Incremental change can "contribute to the erosion and undermining of the existing
institutional architecture and the construction of new arrangements," even
though "their intent may be obscured" (Ashbee 2014, 85).[9]

That there was no demonstrable rupture with existing policy routines or highly visible punctuation of the existing policy equilibrium is not surprising – policy makers deliberately avoided doing so. Daguerre (2011, 401) describes the strategy underpinning the social policy elements of the Recovery Act as representing "expansion by stealth." Skocpol and Jacobs (2011, 38), assessing the first two years of the Obama administration, would concur: "Obama's agenda for policy change progressed quite remarkably during 2009 and 2010 ... But much of what happened was either invisible or ominously incomprehensible to most citizens." Nowhere is this clearer than with unemployment insurance benefit expansion. The expansion and extension of benefits in the 2008 stimulus bill was clearly framed as a one-off. Moreover, it was overshadowed by other elements of a huge and diverse stimulus package – especially the broadly applied tax cuts. Nevertheless, even if the Obama administration failed to provide visible leadership on this issue, these shifts were significant, and a social Keynesian frame came to dominate. When told by a junior congressman that the bill was the "best anti-poverty bill in a generation," Michelle Obama is reported to have replied "shhhhh" (Alter 2011, 101).

Certainly, low-visibility changes undoubtedly have different political effects than high-visibility ones – making them less likely to encounter full-out opposition but also less likely to shape and lead public opinion. As Daguerre (2011, 404) notes, "the Recovery Act failed to win over impoverished Americans to the cause of social spending precisely because it was not bold enough to visibly improve the daily experiences of these citizens." Along this line of reasoning, the choice to pursue social policy expansion by stealth might have come with considerable political opportunity costs.

Ideational Implications

This is not to say, however, that the thinking behind those initiatives did not mark a relatively radical departure from existing policy approaches. McCarty (2012, 226) baldly states that "the crisis appeared to do little to change the distribution of beliefs among elected leaders about free markets and the role of government intervention." In contrast, Ashbee (2014, 89) argues that the crisis was perceived by senior advisers and policy makers as a "special case" requiring the use of "overwhelming force" in which "fiscal measures had to be large enough to sway the economic decisions of both firms and households." This portrayal fits with the more general conclusion of Pontusson and Raess (2012, 18) across advanced capitalist countries regarding "the sudden and surprising revival of Keynesianism." In this sense, policy makers' perception of the crisis and its

Gerard W. Boychuk

required solution was relatively radical, and, as Ashbee (2014, 89) asserts, "such representations laid the basis for ARRA."

However, enactment of this vision and its policy prescriptions was constrained, according to Ashbee (2014, 89), by an internalized sense among policy makers of institutional constraint: "Their thinking was, however, constrained by an internalized recognition of the ways in which institutionalized veto points put limits on their capacity for action, despite the unambiguous character of the November 2008 election results."[10] Thus, those who sought reform, to some degree, deliberately adopted a strategy of conversion, layering, and drift – consistent with Daguerre's (2011, 401) interpretation that the stimulus package represented social policy expansion by stealth (see also Ashbee 2014, 85). Thus, despite the appearance of a muted response, Philip (2014, 200) concludes that the primary effect of the financial crisis of 2008 was its "role in reshaping political attitudes": "Political institutions in the US have not changed by much since 2008, but the mentality of its policy makers has indeed."

This depiction of relatively radical thinking deeply tempered by strategic calculation differs significantly from portrayals suggesting that a fundamental ideational shift among policy makers away from Keynesian policy approaches occurred shortly after their brief flirtation with it. Kregel (2011, 25), for example, asserts forcefully that "the resurgence of support for Keynesian expenditure policies has been extremely short lived, and the pages of every newspaper and every news broadcast have turned to a discussion of the risks facing the global economy and in particular the US economy from the impact of the stimulus measures on the size of government debt." He concludes sharply: "Rather than a resurgence of influence, Keynesian policies are now considered as discredited and outmoded." Writing early in 2012, D'Ippoliti stated that, "after a rapid surge in Keynesianism in the USA ... in the wake of the financial and economic crisis, the cultural and political debate has already turned to fiercely opposing it" (3). Such conclusions seem to be partial at best and likely premature. As just one example, in policy announcements in the fall of 2013, the Federal Reserve Board could not have stated it more clearly: "Fiscal policy is restraining economic growth." At the same time, the board voiced its concern that a potential future turn for the worse in the broader economy could result from cuts in federal spending (Appelbaum 2013).

Potential Institutional Shifts

In addition to simply enhancing benefits, the extension and expansion of unemployment insurance entailed two major incidental effects. The first effect was increasing the financial responsibility of the federal government for unemployment (and unemployment insurance) relative to the states. The federal government had adopted full financial responsibility for emergency benefits but also for pre-existing extended benefits that had been formerly funded on a fifty-fifty basis between states and the federal government.

The second effect was an increasing reliance on general revenues rather than unemployment insurance trust funds (generated by earmarked state payroll taxes and an earmarked federal payroll tax). In contrast, emergency unemployment benefits have been fully funded by general federal revenues, and even extended benefits (previously funded on a fifty-fifty basis by state and federal governments) are now (at least temporarily) fully funded by the federal government from general revenues. The latter shift has an ancillary implication. To the degree that benefits have been increasingly funded from general revenues, the overall program has become more progressive since general taxes are relatively more progressive than payroll taxes. One can argue that shifting the relative balance of responsibilities between the federal government and state governments in a policy area, shifting the manner in which benefits are funded, and shifting the progressivity of the overall program of benefits would also shift the politics of those benefits.

For example, the choice to fund expansion almost exclusively through general revenues bypassed the zero-sum politics that would have undoubtedly been generated if changes to unemployment insurance had been self-funding. As a recent Congressional Budget Office (Bermeo and Pontusson 2012b, 23) report notes, the limit on earnings used to calculate contributions has remained the same since 1983 in the United States and could be increased and/or indexed. Such changes, however, would have important direct implications for the way that income is redistributed through the unemployment insurance system. The reversion to funding through general revenues helped to ease the zero-sum nature of the changes.

Interestingly, a CBO report released in November 2012 raised (among a wide range of potential reforms) a number of suggestions for changing the structure of the unemployment insurance system for the longer term. Noting that "most of the increase in federal spending on unemployment insurance occurred through new policies," the CBO raised the possibility of regularizing expenditure increases: "Increases in federal funding during and after recessions could be made more formulaic by automatically tying more funding to state and national unemployment rates ... instead of relying on new policies" (2012b, 22). In essence, this would entail a shift in focus at the federal level toward truly automatic stabilizers rather than discretionary stabilizers. At the

Gerard W. Boychuk

same time, it would make permanent (subject to unemployment rates) the incidental effects outlined above – a greater degree of financial responsibility for unemployment borne by the federal government, a greater reliance on general revenues rather than social insurance funds, and, given the latter, *ceteris paribus* a more progressive system.

Even more radically, in its discussion of possible structural changes to make state programs more uniform, the report noted the possibility that policy makers "could federalize the US system by collecting taxes and administering benefits at the federal rather than at the state level" (CBO 2012b, 22). The report noted, in its discussion of this possibility, that, "in virtually all countries in Western Europe, UI policies are administered at the national level" (22). This is not to say that either option appears to be politically feasible at this time; rather, this illustrates that discussions of such options can emerge onto the political agenda in a context of persistent high unemployment and massive expansion of the unemployment insurance system.

Potential for Future Political Coalitions

One possible avenue for change is the reconfiguration of interests. As Kahler and Lake (2013, 18) outline, "it is the reshuffling of interests and coalitions that produces potential policy change rather than the direct influence of the crisis." Pinto (2013, 108) concludes, in agreement with earlier conclusions of Gourevitch, that "coalitional dynamics trump ideology, institutions, and international factors in explanations of policy choices." The long-term implications of discursive shifts for how various groups perceive their own interests comprise one example. As Hall and Lamont (2013, 10) note, "by framing their demands in new terms, many groups could advance longstanding purposes. Over time, however, these shifts in strategy often affected the character of politics and what it secured ... Even when they did not change underlying preferences, they often altered what actors could achieve."

In their assessment of the changing prospects for coalitional realignment in the United States, Bermeo and Pontusson (2012, 28) conclude that, "though an assortment of actors are mobilizing sporadic protests in the United States ... no successful new redistributive coalitions have yet emerged." Skocpol and Jacobs (2011, 39) are undoubtedly correct that "economic troubles, especially long-term unemployment, remain the true elephant in the room." As Bermeo and Pontusson (2012, 28) similarly conclude, "should current economic difficulties persist, new coalitions with a redistributive agenda may yet emerge." Both assessments might be right; however, it seems to be increasingly unlikely that additional pressures from long-term unemployment will come to bear in the immediate future. The questions become, rather, whether policies in the post-crisis period will revert to existing policy routines during periods of moderate unemployment and whether the crisis response will have any significant impact on how future bouts of high unemployment are experienced and perceived. That is, will responses to this crisis create change that will affect the experience of the next "crisis"? The potential for different future political coalitions is undoubtedly crucial in this regard.

In examining these possibilities, Bermeo and Pontusson (2012, 28) offer their assessment of the potential shifts in a relatively dichotomous balance between coalitions in favour of redistribution and those against it:

> New coalitions with a redistributive agenda may yet emerge, but if they do, they will have to confront an already established and powerful cross-class coalition that resists a more activist role for the state. This coalition is dominated by finance capital but it is clearly supported by more modest and more numerous property owners who seek shelter from taxes and from state control more generally. With governments in many rich democracies now implementing harsh austerity programs, this is the coalition that seems to have seized the latest opportunity for change.

It seems somewhat too simplistic to focus solely on the potential for a new coalition with a redistributive agenda to confront an existing coalition opposed to state activism. Rather than focusing exclusively on support for or resistance to redistributive policy, Rajan (2010) presents a fundamentally different analysis of coalitional politics. In his analysis of the period leading up to the crisis, he focuses on the coalescence of interests around a policy of "easy credit" to address the problem of rising inequality at the same time that forging a countervailing coalition around the main policy alternative (more redistributive social and taxation policy) was significantly more difficult. Thus, it seems crucial to consider the relative ease of assemblage and likely durability of various coalitions supporting, alternatively, addressing rising income inequality through expansive social policy, addressing rising income inequality by promoting access to credit, or resisting either approach in favour of accepting ostensibly "market-generated" inequalities. In doing so, the perception of interests is key. Rajan describes a more easily assembled and perhaps more durable political coalition behind easy credit than what would have been required to undertake permanent changes to social programs (see also Thompson 2012). So the question does not seem to be as straightforward as simply assessing the potential for coalition building by interests with a "redistributive agenda" versus interests that "resist a more

Gerard W. Boychuk

activist role for the state" but between interests willing to countenance growing income inequality without ameliorative measures and those with an interest in ameliorating inequality. However, among the latter are interests that would address growing inequality through redistributive social policy and taxation and interests that would address growing inequality through easy credit. The financial "crisis" dislodged the latter. Following the logic of Rajan's assessment, the long-term prospects of rising inequality will generate pressure on the two alternative solutions of easy credit versus more highly redistributive social benefits (and the associated taxation to fund them), with the former having suffered significantly in the most recent crisis.

Conclusion

Many observers continue to see the United States as the exception to the more general trend of countries "deeply affected" by the global financial crisis to embark on programs of austerity (see Kelsey 2013, 273–74). As Béland and Waddan (2013, 102) conclude, "by contrast no coherent austerity policy has emerged in the context of 'divided government' in the United States. The 2012 elections reinforced the pattern of divided government, which means that the argument over the merits of a programme of austerity as against a more progressive approach to fiscal and social policy in difficult economic times is likely to continue." Starke, Kaasch, and van Hooren (2013, 185) concur: "Against the background of record indebtedness, austerity measures have entered political debate more recently. More wide-ranging austerity measures, however, have failed to be implemented due to the high level of political polarisation between the main players in the US Congress. So far at least, welfare state measures have been largely off-limits."

It is not simply a matter of the degree of political polarization but the nature of the differences, the range between the poles, and the positioning of the edges of the mainstream consensus that help to indicate possible directions for change. For example, as noted by Baker (2013), congressional discussions in late 2013 regarding increasing Social Security benefits have been argued to indicate "a remarkable turn of events." This was not necessarily because of the prospects for success but because of what it indicated about the terms of the debate: "For over a decade the only discussion of Social Security ... was over how much to cut it and when. The extreme left position was 'about right.'" Proposals for benefit enrichment are argued to have "changed the debate." Similarly, significant social policy expansionism in immediate response to the financial crisis and Great Recession might have shifted the ideational terms of the debate, the institutional landscape on which that debate takes place, and the long-term prospects for political coalitions that might underpin future social policy developments. In arguing that "the nature of the financial crisis of 2008 ... has deepened political cleavages in the United States over the role of the government in the economy, on the one hand, and economic inequality, on the other," Kahler and Lake (2013, 16) conclude that, "bracketed by the Tea Party and the Occupy Wall Street movements, the seeds of political change are certainly present in the United States."

Notes

1 Pontusson and Raess (2012, 31) distinguish between "liberal Keynesianism" and "social Keynesianism" as follows: "Whereas social Keynesianism emphasizes public spending and redistributive measures to sustain long-term prosperity, liberal Keynesianism focuses on demand stimulation during economic downturns and favors tax cuts over spending increases." Their overall argument is that the policy response to the Great Recession in the United States (as well as in France, Germany, Sweden, and the United Kingdom) can be characterized as liberal Keynesianism and marks a retreat from social Keynesianism, which characterized earlier policy responses to the Long Recession of 1974–82.

2 This proportion depends on how Medicaid transfers to states are classified (either as state transfers or as transfers to individuals).

3 The threshold was a total unemployment rate of 6 percent, which the CBO estimated would be reached in enough states to cover roughly one-quarter of all beneficiaries. CBO Cost Estimate, HR 5749 Emergency Extended Unemployment Compensation Act of 2008, 17 April.

4 CBO Cost Estimate, HR 6867 Unemployment Compensation Extension Act of 2008, 22 December.

5 CBO Cost Estimate, HR 1 American Recovery and Reinvestment Act of 2009, 26 January.

6 Transfers to minimum-wage earners can be undertaken only with considerable caution since minimum wages differ between the two countries in terms of their value relative to the average wage. In the United States, the minimum wage was 28 percent of the average wage in 2005, whereas in Canada it was 38 percent.

7 In neither country has there been any significant change in the level of minimum cash income, though minimum transfer income has decreased very moderately in Canada and increased very moderately in the United States. Thus, Canada continues to provide a significantly higher level of minimum cash income to people in this group in comparison with the minimalist level of protection provided in the United States, and the pattern over time in this regard has been continuing distinctiveness between the two countries. A relatively similar picture emerges when considering minimum transfer income for families with children. There has been a moderate increase in minimum transfer income to these families in both countries. As a result of these parallel developments, the overall pattern between the two countries is continuing distinctiveness.

8 SNAP was formerly known as the Food Stamps program.

9 As Ashbee (2014, 85–87) outlines, conversion, layering, and drift themselves can be congruent or incongruent, and the challenge then becomes distinguishing between congruent and incongruent forms of incremental change.

Gerard W. Boychuk

10   Bermeo and Pontusson (2012, 15) conclude that, "in the United States, the Democratic
     Party was forced to make dramatic cuts to its original stimulus proposal because super-
     majoritarianism and other institutional veto points allowed it no alternative."

References

Alter, Jonathan. 2011. *The Promise: President Obama, Year One*. New York: Simon and
     Schuster.
Appelbaum, Binyamin. 2013. "In Surprise, Fed Decides to Maintain Pace of Stimulus." *New
     York Times*, 18 September.
Ashbee, Edward. 2014. "The United States: Institutional Continuities, Reform, and 'Critical
     Junctures.'" In *Moments of Truth: The Politics of Financial Crises in Comparative
     Perspective*, edited by Francisco Panizza and George Philip, 82–100. New York:
     Routledge.
Baker, Dean. 2013. "The End of the Assault on Social Security and Medicare." Truthout,
     16 December. http://truth-out.org/news/item/20653-the-end-of-the-assault-on-social
     -security-and-medicare.
Béland, Daniel, and Alex Waddan. 2013. "The New Politics of Austerity in the United
     Kingdom and the United States." In *Retrenchment or Renewal: Welfare States in Times
     of Economic Crisis*, edited by Gudmundur Jonsson and Kolbeinn Steffanson, 87–105.
     Helsinki: Nordic Centre of Excellence Nordwel.
Bermeo, Nancy, and Jonas Pontusson. 2012a. "Coping with Crisis: An Introduction." In
     Coping with Crisis: Government Reactions to the Great Depression, edited by Nancy
     Bermeo and Jonas Pontusson, 1–31. New York: Russell Sage.
–. 2012b. *Unemployment Insurance in the Wake of the Recent Recession*. CBO Publication
     No. 4525. Washington, DC: CBO.
Cooper, Michael. 2010. "From Obama, the Tax Cut Nobody Heard Of ..." *New York Times*,
     18 October.
Daguerre, Anne. 2011. "US Social Policy in the 21st Century: The Difficulties of Compre-
     hensive Social Reform." *Social Policy and Administration* 45, 4: 389–407. http://dx.doi.
     org/10.1111/j.1467-9515.2011.00781.x.
D'Ippoliti, Carlo. 2012. "There Is More to Keynesianism than Spending Alone." *PSL
     Quarterly Review* 65: 3–10.
Hacker, Jacob. 2004. "Privatizing Risk without Privatizing the Welfare State: The Hidden
     Politics of Social Policy Retrenchment in the United States." *American Political Science
     Review* 89, 2: 243–60.
Hall, Peter A., and Michèle Lamont. 2013. "Introduction." In *Social Resilience in the Neo-
     liberal Era*, edited by Peter A. Hall and Michèle Lamont, 1–32. New York: Cambridge
     University Press. http://dx.doi.org/10.1017/CBO9781139542425.003.
Jonsson, Gudmundur, and Kolbeinn Steffanson. 2013. "Introduction." In *Retrenchment or
     Renewal: Welfare States in Times of Economic Crisis*, edited by Gudmundur Jonsson and
     Kolbeinn Steffanson, 13–28. Helsinki: Nordic Centre of Excellence Nordwel.
Kahler, Miles, and David A. Lake. 2013. "Anatomy of Crisis: The Great Recession and
     Political Change." In *Politics in the New Hard Times: The Great Recession in Comparative
     Perspective*, edited by Miles Kahler and David A. Lake, 1–16. Ithaca: Cornell University
     Press.
Kelsey, Jane. 2013. "Ulysses versus Polani: Can Embedded Neo-Liberalism Prevent a 'Great
     Transformation'?" In *Retrenchment or Renewal: Welfare States in Times of Economic*

Crisis, edited by Gudmundur Jonsson and Kolbeinn Steffanson, 273-92. Helsinki: Nordic Centre of Excellence Nordwel.

Kregel, Jan. 2011. "Resolving the US Financial Crisis: Politics Dominates Economics in the New Political Economy." *PSL Quarterly Review* 65: 23-37.

McCarty, Nolan. 2012. "The Politics of the Pop: The US Response to the Financial Crisis and the Great Recession." In *Coping with Crisis: Government Reactions to the Great Depression*, edited by Nancy Bermeo and Jonas Pontusson, 201-32. New York: Russell Sage.

Philip, George. 2014. "Conclusion." In *Moments of Truth: The Politics of Financial Crises in Comparative Perspective*, edited by Francisco Panizza and George Philip, 194-200. New York: Routledge.

Pinto, Pablo M. 2013. "The Politics of Hard Times: Fiscal Policy and the Endogeneity of Economic Recessions." In *Politics in the New Hard Times: The Great Recession in Comparative Perspective*, edited by Miles Kahler and David A. Lake, 102-26. Ithaca: Cornell University Press.

Pontusson, Jonas, and Damien Raess. 2012. "How (and Why) Is This Time Different? The Politics of Economic Crisis in Western Europe and the United States." *Annual Review of Political Science* 15, 1: 13-33. http://dx.doi.org/10.1146/annurev-polisci-031710-100955.

Rajan, Raghuram G. 2010. *Fault Lines: How Hidden Fractures Still Threaten the World Economy*. Princeton: Princeton University Press.

Rueda, David. 2012. "West European Welfare States in Times of Crisis." In *Coping with Crisis: Government Reactions to the Great Depression*, edited by Nancy Bermeo and Jonas Pontusson, 361-98. New York: Russell Sage.

Skocpol, Theda, and Lawrence R. Jacobs. 2011. "Reaching for a New Deal: Ambitious Governance, Economic Meltdown, and Polarized Politics." In *Reaching for a New Deal: Ambitious Governance, Economic Meltdown, and Polarized Politics in Obama's First Two Years*, edited by Theda Skocpol and Lawrence R. Jacobs, 1-49. New York: Russell Sage.

Starke, Peter, Alexandra Kaasch, and Franca van Hooren. 2013. *The Welfare State as Crisis Manager: Explaining the Diversity of Policy Responses to Economic Crisis*. Houndmills: Palgrave Macmillan. http://dx.doi.org/10.1057/9781137314840.

Thompson, Helen. 2012. "The Limits of Blaming Neo-Liberalism: Fannie Mae and Freddie Mac, the American State, and the Financial Crisis." *New Political Economy* 17, 4: 399-419. http://dx.doi.org/10.1080/13563467.2011.595481.

United States. Federal Reserve Board. 2013. Press release, 18 September. http://federalreserve.gov/newsevents/press/monetary/20130918a.htm.

Gerard W. Boychuk

Conclusion

GERARD W. BOYCHUK, RIANNE MAHON, AND STEPHEN McBRIDE

There is broad agreement among the contributors to this volume that the financial crisis and Great Recession opened up at least the possibility of social policy change in the directions of both social policy retrenchment and expansion. In examining the degree to which the prospects for progressive social policy have shifted, these chapters collectively examine whether the broader neo-liberal landscape has shifted in response to crisis. The volume also examines whether it is even possible to discern broad trends in social policy responses to crisis or whether diversity in national experiences and policy responses thereto make it impossible to generalize except at the broadest level. The two questions are distinct but not unrelated.

The views presented here range from those that argue that the financial crisis contributed to a neo-liberal consolidation, to those that are skeptical about whether the crisis generated significant opportunities for progressive social policy reform, to those that are more optimistic about possibilities opened up by the crisis for more progressive social policy. Few anticipated a whole-sale overturning of neo-liberalism. This is not particularly surprising. Even in the context of the Great Depression, Polanyi (1944, 149) would categorically conclude that "secular tenets of social organization ... are not dislodged by the events of a decade."[1] Nevertheless, those who see neo-liberalism as having been strengthened by the crisis are joined here by those who continue to see increased possibilities post-crisis for disruptions at the margins of neo-liberal hegemony.

Despite this variation, there is also general caution among the contributors about where things currently stand. Those who consider neo-liberalism to have been successfully consolidated in the wake of the crisis, with austerity programs coming to dominate over more expansive social policy, acknowledge that the possibility of significant change in a more progressive direction continues to exist. Conversely, those who argue that we might be on the threshold of a Polanyian moment allow that its further development is highly contingent on a variety of factors and by no means assured.

To some extent, these interpretations rest on different readings of the substantive content of the alternatives that have developed. Most notably, authors differ on whether the social investment approach (or the global social protection floor, for that matter) is an alternative to neo-liberalism or simply a modification thereof that leaves the fundamentals intact (see Mestrum 2012). To some extent, these differences also depend on divergent readings of whether these ideational paradigms (both consolidated neo-liberalism and various alternatives to it) have actually been translated into formal policy (e.g., in the form of policy resolutions and communiqués) and, in turn, from formal policy pronouncements into programs and practices on the ground.

A Shifting Neo-Liberal Landscape?

Jenson and McBride are complementary in the degree of emphasis that they place on the role of ideational paradigms; they differ, however, on the question of whether neo-liberalism faces a fundamental challenge. McBride argues that neo-liberalism's predominance has not been successfully challenged and remains the guide to action of important states and global institutions. In contrast, Jenson posits that we might have reached a Polanyian moment in which a significant change of direction is occurring. Coherent rationales for state spending and intervention in the name of social investment and inclusive growth have emerged across a range of venues and actors, from northern-based international organizations such as the OECD to states in the global South heralding opportunities for significant policy change.

As Starke, Kaasch, and van Hooren (2013) note, the construction of this transnational political-intellectual climate is one of the main contributions of international organizations, and it is to a consideration of them that we now turn.

At the global level, old divisions among international organizations persist and in fact might have deepened, for international financial institutions such as the IMF but also the ILO appear to be enjoying a resurgence. As Vetterlein

Gerard W. Boychuk, Rianne Mahon, and Stephen McBride

shows, contrary to its role in the Asian financial crisis, when the IMF was prepared to take social questions seriously, a resurgent IMF has renewed its traditional focus on promoting macroeconomic stability and balance-of-payment problems – even if this requires imposing austerity while leaving social policy concerns to others. Consistent with this interpretation, as Ayhan and McBride argue, the influence of international and supranational institutions is clear from the conditions imposed by the IMF, ECB, and European Commission on Ireland, Greece, and Portugal. The result in these three countries has been significant social policy austerity.

At the same time, the ILO was able to use the crisis to capture the global social policy agenda. The threatened social meltdown generated demand for its expertise in labour market and social policy. It has used the opportunity to augment its role in global governance, and, as Deacon notes, it was instrumental in getting the global social protection floor proposal adopted by the G20, United Nations, and World Bank. Yet important questions remain. Most directly, it is not clear that the version favoured by the ILO will prevail in the implementation stage by other bodies, such as the World Bank, which might favour a more residual version. Hall's examination of the role of the World Bank in promoting conditional cash transfers adds to this complexity. Although CCTs can be seen as a prime example of social investment, as implemented in practice they have tended to reinforce the emphasis on piecemeal programs focused on poverty at the expense of the kind of universal and comprehensive approach advocated by the ILO. Moreover, Hall cautions against overemphasizing the ability of the World Bank, and by extension international organizations more generally, to promote particular policy approaches unless they are seen to be of domestic political benefit to client governments.

The broader role of the ILO remains an open question. Whether the ILO can regain its lost role and contribute to a shift in global social policy in a progressive direction will, as Deacon suggests, depend on a number of factors. Haworth and Hughes agree that, in the longer term, the ILO's agenda might enjoy a resurgence. Nevertheless, their analysis suggests that a combination of factors challenges short-term adoption of the ILO's preferred alternative: the orthodox economic and institutional underpinnings of neo-liberalism remain strong, and the willingness, let alone ability, of nation-states to commit to the ILO agenda cannot be assumed. Moreover, as noted above, it has to contend with a resurgent and refocused IMF.

The transnational political-intellectual climate can also be strongly shaped at the regional level. As Mahon argues, the near-continent-wide scale of social policy progress in Latin America suggests the need to develop a focus at the regional scale. Over the past decade, CEPAL's discourse has come to incorporate a strong social dimension. This opening was made possible not only by shifts in the global universe of social policy discourse, such as those described by Deacon and Jenson, but also, and more importantly, by the failure of neo-liberal reforms to deliver promised trickle-down benefits, a failure highlighted by popular protests and the electoral "pink tide" across the region. Thus far, the financial crisis and austerity policies elsewhere in the globe have not dampened this thrust.

All of these analyses suggest that the broader transnational context, in which national social policy responses are being crafted, is important. At the same time, the context is turbulent and in flux. A similar degree of complexity is evident in the diversity of national social policy responses outlined in this volume.

Diversity in National Social Policy Responses

Farnsworth and Irving compellingly contend that the economic crisis did not represent a singular window of opportunity for either social policy expansionism or retrenchment across national contexts. The analyses below agree that each country's response was predicated on the extent of financial integration and vulnerability, pre-existing social protection systems, and contemporary political alignments. Consistent with this is the picture of cross-national diversity portrayed in the chapters examining the situation on the ground – the actual policy responses adopted by states.

The broad picture in the chapters on specific countries of the global South is that the Great Recession has not created major turning points in social policy in the direction of expansion or austerity. At the same time, of course, each country examined experienced the crisis in ways shaped by a distinct constellation of domestic forces. The crisis had an impact on China, but that country's social policy continues to develop in ways that reflect its national characteristics and policy priorities, of which maintaining social and political stability in a time of rapid economic growth and social change is primary (Cook and Lam, this volume). For Mexico, the impacts of successive crises have left imprints on its social policy, seen as a key tool to promote social stability, though poverty and inequality have been little improved. The latest crisis has produced policy incoherence as a clientelist approach, typical of pre-1980s Mexico, has been grafted onto the neo-liberal reforms of the 1980s and a (limited) social investment approach in the 1990s. In South Africa, the crisis exposed the limitations of the country's social policy and programs; however, though major reform is

Gerard W. Boychuk, Rianne Mahon, and Stephen McBride

needed, South Africa's current neo-liberal economic model constitutes a major obstacle to achieving it (Clarke, this volume). In Latin America, the "global" financial crisis has been associated not with austerity and social policy cuts, as it has in many countries of the global North and in some of the global South, but with ongoing social policy development. Despite the crisis, Latin America has continued to move in the opposite direction from most parts of the world, making visible progress in reducing inequality on a near-continent-wide scale (Mahon, this volume).

The direct effects of the economic crisis were more powerful in countries of the global North, where there has also been significant diversity in crisis responses. One set of experiences is those of hard-hit European countries subjected to troika conditions – Ireland, Greece, and Portugal – in which austerity has been imposed (Ayhan and McBride, this volume). In contrast, countries such as Australia, Canada, and the United Kingdom, which could have opted for expansion, have instead chosen austerity (Whiteside, this volume). In the specific case of Canada, austerity represents not a radical departure from but a reinforcement of neo-liberal trends existent before the onset of the crisis. The crisis merely provided new justifications for the deepening of neo-liberal social policy reforms (Labonté and Ruckert, this volume). This is in marked contrast to the United States, which has charted a different course, opting for fiscal and social policy expansionism "by stealth" (Boychuk, this volume). It is still unclear whether social policy expansionism will contribute to institutional shifts, long-term shifts in public or elite opinion, or conditions for the emergence of a constellation of interests that could sustain and deepen this turn in US social policy.

Conclusion

Writing before the crisis, Deacon contested the observation that "powerful states (notably the USA), powerful organisations (such as the IMF), and even powerful disciplines (economics) exercise their power largely by 'framing': which serves to limit the power of potentially radical ideas to achieve change" (Boas and McNeil 2004, 1). Instead, Deacon (2007, 16) asserted that a "more nuanced and accurate" depiction is that these actors "contend with other powerful states (the EU, China, Brazil), other powerful organisations (such as the ILO), and other disciplines (such as social and political science) to engage in a global war of positions regarding the content of global social policy." Whether this second depiction is indeed more accurate, as Deacon claims, remains an open empirical question. Nevertheless, such empirical work, requiring an examination of the "grinding and uneven [neo-liberal] struggle to make the world conform" while recognizing "the limitations and failures of this project," is crucial to avoid "confirming the neoliberal illusion of inevitability" (Clarke 2004, 102).

These dictates pose the central challenge in empirically assessing the effects of the financial crisis and ensuing Great Recession on social policy. To be sure, the financial and economic crisis has shifted the policy stances of various powerful states, the relative influence and policy stances of powerful organizations, and even the relative dominance of different disciplines. The empirical question that remains is whether such shifts taken together have been more favourable to the forces of neo-liberalism or to the forces arguing for strengthened social protection. Taken together the chapters of this volume begin – but only begin – to answer such questions.

As Farnsworth and Irving lead us to expect, the picture is indeed complex. The Great Recession might be global in its reach, but its impact seems to have been the greatest in the traditional centres. That said, its "structural" impact seems to have been the greatest in the peripheral countries of Europe, where it has served to reinforce, rather than challenge, neo-liberal orthodoxies. In yet other countries of the North, the crisis has been used politically to reinforce tendencies toward austerity by choice – as opposed to structural constraint leading to similar outcomes. Interestingly, however, it seems to have spurred an important, if incremental, social policy shift in the United States – the "ground zero" of the financial crisis. At the same time, the crisis has not been as strongly felt across the global South, especially in the "emerging" countries, for which previous crises – the "lost decade" of the 1980s in Latin America, the Asian financial crisis of the late 1990s – proved to be far more influential. The discussions in these chapters, then, do not resolve these debates; however, we hope that they do contribute to their fruitfulness – recognizing, of course, that there is further work to be done.

Note

1 Rather, Polanyi (2001, 149) argued that the failures of economic liberalism that became so evident in the Great Depression and its "partial eclipse" in material reality might "have even strengthened its hold" as an ideational paradigm.

References

Boas, Morten, and Desmond McNeil. 2004. *Global Institutions and Development: Framing the World*. New York: Routledge.

Clarke, John. 2004. *Changing Welfare, Changing States: New Directions in Social Policy*. London: Sage.

Deacon, Bob. 2007. *Global Social Policy and Governance*. London: Sage.

–. 2013. *Global Social Policy in the Making: The Foundations of the Social Protection Floor.* Bristol: Policy Press.

Mestrum, Francine. 2012."Social Protection Floor: Beyond Poverty Reduction?" Global Social Justice. http://www.globalsocialjustice.eu/index.php?option=com_content&id=223:social-protection-floor-beyond-poverty-reduction&Itemid=6.

Polanyi, Karl. 2001. *The Great Transformation: The Political and Economic Origins of Our Time.* Boston: Beacon.

Starke, Peter, Alexandra Kaasch, and Franca van Hooren. 2013. *The Welfare State as Crisis Manager: Explaining the Diversity of Policy Responses to Economic Crisis.* Houndmills: Palgrave Macmillan.

Contributors

Berkay Ayhan is a PhD candidate in the Political Science Department of McMaster University in Hamilton, Canada. He received his bachelor's degree from the Economics Department of Gazi University and his master's degree from the Political Science and Public Administration Department of the Middle East Technical University. His research interests are financial literacy, corporate social responsibility, and international political economy.

Gerard W. Boychuk is chair of the Department of Political Science at the University of Waterloo and a professor at the Balsillie School of International Affairs. He is co-editor of the journal *Global Social Policy,* co-editor of the book series American Governance and Public Policy (Georgetown University Press), and author of *National Health Insurance in the United States and Canada: Race, Territory, and the Roots of Difference,* winner of the 2009 Donald Smiley Prize.

Marlea Clarke teaches in the Department of Political Science at the University of Victoria and is a research associate with the Labour and Enterprise Research Project (LEP) at the University of Cape Town. Her work has focused on labour market restructuring in post-apartheid South Africa and labour's role in shaping the country's transition. She has published articles in *Law, Democracy, and Development, Canadian Journal of African Studies,* and *Work, Organisation, Labour, and Globalisation,* and she is co-author of *Working without Commitments* (McGill-Queen's University Press).

Sarah Cook is currently director of the United Nations Research Institute for Social Development (UNRISD). Her research has focused on the social impacts of China's post-Mao economic transformation. Recent publications include "Harsh Choices: Chinese Women's Paid Work and Unpaid Care Responsibilities under Economic Reform" (with Xiao-yuan Dong) in *Development and Change* 42: 4 (July 2011) and "Rebounding from Crisis: The Role and Limits of Social Policy in China's Recovery" in *The Global Crisis and Transformative Social Change*, ed. P. Utting and S. Razavi (London: Palgrave Macmillan for UNRISD, 2012).

Bob Deacon is professor emeritus of international social policy at the University of Sheffield, United Kingdom, and recently held the UNESCO-UNU Chair in Regional Integration, Migration, and the Free Movement of People at UNUCRIS in Bruges. He is Honorary Professor of Global Social Policy at the University of York, United Kingdom. His most recent books are *Global Social Policy in the Making* and *Global Social Policy and Governance*. He is founding editor of the journals *Critical Social Policy* and *Global Social Policy*. He has acted as an adviser to several UN agencies. He now lives in Hebden Bridge, West Yorkshire, United Kingdom.

Kevin Farnsworth is a senior lecturer in international social policy at the University of York, United Kingdom. He has published widely on issues related to the political economy of the welfare state, including economic crisis, austerity, corporate power, and corporate welfare. He is co-editor (with Zoë Irving) of the *Journal of International and Comparative Social Policy* and *Social Policy in Challenging Times* (Policy Press, 2011). His other books include *Corporate Power and Social Policy* (Policy Press, 2004) and *Social versus Corporate Welfare* (Palgrave Macmillan).

Anthony Hall is professor of social policy at the London School of Economics. His current research focuses on social protection and related areas of climate change mitigation in Latin America, especially Brazil, with particular reference to the role of international financial institutions. His latest book is *Forests and Climate Change: The Social Dimensions of REDD in Latin America* (Edward Elgar, 2012).

Nigel Haworth is professor of human resource development at the University of Auckland, where he is also head of the Department of Management and

International Business. Apart from his long involvement in international labour studies in general, and the International Labour Organization in particular, he has published on a variety of issues, including New Zealand employment relations, Maori business development, and workplace partnership. He is currently working on the global value chain in the fishing industry and labour standards.

Steve Hughes is professor of international organizations at Newcastle University Business School. He teaches global political economy and has a research focus on executive leadership and institutional development in the ILO. He publishes regularly in leading international texts and journals and contributes commentary on global issues to the media. He is on the Editorial Board of the *British Journal of Management* and serves as an external adviser to the UN Joint Inspection Unit.

Zoë Irving is a senior lecturer in comparative and global social policy at the University of York, United Kingdom. Her current research interests are in the politics of economic crisis and austerity and in the development of comparative welfare theory that accounts for population size. She is co-editor with Kevin Farnsworth of the *Journal of International and Comparative Social Policy* and *Social Policy in Challenging Times* (Policy Press, 2011), and she is co-author with Michael Hill of *Understanding Social Policy* (Wiley Blackwell, 2009).

Jane Jenson was awarded the Canada Research Chair in Citizenship and Governance at the Université de Montréal in 2001, where she is professor of political science. She has also been a senior fellow of the Successful Societies program of the Canadian Institute for Advanced Research since 2004. Her research focuses on comparative social policy. For further information and some publications, see http://www.cccg.umontreal.ca and http://pol.umontreal.ca/repertoire-departement/vue/jenson-jane/.

Ronald Labonté holds a Canada Research Chair in Globalization and Health Equity and is a professor in the Faculty of Medicine at the University of Ottawa. He has over 200 scientific publications and several hundred articles in popular media. His recent books include *Globalization and Health: Pathways, Evidence, and Policy,* co-edited with Ted Schrecker, Corinne Packer, and Vivien Runnels (Routledge, 2009); *Critical Public Health: A Reader,* co-edited with Judith Greene (Routledge, 2007); and *Health Promotion: From Community Empowerment to Global Justice,* co-authored with Glenn Laverack (Palgrave Macmillan, 2007).

Wing Lam is a development policy researcher based in Hong Kong. As part of her studies at the Institute of Development Studies (Sussex, UK), she conducted field research in China on poverty and food security policy in the country. After her graduation, she affiliated with development NGOs and specialized in policy research and advocacy programs in the areas of poverty, human rights, and sustainable development. Her research interests include social policy reform and closing the rich/poor gap in China.

Lucy Luccisano is associate professor and chair of the Department of Sociology at Wilfrid Laurier University, Waterloo, Canada. She has published on Mexican social policy, specifically on Mexico's CCT program, within the context of neo-liberalism, decentralization, clientelism, and its implications on citizenship, gender, and democracy. She has also done comparative work examining Mexican federal and Mexico City social policies and security. Her current research is on comparing local-level social policy and security in North American cities.

Laura Macdonald is professor of political science and political economy at Carleton University, Canada, and director of the Institute of Political Economy. Her work focuses on issues such as the role of contentious politics of trade in the Americas, citizenship struggles in Latin America, Canadian development assistance, political economy of the North American Free Trade Agreement, Mexican politics, and Canada–Latin American relations.

Rianne Mahon holds a CIGI Chair in Comparative Social Policy at the Balsillie School of International Affairs and is a professor in the Department of Political Science at Wilfrid Laurier University, Canada. She is co-editor (with Stephen McBride) of *The OECD and Transnational Governance,* co-editor (with Roger Keil) of *Leviathan Undone?,* and co-editor (with Fiona Robinson) of *Feminist Ethics and Social Politics.*

Stephen McBride is professor of political science and Canada Research Chair in Public Policy and Globalization at McMaster University, Canada. He is co-author (with Heather Whiteside) of *Private Affluence, Public Austerity: Economic Crisis and Democratic Malaise in Canada* and co-editor (with Donna Baines) of *Orchestrating Austerity: Impacts and Resistance.*

Arne Ruckert is a senior research associate and part-time professor at the University of Ottawa, Canada. His principal areas of research include international financial institutions, international aid architecture, financial crisis and health equity, social determinants of health, and global health diplomacy and governance. He has published widely in the areas of international development and global health and has co-edited (with Laura Macdonald) *Post-Neoliberalism in the Americas* (Palgrave Macmillan, 2009).

Antje Vetterlein is associate professor in the Department of Business and Politics at Copenhagen Business School. Her research is located within international political sociology, with particular interests in global governance, the politics of development, and the relationship between economy and society, focusing on political actors and practices at the transnational level and the role of ideas and norms in international politics. Her latest publications include (with Susan Park) *Owning Development: Creating Global Policy Norms in the IMF and the World Bank* (Cambridge University Press, 2010) and "Seeing like the World Bank on Poverty," *New Political Economy* 17, 1 (2012): 35–58.

Heather Whiteside is assistant professor of political science at the University of Waterloo, Canada. Her research focuses on political economy analyses of privatization, austerity, and financialization. Her books include *Purchase for Profit: Public-Private Partnerships and Canada's Public Health Care System* (forthcoming, University of Toronto Press) and *Private Affluence, Public Austerity: Economic Crisis and Democratic Malaise in Canada* (co-authored with Stephen McBride).

Index

Note: "(f)" following a page number indicates a figure; "(t)" following a page number indicates a table. "GFC" refers to the global financial crisis of 2008.

China, 216–34; about, 13, 216–17, 229–30; Asian financial crisis, 9, 220, 230n2; banking crisis costs, 64, 65(t); economic restructuring, 226–28; environmental issues, 227; Five-Year Plans (2011–15), 219, 225–26; gender issues, 228; GFC's impact on, 13, 216, 220–22, 226, 316; historical background, 218–20; neo-liberalism, 6, 218–19, 230; social stability priorities, 218–20, 226–30, 316; social unrest, 228–29; stimulus packages, 9, 216, 220–22, 221(t), 225–27

China, social programs: about, 9–10, 216–18; expansion of, 216, 222–30, 222(t), 225(t); food insecurity, 225; funding, 216, 220–25, 221(t), 230n5; health, 222(t); housing, 225–26; pensions, 222(t), 223–24(t); political dimensions, 219–20, 227–29; social assistance *(dibao)*, 218–19, 222(t), 223–25(t); social citizenship, 228–29; social insurance, 218–20, 222(t), 223; social protection floor, 9–10; unemployment insurance, 222(t); urban vs rural, 219–20, 222–24, 222(t), 224(t), 225(t)

Cichon, Michael, 110–12, 114–15, 118

Clarke, Marlea, 13, 197–215, 320

Closing the Coverage Gap (Holzmann), 107–8

Cohen, Michael, 10

Colombia, 144, 145, 153, 183

common-sense worldview, 14, 255–58, 260, 265

conditional cash transfers. *See* CCTs (conditional cash transfers)

CONEVAL (National Council for the Evaluation of Social Development Policy), 186–87

Cook, Mitchell, 10

Cook, Sarah, 13, 216–34, 321

Cox, Robert, 22

crises and social policy: about, 5–6, 11, 21–22, 40, 313–18; Bourdieu's fields, 89–91, 93, 97, 100–1; coalitional realignments, 307–8; cognitive lock-in, 32–33, 286; exogenous shocks, 5, 22,

32, 88–89; factors in, 22–24; historical background, 59–62; ideas as factors, 32–34, 41–42; IMF's responses, 91–93; and institutionalism, 41–42, 54n1, 101n1; interpretation of, 22–24; labour's weakening, 29, 33; measurement of change, 89, 101n1; neo-liberalism, 21, 28–34, 286; policy change, 22, 24; power relations, 24, 33–34, 34n15; social cohesion, 40; social dialogue, 121, 135–37; types of policy change, 24, 30; variation in, 11, 62, 70–72, 81–83, 88–90, 101n1, 316–17; veto players, 32–33, 304, 310n10. *See also* Polanyian moment

Cuba, 166

Deacon, Bob, 11–12, 22, 105–20, 137, 315–16, 317–18, 321

debt, sovereign. *See* sovereign debt

democracy: about, 72–73; political polarization in US, 27, 73, 293–94, 309, 310n10; politics of austerity, 74–76, 82–83, 249–50, 254–55, 259–60, 266–67; remoteness of power, 25, 33–34; structural restraints on, 72–74

Denmark: austerity measures, 77(f); debt (2006–16), 67, 68(t)–69(t), 79–80

Depression. *See* Great Depression

Divided We Stand (OECD), 50

Dorfman, Mark, 109

EC. *See* European Commission (EC)

ECB. *See* European Central Bank (ECB)

ECLAC. *See* CEPAL (Economic Commission for Latin America and the Caribbean)

Economic Commission for Latin America and the Caribbean. *See* CEPAL (Economic Commission for Latin America and the Caribbean)

economic crisis of 1997–98. *See* Asian financial crisis (1997–98)

economic crisis of 2008. *See* global financial crisis of 2008 (GFC)

Economic and Monetary Union (EMU), 238–42

G7 and G8 economies: debt (2006–16), 64, 67, 68(t)–69(t), 79–80; funding of IMF, 93; neo-liberalism, 26, 31

G20 economies: austerity measures, 257–58; debt (2006–16), 67, 68(t)–69(t), 79–80; ILO's influence on, 28, 113, 118, 123–24; IMF's emergency response to GFC, 98, 100; neo-liberalism, 5, 26, 30, 31; social protection floor, 12, 105, 113–18; trade protectionism, 28

gender issues: Bachelet Report, 51; in Canada, 285; cash transfer programs, 169, 173; CEPAL, 170–75; child-centred policies, 45, 46, 48; in China, 228; in European Union, 55n16; in Greece, 135, 241; in Ireland, 244; male breadwinner model, 46, 170, 172, 188; maternal roles, 169, 174; in Mexico, 188; new social risks, 177n18; pensions, 203; in Portugal, 241; and power relations, 174; social protection floor (SPF), 51; in South Africa, 203; unpaid and paid work, 173, 174

General Agreement on Tariffs and Trade, 164, 273

Germany: austerity measures, 5, 75, 77(f); banking crisis costs, 64, 65(t); core-periphery dynamics, 239–40, 242, 250n2; debt (2006–16), 67, 68(t)–69(t), 79–80; GFC's impact on, 4; influence in IMF, 97; unification and policy change, 89

GFC. See global financial crisis of 2008 (GFC)

global financial crisis of 1997–98. See Asian financial crisis (1997–98)

global financial crisis of 2008 (GFC): about, 3–5, 62–63, 274, 313–18; banking crisis, 63–64, 65(t)–66(t), 81–83; compared with Great Depression, 123–24, 303; interpretations of, 22–24; lack of international coordination, 82–83; structural constraints, 72–74; variation in, 4, 62–64, 70–72, 81–83, 316–17; waves in, 62–64, 67, 70–71, 98. See also austerity measures; neo-liberalism

global financial crisis of 2008 (GFC) and social policy: about, 3–5, 81–83, 117–18, 313–18; actors in, 8–10, 41–42; coalitional realignments, 307–8; existing social policies as factor, 70–72; international organizations, 8–10, 117–18; interpretations of, 22–24; OECD's recommendations, 30–31; variation in, 60–62, 70–72, 81–83, 101n1, 316–17. See also crises and social policy; Polanyian moment

Gough, Ian, 23

government debt. See sovereign debt

Gramsci, Antonio, 26, 174, 255

Great Depression: compared with GFC, 123–24, 303; impact on health, 285–86; Keynesian welfare regimes, 40; Polanyian moment, 7; Prebisch on, 164

Great Recession. See global financial crisis of 2008 (GFC)

Greece, 125–31; about, 12, 13, 241, 247–48; austerity measures, 75–76, 77(f), 83n2, 125–26, 242, 247–50, 250n6; banking system, 63–64, 65(t), 67; core-periphery dynamics, 13, 237–40, 238(t), 242, 248–50, 250n1; debt (2006–16), 67, 68(t)–69(t), 70, 79–80; debt crisis, 242, 247–49, 255; gender issues, 135, 241; GFC's impact on, 63, 125–26, 237–38(t), 242; historical background, 76, 121–22; labour markets, 125, 135, 238(t), 242, 247–48; labour-employment relations, 126–29, 135; neo-liberalism, 27, 121, 136–37, 247–49; politics of austerity, 76, 125–26, 249–50; small enterprises (SMEs), 127, 129; social dialogue, 12, 121–23, 125–31, 134–37; social programs, 247–48; social unrest, 125, 135, 248, 250n6; troika's policies, 125–30, 135–36, 247–50, 250n6, 315

Growing Inequality (OECD), 50

Hacker, Jacob, 303

Hall, Anthony, 12, 140–58, 315, 321

Hall, Peter, 22, 24, 30, 54n1, 89

Haworth, Nigel, 12, 121–39, 315, 321–22

health: and austerity measures, 285–86; in Australia, 264; and CCTs, 145, 148, 152, 173; in Mexico, 186, 189, 190, 192; social protection floor (SPF), 53, 105–6; in South Africa, 207; in United Kingdom, 261–62; in United States (ARRA), 299(f). *See also* social determinants of health (SDH); WHO (World Health Organization)

Hemerijck, Anton, 61–62

Herndon, Thomas, 23, 258, 267n5

Hirsch, Martin, 114

Holzmann, Robert, 107–8

Hughes, Steve, 12, 121–39, 315, 322

Hulme, David, 110, 141

Hungary, financial crisis, 64, 65(t)

hunger. *See* food insecurity

Iceland: banking system, 26, 63, 72–73; debt (2006–16), 67, 68(t)–69(t), 79–80; GFC's impact on, 63, 71, 72–73

IDB (Inter-American Development Bank), 144, 166, 176n13, 192

IFIs. *See* international financial institutions (IFIs)

ILO (International Labour Organization), 105–20; about, 8–10, 11–12, 105, 116–18, 121–22, 135–37, 315; and CCTs, 154–55; complaints mechanism, 124–25; Decent Work, 122–24, 169; G20 and, 113, 118, 123–24; GFC's impact on, 8–10, 110–12, 117–18, 121–23; historical background, 105–7, 109–11, 121–23; influence of, 8–9, 11–12, 28, 116, 314–16; neo-liberalism, 26, 28, 121–23, 135, 314–16; public relations, 124–25; social dialogue in Greece, 12, 121–23, 125–31, 134–37; social dialogue in Italy, 130–33, 134–37; social dialogue in Spain, 133–37; social protection, 8, 28, 110–11, 116–18, 123, 154–55; World Bank/ILO board for SPF, 105, 112–16; World Bank's rivalry with, 105–7. *See also* social protection floor (SPF)

IMF (International Monetary Fund), 87–104; about, 11, 87–88, 100–1; and Asian financial crisis, 11, 87–88, 91, 93–97, 99, 100–1, 101n2, 315; austerity measures, 11, 28, 31, 80, 267n3; austerity warnings by, 259, 266, 286; banking crisis costs, 64, 65(t)–66(t); Bourdieu's fields, 89–91, 93, 97, 100–1; compared with World Bank, 87–88, 92, 101, 149; country ownership of issues, 94, 95, 99–100; crises and policy changes, 87–90; exogenous shocks facility (ESF), 98; fiscal targets, 28, 67, 68(t)–69(t), 79–80; funding of, 93, 97–98; G20's response to GFC, 98, 100; GFC and social policy, 8–10, 88, 96–100; governance reform of, 97–98; Greek crisis, 125–30; historical background, 87–88, 91–92, 101; influence of, 87, 315; loans and conditionality, 99–100; low-income countries (LICs), 87, 92–93, 96, 98, 101; management of, 19–20; neo-liberalism, 6, 26–28, 167, 273; NGO influences on, 88, 93, 95, 100; position-takings, 88–91, 317–18; poverty reduction, 87–88, 91–94, 96, 99–101; poverty reduction and growth facility (PRGF), 94–99; poverty and social impact analysis (PSIA), 95; social safety nets (SSNs), 92–94, 99–101, 101n2; structural adjustment facilities (SAF and ESAF), 92, 93–96, 273; World Bank's poverty reduction initiative (PRSP), 87, 93–96, 99–101. *See also* troika (ECB, EC, and IMF)

import-substituting industrialization. *See* ISI (import-substituting industrialization) programs

inclusive growth: about, 41, 43–44, 47–49; Bachelet Report, 52–53; discourse and policy, 51–54; employment goals, 53–54, 55n9; EU's policies, 49–50; future payoffs, 54; historical background, 49; and institutionalism, 41–42; OECD's policies, 43–44, 50, 52; as post-neo-liberal policy, 53–54; and poverty, 43–44, 49; and social investment, 41, 47–48, 53–54; and social protection floor (ILO), 43, 53–54; World Bank's policies, 43, 55n9. *See also* social investment

response to GFC, 4–5; and social dialogue, 136; and social investment, 45; social Keynesianism, 83, 292, 304, 310n1

Korea: banking crisis costs, 64, 65(t); debt (2006–16), 67, 68(t)–69(t), 79–80; influence in IMF, 97; social policy, 9, 113, 223

Krugman, Paul, 26, 258

Labonté, Ronald, 14, 272–91, 322

labour: access to benefits through, 54; austerity controls on, 255; challenges to neo-liberalism, 26, 29; Greek labour-employment relations, 126–29, 135–36; ILO's Decent Work, 122–24, 169; Italian labour-employment relations, 130–33; social dialogue, 126–27, 135–37; weakening of, 29, 33, 34n15, 62–63; working poor, 47, 54; World Bank policies, 108. *See also* ILO (International Labour Organization)

labour markets: flexible markets, 25–26, 31, 33, 53, 62–63; flexicurity and re-regulation of, 172, 174; GFC's impact on, 238(t), 300(t); neo-liberalism's impact on, 25–26, 135; rights of weaker actors, 174; workfare, 9, 25, 31

Lagarde, Christine, 80

Lam, Wing, 13, 216–34, 323

Lamy, Pascal, 117

Latin America: CCTs in, 110, 140–43, 142(f), 144, 146–47, 151–53; GFC's impact on, 4, 9–10, 183; ILO's influence on, 124; neo-liberalism, 6, 27, 162, 166, 167, 316; political dimensions of CCTs, 151–53; poverty, 161; social policy innovation, 10, 46, 110, 315–16, 317; social unrest, 162; taxation, 177n14; unemployment, 183; wealth inequality, 161, 317. *See also* CEPAL (Economic Commission for Latin America and the Caribbean)

Lew, Jack, 76

low-income countries (LICs): CCT programs, 143–44; IMF policies, 87, 92–

93, 96, 98, 101; pensions, 107–8; social protection floor, 114

Luccisano, Lucy, 12–13, 181–96, 323

Lula da Silva, Luiz Inácio, 46, 113, 151

Macdonald, Laura, 12–13, 181–96, 323

Mahon, Rianne, 3–17, 12, 161–80, 323

Making Growth Inclusive to Tackle Rising Inequality (OECD), 54n1

McBride, Stephen, 3–17, 237–53, 314, 315, 323

Mesa-Lago, Carmelo, 188

Mexico, 181–96; about, 12–13, 181–82, 193–94; austerity measures, 267n4; crime, 181–82, 185–86, 191; economy, 181–85, 191–93; financial crises, 13, 182–83, 187–88, 193–94; GFC's impact on, 4, 13, 63, 181–84, 186–87, 194; historical background, 13, 181–83, 187–88; influence in IMF, 97; ISI model, 183, 189; neo-liberalism, 6, 13, 181–86, 189, 193, 316; poverty, 186–87, 191; reforms needed, 187; stimulus measures, 185, 267n4; taxation, 185–86, 192; unemployment, 183–84; wealth inequality, 187, 188t. *See also* Oportunidades (Mexico)

Mexico, social programs: about, 181–82, 187–88, 193–94; CCT programs, 13, 169, 182–83, 190; clientelism, 13, 182, 191, 316; evaluation of, 186–87; food insecurity, 13, 182, 187, 189–92; funding, 186; gender issues, 188; health, 186, 189, 192; human capital development (Progresa), 190; hybrid of old and new, 193–94, 194n1; infrastructure (PRONASOL), 189–90; pensions, 186, 189, 192; politicization of, 182, 188–92; public-private partnerships, 13, 191–92; rural vs urban, 187, 189; social insurance vs social assistance, 189, 193–94; unemployment insurance, 187, 188, 192. *See also* Oportunidades (Mexico)

Middle East and CCTs, 142(f), 143

middle-income countries: CCT funding, 143–44; pensions, 107–8; wealth inequality, 52; World Bank's support, 143–44, 146–47

Millennium Development Goals (MDGs), 95, 155

Monti, Marlo, 132–33

Moreno-Brid, Juan Carlos, 183–85

Moschella, Manuela, 89, 90

NAFTA (North American Free Trade Agreement) and Mexico, 182–84

nation-states: federalism and political discourse, 42; influence of IOs vs nation-states, 153–55; neo-liberal domination of, 24, 274–75; neo-liberalism and IOs, 30–32; politics of austerity, 254–55; and post-neo-liberal policy, 54; power of elites in, 24, 29, 33–34; response to GFC, 8–10; role in social investment, 45–46, 153–55

National Council for the Evaluation of Social Development Policy (CONEVAL), 186–87

neo-liberalism: about, 6, 21, 24–28, 273–76; actors for, 8–10, 26–27; alternatives to, 6, 136–37, 167, 286; basic elements of, 6, 24–25, 33–34, 273–76; as common-sense approach, 14, 255–58, 265; de-regulation and reregulation, 25, 63, 71–72, 273; failures of, 162, 168, 274, 286–87, 316; GFC's impact on, 4–5, 274; historical background, 8–10, 34n5, 273–76; and intellectuals, 26–27, 29; labour market flexibility, 25, 53, 167; labour's influence on, 29, 33; media promotion of, 286; persistence of, 6, 11, 21, 28–34, 82–83, 121, 135–37, 286, 313–14; post-neo-liberal policies, 45–46, 53–54, 117–18, 148, 169, 314; poverty, 25, 43–44; power of elites, 24, 29, 33–34, 42; privatization, 25, 273, 303–4; Reinhart-Rogoff thesis, 23–24, 26, 257–58, 267n6; social unrest, 26, 168, 258, 274; variation in, 6, 25; wealth inequality, 25, 43–44. See also austerity measures; Polanyian moment; structural adjustment

Netherlands: austerity measures, 75, 78(f); banking crisis costs, 64, 65(t)–66(t); core-periphery dynamics, 239–40; debt (2006–16), 67, 68(t)–69(t), 79–80

New York City, CCT program, 141

New Zealand, debt (2006–16), 67, 68(t)–69(t), 79–80

NGOs (non-governmental organizations): Bourdieu's fields, 89–91, 93, 97, 100–1; crises and policy changes, 88–89; and IMF's policy development, 95, 100; influence of, 90, 95; poverty reduction, 93; social protection floor, 115

Nicaragua, CCT programs, 145

North American Free Trade Agreement (NAFTA) and Mexico, 182–84

Norway: banking crisis costs, 64, 65(t)–66(t); debt (2006–16), 67, 68(t)–69(t), 79–80

Obama, Barack, administration, 113, 304

Occupy movement, United States, 274, 310

OECD: about, 30; austerity measures, 30, 75, 80–81; austerity warnings by, 259, 266, 286; challenges to neo-liberalism, 26, 30; debt (2006–16), 67, 68(t)–69(t), 79–80; GFC's impact on, 237–38(t); inclusive growth, 43–44, 47, 50, 52; labour markets, 238(t); labour's influence on, 26, 29; public finance, 238(t); social investment policies, 46–47, 50, 52; social protection floor, 114; taxation, 177n14; wealth inequality, 43, 52, 54n3, 71

Ontario, Canada, 263–64, 280–83, 285

Oportunidades (Mexico): about, 13, 182, 190–94; conditions on, 151, 182; cost, 152, 193; expansion of, 190, 192, 193; food insecurity (PAL), 13, 190; funding for, 140, 152, 190, 192; global model, 141, 169; historical background, 182, 190; political dimensions, 153, 190–91; rural vs urban residents, 187, 190;

World Bank's support for, 140, 146. *See also* CCTs (conditional cash transfers)

Orenstein, Michael, 54*n*2, 105, 107

Organisation for Economic Co-operation and Development. *See* OECD

Ortiz, Isabel, 115

Palacios, Robert, 109

Palme, Joakim, 9, 171, 177*n*20

Peña Nieto, Enrique, 181–84, 191–94

pensions: in Africa, 110, 212*n*2; in Canada, 263; in China, 223–24(t); gender issues, 203; GFC's impact on, 106–7, 109; historical background, 105–9, 116; ILO's policies, 105–6, 109–11; in Mexico, 186, 189, 192; pay-as-you-go systems, 106–9, 116; privatized, 106–7, 109, 116, 203; social protection floor (SPF) programs, 105–10; in South Africa, 199, 200, 201, 203–4, 207, 212*n*2; World Bank's policies, 106–9, 116

Peru, social investment, 46

Philippines, CCT programs, 144, 146, 152

Pierson, Paul, 61

Pinheiro, Vinicius, 114

Pinto, Anibal, 166, 167–68, 175, 176*n*5

Pinto, Pablo, 307

Poland, banking crisis, 64, 65(t)–66(t)

Polanyi, Karl, 7, 40, 313, 318*n*1

Polanyian moment: about, 5, 7–8, 40; discourse and policy, 54, 117–18, 136, 314; GFC and social policy, 5, 7–8, 136, 313–14; in Greece, Spain, and Italy, 136–37; social protection floor, 117–18

politics of austerity, 74–76, 82–83, 249–50, 254–55, 266–67. *See also* austerity measures

Pollin, Robert, 23, 258, 267*n*5

Pontusson, Jonas, 59–60, 80, 294, 304, 307, 310*n*1, 310*n*10

Portugal: about, 13, 241–42, 245–47; austerity measures, 75, 78(f), 245–47, 249–50; banking system, 63–64, 65(t)–66(t), 67, 245; core-periphery dynamics, 13, 237–42, 238(t), 242, 248–50, 250*n*1; debt (2006–16), 67, 68(t)–69(t), 70, 79–80; gender issues, 241; GFC's impact on, 13, 63–64, 237–38(t), 242; labour markets, 238(t), 241, 245, 247; neo-liberalism, 246, 249; politics of austerity, 249–50; social programs, 245–47; stimulus measures, 245, 249; taxation, 246; troika's policies, 13, 245–47, 247–50, 315

poverty: about, 43–45; cash transfer programs, 144; discourse and policy, 51–54; and equality of opportunity, 48; EU policies, 49–50; ILO's report on, 50–52; and inclusive growth, 43–44, 49–50; IPC-IG policies, 49; and market insufficiency, 47; measurements of, 48, 276; neo-liberalism as factor, 43–44; new social risks, 44, 47, 172, 177*n*18; OECD's policies, 43–44, 54*n*1; working poor, 47, 54; World Bank's influence, 43–44, 144. *See also* cash transfer programs; food insecurity; wealth inequality

Poverty Reduction Strategy Paper (PRSP), 87, 93–96, 99, 101

Prebisch, Raúl, 163–65, 176*n*8

Productive Development in an Open Economy (CEPAL), 172

public-private partnerships (P3s), 191–92, 263–64, 266, 285

quantitative easing: about, 14*n*1, 266; in Canada, 278; in UK, 266, 268*n*14; in US, 4, 27, 293; wealth inequality, 268*n*14

Raess, Damien, 304, 310*n*1

Recovery Act. *See* American Recovery and Reinvestment Act (ARRA)

Reinhart-Rogoff thesis, 23–24, 26, 257–58, 267*n*6

Republic of South Africa. *See* South Africa

Rogoff, Kenneth. *See* Reinhart-Rogoff thesis

South Africa, social programs: about, 197, 203–4, 211–12; child-centred policies, 199, 200, 203–5; food insecurity, 199, 209; gender issues, 203; health, 203, 207; historical background, 200–3; inclusive growth, 49; pensions, 199, 200, 201, 203–4, 207, 210; racial issues, 200–2, 206, 210–11; reforms needed, 206, 210–12; social grants, 203–5, 210–11; social security, 197, 202–7; unemployment insurance, 199, 201, 203, 207, 209–10; urban vs rural, 205

South Korea. *See* Korea

sovereign debt: and contraction of the state, 29; debt as percentage of GDP, 23; drivers of, 23–24, 64; GFC's impact on, 23, 59–60, 64, 67, 70; IMF's fiscal targets, 79–80; in OECD (2006–16), 67, 68(t)–69(t), 70, 79–80; Reinhart-Rogoff thesis, 23–24, 26, 257–58, 267n6

Spain: austerity measures, 75, 78(f)–79(f), 133–34; banking system, 63–64, 65(t)–66(t), 67; core-periphery dynamics, 239–40, 250n1; debt (2006–16), 67, 68(t)–69(t), 70, 79–80; EU's policy constraints on, 80; GFC's impact on, 63–64, 133–34; labour-employment relations, 133–34; social dialogue, 133–37

SPF. *See* social protection floor (SPF)

states. *See* nation-states

Stiglitz, Joseph, 22, 26

Strauss-Kahn, Dominique, 97, 99, 130

structural adjustment: basic elements of, 23, 30; Greek crisis, 125–30; OECD's policies, 30, 44; troika's policies, 31. *See also* neo-liberalism

Stuckler, David, 285–86

Sweden: austerity measures, 75, 82; banking crisis costs, 64, 65(t)–66(t); debt (2006–16), 67, 68(t)–69(t), 79–80

Switzerland: banking crisis costs, 64, 65(t)–66(t); debt (2006–16), 67, 68(t)–69(t), 79–80

Taylor, Rosemary, 54n1

Therborn, Göran, 277

Time for Equality (CEPAL), 173–74

trade: GATT, 273; NAFTA, 182–84; neo-liberalism and liberalization, 273; protectionism, 27–28; regional agreements, 29; WTO, 28, 114, 130, 259, 273

troika (ECB, EC, and IMF): austerity measures, 31, 79–80, 135–36, 237–38(t), 257; core-periphery dynamics, 13, 31, 237–38(t), 248–50; Greek crisis, 125–30, 135–37; ILO's influence on, 136; social dialogue, 135–36. *See also* European Central Bank (ECB); European Commission (EC); IMF (International Monetary Fund)

Turkey, 64, 65(t)–66(t), 97

UCTs (unconditional cash transfers): about, 140–41, 143, 153–55; effectiveness of, 144–48; funding for, 143, 145–46; research and technical assistance for, 146–48; World Bank's support for, 143(f), 145–50. *See also* cash transfer programs

UN Children's Fund (UNICEF), 12, 105, 111, 115

UN Department of Economic and Social Affairs (UNDESA), 111, 115

UN Development Programme (UNDP), 49, 113–15, 117

UN ECLAC. *See* CEPAL (Economic Commission for Latin America and the Caribbean)

UN Economic and Social Council (ECOSOC), 118, 162, 164–65

UN Educational, Scientific and Cultural Organization (UNESCO), 167

UN International Policy Centre for Inclusive Growth (IPC-IG), 49

United Kingdom: about, 14, 260–62; austerity measures, 14, 28, 74–75, 79(f), 80, 255–56, 260–62, 265–66; austerity warnings to, 258; banking system, 63–64, 65(t)–66(t), 72–73, 261; common-sense governing, 14, 256, 265; debt (2006–16), 67, 68(t)–69(t), 79–80; GFC's impact on, 63, 72–73, 260–61,

300(t); IMF's fiscal targets, 28; international aid for CCTs, 144; neo-liberalism, 6, 28, 34n15, 256, 260; politics of austerity, 72, 74, 82, 260–61, 265–66; quantitative easing, 14n1, 266, 268n14; social policies, 261–62; stimulus packages, 260–61; taxation, 260–62; unemployment, 256, 258, 261, 300(t)

United Nations: inclusive growth, 47; influence on CEPAL, 169, 171; poverty reduction, 93; rights-based discourse, 169, 171; social protection floor (SPF-I), 12, 105, 111–18

United States, 292–312; about, 14, 292–93, 309; austerity measures, 27, 75–76, 309; banking crisis, 63–64, 65(t)–66(t), 71–73; coalitional realignments, 307–8; compared with Canada, 300–3, 300(t), 301(f)–302(f), 310nn6–7; debt (2006–16), 67, 68(t)–69(t), 79–80; GFC's impact on, 4, 14, 30, 63, 71–72, 81–83, 293–94; housing crisis, 63, 70–71; influence in IMF, 97; NAFTA's impact, 182–84; neo-liberalism, 27, 304–5; political dimensions, 304, 307–9; political polarization, 27, 73, 293–94, 309, 310n10; politics of austerity, 72–76; quantitative easing, 14, 27, 293; social unrest, 274; stimulus measures, 27, 30, 74, 293–95(f), 298, 304–5; taxation, 292, 294–95, 304–6, 308; unemployment, 300(t); wealth inequality, 71, 308–9. *See also* American Recovery and Reinvestment Act (ARRA)

United States, social policy, 292–312; about, 14; CCTs in NYC, 141; coalitional realignments, 307–8; compared with Canada, 292–93, 300–3, 300(t), 301(f)–302(f), 310nn6–7; differing assessments of, 293–94, 303–5; expansionism, 14, 292–300, 299(f), 303–6, 317; federal/state responsibilities, 305–7; liberal vs social Keynesianism, 310n1; pensions, 107; political dimensions, 307–9; privatization of risk, 107, 303–4; social protection, 71; Social Security benefits, 309; transfers to low-

earners, 301–3, 301(f)–302(f), 310n6; unemployment insurance, 14, 292–93, 298, 305–7. *See also* American Recovery and Reinvestment Act (ARRA)

van Kersbergen, Kees, 61–62
Venezuela, GFC's impact on, 183
Vetterlein, Antje, 11, 87–104, 89, 90, 324
Vietnam, social programs, 230n5
Vis, Barbara, 61–62
Vuskovic, Pedro, 165–66, 176n5

wealth inequality: about, 71; CCTs' effectiveness against, 145; CEPAL's survey on, 168; discourse and policy, 48, 51–54; and equality of opportunity, 48; GFC's impact on, 274; GINI coefficient, 49, 52, 145, 161; ILO's report on, 50–52; and inclusive growth, 41, 43; in Latin America, 161; middle-income countries, 52; and neo-liberalism, 25, 26; and OECD, 43, 52, 71; and political change in US, 308–9; and quantitative easing, 268n14; and weakening of labour, 33–34; World Economic Forum on, 136. *See also* inclusive growth

Whiteside, Heather, 14, 254–71, 324
WHO (World Health Organization), 52–53, 111, 114, 115, 154
Wilson, Christopher, 187, 188
Wolf, Martin, 80, 255–56, 259
World Bank: about, 12, 107–9; austerity warnings by, 259; CCT programs, 140–50, 142(f)–143(f), 153–55; compared with IMF, 87–88, 92, 101, 149; development policy loans (DPLs), 145; evaluation of social programs, 115, 145, 146–48; GFC and social policy, 8–10, 111–12, 118; historical background, 105–6, 116; and ILO, 28, 105–7, 117–18; ILO/WB board for SPF, 105, 112–16; inclusive growth, 43, 55n9; loans to middle- vs low-income countries, 143–44; management of, 149–50; neo-liberalism, 6, 167, 273; pension systems, 106–9, 116; poverty reduction, 43–44, 92–93; Poverty

Printed and bound in Canada by Friesens

Set in Myriad SemiCondensed and Minion
by Artegraphica Design Co. Ltd.

Copy editor: Dallas Harrison

Proofreader: Lana Okerlund

Indexer: Judy Dunlop

Cartographer: Eric Leinberger